Urban Cultures in (Post)Colonial Central Europe

Comparative Cultural Studies,
Steven Tötösy de Zepetnek, Series Editor

The Purdue University Press monograph series of Books in Comparative Cultural Studies publishes single-authored and thematic collected volumes of new scholarship. Manuscripts are invited for publication in the series in fields of the study of culture, literature, the arts, media studies, communication studies, the history of ideas, etc., and related disciplines of the humanities and social sciences to the series editor via email at <clcweb@purdue.edu>. Comparative cultural studies is a contextual approach in the study of culture in a global and intercultural context and work with a plurality of methods and approaches; the theoretical and methodological framework of comparative cultural studies is built on tenets borrowed from the disciplines of cultural studies and comparative literature and from a range of thought including literary and culture theory, (radical) constructivism, communication theories, and systems theories; in comparative cultural studies focus is on theory and method as well as application. For a detailed description of the aims and scope of the series including the style guide of the series link to <http://docs. lib.purdue.edu/clcweblibrary/seriespurdueccs>. Manuscripts submitted to the series are peer reviewed followed by the usual standards of editing, copy editing, marketing, and distribution. The series is affiliated with *CLCWeb: Comparative Literature and Culture* (ISSN 1481-4374), the peer-reviewed, full-text, and open-access quarterly published by Purdue University Press at <http://docs.lib.purdue.edu/clcweb>.

Volumes in the Purdue series of Books in Comparative Cultural Studies
<http://www.thepress.purdue.edu/comparativeculturalstudies.html>

Agata Anna Lisiak, *Urban Cultures in (Post)Colonial Central Europe*
Representing Humanity in an Age of Terror, Ed. Sophia A. McClennen and Henry
   James Morello
Michael Goddard, *Gombrowicz, Polish Modernism, and the Subversion of Form*
Shakespeare in Hollywood, Asia, and Cyberspace, Ed. Alexander C.Y. Huang and
   Charles S. Ross
Gustav Shpet's Contribution to Philosophy and Cultural Theory, Ed. Galin Tihanov
Comparative Central European Holocaust Studies, Ed. Louise O. Vasvári and Steven
   Tötösy de Zepetnek
Marko Juvan, *History and Poetics of Intertextuality*
Thomas O. Beebee, *Nation and Region in Modern American and European Fiction*
Paolo Bartoloni, *On the Cultures of Exile, Translation, and Writing*
Justyna Sempruch, *Fantasies of Gender and the Witch in Feminist Theory and Literature*
Kimberly Chabot Davis, *Postmodern Texts and Emotional Audiences*
Philippe Codde, *The Jewish American Novel*
Deborah Streifford Reisinger, *Crime and Media in Contemporary France*
Imre Kertész and Holocaust Literature, Ed. Louise O. Vasvári and Steven Tötösy de
   Zepetnek
Camilla Fojas, *Cosmopolitanism in the Americas*
Comparative Cultural Studies and Michael Ondaatje's Writing, Ed. Steven Tötösy de
   Zepetnek
Jin Feng, *The New Woman in Early Twentieth-Century Chinese Fiction*
Comparative Cultural Studies and Latin America, Ed. Sophia A. McClennen and Earl E. Fitz
Sophia A. McClennen, *The Dialectics of Exile*
Comparative Literature and Comparative Cultural Studies, Ed. Steven Tötösy de Zepetnek
Comparative Central European Culture, Ed. Steven Tötösy de Zepetnek

Agata Anna Lisiak

Urban Cultures in (Post)Colonial Central Europe

Purdue University Press
West Lafayette, Indiana

Library of Congress Cataloging-in-Publication Data

Lisiak, Agata Anna, 1979-
  Urban Cultures in (Post)Colonial Central Europe / Agata Anna Lisiak.
     p. cm. -- (Comparative cultural studies)
  Includes bibliographical references and index.
  ISBN 978-1-55753-573-3
  1. Sociology, Urban--Europe, Central. 2. Sociology, Urban--Former communist
countries. 3. Postcolonialism--Former communist countries. 4. Post-
communism--Social aspects--Europe, Central. I. Title.
  HT131.L57 2011
  307.760943--dc22
                              2010011246

To my family, old and new

Contents

List of Illustrations

Acknowledgements

I am grateful to my friends—particularly Gal Beckerman, Jacob Birken, Rebecca Dolgoy, Florian Duijsens, Debbie Kolben, Jacek Kołtan, Agnieszka Leszczyńska, and Filip Litewka—who helped me along the way with their insightful comments and words of encouragement. Although it may not strike the reader as obvious, this book—as well as my other writings on cities—has been greatly inspired by the work of Marshall Berman and the few conversations I have been fortunate to share with him in Berlin and New York. I am especially indebted to my partner, Christoph Cico Nicolaisen, who made countless cups of coffee, cooked dinners, and helped me in a thousand different ways. This book would not have been possible if not for Steven Tötösy de Zepetnek, who has provided support throughout my research and writing process both as a scholar and as the series editor of the Purdue University Press monograph series of Books in Comparative Cultural Studies, where my work found its home. I thank Steven for the long hours we spent discussing my work. Finally, I thank the anonymous readers of the manuscript for their comments and Purdue University Press for the interest in and support of my work.

Acknowledgements

[faded, largely illegible text]

Chapter One

Introduction

In *Urban Cultures in (Post)Colonial Central Europe* I present an analysis of post-1989 images of four Central European cities: Berlin, Budapest, Prague, and Warsaw. After the demise of communism these cities had to redefine their identities. More than forty years of communism, the prevalent presence of foreign military powers, political and economic dependence on the Soviet Union, and Soviet cultural and architectonic influences had, among other factors, enormous and long-lasting impact on these cities. How do the cities deal with this legacy? How do they respond to the transformation processes that shaped the most recent past—the demise of the Cold War division and all-encompassing globalization? What images do they use to express their newly (re)found identities? How do their official self-representations communicated through municipal media relate to literary and film portrayals of post-1989 urban identities?

One of the leading hypotheses of my book is that Berlin, Budapest, Prague, and Warsaw are not only Central European but also (post)colonial spaces and that the proof of their (post)coloniality can be found predominantly in the works of contemporary architecture, literature, and film. While the (post)colonial character of these cities escapes a clear definition, their Central Europeanness is hardly a troubling notion (even if the idea of Central Europe remains contested). Milan Kundera defines Central Europe as located geographically in the center, culturally in the West, and politically—after 1945—in Eastern Europe. According to Kundera, the tragic fate of Central Europe stems from its location between Russia and Germany; however, he focuses much more on the former than the latter and defines Central Europe in opposition to Russia: whereas Central Europe is based on the rule of maximum diversity in a minimum of space, Russia is characterized by minimum diversity in a maximum of space. This theory seems especially plausible when we think of Central European cities as being shaped by centuries of cultural and ethnic diversity. Kundera's understanding of Central Europe fails to include the former German Democratic Republic—and, thus, (East) Berlin—in the group of Central European countries, despite the fact that it belonged politically to the Soviet bloc while belonging geographically and historically to Central Europe. I propose that the word "Central"

1

signifies (in this case) a location between east and west. This "in-between" position of Central European capitals gained on importance after 1989: the cities have increasingly fallen under Western economic and cultural influence, but they continue to possess distinctly Eastern and (post)Soviet qualities. Interestingly, the perception of the Central European city as a bridge between east and west has been applied in urban marketing strategies. Berlin Partner GmbH, the city contracted consulting agency for potential investors, describes the German capital as *Ost-West-Metropole*.

Chapter 2 is devoted to the theories I find particularly useful in my research and analysis. I apply an interdisciplinary take on urban cultures as advocated by Roland Barthes and, thus, rely in my work on methods and frameworks that allow for an interplay of several approaches. I ground my analysis in comparative cultural studies developed by Steven Tötösy de Zepetnek, explain why postcolonial studies can (and should) be applied in analyses of Central European (urban) cultures, and discuss selected approaches from the field of broadly understood urban studies. I elaborate on the impact of two cultural centers (West Europe and the Soviet Union) upon the region, as suggested by Tötösy de Zepetnek in his notion of "in-between peripherality." Furthermore, I include an analysis of the United States' influence and the discussion of the "Americanization" of Central European societies as opposed to their former "Sovietization." Although highly respected Central European authors refer to it indirectly in a number of publications, the perception of the Soviet Union as a colonizer remains a controversial view. Czesław Miłosz describes the postwar division of Europe as follows: "independent states of half of Europe were converted into colonial satrapies controlled from outside" (103). According to Péter Esterházy, it was exactly the colonizing Soviet power that linked the otherwise diverse countries of Central Europe into one organism and kept Kundera's definition alive. Finally, Claudio Magris defines Central Europe as a metaphor of protest—against the Soviet rule over Eastern Europe and against the American way of life in Western Europe.

In chapter 3 I focus on the (post)colonial character of Central European capitals. I address such questions as: What is a (post)colonial city? Are Central European cities equally (post)colonial? What historical and cultural processes have influenced their identities? How has the system transformation shaped new urban realities? How have these cities been developing and communicating their identities since 1989? In order to better understand the current situation I describe the cultural, political, economic, and social developments of the cities first before and then after the fall of communism. Berlin strikes as a particularly interesting case since it can be described as both post-Soviet and "post-Allied" and since for years it has remained under heavy economic and cultural influence of (the former) West Germany. Furthermore, Berlin has an unusual status as the former capital of the GDR and the former island of the *Bundesrepublik*: after the collapse of communism, Berlin continues to function as the capital (of re-united Germany) although the state it used to be the capital of ceased to exist. Warsaw is strictly post-Soviet, but its developments after 1945 in many ways resemble those of Berlin. Almost completely destroyed in World War II, Warsaw was rebuilt in a Soviet fashion, which is visible today and continues to determine people's lives, thus, contributing to a specific communist (and now postcommunist) urban angst (see, for example, Tadeusz Konwicki's descriptions of Warsaw in *A Minor Apocalypse*). After 1989, Warsaw experienced an inflow of Western or global capital, but, unlike Prague and Budapest, did not develop an expatriate community of any remarkable size. Budapest and Prague are also post-Soviet (both were especially affected by the brutally repressed revolutions of 1956 and 1968, respectively, both scarred by prefabricated apartment buildings, Prague was home to the biggest statue of Stalin in the whole Soviet world, etc.), but they are also post-Habsburg since they used to belong to the most important cultural centers in the Austro-Hungarian Empire and continue to be associated with the Habsburg monarchy because of their architecture, culture, and urban traditions.

In chapter 4 I analyze how the municipalities of Berlin, Budapest, Prague, and Warsaw communicate their post-1989 identities. This section responds to following questions: What imagery do they use to express their urbanities and what meanings do these images convey? What (new) media tools do they implement and what audiences do they address? How do official municipal images respond to the realities of every day life and the former and present colonial influence in these cities, if at all? I start my analysis with the oldest city symbols—coats of arms and flags—and move on to more modern types of images such as logos and brand campaigns. Next, I look at selected elements of electronic and print municipal media: their web design, the photographs illustrating information about the city, the design of city maps, city guides, and city tourist cards as well as the images used therein. The images and texts published in municipal media represent the discussed cities on three levels: as independent cities, nation's capitals, and (Central) European metropolises. Invariably, it is the city's dominant role within the country and the region that is most strongly influenced.

In chapter 5 I look into the elements of Central European cities' pasts which have been remembered and which have been forgotten. Predictably, many material remnants of the socialist regime have been destroyed or hidden from the public eye. My interest lies not only in which buildings and monuments had to go, but also in why and how they disappeared. I discuss which urban or national pasts have been considered worthy of commemoration and how they have been commemorated. Furthermore, I analyze the impact of the newest architecture and urban planning on the cities' landscapes and cultures. How do the new buildings and monuments influence the image of Central European capitals? What meanings do they convey? How do they respond to the remnants of the Soviet architectural and cultural legacy? Most recent changes in the urban landscapes of Berlin, Budapest, Prague, and Warsaw are influenced predominantly by global developments in architecture: even if architects and constructors claim they tailor their products to fit local peculiarities and cultural traditions, their buildings appear increasingly standardized. The growing aestheticization of urban space and, consequently, a shift of attention from the content to the form have had a remarkable affect on urban planning and architecture in Central European cities.

In chapter 6 I analyze how literature responds to recent cultural, political, and economic transformations and what types of city images are conveyed in post-1989 works of fiction set in Berlin and Warsaw. The exceptional position of these two cities derives largely from the fact that their urban identities are shaped predominantly by the historical events of the twentieth century (the terror and destruction of the Second World War and the postwar urban reconstruction conducted in compliance with the Soviet regime), while Budapest and Prague are defined largely through the architectonic and cultural achievements of their golden age, that is, when they were part of the Habsburg empire. The novels, short stories, and plays I discuss mirror the (post)colonial character of Berlin and Warsaw in that they respond to the Soviet past, but also remain attentive to the feeling of euphoria, loss, or confusion at the postcommunist developments. Some of the authors whose works I discuss in this chapter include Wladimir Kaminer, Inka Parei, Kathrin Röggla, and Jens Sparschuh, who write about Berlin, and Dorota Masłowska, Tomasz Piątek, and Krzysztof Varga, who set their fiction in Warsaw.

In chapter 7 I analyze how film relates to the (post)colonial character of Central European cities in general and Berlin and Warsaw in particular. Aside from interweaving with the issues thematized in literature, post-1989 film representations of Central European cities relate to all the topics discussed in the previous chapters, that is, the newest history, the official images of Central European cities as communicated in municipal media, and the transformations of and in urban landscapes and city texts. I demonstrate how the post-1989 urban space is represented in film and what are some of the most recurring themes and motifs in the new Central European urban cinema. The films I analyze depict those urban phenomena that are uncomfortable to city promoters: the void, the neglected prefabricated apartment blocks, and other not always positive developments. The feature films analyzed in the chapter include Wolfgang Becker's *Good Bye, Lenin!* (2003), Michael Klier's *Ostkreuz* (1991), Dani Levy's *Alles auf Zucker!* (2004), Tom Tykwer's *Lola Rennt* (1998), Dariusz Gajewski's *Warszawa* (2003), Marek Koterski's *Dzień świra* (2002), Márta Mészáros' *Córy szczęścia* (1999), and Mariusz Treliński's *Egoiści* (2000), among many others.

In *Urban Cultures in (Post)Colonial Central Europe* I aim at determining whether a common (post)colonial urban identity can be distinguished in Central Europe and, if so, what it entails. Field work in Berlin, Budapest, Prague, and Warsaw has proven particularly beneficial for my research and allowed for a thorough examination of the sometimes elusive aspects of the cities' (post)colonial nature. I propose that my work is innovative because of my attention to and execution of theoretical development, interdisciplinarity, and, importantly, the approach and presentation of a theoretical framework, which demonstrates the social relevance of humanities scholarship. I argue that my approach and analysis represent a much needed change of paradigm within the existing scholarship examining Central Europe. In addition, this theoretical development is applied in the analysis of a topic relevant not only in current scholarship, but also in current political and social discourse, namely, the urban cultures of Central Europe, a region whose importance within the European Union on all levels proves not only relevant but also most urgent.

Chapter Two

Theoretical Background

The interdisciplinary character of my research justifies the use of theories that include a broad definition of culture and, hence, provide a viable framework and methodologies for an analysis of various aspects of Central European cultures after 1989. Since culture is not an isolated phenomenon, but remains closely interdependent with other areas of life, such as, though not exclusively, the political and economic spheres, inclusion of these outside factors contributes to a thorough understanding of cultural processes. I ground my discussion and analysis in the framework of comparative cultural studies, a framework and methodology developed by Steven Tötösy de Zepetnek, itself based in Siegfried J. Schmidt's empirical study of literature (about ESL, see in particular Schmidt "Literary Studies") and Itamar Even-Zohar's polysystem studies. Further, postcolonial theories developed by Edward W. Said, Homi K. Bhabha, and Gayatri Chakravorty Spivak, among others, are particularly significant with regards to political and cultural changes in Central Europe as they help to understand the impact of two cultural centers (Western Europe and the United States on the one hand and the Soviet Union on the other hand) on the region, as suggested by Tötösy de Zepetnek in his notion of "in-between peripherality" (see, e.g., "Comparative Cultural Studies"). Since cities are the main object of my study, selected concepts from the field of broadly understood urban studies—such as those developed by David Harvey, Kevin Lynch, and Wolfgang Kaschuba, among others—have proven particularly beneficial for my analysis. What all these theories have in common is an inclusive understanding of culture, which is particularly important if we take into consideration the technological progress and ensuing cultural changes that have taken place in the last two decades. Consequently, they provide adequate tools for a complex analysis of miscellaneous aspects of contemporary Central European urban cultures.

Comparative cultural studies and "in-between peripherality"

Comparative cultural studies is rooted in empirical and systemic theories in general and in empirical study of literature and polysystem studies in particular. Before I

move on to discuss Tötösy de Zepetnek's interdisciplinary framework and methodologies, I briefly look at those of Schmidt's and Even-Zohar's concepts that appear
especially viable on the development of comparative cultural studies as well as the
subject and nature of my research.

Unlike most traditional literary studies, the empirical study of literature (ESL)
does not limit itself to literary texts and their interpretations, but crosses the borders of hermeneutics and applies approaches and methods characteristic of areas of
knowledge other than literature, for example, psychology, social sciences, reception
theory, and cognitive science. Consequently, ESL not only offers a broad and deep
view on literature, but also proposes an extended understanding of the word "literature." Developed by Siegfried J. Schmidt in the late 1970s, ESL questions and
rejects the established distinction between the humanities and the natural sciences.
It also advocates application of empirical methods onto the field of literary studies, which—according to Schmidt—could help refresh literary scholarship, bring
it closer to other disciplines, and render it more socially and intellectually relevant.
Further, a theory is viable only when it relies on "explicit methods whose correct
application yields results which—in principle—can be obtained and checked by
anyone applying the same procedures" (Schmidt, "Empirical Study of Literature"
139). In opposition to hermeneutic claims of inherent properties of literature, ESL
focuses not merely on the text, but also on actions and processes that are related to
it, such as production, distribution, reception, and imitation. In this sense, ESL is not
interested in literature in the traditional meaning of the word, but rather in "the social
system 'literature'" (141), that is, psychological, social, cultural, political, and other
contexts, in which literature exists.

Not only does ESL augment the definition of literature, but also that of culture,
which encompasses not only the "traditional concept of culture which is primarily
related to art, science, and religion" (Schmidt, "Empirical Study of Literature" 141),
but also other phenomena, which have only recently (and rather reluctantly) been
acknowledged as culture: popular culture, subculture, alternative culture, media culture, and so on. ESL perceives literature as one of many types of media that remains
in a close relation not only to other print media such as newspapers, magazines, and
journals, but also to electronic audiovisual media such as television, satellite and
cable television, video, DVD, CD-ROM, and the internet with its blogs, chat rooms,
and forums. Schmidt argues that owing to the growing importance of the mass media, "the medium of print" has lost its hitherto dominant position and has become
"one medium among others, which has to compete with other media for its cultural
position" (146), which justifies—if not necessitates—the transformation of literary
studies into a branch of a bigger framework of cultural or media studies (141).

Polysystem studies also does not focus on literature in its traditional sense,
but relates to it as part of a larger system. In the polysystem approach developed by
Itamar Even-Zohar "literature is . . . conceived of not as an isolated activity in society, regulated by laws exclusively (and inherently) different from all the rest of the
human activities, but as an integral—often central and very powerful—factor among

the latter" (2). In polysystem studies, literature, language, culture, society, and other semiotic phenomena are perceived and analyzed as interrelated systems, which Even-Zohar describes as heterogeneous and dynamic. Polysystem studies borrows from modern sciences that make use of functional approaches and analyze relations between objects rather than focus on their substance. Even-Zohar differentiates between static functionalism (associated with Ferdinand de Saussure and the Geneva School), which he considers insufficient to thoroughly analyze complex systems, and dynamic functionalism (related to Russian Formalism and Czech Structuralism), which he uses as an ideological and structural basis for polysystem studies (9-12). Apart from the formalist and structuralist theories, Even-Zohar's work has been influenced by Pierre Bourdieu, in particular by his concepts of field and habitus (Even-Zohar 3).

Even-Zohar rejects the idea that uniformity is a prerequisite for a system to function (12)—on the contrary: systems are complex and their interrelations multifarious. As a system, culture is heterogeneous, which is especially noticeable in bi- or multilingual societies (12). This diversity is also detectable in seemingly more uniform societies if we take into consideration their many layers. For instance, in pre-1989 Central Europe there was a clear gap between the official (mainstream) culture imposed and controlled—in some countries more than in others—by the Soviet Union and the unofficial (underground) cultures, rejected or censored by the state and usually praised by the political or religious opposition. After 1989, the various layers of culture became even more evident as the hitherto neglected groups (ethnic, religious, and national minorities, gay men and lesbians) began to remind or inform the rest of society of their existence. Like any other system, a culture needs "a regulating balance in order not to collapse or disappear" (Even-Zohar 16). The dominant culture changes together with historical, economic, social, and scientific circumstances. The canon needs to adjust in order to include what were once considered to be noncanonical works; otherwise it fails to represent the dominant culture. This transformation may be gradual, as in case of Latin being slowly replaced by national languages (Even-Zohar 16), or rapid (and chaotic), as in case of the peaceful revolutions of 1989. Even-Zohar's approach is anti-elitist and anticanonical. He postulates that literary studies should go beyond analysis of generally acknowledged works and pay attention to various branches of literature that until recently have been fully excluded from the scholarship, such as mass-produced literature (13). If we perceive culture as a complex system, we should also think of literature as heterogeneous and multifaceted.

Among Even-Zohar's concepts, literary—and, by implication, cultural—interference is particularly interesting when discussing post-1989 Central European cultures: "Interference can be defined as a relation(ship) between literatures, whereby a certain literature A (a source literature) may become a source of direct or indirect loans for another literature B (a target literature)" (54). A source literature may be selected by its prestige: its attractiveness appeals to a target literature and induces it to adapt parts of the source literature onto its ground. Also, interference will take place when a literature lacks certain elements that are necessary to express new cultural developments, whereas another literature seems to possess them (69)—for example, where domestic playwrights by and large failed to deal convincingly with the prevailing confusion tormenting the modern urban individual, contemporary Central European theater readily embraced the texts of British author Sarah Kane. It may also happen that "a source literature is selected by dominance" (68), as in the case of colonialism or other types of political, economic, or cultural supremacy. In its most extreme form, literary dominance penetrates all aspects of a target literature including the language, as in case of literatures in the former British and French colonies. Cultural supremacy may also be engineered through more subtle influences. The Soviet Union did not demand that its satellites produce literature in Russian, but made it clear—through censorship as well as by the means of literary workshops and scholarships—what kinds of genres and texts fit into a social-realist aesthetics. In most cases, however, a target literature adapts only certain elements of a source literature rather than a whole system.

New theories are usually conceived from dissatisfaction with the existing systems of ideas. Polysystem studies originated in Even-Zohar's frustration with translation studies that lacked a complex framework that would explain multidimensional relations between the original text and its translations as well as between the source and target literatures. Schmidt's conviction that hermeneutics not only is insufficient for a thorough analysis of literature but also contributes to the decline of literature as an academic discipline resulted in the concept of empirical studies of literature. Similarly, Steven Tötösy de Zepetnek's observation that comparative literature experiences an intellectual and institutional downfall while cultural studies enjoys progress led to the formation of comparative cultural studies (see *Comparative Literature*).

Tötösy de Zepetnek argues that cultural studies owes its success partly to theoretical approaches borrowed from comparative literature and that comparative literature has a long and rich tradition of "cross-cultural and interdisciplinary study of literature and culture," including studies of popular culture and film studies ("From Comparative Literature" 235). Therefore, cultural studies is not as innovative in its methods as it may appear to someone unfamiliar with achievements of comparative literature. Nevertheless, Tötösy de Zepetnek acknowledges that "cultural studies has acquired both intellectual and institutional standing" and—admittedly, partly for political reasons (236)—proposes to consolidate the most viable aspects of comparative literature and cultural studies into a new theory:

> Comparative cultural studies is field of study where selected tenets of the discipline of comparative literature are merged with selected tenets of the field of cultural studies meaning that the study of culture and culture products—including but not restricted to literature, communication, media, art, etc.—is performed in a contextual and relational construction and with a plurality of methods and approaches, inter-disciplinarity, and, if and when required, including team work. In comparative cultural studies it is the processes of communicative action(s) in culture and the how of these processes

that constitute the main objectives of research and study. However, comparative cultural studies does not exclude textual analysis proper or other established fields of study. ("From Comparative Literature" 262)

The broad definition of culture and the focus on the "how" of the processes unavoidably call to mind Schmidt's and Even-Zohar's theories. Apart from polysystem studies, Tötösy de Zepetnek adapts methods available in other systemic theories, such as the concepts of literary institution (Jacques Dubois) and literary field (Pierre Bourdieu) as well as Niklas Luhmann's theory of literature as a system (see Tötösy de Zepetnek, *Comparative Literature*). No wonder then that Tötösy de Zepetnek defines comparative cultural studies as a "composite approach" ("Constructivism" 7), that is, composed of aspects of various other theories. It is also important to bear in mind that systemic and empirical approaches borrow from each other (as in the case of Even-Zohar's adaptation of Bourdieu's concepts of field and habitus) or intersect at vital points (as in case of broad definitions of culture present both in Schmidt and Even-Zohar). Furthermore, all these theories derive from constructivism while, at the same time, provide a framework for operational constructivism, that is, a form of cognitive constructivism, in which literature is considered "a subsystem of culture [that] occurs and functions in a soft, semi-permeable, and self-referential system of human and social interaction characterized by (cognitive) aesthetic and polyvalence conventions" (Tötösy de Zepetnek, "Constructivism" 6).

Another feature that the systemic and empirical theories—and, consequently, comparative cultural studies—have in common is their theoretical competence and readiness to embrace new types of media which constitute cultural subsystems. The flexible framework allows for the application of theories onto emerging cultural phenomena. Therefore, comparative cultural studies is a methodological framework that swiftly detects changes in culture and is adequately equipped with the tools to thoroughly analyze them. Additionally, the approach proposed by Tötösy de Zepetnek is deeply contextual and, hence, encourages the relation of a cultural product to other cultural products or areas of culture, society, science, art, politics, and economy in order to better understand its meaning and role in a cultural (poly)system. Importantly, culture here stands for "all human activity resulting in artistic production" (Tötösy de Zepetnek, "Constructivism" 7). Tötösy de Zepetnek explicates the framework of comparative cultural studies in the form of ten general principles (here quoted from Tötösy de Zepetnek, "From Comparative Literature" 259-62) enumerated in a condensed form below:

1. Comparative cultural studies focuses on the "how" of cultural processes. Hence, it is not a cultural product as such, but rather its interactions with the environment are interesting for the study of culture. Furthermore, Tötösy de Zepetnek emphasizes that "to 'compare' does not—and must not—imply a hierarchy," that is, in a comparative analysis it is the method in use rather than the studied matter that is of crucial importance for the study of literature and culture.

2. "Attention to other cultures . . . is a basic and founding element and factor of the framework" of comparative cultural studies. This principle encourages an intercultural and interdisciplinary dialogue. Here, dialogue is understood as "inclusion," which "extends to all Other, all marginal, minority, and peripheral."

3. It is necessary for the scholars working in the field of comparative cultural studies to inquire background in several languages, disciplines, and cultures before moving on to the study of theory and methodology.

4. Comparative cultural studies focuses on the study of culture both in parts (literature, film, popular culture, television, the internet, etc.) and as a whole "in relation to other forms of human expression and activity as well as in relation to other disciplines in the humanities and social sciences." Such a complex approach enables a thorough contextual cultural analysis.

5. Comparative cultural studies focuses on English as the contemporary lingua franca of communication, business, technology, and so on. Therefore, Tötösy de Zepetnek stresses, the focus on English does not mean "Euro-American centricity." On the contrary, the broad use of English as an international language of scholarship allows scholars from outside North America and Europe to present their works on an international forum and be understood by their colleagues from other countries.

6. Comparative cultural studies focuses on "evidence-based research and analysis," for which—in Tötösy de Zepetnek's opinion—the systemic and empirical studies present the most advantageous methodologies and framework.

7. Comparative cultural studies insists on a methodology involving interdisciplinary study with "three main types of methodological precision: intra-disciplinarity (analysis and research within the disciplines in the humanities), multi-disciplinarity (analysis and research by one scholar employing any other discipline), and pluri-disciplinarity (analysis and research by team-work with participants from several disciplines)." Importantly, all these types are "built-in in the framework and methodology of the systemic and empirical approach to culture."

8. Comparative cultural studies is "a global and inclusive discipline of international humanities" and, as such, acts against the paradox of globalization versus localization.

9. Comparative cultural studies "advances our knowledge by a multi-faceted approach based on scholarly rigour and multi-layered knowledge with precise methodology."

10. Comparative cultural studies—as demonstrated in its principles—attempts to reverse the intellectual and institutional decline of the humanities and their marginalization.

As the ten principles clarify, the framework and methodologies of comparative cultural studies can be used in analysis of various literatures and cultures such as, for example, Latin American culture (McClennen and Fitz) or Michael Ondaatje's writing (Tötösy de Zepetnek). What is most interesting from the viewpoint of my project, however, is Tötösy de Zepetnek's application of his theories to the field of Central European cultures (see, e.g., *Comparative Central European Culture*; for further studies where the framework has been applied, see the peer-reviewed humanities and social sciences quarterly *CLCWeb: Comparative Literature and Culture*, as well as the Purdue University Press monograph series of books in Comparative Cultural Studies; see also Tötösy de Zepetnek, "Bibliography for Work," "Systemic Approaches").

To Tötösy de Zepetnek, Central European culture is "a combination of geography, history, economics, cultures, politics," and "a landscape of cultures of spaces ranging from Austria, the Czech and Slovak Republics, Hungary, Poland, Romania, Bulgaria, West Ukraine, former East Germany, and the countries of former Yugoslavia" ("Comparative Cultural Studies" 8). In his article "Comparative Cultural Studies and the Study of Central European Culture" Tötösy de Zepetnek applies his theoretical framework and methods to fragments of second-generation North American Jewish memoirs about Central Europe as well as to parts of contemporary East German and Hungarian fiction. In so doing, not only does he prove that comparative cultural studies is a viable theory that helps analyze Central European cultures, but he also shows possible ways of applying these theories. In what follows, I argue why, in my opinion, the general principles developed by Tötösy de Zepetnek provide a functional theoretical background for the study of Central European (urban) cultures.

The focus on the "how" of cultural processes is an indispensable condition for understanding the political, economic, and cultural transformations that have taken place in Central Europe after 1989. Evidently, the region has been subject to drastic changes, which have been frequently described by a number of scholars—perhaps most famously by Timothy Garton Ash (see, e.g., *We The People*). However, less obvious and less discussed is "how" these metamorphoses have been happening. Comparative cultural studies advocates the inclusion of "how" as a priority question—next to "what" or "who"—and thus contributes to the better understanding of the mechanisms behind cultural processes (principle 1).

In a comparative analysis of Central European (urban) cultures it is necessary to discuss various national or regional cultures in relation to one another as well as in relation to the cultures from outside the region that have particularly influenced the analyzed area (the Soviet Union, West Europe, the United States). Since Central European cities include miscellaneous ethnic and religious groups, the inclusion of all Others is essential for a thorough analysis of the said cultures (principle 2). Furthermore, knowledge of more than one Central European culture (thus, by implication, knowledge of several Central European languages, literatures, political and economic situations, etc.) helps create a bigger, more complex picture of the analyzed region. More often than not, understanding of Central European languages is a prerequisite for a comprehensive study as many materials and sources (fiction, film, secondary literature, daily news information, etc.) are unavailable in translation (principles 3 and 4). Keeping the latter in mind, Central European scholars may find it advantageous to publish their work in English. As such, not only do they make their academic findings available for their Central European colleagues who do not speak the source language, but they also increase their chances of publishing in other parts of the world and, thus, render the peripheral position of Central European cultural studies more central (principle 5). Through the aforementioned application of his theories onto parts of Central European (or Central Europe related) prose, Tötösy de Zepetnek demonstrates that research and analysis based on evidence (principle 6) are viable ways of examining Central European culture(s). Interdisciplinarity (principle 7) and application of innovative framework and methodologies increase attractiveness of the studies of Central Europe not only on the local, but also on the global level (principle 8).

Additionally, the interdisciplinary nature of Tötösy de Zepetnek's framework allows for a multilayered analysis of the aspects of Central European (urban) cultures that are of particular interest to my study, namely, the images produced and communicated in and through new media. In accordance with the principles of comparative cultural studies, my investigation into what I describe as municipal images (coats of arms, logos, image campaigns, photographs, etc.) focuses not on the visual symbols as such, but rather on how they respond to and interact with each other and their environment (principle 1). Furthermore, my analysis includes work from various urban cultures, milieus (principle 2), and four Central European languages (Czech, German, Hungarian, and Polish) translated into English (principles 3 and 5). These images are discussed both as part of the cities' marketing and tourist campaigns and in relation to other disciplines such as media and communication studies, urban studies, literature, and film (principle 4) and my research on municipal images and their analysis are evidence based (principle 6) as well as intra- and multidisciplinary (principle 7).

Another interesting aspect of comparative cultural studies in relation to Central European (urban) cultures is the attention the framework receives among international scholars of Central European origin. Nearly all contributors to Tötösy de Zepetnek's 2002 volume, *Comparative Central European Culture* (Susan Rubin Suleiman, Roumiana Deltcheva, Andrea Fábry, Peter Petro, Hana Pichova, among others), as well as the editor himself, come from Central Europe, but work predominantly in Canada and the United States. The authors see their countries of origin as part of a larger cultural framework, even when their articles focus on individual countries. This tendency proves Tötösy de Zepetnek's claim that the idea of Central Europe as one—although diverse—entity is much more accepted outside the region: "the locus of observation and perception plays a crucial role" ("Comparative Cultural Studies" 6). Whereas Central Europeans living in Central Europe are—as Milan Kundera noticed in his famous 1984 essay—skeptical about the notion of Central Europe, the idea seems attractive and plausible to Central European émigrés in the West, particularly in North America. "Thus," according to Tötösy de Zepetnek, "Czechs and Hungarians . . . discover kinship and the Central European dimension, when they live in Toronto or Berlin" (6). I suggest that we see this more in Toronto as Berlin is itself geographically—but also culturally and politically—Central European. Apparently, the further away we go, the more integrated Central Europe appears to be.

The above should not imply that Tötösy de Zepetnek's comparative cultural studies and its application in parts of Central European cultures are fully rejected by the scholars working in the region. Considerable interest in Tötösy de Zepetnek's work has been shown, for example, in the former East Germany (Reinhold Viehoff and Werner Nell at Halle), Hungary (Györgyi Horváth at Balassi), Macedonia (Sonja Stojmenska-Elzeser at Skopje), Romania (Carmen Andras at Sincai), and Poland (Bogusław Bakuła at Poznan and Dariusz Skórczewski at Lublin), for example. Taking into consideration the topic and theoretical framework of my project, I would like to comment shortly on Skórczewski's reaction to Tötösy de Zepetnek's work. Skórczewski embraces Tötösy de Zepetnek's idea of "in-between peripherality" and discusses it in relation to Poland, but perceives the construct as a postcolonial theory rather than a product of the framework and methodologies of comparative cultural studies (Skórczewski 104-05). He is partly right, as Tötösy de Zepetnek himself cites such postcolonialists as Amin Malak, Homi K. Bhabha, and François Paré among his inspirations ("Comparative Cultural Studies" 4). Nonetheless, Tötösy de Zepetnek claims that "while postcolonial paradigms of 'centre/periphery' and 'centre/margin' are useful and partially applicable in the study of Central and Eastern European culture(s), they lack methodology and precise taxonomy and are often political or rhetorical in nature" ("Comparative Cultural Studies" 5). For this reason, the notion of "in-between peripherality" is rooted in Even-Zohar's polysystem framework and additionally influenced by the concepts of "center/margin" developed by Tomislav Longinović, Marcel Cornis-Pope, and Anna Klobucka (Tötösy de Zepetnek, "Comparative Cultural Studies" 14-15). Although the idea of "in-between peripherality" does include aspects of postcolonial theories—which are discussed in the following section of this chapter together with Tötösy de Zepetnek's and Skórczewski's other views on postcoloniality of Central Europe—I follow Tötösy de Zepetnek's suggestion and look at it as part of comparative cultural studies.

In a polysystemic analysis of a culture "one must not think in terms of one center and one periphery, since several such positions are hypothesized" (Even-Zohar 14). Therefore, cultural phenomena are not simply driven from the center to the periphery (or the other way around), but may move in all possible directions: from a periphery of one system to a periphery of another system, from a center of one system to a center of another system, and so on (Even-Zohar 14). Tötösy de Zepetnek agrees with this view and borrows some of its parts for his notion of "in-between peripherality." For example, Tötösy de Zepetnek claims that Even-Zohar's explanation of relations between a dominant culture and subjugated cultures may also be applied to Central Europe; however, with an extension: "When the indig-

enous culture is in content and form self-centered and self-referential—as in the case
of Central and Eastern European cultures and literatures—the leverage and power
of a superseding colonialist centre, that is, a dominant culture, is not immediately
obvious or clear. This is especially the case from the perspective of the subjugated
community" ("Comparative Cultural Studies" 5). The last point of Tötösy de Zepetnek's argument is especially important since it partly explains the unwillingness of
Central Europeans to see their national cultures as subjugate. Moreover, Tötösy de
Zepetnek remarks that whereas West European influences on Central and Eastern
European cultures are largely considered natural and welcome, the very possibility
of a cultural impact of the former Soviet Union is more often than not rejected (5).
Although Tötösy de Zepetnek generally agrees with Even-Zohar's understanding of
"center/periphery," he notes that Even-Zohar's concept focuses predominantly on aspects of the periphery and, as such, is "not entirely applicable" in the case of Central
Europe (5). The cultures of the region are not completely marginal owing to their
"national self-referentiality and relative sovereignty" (5). Furthermore, Central Europe is located—not only geographically, but also culturally and politically—on the
margins of Western Europe and the former Soviet Union, which, in turn, renders the
region peripheral from both sides, or, to use Tötösy de Zepetnek's term, "in-between
peripheral."

To conclude, according to Tötösy de Zepetnek, Central European cultures are
influenced by three centers: "the self-referential national culture that in reality is never as homogeneous as proclaimed and propagated" ("Comparative Cultural Studies"
5) and includes various influences that are visible in literature, language, fine arts,
politics, economy, and so on (e.g., Austrian influences in Hungary, German influences in the Czech Republic and Poland); the Western countries, mainly Germany and
France, but also, especially in the 1990s, the United States, and the Soviet Union.
Clearly, Tötösy de Zepetnek's perception of Central European cultures is inspired by
postcolonial theories, but the concept of "in-between peripherality" is methodologi-
cally rooted in systemic and empirical theories rather than in postcolonial studies.

Interest in the way of looking at Central Europe proposed by Tötösy de Zepetnek has increased in the last couple of years, especially regarding the 2004 and 2007
enlargements of the European Union. Owing to its flexible framework, Tötösy de
Zepetnek's notion of Central European "in-between peripherality" remains viable
despite substantial political and economic transformations happening in the region.
Furthermore, what makes Tötösy de Zepetnek's concept particularly attractive is that
it takes into consideration various aspects of culture (literature, film, publishing industry, the internet, etc.) as well as political and economic factors influencing it
and, therefore, provides an all-encompassing structure for a cultural analysis of the
region. I propose that "in-between peripherality" adapts itself to various historical
developments and succeeds at explaining the specificity of Central European (urban)
cultures as "in-between" and "peripheral" throughout centuries.

During the four decades of Soviet supremacy the position of Central European
countries was also "in-between peripheral," although in a different sense than today.

Geographically—and, arguably, culturally—the region was located on the periphery of Europe. Politically and economically, however, Central European countries were rarely considered anything more than mere satellites of the Soviet Union, and un-European. In mainstream Western discourse during the Cold War, Western Europe became synonymous with Europe and everything behind the iron curtain was described in political rather than geographic or cultural terms: the Soviet bloc. The situation changed together with the fall of the Berlin Wall. The border between West Germany and East Germany ceased to exist (although at first more physically than mentally and culturally) and, consequently, the border between the west and the east, or Europe and non-Europe, had to be redefined. Democratic changes brought the former Soviet satellites closer to the Western world. Still, except for the former German Democratic Republic (GDR)—which was fully incorporated into the Federal Republic and, consequently (and unconditionally), into the European Union (EU)—Central European countries continued to lack an adequate definition. The initial enthusiasm at the end of the Cold War and the feeling of righteous victory prompted verbal generosity in the West: the former Soviet bloc countries were labeled new democracies or young democracies—political rather than cultural, the labels emphasized patronizingly the eminence of Western economic and political systems that the freshly liberated countries should (and would) aspire to acquire.

In the early 1990s, a number of Central European countries (including the Czech and Slovak Republics, Poland, Hungary) were offered the prospect of becoming EU members, provided they "behave properly," that is, meet all the necessary requirements, adjust their legal, political, and economic systems to EU standards, and open their markets to EU products and services. More often than not these adjustments proved to be advantageous for the countries undergoing transformation. At the same time, however, they created new divisions: some Central European countries (the Czech Republic, Hungary) were achieving desirable results faster than others (Bulgaria, Romania), who at that point were not even invited to negotiations with the EU. The new break-up line in the former Soviet bloc ran between candidates and noncandidates for the EU membership. This division consisted in turn of various subcategories: some candidate states (Hungary) were enjoying more praise for their performance from the West than others (Poland), some noncandidates (Ukraine) remained under the Russian influence even after gaining independence and, thus, their chances for ever joining the EU were smaller than those of other noncandidates. Consequently, in the late 1990s the region under scrutiny became increasingly described in the West as Central East Europe, whereby "Central" often implied more economically developed, more democratic, and, hence, more European and "East" stood for underdeveloped, problematic, un-European. These divisions and subdivisions further problematized the location of a periphery and created peripheries within a periphery (e.g., West Ukraine, Romania, Bulgaria became peripheries of peripheral Central Europe). Keeping the above in mind, the urban cultures I analyze in the following chapters—Berlin, Budapest, Prague, and Warsaw—are decidedly Central European.

The recent EU enlargements introduced new developments in the perception of Central Europe as peripheral. The language has changed: the countries that joined the European Union in 2004 and 2007 are mainly described as "the new Member States" (see, e.g., official reports of the European Commission or the European Central Bank) or "New Europe" (see, e.g., Lungescu). Clearly, most Central European states are still not considered equal with the "old" member states (which is also mirrored in limitations of free movement of labor among other restrictions) and continue being lectured on how to conduct politics. Geographies have shifted again and now the countries that used to be perceived as the westernmost parts of Central Europe have become the easternmost region of the European Union; what has remained the same, however, is the "peripheral" and "in-between" condition of the region. I predict that the notion of "in-between peripherality" will continue to remain viable even after further enlargements of the EU. If Ukraine is ever allowed to join, the EU borders will shift further east, which is likely to cause Central Europe appear more Western—especially in the eyes of its eastern neighbors. According to the Ukrainian writer Yuri Andrukhovych, Ukrainians already perceive the Czech Republic and Poland as part of the West, owing to their NATO and EU membership. The last point once again proves Tötösy de Zepetnek's claim of Central European "in-between peripherality": seen from the West, it is Eastern European; seen from the East, it is Western European; seen from the inside, it hardly exists.

Postcolonial theories

On several occasions I have touched upon concepts from the field of postcolonial studies. Even-Zohar's discussion of the dominant and subjugate cultures and the source and target literatures has a strong underlying postcolonial context (53-72). Tötösy de Zepetnek's notion of "in-between peripherality" openly borrows from postcolonial theories and, on top of that, advocates a postcolonial analysis of Central and Eastern Europe ("Comparative Cultural Studies" 4-5). Nevertheless, a postcolonial reading of Central European cultures is hardly a popular practice: the word "postcolonial" is still predominantly associated with former European overseas colonies and, therefore, postcolonialism is customarily related to problems resulting from racial and linguistic dominance of one culture over another, as, for example, in the case of the former British colonies in Africa. Although the focus on the issues of race and language overshadows other aspects of postcolonial theories, I argue that they are applicable and viable in a discussion on Central European (urban) cultures.

The term "postcolonial" implies that colonial elements continue to shape the culture of the former colony even after its formal liberation. The persisting influence of the excolonizer is often observable, for example, in the official language (Kenya), bureaucratic practices (India), or the educational system (Pakistan). A postcolonial status is also characterized by traumatic or nostalgic memories of the colonial past, the love-hate relationship with the former colonial center, and the popularity of nationalistic ideologies—interestingly, all of these features are widespread in the cultures of Central and Eastern Europe.

Nostalgia for communism—and, hence, by implication, for the colonial past—typifies not only Central and Eastern European literatures, but also the moods prevailing in postcommunist societies after 1989 (see Modrzejewski and Sznajderman). Simona Popescu claims that if we look at communism as a definitively closed chapter in history, then we may find a certain charm to it (Paweł Śpiewak, on the contrary, suffers from an apparently incurable allergy to everything related to the Soviet colonial past). In the absence of the Soviet Union, many Central European hardline politicians exchange their anticommunism for open hostility towards the former colonizer's heir—Russia. Such practices frequently result in deterioration of international relations, but remain a popular way of gaining votes at home. Russophobia is often accompanied by other types of xenophobia. The alarmingly growing popularity of nationalist ideologies in Central and Eastern European countries is a natural consequence of a colonial experience. According to one of the major theoreticians of postcolonialism, Edward W. Said,

> In time, culture comes to be associated, often aggressively, with the nation or the state; this differentiates "us" from "them," almost always with some degree of xenophobia. Culture in this sense is a source of identity, and a rather combative one at that, as we see in recent "returns" to culture and tradition. These "returns" accompany rigorous codes of intellectual and moral behaviour that are opposed to the permissiveness associated with such relatively liberal philosophies as multiculturalism and hybridity. In the formerly colonized world, these "returns" have produced varieties of religious and nationalist fundamentalism. (*Culture and Imperialism* xiii-xiv)

In Central Europe, "multiculturalism and hybridity" are customarily associated with Western EU countries, which are often described as immoral or decadent by those who oppose the idea of EU membership (Zając). Interestingly, many Central European populist politicians and clerics as well as their followers criticize the European Union for its inclination towards political, economic, and cultural dominance over Central and Eastern European countries and compare Brussels to the Soviet Moscow (Zając). Their rhetoric is genuinely anticolonial as they reject both types of colonialism as evil and advocate "return" to the roots, that is, to the national culture or religion, which is often synonymous with cultural essentialism and exclusion of all Others from the public discourse (Krzemiński).

In recent years Central European societies proved their postcoloniality by voting for nationalist politicians. In September 2006 the German Nationalist Party (*Nationaldemokratische Partei Deutschlands*, or *NPD*) won a number of seats in the local parliament in Mecklenburg-Vorpommern in the former East Germany. Earlier that year, parties openly expressing nationalist sympathies were invited into coalition governments in Poland (*Liga Polskich Rodzin*—League of Polish Families— an ideological successor of the prewar National Democratic Party infamous for its anti-Semitism) and Slovakia (*Slovenská národná strana*—Slovak National Party—a self-proclaimed heir of the Slovak National Party that helped establish the clerical-fascist Slovak State in 1939). Moreover, in both cases, top members of these parties (Roman Giertych in Poland and Ján Mikolaj in Slovakia) were appointed ministers of education, which raised justifiable protests in and outside Central Europe. The beautiful icon of the Ukrainian 2004 Orange Revolution, Julia Tymoshenko, embraced patriotic rhetoric verging on nationalism and proudly displayed her love for Ukrainian folklore in that she paraded in traditional clothes and wove her hair in a thick braid. The 2009 elections for the European Parliament disclosed another wave of nationalistic phenomena in Central Europe. The Czech National Party (*Národní Strana*) launched a television spot, in which, among other extremist right-wing statements, it promised "a final solution to the Gypsy problem" (Johnstone). Shockingly, the spot was broadcasted by the Czech public television, which promptly removed the xenophobic clip after an intervention by Czech prime minister Jan Fischer. Whereas the discredited Národní Strana failed to enter the European Parliament, the Movement for a Better Hungary (*Jobbik Magyarországért Mozgalom*), a radical nationalist party also known as *Jobbik*, managed to win three seats. Since its establishment in 2003, Jobbik has been linked to numerous homophobic, anti-Semitic, and anti-Roma incidents in Hungary, thus, gaining internationally the reputation of a fascist party (Schmidt-Häuer 3). Although Slavoj Žižek is right to notice that "nationalist populism, far from being peculiar to Eastern Europe, is a common feature of all countries caught in the vortex of globalization" (10), in the case of Central European societies, the factors determining the rise of nationalist sympathies differ from those in Western European countries and, I argue, are more directly rooted in the fall of communism and the ensuing new political and economic order rather than in globalization.

As demonstrated above, Said's definition of a postcolonial culture can be successfully applied in an analysis of Central and Eastern European countries. Said goes far beyond a simplistic understanding of colonialism as the political, economic, and cultural domination of a white European man over an Asian or African man of color: "Neither imperialism nor colonialism is a simple act of accumulation and acquisition. Both are supported and perhaps even impelled by impressive ideological formations that include notions that certain territories and people *require* and beseech domination, as well as forms of knowledge affiliated with domination" (*Culture and Imperialism* 8). Arguably, the Soviet Union reached near-perfection regarding the creation of an ideological apparatus and propaganda facilitating colonial practices. Whereas the nineteenth-century empires used such words as "'inferior' or 'subject races,' 'subordinate peoples,' 'dependency,' 'expansion,' and 'authority'" (*Culture and Imperialism* 8), which helped create and cement colonial systems, the Soviet empire popularized such slogans as "Liberation of the working class," "Proletarians of all countries, unite!" or "At home and at work—economize!" Therefore, the Soviet Union employed methods essentially similar to those of the nineteenth-century colonizers, only instead of the vocabulary of dominance, it (ab)used the language of comradeship.

Said made his acknowledgement of postcoloniality of Central Europe explicit in saying that his lack of preoccupation with the former Soviet bloc was "not at all meant to suggest that Russia's domination of Central Asia and Eastern Europe

. . . have been either benign (and hence approved of) or any less imperialist" (*Culture and Imperialism* xxv). Although he recognized the colonial nature of the Soviet Union as well as other empires—"the Austro-Hungarian, . . . the Ottoman, and the Spanish and Portuguese" (xxv)—Said never discussed its effects at length. His focus on former British and French colonies may be explained by Said's Palestinian heritage and first-hand knowledge of Middle Eastern cultures as well as his devotion to relationships between the Oriental East and the Occidental West (see, e.g., Said's *Orientalism*).

In the case of other prominent postcolonial theoreticians, such as Homi K. Bhabha and Gayatri Chakravorty Spivak, application of their concepts onto Central and Eastern European cultures proves to be more problematic, as they concentrate on the issues of race, color, and ethnicity, which are of marginal importance in the discussion of Central European postcoloniality. Nevertheless, Bhabha's notion of hybridity (see, e.g., *Location of Culture*) may be also partly applied in the former Soviet colonies. In Central Europe, however, hybridity—that is, the intermixing of dominant and subjugate cultures—happened mostly on the ideological level rather than on the social or racial level as in India or in the Caribbean. In other words, Central European hybridity was not an effect of interracial relationships, but rather an amalgam of various—often contrasting—systems of beliefs such as communism, socialism, Catholicism, and nationalism. One of the products of this ideological confusion is, I suggest, the famous Polish workers' organization *Solidarność* (Solidarity): although a trade union is a traditionally socialist formation, of which one could expect left-wing sympathies, Solidarność has positioned itself on the right side of the political scene. It is true that these left-wing/right-wing incongruities were mostly overlooked during Solidarność's struggle against communism in the 1980s; however, they gained in importance after 1989, when part of Solidarność transformed into a political party and, I argue, led to its eventual decline precisely because of its confused and confusing ideological agenda.

Even if Central European postcoloniality hardly refers to the issue of race, which is customarily associated with postcolonial cultures, many aspects of postcolonial theories are—as I have demonstrated above—applicable in the countries of the former Soviet bloc. Spivak reminds that "every postcoloniality is situated and therefore different" (828). Furthermore, Spivak proposes a rethinking of post-Soviet studies as postcolonial studies (828) and, thus, gives a green light for a postcolonial reading of Central and Eastern European cultures. Spivak's readiness to label post-Soviet cultures as postcolonial results from and gives evidence to a flexible understanding of postcolonialism she proposes: "When an alien nation-state establishes itself as ruler, impressing its own laws and systems of education and rearranging the mode of production for its own economic benefit, 'colonizer' and 'colonized' can be used. The consequences of applying them to a wide array of political and geographic entities would be dire if colonialism had only one model. On the other hand, if we notice how different kinds of adventures and projects turn into something that fits the bare-bones description given above, we will have a powerful analysis of the politics of progressivism, of one sort or another" (828). If we follow Spivak's definition, the Soviet Union can be definitely identified as a "colonizer" and Central and Eastern Europe as a formerly "colonized" region, thus, currently postcolonial.

Nevertheless, despite her recognition of miscellaneous types of postcolonialism, Spivak warns that attempts to apply the postcolonial framework to Central and Eastern Europe may (and do) face formal problems. Today the strongest postcolonial models deal with the Middle East, South Asia, and Latin America (Spivak 829): all of these regions used to be overseas colonies of European powers "as exploration and conquest nourished mercantile capitalism" (829). The Soviet (as well as earlier Ottoman and Habsburg) type of colonialism was more political than economic and involved inland expansion rather than conquest of distant lands. Another difficulty is, in Spivak's mind, "the presence of an articulated ideal" (829), lacking in the countries of the former Soviet bloc. For example, the colonizing activities in British and French overseas provinces where often accompanied by "civilizing missions" (Spivak 829) that were not necessarily related to the political or economic authorities. In the Soviet Union, on the contrary, there were few people who—either individually or self-organized—strove to educate Central and Eastern European societies on the greatness of Soviet socialism. First, individualism and self-initiative were strongly condemned in the Soviet Union. Second, more often than not, citizens of the Soviet Union experienced much worse economic and political conditions than their western neighbors and were hardly anxious to display their misery.

Despite these and other difficulties with the application of postcolonial theories in Central and Eastern Europe, I have shown that they are not only feasible but also increase the thoroughness of an interdisciplinary analysis of the cultures of the region. Still, a postcolonial approach towards post-1989 Central European cultures is a new field, which has, until now, scarcely been researched. One of the reasons for the scarcity of postcolonial research done on the discussed region is that Central European scholars are reluctant to look at their national cultures as part of a bigger postcolonial framework with the Soviet Union as the former colonizer and Western Europe and the United States as the present centers of colonial influence. Tötösy de Zepetnek claims this academic opposition is based on "the perception and insistence that Soviet colonialism exerted no direct cultural influence while the notion that the center's primary colonialism, that influenced the region's cultures and literature(s) (and was followed by a secondary colonialism and thus filtered impact, that occurred in the process of culture) was also consequently rejected" ("Comparative Cultural Studies" 5).

Instead of accepting the possibility of Soviet communist influences on the cultures of the region, Central European scholars prefer to label recent developments in their national cultures as "postmodern" or "postindustrial." For example, Halina Janaszek-Ivaničkova argues that Central European literatures are "postmodern" rather than "postcolonial" because they were already changing dramatically even before the end of the alleged Soviet colonialism (806). Whereas it is true that literature (as well as other types of media) underwent remarkable transformations in the

1980s, this fact does not exclude Soviet influences, but proves, rather, that cultural parallels between the colonial center and the "provinces" existed, as similar changes took place in the USSR with the advent of Gorbachev's *perestroika* (see Tötösy de Zepetnek, *Comparative Literature*). Furthermore, the term "postcolonial" describes a culture not only after it has been liberated, but it is also used to cover the whole period of political, economic, and cultural influences executed by an imperial power, that is, from the moment of colonization to the present (see Ashcroft, Griffiths, and Tiffin). Keeping the above in mind, the cultural changes experienced in Central Europe in the 1980s may be seen as both postcolonial and postmodern.

In Austrian scholarship (see Müller-Funk, Plener, and Ruthner) Central and Eastern Europe is viewed as a postcolonial space, but in relation to the Habsburg empire rather than to the more recent influences of the Soviet Union or Western Europe. Still, even in relation to the nineteenth-century superpower that ruled over most of Central Europe, Wolfgang Müller-Funk shies away from using the term "colonial" and proposes a more compromising and safer "quasi-colonial" instead (19). Müller-Funk claims that the differences between the sea powers traditionally perceived as colonizers and the European inland "colonizers" are of crucial importance and implies that only the former have the right to be described as colonizers. Further, Müller-Funk argues that while the maritime imperialism was based on the dichotomy between European versus non-European (overseas) cultures, the inner-European "colonialism" was shaped by such parameters as the level of industrial and technical development established along west-east relations, the opposition between Protestantism and Catholicism or Western Christianity and Orthodox Christianity, and the contrast between German and non-German cultures (20). Still, despite the crucial differences between "classical colonialism" and Habsburg imperialism, Müller-Funk acknowledges certain similarities between them: for example, in both cases the colonizing elites embark on a "civilizing mission," thus, imposing their culture on the subjugated countries (22-23). It is also important to remember that besides clearly positive changes such as the introduction of industrial progress to the occupied territories and the improvement of infrastructure, Habsburg authorities hurt the national and cultural pride as well as the self-governing rights of Central and Eastern European peoples (Müller-Funk 23), just like the British administration robbed Indians of their dignity and sovereignty.

The common colonial experience in the nineteenth century certainly constitutes one of the contact points between Central European countries (especially regarding the development of culture in urban centers such as Prague, Budapest, and Kraków); however, the unity of this philosophically, literarily, artistically, and socially discursive tradition as well as its ethos were lost with the end of the geographical and political unity of the Habsburg empire and with the events that accompanied its downfall. After 1918, the urban centers were incorporated into different nation states and the rich network of exchanges, contacts, and relationships was disrupted. Therefore, while an analysis of Habsburg colonialism—or, as Müller-Funk writes, "cultural asymmetry"—helps understand the beginnings and the historically complex postcolonial nature of Central and Eastern Europe, it is insufficient to explain the present cultural, political, and economic relations between Central and Eastern European countries, or their external relations with the former Soviet Union and Western Europe.

Keeping in mind the differences between the classical or overseas type of colonialism and Soviet colonialism, Tötösy de Zepetnek proposes that the latter be understood "not only within the traditional definition of colonialism, but also in terms of [what he defines as] 'filtered colonialism,' a type of colonialism that manifested itself in a secondary colonization through ideological, political, social, cultural, and other means during and after the forty-year period" of the Soviet rule ("Comparative Cultural Studies" 4). Filtered colonialism is a result of primary colonialism: whereas the latter is to be understood as the direct or indirect ideological, military, political, and economic "leadership-by-force of the Soviet centre," filtered colonialism is to be identified with "penetration and imprint of cultural processes and behaviour" (4).

What Tötösy de Zepetnek suggests is that while a political, institutional, and economic dominance is of a primary nature and, hence, easily detectable as colonial, cultural influences of the colonial center are indirect and, thus, not always obvious. Skórczewski argues against the idea of filtered colonialism as undermining the importance of Soviet cultural dominance in Central Europe, which, to him—with the exception of Romania and Yugoslavia—was equally as powerful and ruthless as the British cultural brainwashing of overseas colonies (105). I disagree with Skórczewski and argue that the Soviet cultural influences in Central Europe were milder than those executed by England in Africa and Asia: for example, while it is true that in the Soviet satellite countries, learning Russian as a second language was obligatory, in India and Kenya, English was the first language of education and, hence, the only way to get to know and create literature. Admittedly, in Ukraine, as well as in other Soviet republics, Russian was the official language and still remains an important means of communication; however, in my discussion of Central European cultures I focus on former satellite countries, not former Soviet republics.

Although Russian never became the language of Central European literatures, Soviet literature and culture were tremendously influential and dictated the (official) literary trends in the region. For example, as Tötösy de Zepetnek argues, postmodernism came to Central Europe from the Soviet Union and was closely related to the cultural and political changes initiated by Gorbachev (see, e.g., *Comparative Literature*). Underground and exile literature of the time was inspired chiefly by Western (predominantly French and German) literatures, which means that already before 1989 Central Europe experienced two types of cultural colonialism: from Moscow as well as from Paris, Munich, Vienna, or New York. The Western influences increased remarkably after 1989, overshadowing the impact of the former Soviet Union; however, the latter did not disappear, but continued "posthumously" to shape Central European cultures. The literatures of the region "show all elements of the postcolonial situation, and can be read as 'narratives of change'" that are characterized by "the emergence of the erotic and sexual in literary texts albeit from a strong patriarchal perspective; the shift in the social status of the male author and its repercussions apparent in literature, and the observation that the themes of urbanity, memory, and sexuality/eroticism are manifested prominently in the texts as 'subjective sensibility'" (Tötösy de Zepetnek, "Comparative Cultural Studies" 11).

Even if in their peculiarities they differ from the former overseas colonies of Western European empires, contemporary Central European cultures bear postcolonial characteristics; moreover, as I demonstrate above, many aspects of the theories developed by Said, Bhabha, and Spivak are applicable in this region. Nevertheless, Central European scholars are still largely reluctant to make use of postcolonial theories and, if they do, they relate them to the Habsburg empire rather than to the more recent colonial influences of the Soviet Union and Western Europe. To date, the most comprehensive theoretical elaboration on the postcolonial nature of Central European cultures has been developed by Tötösy de Zepetnek.

Urban studies

In my research and analysis, I take an interdisciplinary approach to the city as advocated by Roland Barthes: "anyone who wants to sketch a semiotics of the city must be at once a semiologist (a specialist in signs), a geographer, an historian, an urbanist, an architect, and probably a psychoanalyst" (191). Aside from the interdisciplinary frameworks of comparative cultural studies and postcolonial studies that have proved particularly viable for my research, I also apply selected notions from the field of urban studies: urban identity, urban image, urban representation, and urban entrepreneurialism.

Despite its wide use in various academic disciplines and public discourse alike, the term "urban identity" remains elusive. Taking into consideration the multitude and diversity of potential analytical perspectives, an attempt at developing a general definition of urban identity would be a rather futile task. Instead, I choose to focus on how urban identity is produced and communicated. Wolfgang Kaschuba distinguishes four models of creating urban identities: *Literarisierung* ("literization"), *touristische Modellierung* ("tourist modeling"), *Medialisierung* ("medialization"), and *Biografisierung* ("biographization") of the city (18-20). Literarization stands for the creation of literary images of the city that, in turn, leads to the mythologization of urban history, culture, and mentality. Beginning with the Renaissance travel literature through French and English novels of the eighteenth century to contemporary novels, poems, and plays set in metropolises, literature shapes our understanding and perception of the city it describes to the point that it becomes nearly impossible to think of a city like New York without keeping in mind its fictional representations created by Edith Warton, Ralph Ellison, or Jonathan Lethem. Naturally, literization is not a widespread phenomenon that affects all cities and towns, but rather a special gift a city may or may not have, namely a *Literaturfähigkeit*, or "capability to be literary." According to Kaschuba, the cities that are able to be literary—and, therefore, possess "aura and authenticity"—belong to an "urban Champions League" (18). Arguably, all of the cities I discuss in this book are "literary" to various extents whereby Berlin has been particularly inspiring not only to German, but also international writers. Owing to a developed network of scholarships and writers-in-residence programs, Berlin has hosted countless authors from Central European cities (as well as other parts of the world) who often feel inspired to produce literary portrayals of the city and, hence, intensify its literization. In chapter 6 I analyze selected works of literature set in Berlin and Warsaw and discuss what types of urban identities they communicate.

In tourist modeling, tourists are "transmitters and interpreters of urban images and myths" (Kaschuba 19—unless otherwise indicated, all translations from Polish, German, Hungarian, and Czech are mine). Kaschuba notes that it is tourists rather than residents who confront what they read and see in travel guides, urban literature, and city marketing materials with what they find in real life cities and, consequently, enter a dialog between the already existing and widely distributed city images and their own individual images of the city. In the age of mass (urban) tourism, the preconceptions city visitors bring with them are powerful enough to transform the city. Tourists appear to Kaschuba as "'city builders': active co-designers of urban images and imaginations, urban worlds and myths" (19). In chapter 4 I discuss city images as communicated by municipal authorities on official city websites and tourist information websites as well as in print materials distributed by tourist information offices. An analysis of these visual and textual self-representations of Central European capitals helps understand what kind of city image the governments of Berlin, Budapest, Prague, and Warsaw strive to communicate in an attempt to lure prospective visitors and investors.

Medialization of the city refers to city images reproduced in and through mass media. Kaschuba argues that distinct buildings, panoramas, and urban landscapes become "unmistakable symbols of urban identity" and are, as such, "staged in film and in the internet" (19). Some most recognizable buildings and structures (e.g., the Brandenburg Gate and the TV tower in Berlin; the Buda Castle Hill in Budapest; the Charles Bridge in Prague; the Palace of Culture and Science in Warsaw) are indeed repeatedly used in mass media as visual metonymies for cities—"the Eiffel Tower 'is' Paris" (Kaschuba 19); I disagree, however, that they possess the ability to solely symbolize urban identities. Only when they appear in a context—that is, for example, as objects rather than mise-en-scène in film (see chapter 7) or when we consider the frequency with which their images pop up on a website (see chapter 4)—can they be understood as representations of urban identities.

Through biographization, the city's history is mythologized and its residents "tribalized" (as Berliners, Budapestians, Praguers, Warsovians, etc.) (Kaschuba 20). Since the city is always "in the making," it constantly redefines itself and adds new features to the already existing ones. Consequently, the same city may reveal many different faces depending on a century or a decade. To Kaschuba, the city appears as "an individual whose fate and personality enable it to create a collective identification," especially today when pop culture and new media add new layers and dimensions to urban biographies (20). Local heroes (Franz Kafka in Prague) and events (the *Berlinale* in Berlin) remain closely associated with a particular city also when they become globally known. Owing to the appearance of ever new cultural, political, and sports phenomena, urban identities are continually changing and can be defined only in a given moment or period in time rather than definitively. As Kaschuba concludes, "urban identity rests on a permanence of cultural negotiations" (24) whereby urban identity is understood as a "form of 'glocal' identity" (24), that is, an identity possessing global and local traits.

According to the US-American urban planner Kevin A. Lynch, the image of the city—or any environmental image for that matter—consists of three components: identity, structure, and meaning: "A workable image requires first the identification of an object, which implies its distinction from other things, its recognition as a separable entity. This is called identity, not in the sense of equality with something else, but with the meaning of individuality or oneness. Second, the image must include the spatial or pattern relation of the object to the observer and to other objects. Finally, this object must have some meaning for the observer, whether practical or emotional" (8). Importantly, the meaning of the urban image is not fixed, but rather depends on the observer—the same image (Lynch gives the Manhattan skyline as an example) may connote various meanings (such as "vitality, power, decadence, mystery, congestion, greatness"), what matters is that its identity remains clear (that is, that the observer does not confuse the Manhattan skyline for the London skyline). Cities that evoke strong images "in any given observer" may be described as highly imageable (9-10). Lynch is quick to explain that "imageability does not necessarily connote something fixed, limited, precise, unified, or regularly ordered" (10). It may happen, of course, that an image strikes as obvious and, thus, boring (Lynch 10), as in the case of cities such as Barcelona or Paris that, according to Rem Koolhaas, oversimplify their identities (1250). Many of Europe's historic cities—including Central European capitals—tend to be highly imageable, that is, "well formed, distinct, remarkable," cities that can be "apprehended over time as a pattern of high continuity with many distinctive parts clearly interconnected" (Lynch 10). Naturally, some of these urban images strike one as more apparent and obvious than others. In chapter 4 I analyze official images of Central European metropolises developed by municipal authorities and discuss some of the possible meanings they communicate.

Urban images are particularly crucial when it comes to the development of urban representations. John Rennie Short and Yeong-Hyun Kim distinguish two discourses of urban representations: "the positive portrayal of a city" and "the identification of the shadow" (97). The former—known, for example, from the official websites of cities—is aimed at attracting investors and visitors and influencing local politics and is closely connected with urban marketing. The latter tends to be "contained, controlled or ignored" in municipal media: "this discourse works through silence, as some issues and groups are never mentioned, and through negative imagery, as some groups and issues are presented as dangerous, beyond the confines of civil debate" (Short and Kim 97). The shadow side of the city—mostly more complex than the positive portrayal—is frequently represented in literature and film (see chapters 6 and 7), thus, confirming Roland Barthes's and Michel de Certeau's observations on literary qualities of urbanities (see Barthes; de Certeau) as well as Walter Benjamin's and Sigfried Kracauer's notes on film as the medium best equipped to refer to the urban experience (see Benjamin, "Work of Art;" Kracauer).

Urban images and urban representations are important tools of urban entrepreneurialism. In his 1989 article "From Managerialism to Entrepreneurialism," David Harvey defines urban entrepreneurialism as a form of urban governance that "typically rests . . . on a public-private partnership" and focuses on "investment and economic development with the speculative construction of place . . . as its immediate (though by no means exclusive) political and economic goal" (8). Particularly widespread in late capitalism, that is, since the 1960s in Western societies (see, e.g., Jameson, *Postmodernism*) and since 1989 in Central Europe, urban entrepreneurialism has four basic options: 1) competition within the international division of labor, that is, "the creation or exploitation of particular advantages for the production of goods and services" (Harvey 8), some of which derive from the resource base or location while others are created through private and public investments and incentives; 2) competition with respect to the spatial division of consumption that rests increasingly on investments aimed at improving the quality of urban life (gentrification, consumer attractions, entertainment, etc.); 3) competition over "the acquisition of key control and command functions in high finance, government, or information gathering and processing" (Harvey 9), which necessitates investments in transport, communication, office space, and so on; and 4) competition over the "redistribution of surpluses through central governments" (Harvey 10). These four strategies are not mutually exclusive, but rather complimentary, and all of them imply "some level of inter-urban competition" (Harvey 10).

Competition between cities has been rendered more acute through the sinking transport costs and the reduction or removal of spatial barriers to movement of goods, people, money, and information (Harvey 10). Consequently, cities compete with each other not only on the national and global levels, but also, increasingly, within international economic communities (EU) or free trade agreements (NAFTA). Owing to the growing inter-urban competition, municipal governments aim at attracting "highly mobile and flexible production, financial, and consumption flows into its space" (11)—in doing so, they often repeat certain "patterns of development (such as the serial reproduction of 'world trade centers' or of new cultural and entertainment centers, of waterfront development, of postmodern shopping malls, and the like)" (10). The question remains, of course, which of these investments make sense in the long run: how many world trade centers does the world really need? Some of the costly entrepreneurialism-induced urban developments flop because the market fails to respond as expected, or simply because their success has been miscalculated. What they all have in common, however, is that they aim at enhancing "property values, the tax base, the local circulation of revenues, and . . . employment growth" (13).

The entrepreneurial city's focus on symbolic economy "associated with finance, media, tourism, heritage, gentrification, and, above all, with consumerism"

(Cronin and Hetherington 2) shapes urban landscapes and cultures and often results in urban transformations. Whereas "redefining" or "reimagining" the city is often an ongoing process or a long-term strategy of place marketing (Cochrane and Jonas 145-46) triggered simply by the city's need to remain competitive on the global arena, large urban transformations are necessitated by dramatic events such as the fall of the Berlin Wall or 9/11 in New York, or, "more typically," come as "a response to years of economic decline and the injection of new money" (Cronin and Hetherington 2) as in the case of Central European cities after the collapse of communism in 1989. Regardless of the factors behind urban changes, the success of the entrepreneurial city relies greatly on the development of a convincing and attractive urban image. Contemporary municipal governments—often in cooperation with associations of private interest groups (hotel and restaurant owners, airlines, entertainment agencies, etc.)—create elaborate image campaigns including logos, slogans, websites, and commercials and attempt to sell thus redefined cities as brands. In chapter 4 I analyze some of the urban marketing tools and branding campaigns recently developed by Berlin, Budapest, Prague, and Warsaw and discuss the urban identities they communicate. Since my focus remains on official urban images commissioned by city governments, it should be understood that whenever I use anthropomorphic phrases in relation to cities (for instance, "cities communicate," "cities decide," "cities prefer"), I mean the authorities responsible for the decisions affecting the cities.

Chapter Three

(Post)colonial Cultures of Central European Cities

Inspired by Marcel Proust and his idea of *memoire involontaire*, Walter Benjamin pronounced the city to be "like an archive of involuntary memory" (qtd. in Patke 292). In Berlin, Budapest, Prague, and Warsaw, memory lingers predominantly in the second half of the twentieth century. Many people still remember city life under the communist regime, and those who are too young to have experienced it live in a culture irrevocably altered by often catastrophic decisions of communist politicians, urban planners, and economists. Since the former Soviet satellite countries may (and, I argue, should) be perceived as postcolonial cultures, it would only be natural to deduce that their cities also bear postcolonial characteristics. Still, the postcolonial identities of Berlin, Budapest, Prague, and Warsaw remain largely unrecognized and the cities are labeled "postsocialist" or "postcommunist" instead (see, for example, Dimitrovska Andrews; Musil; Tosics; Stanilov). They are postcommunist or postsocialist, of course, but an additional postcolonial perspective yields a deeper insight into their complex identities and therefore should be encouraged. The reason why there has been virtually no comprehensive analysis of their postcolonial character may be explained by the already discussed general reluctance to look at Central Europe from a postcolonial perspective intensified by the fact that postcolonial urbanism and postcolonial geography are relatively new branches of postcolonial studies (see Blunt and McEwan). Whereas postcolonial studies has enjoyed a scholarly presence at least since Edward W. Said's 1978 *Orientalism*, it has focused mostly on language and literature, political science, sociology, and cultural anthropology. A more specific research on postcolonial urban cultures has emerged only recently (see Bishop, Phillips, and Yeo) and revolves around Europe's former overseas colonies. In this chapter, I confront some of the existing definitions of and views on the postcolonial city and demonstrate how they can be applied to Berlin, Budapest, Prague, and Warsaw. An analysis of the postcolonial and colonial characteristics of these cities has inspired me to create a definition of the (post)colonial city. I discuss the new concept in historical, cultural, and political contexts, which lead to a broader understanding of the developments of the Central European urban identity.

What is the (post)colonial city?

In simplest terms, the postcolonial city could be defined as a city whose politics, economy, society, and culture used to be shaped by a colonial power and where colonial influences remain visible; however, as M. Satish Kumar notes, "postcolonial urban space is not simply a physical entity, but is also a relational identity, created by interactions . . . between the colonized and the colonizer" (85). Kumar's remark underlines a crucial aspect of the postcolonial city's identity, namely, the mental relations between the former colonizer and the formerly colonized inhabitants that often outlive colonial monuments, economy, and politics. As I later demonstrate, this proof for a postcolonial condition is to be found predominantly in cultural products such as literature and film and, naturally, in the urban atmosphere that those works depict and communicate. The former colonial dependencies had an intense impact on the identities of Central European cities, especially in the 1990s, but also, to a lesser extent, in the 2000s and deserve a closer analysis.

In Berlin, Budapest, Prague, and Warsaw, Soviet influences were mostly indirect and conducted through the puppet state and local authorities, as well as through the ideological cum political impact of colonization. The politics and economy of Central European cities were largely designed in Moscow, especially in the first two decades after the end of World War II, but instructions and orders were executed by obedient local governments in a failed attempt to blind society with an illusion of self-governance. The only institution with any decision-making power was the communist party, and even its competence was not real, as the party had to report to its big sister in Moscow. If the colonized interacted directly with the colonizer, it was due to the presence of Soviet troops, officials, and secret agents in Central European cities. Needless to say, the Soviet leaders did not hesitate to intervene whenever disobedient "natives" put the colonial rule in jeopardy (e.g., in Plzeň and Berlin in 1953, in Poznań and Budapest in 1956, in Prague in 1968). Memories of mental subjugation and physical terror have outlived the Soviet regime and constitute a preeminent aspect of a postcolonial identity.

The direct and indirect relations between the colonized and the colonizer were also influenced by the surroundings in which they took place: "Colonization captured space and therefore established boundaries across which there were multiple interactions" (Kumar 85). After 1945, Berlin, Budapest, Prague, and Warsaw began experiencing a remarkable shift in the design and use of living and working space. The late 1940s and the early 1950s were dominated by monumental Stalinist architecture (such as the Soviet Embassy and Stalinallee in Berlin, the Palace of Culture and Science in Warsaw, Stalin's monuments in Budapest and Prague), which soon turned out to be too costly and—after Khrushchev's critique of Stalin in 1956—ideologically uncomfortable and gave way to cheap prefabricated housing and office buildings. Importantly, since most of the older buildings were in poor condition, with no central heating and outdoor bathrooms, the *Plattenbauten* became instantly popular among city residents and newcomers. Wladimir Kaminer reminds that in the

Soviet Union—but also in the whole socialist block—the prefabricated apartment complexes were "an attempt at fulfilling the dream of a happy and carefree life for all. 'An apartment with water access for each worker,' was the slogan of the building and construction policy'" (Kaminer 169-70). The leisure areas and entertainment centers were also constructed according to the Soviet design policies. Consequently, the urban population worked, lived, and rested in a world arranged by a socialist ideology and the rules of central planning. Community-building initiatives were discouraged or simply banned and social life was organized around the place of work (Węcławowicz 227), which allowed the party greater control over society.

In his postcolonial analysis of Madras, Kumar observes that "colonial urban forms and spaces were constantly resurrected and reworked to express the aspirations of the imperial metropolis" (86). The same is true of Central European cities. Almost every new tenement building, school, or retail center was enveloped in socialist ideology, be it by its design, the name of its patron, or the glorious party career of its architect. Owing to the poor quality of construction materials, outdated technologies, and inefficient working methods, the socialist buildings proved to be mostly dysfunctional and, hence, indicative of the whole political and economic system. Life and work in those edifices was often a struggle and symbolized the mental condition of the repressed society. Moscow's urge to shape urban developments in Central Europe was a typically colonial desire to control the conquered societies. Where the Soviet Union differed from other empires was that "the imperial center was actually poorer and more backward than its subjugated periphery" (Judt 167), a phenomenon unthinkable in Madras.

So far I have demonstrated that Central European cities have been shaped by interactions between the colonizer and the colonized in a colonized space. For historic and cultural reasons, the paths of colonization in Central Europe differed from those in European overseas colonies. Soviet satellite states were allowed to keep their national languages and religions (although religious practices were discouraged as incompatible with Marxism-Leninism) and seemingly enjoyed a range of other freedoms; in reality, however, they were captured in the unpredictable and malfunctioning Soviet imperial machinery. Even if Soviet officials did not directly govern Central European cities, it was not the society, but the communist party that appointed the mayor, for example. Therefore, "the mayor represented the interests of the state against the citizens, rather than the interests of the citizens against authority" (Węcławowicz 227). Furthermore, the state often represented the interests of the Soviet Union; the party or Moscow had to be consulted with regards to every major urban decision. Soviet politics changed the social and economic patterns of these cities. Prague, for example, underwent a Soviet-imposed process of re-industrialization and changed from a city formerly specializing in services into a factory town, in which, in the 1960s, 61 per cent of the economically active population were working class, half of them in engineering (Musil, "Prague Returns" 285). More often than not, Soviet directives determined what goods should be produced by which city, often completely irrespective of their industrial traditions and the skills of local workers. Whereas Warsaw and Budapest had already developed a remarkably big public sector before World War II as a means of protection from German economic expansion (Judt 168), the forced nationalization of companies and factories was deeply felt in Prague and Berlin, both of which had a long history of private businesses. In the early 1950s, the Soviet occupying powers took control of more than 200 private enterprises in Berlin and turned plants into "inefficient combines whose sole purpose was to produce goods for the Soviet Union" (Richie 680). Also, in the later decades Berlin workers themselves could hardly profit from their economic success (even if the success was measured against Albania, not West Germany) as "over half of their goods were exported to the Soviet Union while the rest went to West Germany" (755). Economic exploitation of subjugated countries and peoples leaves little doubt about the colonial nature of Soviet presence in Central Europe.

Moscow used the local communist parties in Berlin, Budapest, Prague, and Warsaw to extend its control not only over politics, culture, and economy, but also over demographics. The cities' growth and diversity were administered from above. "Only people who, from the perspective of the planners, were 'needed' in Prague"— but also in Warsaw (see Węcławowicz 227)—"were allowed to move and acquire a dwelling there" (Musil, "Prague Returns" 284-85). Similar practices took place in Madras, where "the ethics of colonial town planning suggested that one could not have access to a properly planned town unless one was 'morally' qualified to utilize its public spaces" (Kumar 89). Naturally, it was the colonizer who specified these moral—or, in the case of the Soviet bloc, ideological—qualities. In overseas colonies Europeans administered the spatial segregation of the population: a designation of separate districts, neighborhoods, buildings, and infrastructure for the colonizer and the colonized was a common practice. In Central European cities there were no such official demarcation lines; however, it was not unusual for the local governments to accommodate top party members and party-loyal public figures in higher-standard houses and apartments, inaccessible for "normal" citizens. Next to class and ideological beliefs, ethnicity was the third factor determining the party's social design of the cities. Whereas the administrators of Europe's overseas colonial cities had to decipher intricate ethnic relations and hierarchies before they could (mis)use them (Kumar 85-94), the Central European communist parties had an easier task as history saved them a lot of work.

After 1945, Central European urban centers, hitherto defined by their ethnic, religious, and national diversities, changed into homogenous cities. This transformation was strongly affected by the Holocaust and also by Stalinist persecutions and purges. Mass expulsions and emigration, which marked the years during and after the Second World War, had a strongly ethnic character; the same was true of many of the Stalinist show trials that resulted in countless deaths and disappearances. Furthermore, it was not unusual for the local people to get involved in "revenge" and "witch hunt" actions that either drove the remaining representatives of ethnic minorities (mostly Jews) out of the country or simply killed them (Judt 43). The loss of cultural heterogeneity had serious repercussions for the cities' intellectual life, entertainment, architecture, economy, and politics. The Jewish and German minorities who had lived in Prague for centuries and "cooperated, competed, and vied together for primacy" with the Czechs nearly completely disappeared (by 1961, Czechs accounted for 97.6 per cent of Prague population, with Slovaks being the largest minority at 1.3 per cent) (Musil, "Prague Returns" 286). Even decades after Central European capital cities had been rendered ethnically homogenous, anti-Semitism, discrimination, and ill treatment of minorities did not completely vanish from the region. In a truly Orwellian manner, the party did not hesitate to use the Jews as scapegoats, which led to an even greater ethnic homogenization of the cities. One of the most drastic examples of discriminative strategies took place in Warsaw in the aftermath of the 1968 demonstrations in favor of party reforms: a "disproportionate number of the students and professors arrested, expelled and imprisoned . . . were of Jewish origin" (Judt 434). The Jews were accused of betraying Poland, dubbed the "fifth column," and encouraged to leave the country (434). As a result, 20,000 of the remaining 30,000 Polish Jews moved to the West or to Israel (435). Vacant government posts and university tenures were readily taken over by party hardliners. In a broader context, the Warsaw events can be seen as part of the official Soviet policy at the time (Levin 652). In 1967, the Soviet Union supported the Arab cause in the Six Day War between Israel and its neighbors and "legitimized vocal criticism of Israel, Zionism—and Jews" (Judt 434). Even if Khrushchev himself did not order the Polish Jews to leave the country, he certainly had no intentions of condemning the expulsions.

Clearly, between 1945 and 1989, the development of Central European cities was largely controlled by the Soviet Union in the image and function of an imperial colonizer that determined urban politics, economy, culture, and social patterns. As I have demonstrated, there are some parallels between Europe's treatment of its overseas colonial cities and Moscow's handling of Berlin, Budapest, Prague, and Warsaw. Still, the Soviet Union did not simply copy the colonial practices of England or France, but, rather, developed its own methods of colonization that responded to regional specifics. Now that the colonial nature of the Soviet bloc cities has been established, I move to an analysis of their post-1989 situation and discuss the extent of their postcoloniality.

To date, one of the most inspiring articles on the postcolonial city is Rajeev S. Patke's 2000 essay "Benjamin's *Arcades Project* and the Postcolonial City." Whereas Benjamin's unfinished work has been analyzed by numerous scholars from various disciplines (see, e.g., Buck-Morss; Hanssen; Witte), Patke's reading is particularly interesting in that it refers not only to the modern city, but also to the postcolonial city: "what is true of any modern city applies to the postcolonial city doubly" (296). Following Benjamin, Patke encourages an exploration of the city life as an experience "stretching across time rather than simply extending in space" (289). Benjamin's city "historicizes space" (Patke 289); no wonder then that the historical aspects of urban development lay at the heart of Patke's approach. The consideration of the past and the relations between the past and the present are especially viable in a discussion of the postcolonial city: "The traces of the colonial dominate the architecture of most Asian cities, especially in its monuments, public buildings, and in the 'linguistic cosmos' of street names. Wherever the nationalist impulse has prevailed, civic managements have rushed to efface such traces. Wherever the past is allowed to remain, it has provided a thread leading the traveler back into the labyrinth of historical awareness" (Patke 292). What Patke writes about Singapore and Hong Kong is also true of Central European capitals. After the peaceful—with the notable exception of Romania—revolutions of 1989, the dismantlement of communist monuments and exchange of street name signs were common practices that enjoyed a large social approval in Warsaw, Prague, and Budapest. In Berlin, the recent past was partly "allowed to remain": Lenin's monument was taken away from *Leninplatz* (Lenin Square) in 1991 and the square itself renamed *Platz der Vereinten Nationen* (United Nations Square in Berlin-Friedrichshain), but the statues of Karl Marx and Friedrich Engels still stand on the Marx-Engels-Forum in the very center of the city; similarly, the *Palast der Republik* (Palace of the Republic), which for over two decades housed the GDR parliament, was torn down, while the gray concrete lamp posts on the monumental *Karl-Marx-Allee* (the former *Stalinallee*) await costly renovation. The decisions on which remnants of the communist past remain and which have to go are often controversial; I discuss some of them at length later.

Taking Benjamin's viewpoints on modernity as the starting point, Patke argues the author of *Arcades Project* "would treat the postcolonial and the postmodern as a three-tiered phenomena: Each is a historical phase of world history, a predicament affecting collectivities, and an attitude or state of mind" (288). While it is true that both the postcolonial and postmodern conditions have a serious effect on whole communities and remarkably determine not only their image of the world, but also their self-image, treating the postcolonial as yet another period in world history seems far-fetched: after all, colonization and decolonization are processes that have been taking place for many centuries, with various intensities and repercussions. Also, not every postmodern is postcolonial, so equating the two would be an exaggeration. In the 1990s, for example, the societies of Central European cities were postcolonial without being postmodern; more than that, they aspired to be postmodern and, hence, by implication, more Western. Associating the postindustrial West with economic progress has been prevalent not only in the former European colonies in Asia (Patke 296) but also in the former Soviet satellite states that felt unjustly excluded from the Western world at least since 1945 and where "[the Western] modes of consumption and culture provide[d] the model for the postcolonial city" (Patke 296). Today, twenty years after the demise of the Soviet empire, Central European cities appear to have achieved their aim: their consumption and entertainment behaviors are hardly distinguishable from those in Western metropolises. This economic and cultural transformation has been accelerated, just like in the postcolonial cities of Asia, by globalization.

Paradoxically, it is globalization and its effects on urban centers that constitute one of the most crucial differences between Central European and Asian postcolonial cities. Whereas the former possess certain "global city functions" (Bishop,

Phillip, and Yeo 6) but they are not global cities, Singapore, Manila, Shanghai, and Hong Kong play important roles on world markets and, hence, actively influence globalization processes (Sassen, "Locating Cities" 15-17). In Europe, it is London, Paris, Frankfurt (but not Berlin), Zürich, Amsterdam, and Moscow that have their say in globalization. When she discusses the economic importance of global cities and relations between them, Saskia Sassen does not include Central European cities in the privileged group of cities that "have the resources . . . that enable firms and markets to be global" ("Locating Cities" 9). The author makes a footnote remark on Budapest, suggesting the Hungarian capital is "rather attractive for purposes of investment, both European and non-European" (32), but does not call it a global city. Sassen is right to note that although the cities of what she calls "Eastern Europe" are indeed important players in the regional economy, their influences hardly ever extend beyond Europe. Therefore, despite their economic importance in and for Central Europe, Berlin, Budapest, Prague, and Warsaw are not in a position to remarkably affect globalization processes. In a globalized world, Central European cities appear provincial in comparison to Singapore, Buenos Aires, and Mexico City, not to mention the three essential global cities: New York, London, and Tokyo, as suggested by the title of Sassen's 1991 breakthrough publication, *The Global City: New York, London, Tokyo*. Whether Berlin, Budapest, Prague, and Warsaw will start playing a more important role on world markets and extend their economic (and, hence, cultural and political) influence beyond Central Europe remains to be seen.

As a predominantly urban phenomenon, economic globalization increases competition between cities over investments and, consequently, encourages local governments to promote and market their cities to potential international investors (see chapter 4). Next to the growth of multinational enterprises and the emergence of new global economic sectors, other factors intensifying rivalry between cities include "competition for international institutions to locate within cities" and "competition for global spectacles such as major sporting events, cultural festivals and trade fairs, which generate considerable economic multiplier effects" (Short and Kim 11). Once we recognize the corporate or institutional forces behind globalization, it becomes clear that the globalization of cities goes hand in hand with their colonization, whereby the global capital takes on the role of the new colonizer. The blurb on the cover of Michael Hardt's and Antonio Negri's *Empire* proclaims that "the new political order of globalization should be seen in line with our historical understanding of Empire as a universal order that accepts no boundaries": even if traditional forms of imperialism and colonialism are virtually extinct, the "Empire" is still doing well. As Krzysztof Nawratek writes, contemporary cities are "spaces colonized by global institutions" and the rank of a city is "determined precisely by the extent of its 'colonization' by international corporations and institutions" (*Miasto* 137-38). Keeping this in mind, I argue that postcolonial cities of Central Europe became colonized anew immediately after their 1989 decolonization. Apart from the impact of global capital on the region, Berlin, Budapest, Prague, and Warsaw have been experiencing intensive Westernization. At this point I find it crucial to make clear that globalization does not equal Westernization: after all, Asian and Latin American cities belong to some of the most important global players. It is true that globalization and Westernization interweave and often take place together, as in the case of Central European cities, but the terms are not synonymous.

To Patke, Westernization is one of the main characteristics of the postcolonial city (294-96). For reasons I explain below, I propose to distinguish two types of Westernization: Westernization from the outside and Westernization from within. The former represents what is conventionally understood by the term "Westernization": a situation in which a non-Western culture is politically, economically, socially, and culturally transformed by (what is associated with) the Western culture, predominantly US-American culture (Americanization), but also, increasingly, the European Union (EU-ization). Westernization from the outside is often considered a hostile force, a negative development leading not only to the loss of national or regional culture and identity, but also to a servile economic and political dependence on the West. In Central European cities, the enemies of Westernization can be found especially among people with extreme right-wing (nationalist) and culturally essentialist sympathies, but also among the extreme left-wing activists who associate Western culture with ruthless capitalism and find it destructive. Condemning Westernization as a whole is hardly justified as it overlooks its positive aspects: a wider choice of products, a greater variety of consumer behaviors, often a higher quality of products and a higher efficiency of production, and so on. Similarly, looking at Westernization as a phenomenon coming exclusively from outside is a simplification of the transformation processes taking place inside a given culture. Westernization from within is a situation in which a non-Western culture aspires to emulate the Western culture and introduces political, economic, social, and cultural developments that are meant to render it more Western. This type of Westernization is based to a large extent on a naïve belief in the infallibility of the West and overlooks the pitfalls of late capitalism. Many West-inspired developments in the postcolonial city tend to result in imperfect copies of Western products, systems, and behaviors, which in turn makes the West look more magical than ever. Westernization from within and Westernization from the outside do not exclude each other; more often than not they are complementary.

Interestingly, postcolonial cities of Central Europe and those of Asia look up to the West for the same reasons: "The enormous material prosperity, military power, high standard of living, and conspicuous consumption of the advanced capitalist societies made it inevitable for the postcolonial nation to define its goals and objectives in terms of the given notion of progress, regardless of reservations at what might be entailed in the pursuit of Utopia" (Patke 294). It is also true of both Central European and Asian postcolonial cities that their aspirations reinforce "an imitativeness learned under colonialism" (294). The difference is that the Asian cities try to copy their former colonizers, while the Central European cities strive to imitate the former enemies of their former colonizer (they had already done so under the socialist regime, now they can continue their emulation of the West without the fear of getting punished by the Soviet Union). To Patke, the imitativeness of the formerly colonized is inherent to the postcolonial condition. Despite being postcolonial, Berlin, Budapest, Prague, and Warsaw do not imitate Moscow, but rather choose to copy Paris, London, Frankfurt, and New York, that is, the centers of the Western culture and global capital.

What emerges is a picture of the Central European city as a place influenced by two powerful phenomena: the postcolonial condition determined by the remnants of the colonial (Soviet) past and Westernization from within on the one hand and the colonial nature of Westernization from the outside and globalization on the other. Therefore, calling the Central European city simply postcolonial or colonial would not entirely convey its complex identity. I propose to call the Central European city (post)colonial, a concept I define as follows:

> The (post)colonial city is a city whose politics, culture, society, and economy have been shaped by two centers of power: the former colonizer, whose influence remains visible predominantly in architecture, infrastructure, social relations, and mentalities, and the current colonizer, whose impact extends over virtually all spheres of urban life. The (post)colonial city is characterized by political, cultural, social, and economic tensions resulting from the condition of being postcolonial and colonial at the same time; the intensity of the tensions is proportional to the differences between the former colonizer and the present colonizer. The postcolonial aspects of the (post)colonial city are strongest immediately after decolonization and become weaker with time, whereby the pace of the decline depends on a complex set of factors ranging from economic cycles to political constellations to urban migration. The colonial aspects of the (post)colonial city are most intensely experienced immediately after colonization; with time, they become identified increasingly as qualities essential to the postmodern city rather than results of colonial influences.

Although the above definition has been inspired by a close analysis of Central European cities, I believe it may also be applied to other cities that have experienced similar patterns of development. Here, the cities of Latin America come to mind: the former Spanish (but also Portuguese, Dutch, and French) colonial cities, which—sometimes decades, sometimes a century after gaining their independence—fell under the influence of US-American economic and political power. Whether a (post)colonial nature of Latin American cities can be demonstrated remains a question to be answered by quite a different research project (see, e.g., Capello; Nascimento).

The (post)colonial character of Central European cities supports Tötösy de Zepetnek's claim that the cultures of Central Europe are "in-between peripheral" (see chapter 2). Berlin, Budapest, Prague, and Warsaw are "in-between" not only because they are located between the west and the east, but also because they are torn between the Soviet colonial past and the Western or global colonial present. The cities are not exclusively postcolonial or solely colonial: they are "in-between" the two predicaments and, hence, are best described as (post)colonial. Furthermore, in a geographical—but also, importantly, cultural—sense, Central European cities are located on the peripheries of Eastern and Western spheres of influences. In their colonial past, the cities were located on the periphery of the Soviet empire: outside the official borders of the Soviet Union and dangerously close to and aspiring to the West. In their colonial present, the cities are located on the periphery of the West: inside the official borders of the European Union and NATO, but dangerously (and excitedly) close to the east. The (post)colonial and "in-between peripheral" identities of Central European capitals complement one another and a discussion of them provides an insightful analysis of the transformation processes that have been shaping the cities after 1989.

The remarkable exception in the analysis of the (post)colonial identity of Central European cities is the former West Berlin: a (part of the) city occupied by Western Allies, which, after rejoining with East Berlin in 1990, experienced another wave of Westernization, this time coupled with globalization. Therefore, it is important to keep in mind that the former West Berlin should be considered postcolonial rather than (post)colonial. In the following discussion on Central European cities before 1989, when I speak of Berlin I mean the east part of the city. I argue that keeping the official name of the GDR capital (it was never called East Berlin within the borders of East Germany), which later, without any nominal change, became the capital of reunited Germany, better illustrates the complex character of the city.

Now that the (post)colonial identity of Central European cities has been defined, I examine how it came into being and how it has been developing. In order to land at a deeper understanding of the economic, political, cultural, and social transformations of and in the cities after 1989, it is crucial to examine the processes that were shaping Berlin, Budapest, Prague, and Warsaw under the Soviet regime. I discuss how the Soviet takeover changed the Central European cities right after World War II and how Moscow continued to influence the capitals of its satellite states until the demise of communism in 1989. I pay attention to the social and political responses of the urban societies captured by "a semi-alien Great Power" (Judt 196) and to developments in the cultural lives of the cities. Next, I demonstrate the importance of Berlin, Budapest, Prague, and Warsaw in the system change of 1989. An analysis of the transformations taking place after the fall of the Berlin Wall not only reveals the diverse aspects of (post)colonial cities, but also prepares ground for further discussion on the communication of their urban identities.

Central European cities under Soviet colonial rule

At the beginning of the twentieth century, Central European cities found themselves at various stages of political, economic, and cultural development. Budapest was, next to Vienna, one of the capitals of the Austro-Hungarian Empire, an immense multiethnic and multinational formation that spread over most of Central Europe. Owing to its railway connections to even the most distant provinces of the Dual

Monarchy, Budapest paid a crucial role in Central European trade, industry, and politics. Prague, the capital of the Czech Lands, was one of the regional centers of the Austro-Hungarian Empire and a "'factory backyard' of Vienna" (Hamilton 81). In contrast to Prague and Budapest, which experienced rapid industrialization and urban growth, Warsaw remained largely underdeveloped. Over a century of Russian colonial rule had led to an increased provincialization of the former Polish capital. To Russia, industrialization equaled "creating a revolutionary urban proletariat that could further fuel Polish nationalism" (Hamilton 82); therefore, Moscow discouraged industrial developments in Central Poland. As the capital of the Second German Reich, a young powerful state established in 1871, Berlin became one of the most powerful political centers not only in the region, but also in the world. The industrial developments and economic boom of the nineteenth century led to an unprecedented growth of population, mostly working class. The housing market responded with the construction of thousands of *Mietskasernen* (tenement buildings), which soon became "a key part of . . . Berlin's identity" (Ladd 100). Like London, Paris, and New York, Berlin of the 1900s "shaped the twentieth century's image of modernity: crowds, lights, noise, machines, buildings, all on a scale that dwarfed the individual" (Ladd 115) and, famously, became immortalized as such by Alfred Döblin in *Berlin-Alexanderplatz* (1929).

Germany's defeat in World War I and the succeeding political and economic chaos did not shake the myth of Berlin as the ultimate metropolis; it was the nazi dictatorship that put an end to the vibrant urban life and precipitated the capital's decline. For the other cities under scrutiny, 1918 brought substantial changes. The Versaille Treaty gave rise to nation states in Central and Eastern Europe, among them Poland and Czechoslovakia. Consequently, Warsaw and Prague became capitals of independent countries, finally free to determine their own politics and economy. Hungary, on the other hand, lost two thirds of its land and population in the Treaty of Trianon in 1920. The decrease of Hungary's population from twenty million to less than nine million greatly increased Budapest's significance: the proportion of the capital's inhabitants to the country as a whole rose from 4.5 per cent in 1918 to nearly 12 per cent in 1920 (Lackó 140). Despite considerable differences in their political and economic situations, Central European cities shared one very important feature: cultural and ethnic heterogeneity. After 1929 they had yet another thing in common: general poverty. Unemployment, homelessness, and hunger became prevalent not only in the already impoverished Berlin, but also in the capitals of the young Czechoslovak and Polish nation states and in the populous Budapest. Hardly did they have the chance to recover after the world economic crisis when the war broke out.

Prague and Warsaw were the first two capitals to be occupied by nazi Germany, in March and September 1939, respectively. Berlin, as the capital of the country that started World War II, became a metonymy for the nazi regime and, as such, universally feared and hated. Hungary also steered to the far right and the government in Budapest opted for an alliance with Hitler. Prague, which suffered little damage during the war, was an exception; Berlin, Budapest, and Warsaw became significantly destroyed by air raids, fires, and street fights. Furthermore, all the cities experienced losses in population owing to the deportations of Jews (but also of non-Jewish inhabitants) to concentration camps, mass expulsions, arrests, exile, and starvation. The largest destructions took place in the last year of World War II. An estimated 150,000-200,000 civilians and 16,000 insurgencies died in the Warsaw Uprising of August and September 1944 and another 550,000 people were expelled from the city by the Germans after Warsaw's capitulation. Almost the whole population vanished, and the vast majority of buildings (estimated at 85 per cent) were completely destroyed by the Germans during and after the uprising (see Geter). Budapest also suffered tremendous destruction: during the Soviet siege in the winter of 1944-45 an estimated 40,000 civilians died, some 74 per cent of all buildings suffered damages, and all the bridges were blown up by the escaping German army (Varga, "Devastation" 196). Berlin was the last city to fall. Its population decreased from 4.3 million before World War II to 2.8 million in 1945 as a result of exile, murder, and the deportation of Berlin Jews, Allies' air raids, starvation, and the death of 100,000 civilians during the Battle of Berlin in April and May 1945 (Richie 632). Almost the whole historic center of the city and over half a million apartments were destroyed (Ladd 177). What had not been destroyed during the war was stolen, damaged, or dismantled and shipped to the Soviet Union by the Red Army, which entered Warsaw, Budapest, Prague, and Berlin in the first months of 1945. At the dawn of the postwar era, Central European cities were impoverished, ruined, and—most importantly—controlled by the vigilant eye of the Soviet "liberators."

Colonization by the Soviet Union is often described as Sovietization. Moscow's influence on Central European countries and their capitals lingered for over four decades, but it was not consistently powerful throughout that time. The first phase of Sovietization that took place in the years 1944-1953 was especially brutal. Stalinization, as this period is also called, abounded in show trials, purges, disappearances of the members of the anti-Soviet resistance, pogroms of the homecoming Jews, and mass arrests that terrorized society. Establishing the Soviet rule in Central Europe was an ambitious task, since the region had been known for its hostility towards the Soviet Union during the interwar period. There were very few communists left in Berlin, Budapest, Prague, and Warsaw, and those who survived were too weak to form a government. Therefore, Czech, Slovak, German, Hungarian, and Polish communist politicians, trained in Moscow and deadly loyal to Stalin, were sent back to their national capitals with the task of installing puppet governments. Klement Gottwald, Walter Ulbricht, Mátyás Rákosi, and Bolesław Bierut, among others, who made it easier for Stalin to take over Central Europe, were awarded with top party positions or crucial ministries, which they used to copy the Soviet system onto the local ground.

The determination to "re-mould eastern Europe in the Soviet image" (Judt 167) was a striking characteristic of Soviet colonialism. Historian Tony Judt notes that this trend was particularly forceful under Stalin's regime: "Stalin set out to . . . reproduce Soviet history, institutions and practices in each of the little states now controlled by Communist parties" (167). The propagation of Soviet customs took its most extreme forms in Berlin, where the Red Army soldiers changed the Berlin clocks to Moscow time and installed street signs in Russian; in May 1945, Berlin became merely "an extension of the Soviet Union" (Richie 609). Stalin's takeover was facilitated by horrendous war destruction on the one side and the general weakness of all political parties on the other side. Even if the communist party did not have many supporters, there were few convincing alternatives and even those would soon be eliminated.

In the first months after World War II, it was the inhabitants of Berlin and Budapest—the capitals of the former enemy countries—who suffered most under the Soviet occupation. According to official rhetoric, Central European cities had not been conquered but liberated by the Red Army. In reality, however, Berliners and Budapestians suffered humiliation from the "friendly" Soviet soldiers who took what they had been promised by the supervisors: mass rapes of women of virtually all ages led to a drastic increase in sexually transmitted diseases, abortions, murders, and suicides; local people were robbed of whatever valuables they had left and it was not unusual to see a Soviet private with a few watches on his wrist; since the Soviet Army had control over the distribution of food to the starving inhabitants, Soviet soldiers misused their privileged position, which led to an even greater growth of corruption that had already substantially risen during World War II. The Soviet occupation, together with new laws introduced by the communist governments, induced large-scale exploitation of the local population. The situation in Warsaw was slightly better: the inhabitants were spared the rapes and plunder, but many of those who openly opposed the communist regime (especially members of the resistance movement) were killed as traitors. Prague, disillusioned with the West after Munich 1938, was the only Central European city that welcomed the Red Army as liberators (Judt 137-38). Still, under the Stalinist regime, even devoted Czechoslovak communists were not safe, as the 1948 coup in Prague demonstrated. Stalin engineered the coup despite substantial support for the Communist Party in Prague (in the free election of 1946, the communists received more than 40 per cent of the vote in Bohemia and Moravia and were likely to win the election planned for 1948) and, importantly, in a "more or less democratic country friendly to Moscow" (Judt 139). The Prague coup may be also seen as a punishment for the Czechoslovak interest in the Marshall Plan, a US-American framework of economic assistance officially rejected by the Soviet Union and its satellite states. The events of 1948 made it clear that Stalin was interested not in unlimited support for communism, but, rather, in total domination.

Control seems to have been the chief driving force behind Stalinist politics. One of the reasons Stalin wanted so badly to "liberate" Central Europe was his urge to control the uranium plants in East Germany and Czechoslovakia that would help the Soviet Union produce nuclear weapons (Judt 118). Furthermore, newly subjugated countries increased Moscow's international prestige and security. As the world was turning into a playground of two powerful empires, the situation in Europe was shaped by feudal-like relations. Judt compares the postwar system divisions to the postreformation order in sixteenth-century Europe: the principle *cuius regio eius religio* perfectly represents the state of affairs in Europe after 1945 (129). Not only did subdued peoples have no say in shaping their political and economic fate, but also any serious interference from behind the Iron Curtain could have been understood as a violation and triggered a war, which no one was prepared to risk.

Although Stalin was "typically indifferent to national variety" (Judt 133-34), I demonstrate below that there were some differences in how the Soviet rule was exercised and how the people of Berlin, Budapest, Prague, and Warsaw reacted to it. As we have already seen, Stalin used a group of Central European communists trained by Moscow to establish Soviet political supremacy in the region. After the purges of the late 1940s, the communist party was the only real political power and determined all areas of life. A party membership card often proved to be a ticket to higher positions in state-owned companies, hospitals, and universities, not to mention public offices. Prevalent nepotism, fraud, and other political crimes left little doubt about the true intentions of the decision makers. Consequently, "politics and government became synonymous with corruption and arbitrary repression, practiced by and for the benefit of a venal clique" (Judt 194). Already in the 1950s the dramatic decline or complete unprofitability of local economies offered a clear sign that substantial transformations were urgently needed. The degeneration of the party and the absurdity of the whole system went to such extremes that even its own members sought internal reforms. Interestingly, while the communists in Budapest (Imre Nagy), Warsaw (Władysław Gomułka), and Prague (Alexander Dubček) advocated changes, those in Berlin (Walter Ulbricht) demanded even greater party domination over society. The zealousness of East German leaders seemed frightening even to the Soviet communist party and Berlin repeatedly met with Moscow's criticism (Judt 310-12; Ladd 186).

Since the central committees of the communist parties were located in capital cities, it is only natural that Berlin, Budapest, Prague, and Warsaw played a crucial role in both the implementation of new restrictions and introduction of reforms. Although Moscow tried to block the economic growth of Prague and Warsaw in favor of a development of middle-size cities (see Musil "City Development"), the capitals remained the most important urban centers in their particular countries, albeit with little freedom. Self-governance was nonexistent and municipal political decisions were decided either by the chiefs of the local communist party or directly by the communist party's central committee. City residents had no say in local politics, economy, or culture and hardly identified with their neighborhoods or districts, which were administered by apparatchiks and observed by secret agents. Politics, the most obvious area of Soviet influence, stretched its tentacles into virtually all spheres of urban life. Meetings with family and friends (and sometimes within religious groups) became the only relatively independent and nonpolitical forms of social gatherings and interactions. The dividing line between city officials and the urban population grew thicker with years, as people became more and more disillusioned with politics. The "us versus them" attitude was dangerous in that "them" happened to stand not only for the local government, but also for the urban developments it introduced. People had no say in what was happening to the space they inhabited and so they stopped caring about the space itself.

Apart from its excessive influence on politics, Moscow extended its influence to other spheres of life in Central European cities: economy, society, and culture. All these aspects of urban existence were, of course, closely interwoven with politics and with one another. The impact of the Soviet Union can hardly be underestimated if we look closely at the effects of Moscow-imposed central planning policies. Despite ubiquitous poverty, Central European cities entered the postwar period at various stages of economic development. Berlin and Prague had long capitalist traditions, skilled workers, a well-developed network of services, and machineries competitive with those in the West. Budapest was a step behind (its progress was hindered by Hungary's territorial losses after World War I), but much more industrially and economically advanced than Warsaw. Four decades of central planning brought all the cities to a very similar level. Thanks to the relative economic liberalism of the Kádár era, Budapest was more advanced than Prague, Berlin, and Warsaw, but altogether the cities had to face similar reforms in 1989. Such deep penetration of local economies would have not been possible if not for the mass nationalization that started soon after the Soviet Army entered the cities.

Budapest and Warsaw had introduced nationalization already in the 1930s, as a reaction to the world economic crisis and the protection of local companies against Germany's economic expansion. Prague joined the trend right after World War II with the decision of a freely elected government: remarkably, already a year before the coup, 93 per cent of the transport sector and 78 per cent of industry in Czechoslovakia had been managed by the state (Judt 71); therefore, the increased nationalization ordered after the 1948 communist takeover was merely another way of manifesting control rather than an introduction of new reforms. Unlike in Prague, nationalization in Berlin was introduced clearly against the will of the people: "All chemical, electrical and textile plants were nationalized, while armed men took over shops and businesses, arrested the owners and turned the property over to the state. Self-employed people had their ration cards ripped up and all manifestations of free enterprise were forbidden" (Richie 680). Mass nationalization combined with central planning allowed the Soviet Union to keep the economies of the satellite states in check and to decide where to allocate industries.

It is no secret that central planning proved disastrous for the economy. "As in the case of non-European colonies, so in eastern Europe: the indigenous economies suffered deformation and under-development. Some countries were prevented from manufacturing finished goods, others were instructed to make certain products in abundance (shoes in Czechoslovakia, trucks in Hungary) and sell them to the USSR. No attention was paid to the economics of comparative advantage" (Judt 171). When it comes to the economic aspects of colonization, the main difference between Central Europe and the overseas colonies of England or France was that the Soviet colonizer's economy was even more underdeveloped than that of the colonized. The five-year plans, first introduced in 1928, gradually destroyed the Soviet economy until the demise of the Soviet Union in 1991. None of the cities under scrutiny suffered as much from centrally planned economy as Moscow.

Poland's capital experienced rapid industrialization right after the war. The "irrational structure of industrial production in Warsaw" had devastating consequences not only for the local economy, but also for the "organization of . . . urban space and the social and natural environment" (Węcławowicz 229). The trend continued until the mid-1970s when it became clear that the factories were not only unprofitable, but also frighteningly backward. The only possible remedy—abandoning central planning—was clearly out of the question. Other measures, such as the import of new(er) technologies from the West (which tremendously increased Poland's foreign debt) and slow de-industrialization, were introduced in the 1970s, but did little to improve the situation. Consumer goods soon became so scarce that the government decided to ration them. Ration cards for sugar—and in the 1980s also for meat, coffee, butter, and so on—were issued and long lines of people waiting in front of empty state-owned stores became endemic on the streets of Warsaw. The capital was no different than other Polish cities. Owing to the state-encouraged development of middle-size cities, Warsaw underwent the same industrialization and de-industrialization processes as the rest of the urban centers in the country.

Apart from having a relatively long prewar tradition of capitalist production, trade, and service systems, Prague profited from the few relaxations of central planning introduced in the late 1960s. Although the complex reform program was reversed after the Soviet intervention in 1968, some changes remained and saved the Czechoslovak economy from the degeneration taking place in Poland (Musil, "City Development" 32-34). Hungary was doing even better than Czechoslovakia (although much worse in comparison to Western European countries, of course) and Budapest kept its traditional dominating position within the country. As Ivan Tosics observes, "the 44 years of Soviet dominance and the imposition of the socialist system created at the beginning very unfavorable conditions for Hungary and its capital, which became very isolated from the Western world. From the 1960s onwards, however, Hungarian politics achieved a gradual opening-up of its foreign relations and by the end of the 1980s, Budapest was almost regarded as a 'European city' again" ("Post-socialist Budapest" 249). Kádárism turned Budapest into the most prosperous city in the Soviet bloc and Hungary into a favorite holiday destination for Central Europeans (mostly East Germans but also Austrians). Also, Western politicians and celebrities often visited the Hungarian capital. The city's Western-like status was decisively sealed by the construction of the first Hilton Hotel in the region in 1976 (Judt 608). Clearly, the economic reforms in Hungary could not have taken place without Moscow's permission. The Soviet leaders recognized that the city's relative prosperity prevented people from rebelling against the system. Further, memories of the brutally crushed uprising in 1956 discouraged any political opposition and there was little need to protest in favor of economic reforms since the state introduced them anyway. In Budapest "life was tolerable" (Judt 608).

Berlin's position as a technologically and economically developed city and a traditional leader on the Central European market was irrevocably lost after the war. In East Berlin, the party imposed drastic production norms on the workers, but the economy hardly profited from the progress in production since the Soviet Union demanded participation in the output; in West Berlin, despite substantial state subsidies from the federal government, no large businesses decided to stay in the insecure environment: banks moved to Frankfurt, the car industry to Stuttgart and Munich, and publishing houses to Munich and Hamburg. Although "East Berlin . . . had been transformed into the absolutely dominant metropolis of the GDR at the expense of the Saxon cities of Dresden and Leipzig" (Häußermann and Kapphan 201), it still had outdated technologies, inefficient methods of production, and extremely high air and water pollution. Comparisons with the West were hardly escapable since East Berliners watched West German television and talked to their families and friends visiting from the West. As in other Central European cities, the party refused to take responsibility for economic problems or attribute them to the malfunctioning system; instead, it preferred to blame imaginary "enemies of the working class" and to label all production delays or disasters as "sabotage" (Varga, "Devastation" 201).

Whereas nationalization and central planning determined how the people of the Soviet bloc worked, communalization affected how they lived. Abolition of private ownership of the land initially helped speed up the process of reconstructing the cities destroyed in the war: since there were no landowners to negotiate with, the state had a free hand in administering renovation and demolition works in the cities (Węcławowicz 222). The party's decisions concerning urban planning were unpredictable: on the one hand, the state encouraged reconstruction of historical buildings such as some of the palaces on Unter den Linden in Berlin, the Castle District in Budapest, and the Royal Castle in Warsaw; on the other hand, the renovation of eighteenth-century villas and nineteenth-century tenement buildings was largely considered unnecessary: they were either razed or simply neglected while the city invested in the construction of new socialist houses. When the renovation of old buildings did happen, it was mostly done with poor means, by incompetent teams, and—with the remarkable exception of Warsaw's Old Town, which was meticulously rebuilt according to old blueprints—with no particular attention to historical detail. In the 1950s, it was not uncommon for the interior of a baroque or neoclassicist palace to receive new enamel-painted walls and PVC floor coverings. With the former landlords absent—dead, expelled, imprisoned, or simply dispossessed—their properties were transformed into caricatures of their former selves.

State monopoly on land ownership rendered the property location within the city irrelevant: "there were almost no incentives to invest in the city centre, to build new firm headquarters, hotels, banks, department stores, etc. This contributed to the stability of the physical patterns of urban cores and to the preservation of many historical buildings, but also to the decay of the city centres" (Musil, "City Development" 39). It was mostly older people and poor families who occupied the old buildings in the historical center, while the ever-growing working class moved to the new socialist tenement blocks. This trend was particularly strong in Prague and Budapest. It was also present in the traditionally poor district of Praga in Warsaw and in the centrally located Jewish district (*Scheunenviertel*) in Berlin, but not to such an extent as in the Czechoslovak and Hungarian capitals, where "old people, low-income households, and Roma people were concentrated (even trapped) in the deteriorating city centers, and in many older residential areas in central urban zones" (Musil, "City Development" 40). Dark and dirty gateways, rotting walls, and bands of stray dogs and cats were hardly inviting, and the infrastructure of those buildings was so outdated (many had neither indoor toilets nor central heating) that hardly anyone wanted to move in. The neglect of the historic center was especially noticeable in Prague, which survived the war without much damage. The core of the city remained largely immune to the socialist type of architecture that was turning Central Europe into one huge gray concrete block, but that also meant that the center hardly took part in the modernization of infrastructure. In Budapest, the political center of the city (and the country), formerly located in Buda, moved to Pest after 1945, while the historic edifices on Castle Hill were being slowly reconstructed from the pile of ruins left by World War II. Consequently, Buda gradually lost importance in comparison with the more dynamic and more working-class Pest, parts of which were being transformed in the Soviet fashion (Ellger 12-16).

Among all Central European capitals, Warsaw and Berlin suffered the most damage during the war (see Davies; Judt). Their historic centers had to be renovated or built anew. In Warsaw, few parts except the Old Town, the Castle, and the surrounding area underwent detailed reconstruction. Many buildings were assessed as irretrievable and soon replaced by brand new structures. The socialist architecture complemented the Soviet-imposed politics and economy in that it was rendering Central European cities increasingly alike. Furthermore, architecture was repeatedly used as a clear sign of Soviet supremacy, the best example of which is the Palace of Culture and Science (*Pałac Kultury i Nauki*) that emerged in central Warsaw in the mid-1950s. It was initially called Joseph Stalin's Palace of Culture and Science (*Pałac Kultury i Nauki imienia Józefa Stalina*), as it was the Soviet leader who initiated the project. Obviously, the Palace lost the Stalin part from its name after Khrushchev's speech in 1956. The edifice, at 230 meters, remains the highest building in Warsaw and in Poland until this day (currently, there are plans to build skyscrapers in the area that would dwarf the Palace—see chapter 5). For decades, the Palace was associated with Soviet dominance and perceived as a hostile element to the city by many. At the same time, it came to symbolize the very center of the city: apart from cultural and scientific institutions, the Palace housed exhibition grounds, a congress hall, and restaurants; it was easily accessible by public transportation and neighbored the most famous shopping center in the capital (*Domy Handlowe Centrum*). In the 1970s, with the construction of Central Station in its direct vicinity, Stalin's gift became not only the core center of Warsaw, but also of Poland.

In Berlin, the whole historic center was incorporated into the Soviet sector of the city. Dominance over the architectural symbols of Prussian, imperial German, and nazi power was crucial to Stalin for ideological reasons. Heavily destroyed in air raids, the center was partly rebuilt and partly razed, but the logic behind the decisions on what to keep and what to tear down remains unfathomable. While some nazi buildings were converted into top GDR offices—the building formerly housing the *Reichsbank* became the seat of the East German communist party and its *Politbüro* (today it belongs to the Ministry of Foreign Affairs) and the massive *Reichsluftwaffeministerium* (Reich Air Ministry) building was transformed into the *Haus der Ministerien* (House of Ministries) serving the Council of Ministers (today it is home to the Ministry of Finance)—the *Stadtschloss* (City Castle) was ordered to be razed as a symbol of Prussian imperialism and militarism. Only a few Prussian buildings were rebuilt, including Humboldt University, the Opera House, and the State Library on Unter den Linden. It was only in the 1980s, as part of the preparations for the 750th anniversary of Berlin in 1987, that the party took more interest in the city's cultural heritage, but even that change was merely part of the propaganda: East Berlin was simply competing with West Berlin to be the more attractive side of the city. Nevertheless, the official image of Berlin as the GDR capital was that of a modern city inhabited by modern socialists, in which the city center played a crucial role: "In East Berlin the centre resumed its function as a base for state political and economic administration as well as high-grade commercial establishments. The more centralized an establishment was, the more important and symbolic its location in the city. Unlike the tendency in capitalist cities to displace residential use from the centre and adjacent quarters by expanding tertiary uses, multi-dwelling buildings in the socialist city were indeed built on purpose in the centre and surrounding districts. Of course, the new, centrally located flats were reserved for top officials only" (Häußermann and Kapphan 191). As the examples of Prague and Budapest demonstrate, Hartmut Häußermann and Andreas Kapphan wrongly attribute the tendency to build multidwelling buildings in the center to all socialist cities. A more general trend shared by all the discussed capitals was the construction of large apartment blocks, "built most often in the outer zones of cities" and destined to change the urban structure "quite considerably" (Musil, "City Development" 39).

After World War II, the whole Soviet bloc experienced a "combination of demographic growth and rapid urbanization" (Judt 386). The postwar growth of urban population may be compared with the demographic developments that followed the nineteenth-century industrial revolutions in that it introduced both new architectural forms and new ways of life: "The result in all these cities, from Berlin to Stalingrad, was the classic Soviet-era housing solution: mile upon mile of identical grey or brown cement blocks; cheap, poorly constructed, with no distinguishing architectural features and lacking any aesthetic indulgence (or public facilities)" (Judt 386). Berlin, Budapest, Prague, and Warsaw were no exceptions; however, the apartment blocks located in these cities were only seemingly identical. The housing developments in Prague and Berlin "showed a relatively high degree of social heterogeneity" (Musil, "City Development" 39) and attempted to create a sense of (centrally controlled) local community through the construction of shops, youth cultural centers, and nurseries. The idea behind the project was to make people of various professions and social backgrounds live together under one roof and interact with one another during everyday errands and Sunday walks in the nearby parks named after great communist heroes. The egalitarian vision of socialist urban planners and architects did not survive the transformations of 1989: those who could afford it immediately left the apartments blocks, ultimately proving that the imposed identification with the local community was delusional. The apartment tenements in Budapest and Warsaw were less socially mixed owing to greater economic and political freedoms that allowed for the construction or renovation of residential homes. Furthermore, not all apartment blocks were equal; those that seemed to be more functional were reserved for people from privileged backgrounds: top party members, television and sport celebrities, famous professionals, or those who bribed the officials issuing registration permits.

In the capitals under scrutiny, the construction of large apartment buildings made of prefabricated parts started in the 1950s. A journey through Central European cities leads to the realization that despite many differences in height and length, most prefabricated tenement blocks are eyesores and create an equally claustrophobic atmosphere. Thin walls prevented privacy, small defective windows looked out to other concrete buildings, malfunctioning heating systems delivered tropical climates to the top apartments and Siberian cold to the ground floor—all these and other small and seemingly trivial everyday obstacles summed up to constant stress, which determined the lives of millions of people in the region. (Most prefabricated apartments remain inhabited until today. After 1989 the buildings underwent considerable renovations and improvements, thus making the lives of their residents more bearable). Although the main reason behind the construction of prefabricated buildings was the desire to accommodate the highest number of people with the lowest production costs, it also responded to the idea of an equal, classless society: a concept monstrously distorted by the Soviet Union and its satellites. Remarkably, prefabricated houses were originally a Western trend first designed by modernist architects after World War I and developed well into the 1960s. The Soviet apartment blocks, however, took the idea of a modern city to the extremes, economizing both materials and space.

Despite the objectionable living conditions they offered, the socialist high- and low-rise apartment houses were still considered better than the neglected buildings in the narrow alleys of Prague, in the old working-class neighborhoods of Berlin and Warsaw, and in the hunted streets of Pest. As late as the 1980s, two-fifths of East Berlin's housing stock was prewar, almost all lacked central heating and at least one-quarter of them had no running water and no indoor lavatory. Maintenance was centrally planned and even the smallest repair had to by applied for to a central body (Richie 756). Patience was definitely one of the crucial survival rules in the socialist Central European city. Commodities were cheap, but scarce; therefore, people had to wait for years not only to receive an apartment, but also to be able to buy a car, a fridge, or a TV set or to obtain access to telephone connection at home. Such shortages and delays created a black market. Barter was not unusual, nor was buying rare products with foreign currencies, especially in Warsaw and Prague, as opposed to Budapest, where inhabitants could purchase commodities with relative ease, and to Berlin, where most people were too afraid of the prevalent secret police to engage in secret endeavors. Next to patience, fear and distrust could be named as other by-products of the Soviet system.

For decades, all Central European capitals were infested not only with Moscow's agents, but also with the national secret police. In Berlin, the infamous *Stasi* (from *Ministerium für Staatssicherheit*, or Ministry for State Security) controlled virtually every single area of life (Judt 697-98; Ladd 131). Established in 1950, the Stasi became most active in Berlin owing to the GDR capital's border with the outpost of the Federal Republic of Germany. "By 1980 every street, important building, café and theater in central East Berlin had its informants and its hidden cameras and microphones. The Stasi had access to over 600 buildings, including over 200 furnished flats set up for clandestine meetings, many with two-way mirrors and bugging devices" (Richie 759). The secret security services active in Prague (*Státní bezpečnost* or *StB*) and in Warsaw (*Służba Bezpieczeństwa* or *SB*) were no less intrusive than those in Berlin: they also controlled telephone conversations and correspondence, spied on prospective oppositionists, fabricated evidence, and forced people to cooperate. However, the Stasi was proportionally much bigger and powerful than the Czechoslovak and Polish secret security agencies: during the Cold War, it became known as the most developed secret service after the Soviet KGB and the US-American CIA. Remarkably, the Hungarian State Protection Authority (*Államvédelmi Hatóság* or *ÁVH*), which facilitated Stalinist show trials and purges, was abolished by János Kádár (himself interrogated by the ÁVH in the early 1950s) after the Budapest Uprising of 1956 and was never entirely reinstalled—instead, the tasks of state security were exercised directly by the Ministry of the Interior.

Whereas the constant fear of being watched led to social paranoia, censorship and self-censorship restrained artistic production. The cultural life of Central European cities suffered substantial downfalls under the Soviet-imposed regime. Again, this trend was not equally powerful in all capitals at all times. The reforms of 1967-1968 abolished censorship and led to a brief cultural revival in Prague. After the Soviet invasion, however, most freethinking writers, filmmakers, painters, and musicians either left Czechoslovakia or were banned from publishing their works and forced to work as window cleaners and janitors. Similarly, Warsaw experienced a relative cultural relaxation after the thaw of 1956; however, a 1968 theater production relating to Russia (and, by implication, to the Soviet Union) as an enemy and occupier was banned from further performances and marked the return of party hardliners to power. Repression, expulsions, and censorship strongly affected the cultural life—especially in comparison with the particularly creative period of the 1920s and 1930s—but it would be an unjust exaggeration to call it nonexistent. Berlin, Budapest, Prague, and Warsaw were still capable of producing valuable works of literature and cinema, insightful theater and dance productions, and inspiring painting and sculptures, but there were hardly any independent cultural institutions that would support them: artists had to rely on public institutes, public television, ministries of culture, and state-appointed curators and publishers. Those who wanted their work to be seen or heard had basically only two options: to comply with the party vision of socialist art or to outsmart the censors and decision-makers by disguising the real meaning of their work. Those who consciously moved underground either earned dissident fame among the few and waited for public recognition until 1989, or simply fell into oblivion.

The party's influence was visible not only in the officially approved culture, but also in everyday life. Stalinist and then Soviet-socialist architecture backed by the local party leaders had a tremendous influence on how people lived, worked, shopped, and interacted with one another. Central planning and nationalization were also party controlled. Furthermore, the party sought to hold sway over leisure time. Private initiatives and independent community groups were strongly discouraged, while socialist workers, youth, and child organizations were vehemently supported. The party was especially interested in recruiting young people, who would later join the communist party and in the meantime wave flags and march joyfully on May 1 parades. Children joined communist youth groups sometimes as early as preschool; teenagers were expected to become members of communist youth leagues: *Československý svaz mládeže* or *ČSM* in Czechoslovakia, *Związek Młodzieży Polskiej* or *ZMP* in Poland, *Freie Deutsche Jugend* or *FDJ* in the GDR, and *Kommunista Ifjúsági Szövetség* or *KISZ* in Hungary. It was no secret that a membership card from a youth league increased the chances of getting into university or acquiring higher positions in offices and factories, especially among the children of bourgeois background who were often prohibited from taking up higher education.

Since all types of private initiatives were discouraged and the centrally planned economy made it impossible for small businesses to prosper, Central European cities fell under the spell of economic numbness, which, in turn, led to the disappearance of their middle classes—with the remarkable exception of Budapest, where "goulash communism" ruled and nourished a middle class consisting of the intelligentsia and bureaucrats. In the absence of the middle class, the urban population in Berlin, Prague, and Warsaw consisted of working-class people (who were often newcomers from the countryside) and students or intellectuals. Therefore, it was these two groups that—separately or together—raised protests against Soviet rule. Almost all the most important demonstrations and uprisings of the Cold War era took place in Berlin, Budapest, and Prague; therefore, the capitals gained in political importance and symbolism not only on the national level, but also abroad. Even today, Budapest and Prague remain associated with violently suppressed revolutionary movements. Warsaw also witnessed mass protests—first in 1956, then in 1968—but they were not as significant as the strikes and demonstrations in other parts of the country, for example, in the Joseph Stalin Metal Industries in Poznań, (1956), in the dockyards of Szczecin (1970), in the Lenin Shipyards in Gdańsk (1980-1981), and in the coalmines and steel works of Upper Silesia (1981).

Remarkably, all mass demonstration in the Soviet bloc took place only after Stalin's death. The subjugated societies were hoping for a relaxation of economic and political restrictions; when their expectations were not met, they went to the streets. After yet another increase in production norms announced by Walter Ulbricht on 16 June 1953, Berlin workers began a strike. The SED Politbüro's decision "had hurt all East German workers but none more than seasonal construction laborers in Berlin, who had only a few months in which to fulfill annual work quotas" (Richie 682-83). The construction workers moved west from the Stalinallee to Haus der Ministerien near Potsdamer Platz. Other exasperated workers and hundreds of by-standers joined the demonstrators on the way and within an hour the group reached 5,000 (Richie 683). What started as a demand to lower production norms, turned into a call for free elections and against the Soviet occupation. Since the demonstration was a spontaneous event, there were no leaders that could guide or manage the crowds. "A handful of men" (Richie 683) got hold of a loudspeaker and called for a general strike on the next day. The news quickly spread out in the whole GDR and on 17 June 1953, 400,000 East Germans gathered on the streets of Berlin, Dresden, Halle, Leipzig, and other cities across the country. Interestingly, Moscow warned the SED Politbüro to accept some reforms in order to "stem the hemorrhage of skilled workers to the West" (Judt 177), but Ulbricht rejected any compromise as a sign of the government's weakness. Eventually, Soviet tanks helped the East German police (*Volkspolizei* or the *Vopos*) brutally disperse the demonstration in Berlin as well as in other cities. Almost three hundred people died in East Germany that day and thousands more disappeared in the hastily set-up "Soviet military tribunals and East German kangaroo courts" (Richie 686). The uprising of 1953 had numerous consequences. First, it increased the "hemorrhage" that Moscow feared: tens of thousands of skilled workers, but also other people, mostly the young and educated, left the GDR right after the failed attempt to introduce reforms. Second, West Berliners realized that the Allied forces stationing in their part of the city would not risk a conflict with the Soviet Union only to protect the people in East Berlin. Later events in Central European cities would confirm that the official strategy of the West was that of nonintervention. Third, West Berlin commemorated the victims of the bloodshed in that it renamed the avenue extending from the Brandenburg Gate to the *Grosser Stern* into *Straße des 17. Juni* and, even more importantly, June 17 was announced a national holiday in the Federal Republic. Finally, as Richie argues, "the Berlin Uprising was now used by Nikita Khrushchev as the excuse to remove Beria from power. As such, it was the catalyst which changed the course not only of East German, but of Soviet history as well" (686).

The course of Hungarian history and the fate of Budapest were changed three years later. After Khrushchev's speech of 25 February 1956, there was even more hope for relaxation of the Soviet system than right after Stalin's death. In Budapest, voices demanding democratic reforms were becoming louder and an informal opposition grouped around Prime Minister Imre Nagy. Whereas the revolt in Berlin was ignited by construction workers, in the Hungarian capital it was students who inspired the society to protest. Although first independent student associations formed in the town of Szeged in mid-October, the students of the Technical University in Budapest played a more important role in the national uprising: on 22 October 1956, they formulated a Sixteen Point manifesto, in which they expressed solidarity with the Polish workers whose protests on the streets of Poznań had been crushed in June 1956 and demanded industrial and agrarian reforms, free speech, and re-appointment of Imre Nagy to prime minister. Students' demonstrations started on Lajos Kossuth Square (also known as Parliament Square) on October 23 and brought Nagy back to power the next day. Workers and other inhabitants, including some soldiers and policemen, joined the students in their protests. The ensuing chaos extended over Budapest and affected even small provincial towns. Violent clashes between police and demonstrators, lynching of party members, and brutal street fights became ubiquitous (Judt 315). The party leaders refused to acknowledge the democratic character of the uprising and named it counterrevolution. Every time Nagy went on the radio, he promised more reforms. His optimism culminated on November 1 when he proclaimed Hungary a neutral country. In the meantime, János Kádár, the secretary general of the Hungarian communist party, was in Moscow plotting the details of the Soviet invasion. On November 3, the Nagy government sent representatives to meet with the Soviet authorities and discuss the withdrawal of the Soviet troops from Hungary. The delegates were arrested and Soviet tanks entered Budapest early the next morning. Despite ardent protests and strong armed resistance, the city was defeated within seventy-two hours.

On November 22, Nagy, his closest associates, and their families were tricked into leaving the Yugoslavian Embassy where they had been granted asylum and were arrested on the spot. Nagy was taken to Romania and after a few months transported to a prison, where he was repeatedly interrogated and, eventually, sentenced to death in June 1958. His body was laid in an unmarked grave and its location would be changed a number of times in order to keep it secret. To István Rév, the unburied body is not only reminiscent of the ancient Greek tragedy, but also symptomatic of the communist regime: "Unlike the power of the bishops of late antiquity that derived partly from the tombs of the saints, the strength of the Communist Party stemmed not only from its dead martyrs, the Communist heroes, but also from the unmarked graves of unburied, nameless victims, the persons not talked about" (32). An estimated 3,000 Hungarians died during the uprising and later by death sentence, 22,000 were sent to prison, 13,000 sent to internment camps, thousands more lost their jobs or were expelled from the universities, and some 200,000 people left the country immediately after the failed revolution (Judt 318). Most of the exiles were young and "many from the educated professional elite of Budapest and the urbanized west of the country" (Judt 318). Their absence was a tremendous intellectual and cultural loss to Budapest and to Hungary and no economic reforms of Kádárism could make up for it.

Presumably, one of the reasons why the Soviet Union opted for military intervention in Hungary was the general unrest in the Soviet bloc. In October 1956, Khrushchev had already, reluctantly, agreed on political reforms in Poland, including bringing to power the relatively progressive Władysław Gomułka, who had spent years in prison under Stalin. While the Soviet leadership was pondering how to respond to the Hungarian uprising, they received reports of student demonstrations in Romania and political unrest among Bulgarian intellectuals: "this was beginning to sound like the start of the contamination effect that the Soviet leaders had long feared, and it prompted them to adopt a new approach" (Judt 316). The fear of the contamination effect was also one of the reasons the Soviet Union decided to stop the reforms taking place in Prague in 1968. Another reason was the certainty of getting away with the military invasion, again. Moscow knew that the West would not intervene in their actions in Prague because, as Judt bluntly remarks, "Washington had its hands full of Vietnam" and, additionally, the United States and the Soviet Union had just signed a Treaty of Nuclear Nonproliferation and "the US was not about to jeopardize such gains for the sake of a few million misguided Czechs" (444).

As in Budapest, it was the students of the Technical University that initiated demonstrations in Prague in late October 1967. The primary reason behind the protest was electricity shortages on the Strahov campus, however, "their calls for 'More light!' were rightly interpreted as extending beyond local housekeeping difficulties" (Judt 440). The demonstration was crashed violently by the police, but it indirectly prompted changes within the Czechoslovak communist party. Since the first secretary and president Antonín Novotný failed to respond to the students' protests, on 5 January 1968, the central committee elected a new leader from the reform wing, Alexander Dubček, who was devoted to the party but anxious to reform the country. In March, Ludvik Svoboda replaced Novotný as the new president and soon after the central committee of the party decided on an Action Program that advocated, among other points, political and economic democratization. Censorship was abolished and new hitherto unthinkable essays, theater productions, and songs reached the general public, celebrating what came to be known as the Prague Spring. Dubček intended to transform the dysfunctional system into "socialism with a human face," which met with general enthusiasm in the society. Judt argues that the people of Prague shared Dubček's convictions: "It would be wrong to suppose, in retrospect, that what the students and writers and Party reformers of 1968 were 'really' seeking was to replace Communism with liberal capitalism or that their enthusiasm for 'Socialism with a human face' was mere rhetorical compromise or habit. On the contrary: the idea that there existed a 'third way,' a Democratic Socialism compatible with free institutions, respecting individual freedoms *and* collective goals, had captured the imagination of Czech students no less than Hungarian economists" (441).

The Soviet leadership, typically, did not share the belief in a third way. Already in July 1968, Brezhnev decided that the Prague Spring was out of the Czechoslovak party's control. A letter signed by the party leaders of the USSR, East Germany, Poland, Hungary, and Bulgaria was sent to Prague with a warning of the contaminating consequences of a counterrevolution. Since Dubček did not budge, 500,000 Warsaw Pact troops (with a notable exception of Romania) marched into Czechoslovakia on 21 August 1968. Unlike in Budapest, the invasion remained unopposed with a number of relatively peaceful street protests in Prague (Judt 444). Almost all reforms were immediately reversed as part of the "normalization" process. After the removal of Dubček from party leadership, mass screenings and purging of intellectuals, artists, and other supporters of the reforms started. A wave of mass emigration followed; those who decided to stay in Prague, but refused to collaborate, were not allowed to continue their former professions and were forced into mundane manual labor.

Emigration of skilled workers as well as students and intellectuals was a natural result of all the upheavals and had substantial effects on social, cultural, and political developments in Berlin, Budapest, and Prague for decades. Another common element binding these three events was the silence of the West: the decision for military intervention was made by the Soviet leaders with a deep understanding of Cold War relations and with a clear certainty that the West would not dare to protest. Apparently, Berlin, Budapest, and Prague were minor elements in a bigger game and could be traded for various purposes. The uprisings of 1953, 1956, and 1968 were loud and clear manifestations of the local people's dissatisfaction with Soviet domination, but they did not shake it. They revealed the dual nature of Soviet power: ideologically and economically weak, it lacked social support, but its military strength made it impossible to eradicate. This dichotomy is perfectly illustrated by probably the most meaningful symbol of the Cold War: the Berlin Wall.

By 1961, over three million East Germans left for the West (Richie 716). To stop the mass emigration, the SED Politbüro (with Soviet permission, naturally) did the simplest and, at the same time, the most unbelievable thing it could: it built a wall around West Berlin and forbade East German citizens to cross it. On the night of 12 to 13 August 1961, the troops of the *Volksarmee* (People's Army) sealed the border with a barbed-wire fence and on the next day started putting together a brick construction (the brick wall was later replaced by the famous gray concrete). Symbolically, the first place to be sealed was Potsdamer Platz: once the busiest intersection in Europe and home to bohemian cafes, almost completely destroyed during the war, after 1945 it lay at the junction of the US, British, and Soviet sectors. Ulbricht's plan to seal off West Berlin was both "one of the best-guarded secrets in GDR history," and "one of the most spectacular blunders in the history of western intelligence" (Richie 717-18). Not only did the West fail to predict the building of the Wall, but it also largely failed to take a decisive stance on the new situation. Mayor of West Berlin and future chancellor Willy Brandt gave a speech that discouraged thousands of demonstrators from storming the Wall. Chancellor Adenauer, however, famous for his dislike of Berlin, refused to make a statement, and President John F. Kennedy simply went sailing after he had heard the news of events in Berlin (Richie 719). The West turned a blind eye on what was happening in the divided city and it was not until 1963 that Kennedy gave his famous speech at the Rathaus Schöneberg in which he supported the people of Berlin by saying "Ich bin ein Berliner."

The Wall dramatically changed life in both parts of the city. In the first years after 1961, communication between East and West Berlin was reduced to a minimum. Thousands of East Berliners lost their jobs in the West, and West Berliners were not able to visit the cheap stores and the Opera House in the east. The routes of the subway and elevated lines were cut in the middle and some stations were turned into flea markets while others simply decayed. Importantly, the Wall was called the wall (*die Mauer*) only on the West side. The official name used in East Germany was the "antifascist protective rampart" (*antifaschistischer Schutzwall*), which also mirrored the GDR's absurd attitude towards Germany's nazi past based on the hypocritical claim that the nazis were only in the West. The use of the word "Mauer" in relation to the Wall was prohibited in the east: "This rule had usually been interpreted as an Orwellian denial of reality, but we must also consider it as an attempt—perhaps equally Orwellian—to control the dangerous implications of figurative language" (Ladd 18). The need to define the Wall and its meaning was equally big in both parts of the city. As Brian Ladd notes, "traditionally, a wall has an inside and an outside; it protects the people on one side from those on the other. But which was the outside of the wall that encircled West Berlin? Who was being walled in, and who kept out? West Berliners, physically surrounded by the Wall, felt they were the ones penned in. But so did most East Germans" (22-23).

In describing and analyzing the developments in Central European capitals embraced by Soviet colonial rule, I have left West Berlin out of my discussion simply because it did not belong in the sphere of Soviet influence. Nevertheless, West Berlin was hardly less colonial than East Berlin. In my opinion, all developments in West Berlin were determined by complex relations between West Berliners and the Allies rather than by periphery-metropolis relations between West Berlin and the federal government in Bonn. As agreed at Yalta, Berlin, like the whole of Germany, was to be divided into four sectors: Soviet (eleven districts), US-American (six districts), British (four districts), and French (two districts). Still, the Red Army that arrived in Berlin in late April 1945 occupied the whole city and refused to leave the Western sectors until July of the same year. "Stalin played for more time. He could not risk refusing the western Allies access to their zones in Berlin but he intended to delay the move so that he could continue to strip the city of 'reparations' and put Communist officials in place before they could reach the city" (Richie 627). When the Allied troops entered their sectors they were greeted not like occupiers who had destroyed the city in air raids, but like saviors by the hundreds of thousands of West Berliners worn out by Soviet rapes, lootings, and propaganda. Soon it became clear, however, that the Allied powers did not come as friends. While West Berliners were starving and freezing to death, US-American, British, and French officers enjoyed abundant dinners in the elegant villas of the former nazi elite. Furthermore, Western soldiers were forbidden to interact with the locals. Not all of them followed the rule, of course, but the regulation itself was reminiscent of colonial practices and, as such, clearly defined the relationship between the Allies and West Berliners.

As early as 1948, the Allies again appeared as heroes and continued to be adored by West Berliners until the late 1960s. After the new currency, the *Deutschmark*, had been introduced in the Western sectors of occupied Germany (and, hence, also in the Western sectors of Berlin) without Stalin's permission, the Soviet Union reacted promptly by closing the road and rail corridors between Berlin and the Western zones on 24 June 1948. For the next eleven months, the Western districts of Berlin were supplied with food, coal, gasoline, clothes, and other products by US-American and British airfreights. Once again, in a very short period of time, the occupiers became saviors. To West Berliners, the airlift, as the action became known, was confirmation that the Allies would not leave them on their own. Stalin unblocked the Western sectors in May 1949, but the partition of the city had already been a fact: in 1948 the city government was divided between Soviet and Western sectors and soon after the end of the airlift, the Federal Republic of Germany was established (the German Democratic Republic was founded a few months later, in October 1949). The line between the former Western and Soviet sectors became a border between two countries. In the 1950s, West Berlin enjoyed the *Wirtschaftswunder* (economic miracle) just like other cities of the Federal Republic and, additionally, experienced a general reconstruction. Western urban planners and architects were extreme in their desire to cut off the troubling past: many still livable nineteenth- and early twentieth-century buildings were replaced by gray blocks, rarely better than the architectural monstrosities being erected in the eastern part of the city.

After the Wall was built, West Berlin began losing its inhabitants. The claustrophobic atmosphere, the constant fear of Soviet invasion, the uncomfortable distance from other West German cities, and the economic lethargy compelled skilled workers and young professionals to leave the city: "Because of the proximity of East Germany the production of goods with even a marginal military significance was forbidden, hindering the development of the new 'high-tech' industries" (Richie 777). The city lost all its economic importance with the exception of the cultural sector, which received substantial federal support (Häußermann and Kapphan 201). Nevertheless, even cultural life, trapped within the concrete wall, had few chances to develop. Compared to New York, London, and Paris, West Berlin seemed provincial: "In some ways West Berliners were their own worst enemy; how could their city be a *Weltstadt* when its shops usually closed at 1 p.m. on Saturday; when punks and drug addicts lined up for their social security cheques in front of neat offices, and when artists were paid in hard cash to bribe them to stay in the city and live a Bohemian lifestyle. When visitors came they did not search out the monuments or the museums or the shops. To Berliners' chagrin they came to see one thing: the Wall" (Richie 802).

West Berlin had proportionally the highest number of pensioners in the Federal Republic, many of whom lingered in old Mietskasernen. To prevent the city from depopulation, the federal government introduced a number of favorable regulations, for example, an exemption from military service. Consequently, thousands of young men from the Federal Republic streamed to West Berlin in search of a way of life that would differ from the boring middle-class order in which they were raised. Another trick to keep West Berlin economically and demographically alive was to invite *Gastarbeiter*, mainly from Turkey and Yugoslavia, to inhabit the desolate pre-war apartments in the traditionally working-class districts of Kreuzberg, Neukölln, and Wedding. Furthermore, many students came to Berlin attracted by the protest culture and the relaxed atmosphere at the Free University in the district of Dahlem.

In the late 1960s, young West Berliners rebelled against their parents' inability to deal with the nazi past, but also—as so many of their peers in other Western cities—against US-American politics in general and against the Vietnam War in particular. Within a few years West Berlin transformed from an American-loving city into "the centre of an anti-American storm which would sweep across Western Europe" (Richie 779). West Berliners protested against US-American (but not Soviet, as Richie is right to remark) nuclear testing, against the Allies' occupation of Berlin, against "Coca-Colonization" and other signs of US-American economic, political, and cultural dominance. In a sense, then, the West Berlin protesters were trying to get rid of a colonial domination just like the demonstrators in East Berlin and Budapest in the 1950s and the Prague reformers a decade later (Richie 779). Hundreds of bigger and smaller organizations, communes, initiatives, and associations were established in the radicalized West Berlin in the 1960s and the trend continued well into the 1990s, after the reunification it simply spread into East Berlin. Despite all the protests, demonstrations, radical manifestos, and brutal clashes with the police, neither the generation of 1968 (commonly called *68ers*), nor those who followed, gave rise to a revolution.

The most spectacular events that marked the end of the Cold War took place in Warsaw, Budapest, Berlin, and Prague. This is not to suggest, however, that the occurrences in these cities were single-handedly responsible for the fall of communism in Central Europe. It cannot be overstated that the relatively peaceful revolutions of 1989 could have never taken place, had it not been for the willingness of the Soviet leadership to introduce reforms in the Soviet bloc. In the 1980s, Moscow itself was experiencing political, economic, and cultural relaxations as a result of perestroika and *glasnost*. Mikhail Gorbachev openly scorned party hardliners not only in the Soviet Union, but also in its satellite states and encouraged reforms. The fall of the Berlin Wall is unthinkable without Gorbachev, who, next to Helmut Kohl, became the main contributor to Germany's reunification: "East Germany's young people had for years been told, *Von der Sowjetunion lernen heisst siegen lernen*—'To learn from the Soviet Union is to learn how to win.' So they did! For several years East Germans had been turning the name Gorbachev, and the Soviet example, against their rulers. And Gorbachev personally gave the last push" (Ash 65). It is unlikely that the Soviet leader could foresee that the reforms he supported would lead to the demise of the Soviet bloc. The need for democratic changes had been present in Central Europe for over four decades; after several failed uprisings, people had been waiting for another good moment to demand freedom and Gorbachev gave them a clear sign that they could proceed.

More than anything else, the events of 1989 abounded in powerful images, momentous proverbs, and historic gestures, but, clearly, they were merely part of the bigger international framework of events, agreements, and compromises that made the fall of the Iron Curtain possible. Still, it is important to stress that the images and words that came to symbolize the demise of the Cold War order came directly from these and no other cities. In Warsaw, actress Joanna Szczepkowska made a historic announcement on Polish Television News: "Ladies and Gentelmen, on 4 June 1989, communism in Poland ended" (Ash 46). In Budapest, the official and celebratory reburial of Imre Nagy and his associates drew hundreds of thousands to the Heroes' Square on 16 June 1989 and the photographs from this gathering came to symbolize the end of communism in Hungary and hope for more changes in the region. Film footages of Berliners celebrating at and on the Wall on 9 November 1989, were broadcasted around the world and the image of the collapsing concrete structure was interpreted as the final fall of the Iron Curtain. Finally, the events in Prague were summarized by one of the witnesses, Timothy Garton Ash, in a smart sentence, later repeatedly used by Václav Havel: "In Poland it took ten years, in Hungary ten months, in East Germany ten weeks: perhaps in Czechoslovakia it will take ten days!" (Ash 78).

Ash closely observed the events in Central European cities and immediately put them down in a neat book titled *We The People: The Revolution of '89 Witnessed in Warsaw, Budapest, Berlin and Prague* (1990). The British historian recalls accompanying his Polish friends on the way to cast a vote in the first (partly) democratic election in Poland after World War II. On 4 June 1989, they walked through the working class district of Żoliborz, where "a steady stream of people flowed across the barren ground between the half-finished high-rise blocks, dodging huge muddy puddles on their way to vote" (26-27). On the way back home, they walked "round the giant muddy puddles, past the half-completed blocks, the tenements of communism, in a glow of quiet but profound satisfaction" (27). I chose to quote this image precisely because it is free of big words and unforgettable gestures, but it does not seem any less meaningful. The detailed portrait of Żoliborz with its derelict prefabricated apartment blocks, missing sidewalks, and prevalent grayness not only conveys the living conditions of the people of Warsaw, but is also a dramatic reminder of why they needed a change.

Less than two weeks after the election in Warsaw that ended in a complete victory for the democratic opposition, Ash went south to Budapest and watched the ceremonies of Nagy's reburial together with over two hundred thousand people: "The great neo-classical columns [of *Hősök tere*/Heroes' Square] are wrapped in black cloth. From the colonnades hang huge red, green and white national flags, but each with a hole in the middle, a reminder of how the insurgents of 1956 cut out the hammer and sickle from their flags" (49). National symbols in combination with famous monuments of the capital city dominated not only in Budapest, but also later in Berlin and Prague. The use of flags, coats of arms, and national heroes signified a clear dissociation with Soviet or Soviet-inspired imagery and the re-embracing of traditional symbols. In Berlin and other East German cities, demonstrators held banners saying *Wir sind das Volk* ("We are the people")—the sentence engraved over the main entrance to the Reichstag and, hence, strongly associated with German democracy—and its paraphrase, *Wir sind ein Volk* ("We are one people"), clearly demanding reunification. In Prague, the demonstrators marched to Wenceslas Square, "the stage for all historic moments of Czech history, whether in 1918, 1948, or 1968," where they were met and, eventually, beaten by "riot police, with white helmets, shields and truncheons, and by special anti-terrorist squads, in red berets" (Ash 80). Demonstrators—mostly students and intellectuals, but later also the general public—were peaceful and patient. One of the most powerful images of the Velvet Revolution, as the November events in Prague came to be known, was a photograph of a woman confronting the police with a single carnation.

Not all images of the 1989 events in Central European cities conveyed a message of political freedom, justice, and love. Some of the most meaningful photographs taken in Berlin in November of 1989 portrayed long lines of East Germans waiting in front of banks, discount supermarkets, and fast food restaurants in West Berlin. The implication was clear: Easterners are finally able to make use of great economic freedoms of the West. Nevertheless, as Ash remarks, the power of one hundred Deutschmarks given to every East German entering West Berlin should not be overplayed: "Most of the estimated two million East Germans who flooded into West Berlin over the weekend simply walked the streets in quiet family groups, often with toddlers in pushchairs" (62). Just like people in other Central European cities, Berliners were excited, curious, and scared of what the future would bring. The commencing changes were enormous and largely unpredictable. The political, economic, social, and cultural transformations, which I discuss below, reshaped Central European cities in every possible respect.

The making of (post)colonial cities

The developments that took place in Central European cities in the first years after 1989 were mostly connected with eradicating the previous political and economic system and quickly replacing it with a new one. Soviet symbols, street names, and monuments were readily dismantled and either destroyed or taken away to communist theme parks. In Berlin, "more than 60 streets and squares, most of them named after socialist politicians, communist philosophers, and anti-fascists, were renamed. A lot of plaques on houses where important socialists once lived or worked disappeared, but neighbors and activists have replaced many of them" (Häußermann and Kapphan 210-11). Apart from being a beehive of apparatchiks, Berlin had a long tradition of Marxist politics (even in West Berlin there was a Karl-Marx-Strasse); therefore, the statues of Karl Marx and Friedrich Engels were allowed to remain, while Lenin's monument was dismantled. In no other Central European city did people demand so vehemently that the signs of the communist past be kept, but, importantly, no other capital was (re)connected with a Western city and incorporated into a Western country. East Berliners sought to keep traces not so much of the communist system as of the history of Berlin as the capital of the German Democratic Republic, a country that ceased to exist.

The democratic reforms introduced in and after 1989 were shaped largely along well-established Western patterns: whereas political developments were inspired by the European Union, economic transformation followed the US-American path. The cities under scrutiny were affected by changes on both national and local levels. As capitals of now independent states, Berlin (the capital of re-united Germany since 1990), Prague (since 1993, after the split of Czechoslovakia, the capital of the Czech Republic), Budapest, and Warsaw took an active part in the development of political infrastructure that included creating new institutions and accommodating them in new or renovated buildings. On the municipal level, the cities experienced the establishment of new local government agencies, organizations, and offices. The general decentralization of politics and the economy and the introduction of Western or West-inspired rules of governance substantially affected the patterns of urban life and culture in Central Europe. Further, regional and local offices of international governmental and nongovernmental organizations that sprang up after 1989 lent an international character to the postcommunist capitals. Virtually all political institutions of the bygone era proved to be corrupt, inefficient, or no longer required. There was no chance of ever accomplishing a system transformation with the bureaucratic and fraudulent relicts still in place. Many employees of the communist regime were dismissed and replaced by not necessarily less corrupt and often completely inexperienced people.

Whereas (East) Berlin and the whole former GDR were immediately incorporated into the EU after the German reunification in 1990, Poland, Hungary, and the Czech Republic had to wait until May 2004 before they could join. Already in the 1990s, Central European countries started preparing for EU membership by adjusting national and regional laws according to Brussels' commands. As Ian E.E. Hamilton notes, "the international integration and 'globalization' of Central and Eastern European cities in the 1990s has occurred largely through 'Europeanization,' or most notably through the process of EU integration and enlargement ('EU-ization'), reinforcing cross-border and historic relations with West European cities and regions" (113). Importantly, in the first years after 1989, the transformation process was based more on copying EU standards rather than adapting them locally, which, understandably, raised protests in those people who felt most negatively affected by the introduced changes.

After 1989, municipal and district governments in Central European capitals were no longer centrally designated, but started getting appointed in free elections. Mayors were chosen to represent the interests of citizens against the state rather than the other way round. Consequently, residents began showing more interest in their cities. Although civic society has been generally slow to develop in Central Europe—mostly owing to the obvious distrust of institutional power inherited from the time of the Soviet domination—the 2000s saw some community groups, urban activists, nongovernmental organizations, and artist collectives successfully influence the municipal politics in Budapest, Prague, and Warsaw. Berlin, again, was an exception: activists in the German capital had been co-shaping local affairs ever since the early 1990s, partly thanks to the tradition of civic activism that spread from West Berlin over the whole city (see Richie; Till, *New Berlin*) and partly because many East Berliners perceived the reunification as colonization and protested against its many forms (see Huyssen).

As Kundera remarks, even under Soviet domination, Central Europe was culturally located in the West (34). With political independence formally (re)gained in 1989, this conviction turned into a quest and Central Europe set out to "return to Europe." Central European cities wanted to catch up with Western metropolises as soon as possible and one of the ways to achieve their aim was a quick economic transformation based largely on Western standards. In the 1990s, economic Westernization was taking place both from within and from the outside. As I quoted earlier, "many of the CEE countries, dedicated to the cause of reform, embraced a strategy that became known as 'shock therapy,' [and] for some of them, it provided a lot of 'shock' with little 'therapy'" (Stanilov 22). The Polish minister of finances Leszek Balcerowicz—trained on Milton Freedman's theories and working closely together with Freedman's disciple, Jeffrey Sachs—released all price controls and state subsidies, which promptly led to hyperinflation, bankruptcies of formerly state-owned companies, and, consequently, unemployment. The negative effects of economic transformation were unavoidable. Nevertheless, it remains questionable whether "shock therapy" was necessary, or if the changes could have been introduced gradually. Naomi Klein, known for her vociferous critique of late capitalism, claims that the economic transformation in Poland was merely another trick of the United States, who took advantage of the post-1989 state of emergency in Central Europe to introduce the type of economy that best served their own goals (180-81). The new democratic governments in Central Europe had few experts in Western economics who could show them alternatives. Consequently, intellectuals in Prague and Warsaw (mostly actors, writers, journalists, and historians) who negotiated reforms had little knowledge of economic matters and chose to rely on the few available advisors or Western specialists such as Sachs.

With the exception of Budapest and Hungary, Central European economies were completely unprofitable and their technologies and work methods outdated and inefficient. The young democratic governments opted for financial help from the International Monetary Fund and the World Bank and, consequently, had to act according to the policies of Western or increasingly global capital: Western financial guidance and control was simply another form of colonization and

> external pressure was applied by Western powers on national governments
> to adopt a market system, through the medium of experts appointed by international organizations such as the International Monetary Fund and the World Bank. The operation of both forces was facilitated by the demise of communism in the USSR and by the break-up of the USSR itself, while the seizure by President Kohl of the unique political opportunities to reunite eastern and western Germany (partly by "buying off" east German voters) led to the rapid integration of the former East Germany into the economic, political, and social space of Germany and the European Union. The replacement in a very short time of the stark old "Iron Curtain" by a perceived glittering "Golden Curtain" between Eastern and Western Europe probably also coloured local opinion in Central and Eastern European countries that

following the West European model and closer integration with the European Union could lead to the "promised land." (Hamilton 91)

Berlin, as the capital of reunited Germany, has received financial help both from international organizations and from the West German federal states in the form of *Solidaritätssteuer* (solidarity tax). Furthermore, the city attracted enormous amounts of foreign investment owing to cheap labor and land; however, this ended as soon as the mid-1990s, when foreign companies moved—in search of yet cheaper labor and land—further east to other Central and Eastern European cities and towns (see Bradshaw). Budapest also experienced an investment boom until the mid-1990s, when it received "far more FDI than other cities in the Central European region (except East Berlin)" (Tosics, "Post-Socialist Budapest" 248). The beauty of Prague and its closeness to Munich and Vienna made it one of the favorite locations for subsidiaries of international or Western companies in Central Europe. Warsaw was neither as economically advanced as Budapest nor as alluring as Prague, but it also drew Western capital owing to its relative closeness to the yet-to-be penetrated former Soviet republics.

On the surface, all of the cities experienced economic progress in the early 1990s. Still, it was only the privileged few who entered the "promised land," while the vast majority of the population struggled to survive in the new conditions, or simply quit the race. Unemployment and its direct consequences, such as increased crime, homelessness, hunger, alcoholism, drug abuse, and other social pathologies reigned in Central European capitals, presenting a hitherto unknown phenomenon. While it is true that in the 2000s, general economic and social conditions did improve across the region, the first few years of transformation caused a drastic pauperization of society (see Szczygieł, *20 lat*). Next to increased poverty, the residents of Central European cities experienced social confusion. The switch from central planning to a free market economy meant a loss of hundreds of thousands of jobs: sometimes whole industrial sectors were wiped out as unprofitable, and their employees were forced to retrain and look for new jobs in completely new corporate environments. Also, the services hitherto sponsored by the state, such as daycare, sports centers, medical care, and subsidized summer vacation had to be paid for and many people could no longer afford them. The effects of the "shock therapy" of the early 1990s fulfilled John M. Keynes's prophesy that "rapid transition will involve so much pure destruction of wealth that the new state of affairs will be, at first, far worse than the old, and the grand experiment will be discredited" (qtd. in Stanilov 22).

To Häußermann and Kapphan, the transformation taking place in Central European cities after 1989 "can be described as 'marketization,' which is the opposite of [their] development for 40 years between 1949 and 1989—'demarketizing' or 'decommodification'" (190). State ownership decreased rapidly, which affected both corporate and private areas of life in the city. Freshly privatized companies often fell under foreign—predominantly Western—ownership that introduced their own modes of management, production, and marketing. New working hours and

Western corporate culture decisively changed the rhythm and nature of city life: rush hours changed, lunch restaurants opened in the vicinity of new or renovated office buildings, business people started communicating in a peculiar combination of business English and the national language, and new stores opened to respond to the needs of the fast growing class of corporate managers. Moreover, mass privatization of public housing had a diversifying effect on urban populations: while the poor dwelled in prefabricated buildings, everyone who could afford to move escaped to the newly renovated turn-of-the-century houses in the downtown areas or built residential homes in the suburbs. In Budapest, for example, in "the prosperous parts of the inner districts (within the central business area or in its immediate vicinity) privatization has been almost wholesale and the rehabilitation of houses is under way, as a large majority of the population can afford to invest in renovation. In the less advantageous high-density areas, private apartments also prevail, but as the low-quality rental units are concentrated in this zone, there is hardly any hope that the new condominiums with mixed ownership will create the uniform will of the owners which is required for reconstruction. Thus, the moving-out of the middle class is quite predictable and it will eventually lead to the deterioration of these areas" (Tosics, "Post-socialist Budapest" 270). Similar trends were also observable in Prague, Berlin, and Warsaw, where city centers and neighboring areas were strongly gentrified and suburbs crowded with family houses. Like the housing projects in US-American cities and the high-rise suburbs (*banlieues*) in France, many prefabricated apartment blocks in Central European capitals have experienced ghettoization that, in turn, has led to a further social ostracism of those areas and the people who inhabit them. Naturally, not all communist housing tenements turn into ghettos. In Warsaw, despite the construction boom, "nearly 30 per cent of inhabitants still live in the pre-fabricated apartment blocks that form large housing estates in all districts" (Węcławowicz 231); calling them all slums would be an unnecessary exaggeration.

All Central European capitals experience social polarization. Gated communities and suburban villas contrast with decaying prefabricated apartment blocks; salaries of corporate professionals (a remarkable number of them from the West, sent over to run Central European subsidiaries of international concerns and Western firms) are many times higher than the wages of the majority of the population; few can afford shopping at designer clothing stores and organic food shops while the rest rely on discount supermarkets and international chain stores. Already in the mid-1990s, enormous shopping malls appeared in Central Europe, first in the capitals, which had "the biggest purchasing power," then in other cities and towns (Tosics, "City Development" 64). As Tosics argues, "the retail sector has special importance in the restructuring of postsocialist cities. On the one hand, retailing was very underdeveloped in the socialist cities both in quantitative and qualitative terms. . . . On the other hand, this sector exhibits in market economies the fastest restructuring in accordance with a high level of capital concentration and rapid globalization. . . . The new retail sector is more based in car use, needs bigger buildings, and is therefore more oriented towards the transitional zones and outskirts of cities and to suburban areas" (64-65). The erection of large shopping centers (often owned by Western or global capital) on the outskirts meant a substantial change for Central European capitals. Whereas "the administrative centre of the city was traditionally also the centre of retail activities" (65), since the 1990s, urban consumers have shopped less in downtown areas and more on the outskirts. When Polus Center, a US-style shopping center, opened in Budapest in 1996, "five per cent of the city's population, 100,000 people, showed up for the mall's first weekend" (Ritzer 41). Malls located on the edge of the city and easily accessible by highways have also proliferated in Prague and other Central European capitals (Ritzer 41). Berlin and Warsaw are important exceptions owing to "numerous vacant open spaces" in the center that create opportunities for construction of shopping malls and huge parking lots for their customers (Dimitrovska Andrews 161). The centers of Prague and Budapest, on the contrary, are densely built up and protected as cultural and historical heritages, which, in turn, limits the possibilities for mass retail development. Moreover, owing to fast-growing rents in the center and the surrounding gentrified neighborhoods, only very rich (and, hence, expensive) retail chains, designer stores, and coffee shops can afford downtown locations; most small family-owned businesses are forced out to poorer areas of the city.

The emergence of shopping malls, chain stores, fast food restaurants, and discounters in Berlin, Budapest, Prague, and Warsaw is particularly striking when juxtaposed with the previous scarcity or absence of Western-style commercial space in these cities, although this is hardly an exclusively Central European phenomenon. These "cathedrals of consumption," as Georg Ritzer calls them, not only contribute to "the general atmosphere of consumptionism," but also "lead in various ways to higher levels of consumption" since "they are designed artistically and scientifically to lure people into consumption" (34). The comparison of shopping malls to sanctuaries suggests that they are characterized by the enchantment needed to attract consumers (Ritzer 9), but also—which is particularly true in Catholic Poland—refers to their size. In the words of Sławomir Sierakowski, Poland's leading left-wing intellectual, Warsaw boasts "the biggest hypermarkets and the biggest churches," which symbolize the basic choice the Polish citizen faces: "God or the market" (Sierakowski and Žižek 1:57-2:14). These (hyper)consumption patterns are uncritically copied from the United States "because American-based corporations are intent on, and aggressive about, exporting American consumer goods and the American way of consuming them"—a process Ritzer describes as Americanization rather than globalization, because the latter "would indicate more of a multidirectional relationship among many nations" (Ritzer 38-39). US-style malls have influenced not only the consumption patterns of city residents, but also the look and functions of whole districts: while "the mall . . . assumes the status of an ersatz city, the city center presents itself more and more as a great open-air shopping mall. . . . Mallified city centers . . . tend to invert the traditional relationship between interior and exterior" (Ghent Urban Studies Team [GUST] 97-98). While the inside of the mall is designed to resemble a shopping street, the refurbished parks and squares in central districts make use of "street furniture intended to evoke an indoor coziness" (97-98). Also, inner-city malls are often erected along or at junctions of the most frequented urban routes and are nearly impossible to avoid: a way through the city becomes a way through the shopping center (Hoffmann-Axthelm 66). Sharon Zukin criticizes these "new spaces for public cultures" and warns that "by accepting [them] without questioning their representations of urban life, we risk succumbing to a visually seductive, privatized public culture" (*Cultures of Cities* 3).

Whereas inner-city malls are easily accessible by public transport, shopping malls on the outskirts created a demand for a different kind of transportation and, consequently, a growing need for changes in urban infrastructure: "The explosion of automobile ownership" increased personal mobility, which can be seen as a positive development; however, it had negative side effects: "the level of public transportation services . . . decreased considerably" (Stanilov 11), while traffic jams and air and noise pollution increased significantly. Suburbanization of offices and housing made the situation even worse. The urban developments in Central Europe in the 1990s call to mind the growth of US-American cities in the 1960s and their reliance on automobile transportation (see, e.g., Berman, *All That Is Solid*; Jacobs). Increasingly, however, another trend known from Western metropolises is taking place in Central European capitals, namely, that of reclaiming the downtown: whereas in the 1990s rich people moved to the suburbs of Central European cities, in the 2000s they prefer to live in luxurious high-rise apartment buildings or gentrified historic houses in the city center, closer to entertainment, government and corporate offices, designer boutiques, and gourmet delicatessens (Murawski 93). Importantly, it was Western expatriates who introduced this trend and rich locals who followed.

The internationalization of Central European cities had numerous consequences that have been mostly visible in city centers. "The growing number of Western employees working in Central and East European capital cities (e.g., 50,000 in Prague) is an important force on the residential market, demanding new or reconstructed 'up-market' housing and thus contributing to change in the built environment" (Dimitrovska Andrews 162). Thousands of Western managers and entrepreneurs who moved to Central European cities in the 1990s sought to make their working and living environment similar to that to which had been accustomed, which more often than not meant a higher standard of housing, infrastructure, and retail. They bought apartments or houses as well as office space in city centers and renovated them. New stores, restaurants, and schools appeared in the area to serve the needs of Westerners and other high-income tenants, while those who had lived in the center for decades—"mainly old and relatively poor" (Musil, "Prague Returns" 307)—were forced to spend long hours in traffic to shop at discount markets located on the outskirts of the city. Consequently, although "eviction is not a common mechanism behind displacement and gentrification" in Central Europe (Sýkora, "Gentrification" 98), in downtown neighborhoods, wealthy newcomers replaced long-time residents of low social status (see, e.g., Musil, "Prague Returns"; Sýkora,

"Gentrification"). These and other developments are clear signs of gentrification, which eventually creates rich and poor enclaves within the city and, hence, intensifies social stratification (see, e.g., Holm; Zukin, *Loft Living*).

The gentrification and commercialization of central areas would not have been possible without the restoration of private ownership. Budapest and Prague introduced restitution right after the system change. Since it was not always possible or socially desirable to give back the land or houses to their original owners, in both cities restitution was often combined with compensation. In Prague, 70 per cent of the buildings in the center returned to their proprietors by 1994 (Dimitrovska Andrews 161). Berlin passed "the *'Investitionsvorranggesetz'* ('priority of investment law') that enable[d] the political authorities to grant the land in the city centre to high capital investors, and merely remunerate the former owners" (Dimitrovska Andrews 161). Consequently, Berlin underwent a construction boom throughout the 1990s and well into the 2000s, while disputed property rights in central Warsaw largely limited developments in the 1990s (Dimitrovska Andrews 161). It was not until the 2000s that a real boom on construction market took place in Warsaw as well as other Polish cities.

The internationalization and Westernization of city centers is also mirrored in architecture. Central European capitals followed the example of other big cities and invited world-known architects to design landmark buildings, which increased the prestige and tourist value of the cities (GUST 51, 99; Koolhaas 1248). Frank Gehry in Prague, Daniel Liebeskind in Berlin and Warsaw, I.M. Pei in Berlin, and Norman Foster in Berlin and Warsaw, among others, created edifices that immediately joined the ever increasing list of the world's most talked about buildings. The same architects who designed the architectural symbols of New York, Los Angeles, Paris, and London created the landmarks of contemporary Berlin, Budapest, Prague, and Warsaw. This phenomenon is more connected with globalization than Westernization and I discuss it at length in chapter 5.

Arguably, the driving force behind the architectural and cultural changes in Central European cities has been the rise of global urban tourism. Since the 1980s, the worldwide trend of mass tourism (see, e.g., Hoffman, Fainstein, and Judd; GUST) has substantially transformed postcommunist metropolises. Since 1989, Prague has been one of the favorite tourist destinations in Europe (Williams and Baláž 226). Hardly damaged in World War II, Prague could offer historic architecture, scenic views, and, initially, cheap accommodation and food; but after almost two decades of Westernization and capitalizing on tourism, the Czech capital is no longer a bargain. Nevertheless, owing to cheap flights by budget airlines, it still attracts large numbers of tourists: "With 3.7 million tourist arrivals a year, Prague constitutes Europe's seventh most visited city, an enormous number for a city with a 1.2 million population" (Dujisin 9). The growth of tourism has had serious economic, social, and cultural implications. On the one hand, Prague's prosperity greatly depends on tourism; on the other hand, the inhabitants feel outnumbered by tourists and annoyed by the negative side of tourism, namely, "rises in crime, crowding, noise, loss of privacy, gambling casinos, and various types of informal economic activities, such as prostitution and street vending" (Musil, "Prague Returns" 308).

Similar drawbacks are visible in the cities with a Habsburg history such as Vienna, Budapest, and Kraków. Tosics argues that these cities should cooperate "to increase the joint capacities of their infrastructure (e.g., cooperation between airports, fast rail link, split of tasks instead of direct rivalry)" ("Post-socialist Budapest" 276-77). While it is true that overseas tourists often choose to visit all these cities during a one- or two-week vacation, Budapest, Kraków, and Prague also attract visitors separately, either as conference centers, historical capitals, or simply as party zones still cheaper than Western cities. To Musil, the decisive factor behind the increasingly international role of Prague has been "its rediscovered attractiveness as a beautiful city" ("Prague Returns" 291). The same can be argued with regard to Budapest, although the Hungarian capital had been a popular tourist destination already before the fall of the Wall. Berlin also draws millions of tourists every year, not necessarily owing to its disputed beauty, but rather because of its troubled history, outstanding museums and galleries, fascinating architecture, relatively cheap night life, and world famous events such as the Berlinale, the Love Parade (from 1989 until 2004 and then again, for the last time, in 2006), and, recently, the FIFA World Cup in 2006 (for more on urban spectacles see, e.g., Harvey; Lefebvre; Short and Kim). Warsaw is the least touristy of the discussed metropolises, which can be explained by its (arguable) visual unattractiveness and its eastern location, among other factors. Compared to other Polish cities, Warsaw plays the role of a business, political, and cultural center, while Kraków and Wrocław are visited for their beauty and history. Generally recognized as a major source of income, mass tourism deeply transforms urban culture and politics; its "economic importance . . . has led to the competitive self-promotion of cities" (GUST 99), which I discuss at length in chapter 4.

Next to tourism, the influx of Western expatriates is an important force that has been changing the social, economic, cultural, and national structures of the discussed capitals. While Westernization is mostly associated with urban professionals, it is important to remember that CEOs and lower managers constituted only one of many groups of newcomers. After 1989, young people from the West, mostly from the United States, streamed to Central European cities in search of the unknown, the unspoiled, or—quite unromantically—the cheap. Prague in the 1990s was "the new Paris" (see Shteyngart); "avant-garde publications, coffee houses, pubs, and foreign language journals" (Musil, "Prague Returns" 300) were significant aspects of social and cultural life in the Czech capital in the 1990s. Furthermore, US-American universities opened branches in Prague, which attracted even more Western youth. In the 1990s, expatriate communities bloomed also in Budapest, Berlin, and—to a lesser extent—in Warsaw. Many Western newcomers were (or at least considered themselves) artists: they came to Central Europe not only to take advantage of cheaper accommodation, ateliers, and general costs of living, but also to find inspiration in the cities undergoing thorough transformations. In Berlin, many of the young newcomers stemmed from the West German province. Unsatisfied with the petit bourgeois atmosphere of their hometowns, they settled in the rundown Mietskasernen of East Berlin (mostly in the districts of Mitte, Prenzlauer Berg, and Friedrichshain) and busied themselves with art, activism, and various alternative ways of living (Häußermann, Holm, and Zunzer 54-58). Remarkably, two decades after their arrival, Prenzaluer Berg has turned from an artistic enclave (before 1989 the district had been popular among GDR bohemians) into a copy of a peaceful and rich small town.

As Musil observes, "the growing number of Western employees and tourists, along with the growing import of Western consumer goods, American movies, and Western TV programmes, started to change the consumption patterns, fashion, lifestyles, and values of the local population. Most of these changes in cultural patterns, mainly those symbolizing the links to the West, are already reflected in the architectural semiotics of the city, the streets, and other public spaces" ("Prague Returns" 299-300). Westernization from the outside was most intensively experienced in Central European capitals in the first decade after the change of system. Later, the cities became increasingly used to Western standards and started perceiving them not as foreign elements, but rather as something related to their own culture. This is not to suggest that Westernization from within was absent before and during the transformation process. There has always been a strong social will to catch up with the West, to "come back to Europe." The West has been associated with progress, and, hence, understood as a positive force.

Nearly all post-1989 political, economic, social, and cultural developments bear traces of colonial practices. In the 1990s, the colonization of Central European cities predominantly equaled Westernization; in the 2000s it has been more closely connected to globalization. Berlin, Budapest, Prague, and Warsaw are strongly affected by globalization processes, but themselves play only limited roles in creating the new global order. Whereas the early reforms could be depicted as "an attempt to make a desperate leap from totalitarian existence to capitalism in a matter of only a few years" (Stanilov 7), the later developments have been more moderate and adjusted to the local specifics. The fact that the intensity of Western or global influences seems to fade away may also be partly explained by the disappearance of differences between the local culture and Western or global cultures. Nevertheless, the impact of the West and globalization continue to be crucial in shaping and reshaping urban cultures in Central Europe.

Judging by the official politics and economy of Central European cities, their architectural developments and urban policies, Soviet influences appear no longer to exist. It would be shortsighted, however, to claim that more than forty years of Soviet colonization disappeared with the arrival of Western chain stores and EU flags. Even if Soviet influences are tangible predominantly in postcommunist architecture and infrastructure, they still determine everyday life in the city. The former colonizer exists not only in people's mentalities, but also, I argue, in works of art, especially in literature and film. Interestingly, this is also where the newest Western or global influences are most openly communicated. In the following chapters I juxtapose the official images of Central European cities with those presented in literature and film in order to pin down the elusive (post)colonial nature of Berlin, Budapest, Prague, and Warsaw.

Chapter Four

Self-representations of Central European Cities through Municipal Media

This chapter is the first of four sections in which I analyze various forms and methods of communicating urban identities. Here, I inquire into official and unofficial images and texts used in municipal media, that is, media controlled and published by municipal authorities or private agencies commissioned or subcontracted by city governments. I start with the oldest city symbols—coats of arms and flags—and move on to more modern types of images such as logos and brand campaigns, both inspired by the corporate sector. Next, I analyze selected elements of (electronic and print) municipal media: I look at their web design, the photographs illustrating information about the city, the design of city maps, city guides, and city tourist cards, and the images used therein. In my analysis of images and designs, I focus predominantly on the choice of depicted objects and the frequency with which they appear in the given media, their symbolic meanings, and the messages they communicate. Given the types and nature of the media, images are of crucial interest in this chapter; however, since some of the most important information about urban identities can be communicated only in words, the chapter also includes an analysis of the texts published on the municipal or official tourist information websites. I look closely at the choice of words and the frequency with which they appear and try to determine which historical events, which aspects of city life, which attributes, and so on are included in the text and, consequently, what kinds of urban identities they mediate. In the final part of the chapter I present a summary of the urban identities of Berlin, Budapest, Prague, and Warsaw as communicated through municipal media, a comparison, and a brief analysis of the contradictions that inevitably surface. The following analysis is based on images and texts published in municipal electronic and print media in 2008. The English language versions of city and tourist information homepages are the main object of my study, but, whenever necessary, I also discuss the websites in their original language versions. The interdisciplinary character of the chapter justifies the use of theoretical frameworks and methods of analysis from such diverse areas of knowledge as urban studies (Harvey; Koolhaas; Lynch), media and communication studies (Highmore; Mitchell), comparative cultural studies (Tötösy de Zepetnek), and marketing (Knowles; Wheeler).

Self-representations of Central European cities through official symbols

Coats of arms and flags

Coats of arms are the oldest and most recognizable city symbols. In Europe, municipal coats of arms started taking shape in the second half of the thirteenth century, together with the development of town privileges. The emblematic images were first used without heraldic shields and appeared mostly on municipal seals; their transformation to coats of arms often took centuries (see Warsaw City Hall). While Budapest's coat of arms dates back to the nineteenth century, the final versions of Berlin's, Prague's, and Warsaw's heraldic symbols developed as late as the twentieth century. Remarkably, the coats of arms in the cases of these cities experienced changes or even spells of nonexistence under socialist regimes and all were restored to their traditional forms after 1989. The imagery used in coats of arms, of general animal and fantasy figures, has always been subject to legends, hypotheses, and speculation.

Berlin's shield of arms consists of a black bear with a red tongue and red claws on a silver background (see figure 1). The bear is standing on its hind legs and its open muzzle displays sharp white teeth. The crest is a golden crown with five leaf-shaped peaks. The tiara has a brick pattern, which, together with the double gate placed in the middle, calls to mind a wall, or, more precisely, the city walls. The heraldic description is as follows: Shield: Argent a bear statant erect Sable armed and

Figure 1. Berlin Coat of Arms. BerlinOnline Stadtportal.

langued Gules; Crest: a mural crown Or. (None of the discussed municipal media provide proper heraldic descriptions of their coats of arms. The heraldic descriptions quoted in this chapter were developed with a kind help of Mr. David B. Appleton of the Royal Heraldry Society of Canada.)

The bear has been used as a symbol of Berlin throughout the whole history of the city, but its origins remain uncertain—one of the plausible explanations is that the bear commemorates the founder of the Margraviate of Brandenburg, Albert the Bear (Richie 6-8). The bear's first appearance on the municipal seal dates back to 1280, but until the early twentieth century it had shared the space on the coat of arms with Brandenburg and (since 1709) Prussian eagles. It was not until the collapse of the German monarchy (1918) and the subsequent establishment of Greater Berlin (1920) that the eagles disappeared from the coat of arms. In 1935 Siegmund von Weech designed a new, graphically modern emblem depicting a black bear on a silver shield. The shield had red double edges and was topped by a red brick crown. The bear's posture was more aggressive than the one used today and corresponded to the official image of Berlin as the capital of the Hitler-dominated world. Despite its hostile look and nazi associations, East Berlin continued using the 1935 coat of arms after the war. The authorities of West Berlin decided to keep the bear as its symbol, but refrained from embracing Weech's design. Instead, in 1952 West Berlin invited artists and heraldrists to present plans for a new coat of arms. Ottfried Neubecker's winning proposal functioned as the coat of arms of West Berlin from 1954 to 1990 and in 1990 was adopted as the coat of arms of the City of Berlin (see BerlinOnline).

In city publications and campaigns and during official city events the coat of arms is often accompanied by the city flag. The Berlin flag consists of three horizontal stripes: red, white, and red (see figure 2). Each outer red stripe composes one fifth of the flag, and the middle white stripe fills out the remaining three fifths. The Berlin bear is visible in the center of the white stripe, but without the shield and the

Figure 2. Berlin Flag. BerlinOnline Stadtportal.

brick crown. As official city colors, red and white are repeatedly used in the imagery representing Berlin such as, for example, the city logo, the city marketing campaign, and tourist information brochures. Unlike the coat of arms, which may be used only with the permission of the Berlin Senate, the city flag may be used everywhere and by everyone as long as its use remains respectful (see BerlinOnline).

The origins of Warsaw's coat of arms can be traced back to several versions of one legend. The most famous one is Artur Oppman's tale about *Syrena* (mermaid), who lived in the Vistula waters at the bottom of today's Old Town. Her beautiful singing perplexed two local fishermen; they went to consult the hermit Barnaba, who suggested they should catch Syrena and deliver her as a gift to the prince residing at nearby Czersk Castle. One full-moon night, when Syrena was sitting on a rock, the fishermen and the hermit caught her in the nets and imprisoned her in a wooden barn. Like Odysseus's companions in Homer's epic, they filled their ears with honey to stay immune to Syrena's irresistible voice. The men decided to delay their journey until the sunrise and, in the meantime, ordered a farmhand named Staszek to keep a close watch on the barn. Once the capturers had gone to rest, Syrena started singing. Since Staszek's ears had not been sealed with honey, he could not possibly resist the unearthly voice. Syrena asked him to untie her and follow her to the river, and Staszek obeyed. Before they disappeared in the Vistula waters, Syrena expressed her disappointment with the village people: "I love you, Vistula bank; I love you, simple people of good hearts. I was your song, the charm of your lives! Why did you imprison me? Why did you want to keep me bound in prince's castle and have me sing on his order? I sing to you, simple people, people of calm and good hearts, but I do not want to and shall not sing when ordered. . . . And when hard times come . . . the Vistula waves will hum a song to your offspring, a song of hope, strength, and victory" (Oppman 14).

Interestingly, although Warsaw's official portal claims to follow Oppman's version of the legend, the text on the city website remarkably differs from the original: in that version of the story it is the people of Warsaw who help Syrena escape from the barn where she had been imprisoned by a rich merchant and the grateful creature promises to defend Warsaw anytime the city needs her help—for this reason, Syrena bears a sword and a shield (see Warsaw City Hall). The text quoted on the official portal presents the people of Warsaw as good-hearted, helpful, and friendly, whereas Oppman's legend depicts the locals as scheming, greedy, and simple-minded. It is hardly surprising, of course, that the city chose to publish the more flattering version of the legend. Although it is true that there exist a few versions of the same story, the city's claim to follow Oppman's famous text is simply false.

Syrena—or *Syrenka*, as she is often endearingly referred to—has functioned as Warsaw's symbol ever since the seventeenth century. Today's version of Warsaw's coat of arms, however, is relatively young: it was designed by Szczęsny Kwarta in 1938 (see figure 3). The red shield features a mermaid who carries a golden sword in her lifted right hand, while her left arm is protected by a round golden shield. The colors of her upper (human) body as well as her fishtail are natural and her hair is

Figure 3. Warsaw Coat of Arms. Warsaw City Hall.

golden (see Warsaw City Hall). The heraldic description is as follows: Shield: Gules a mermaid proper maintaining in the dexter hand a sword fesswise and in the sinister hand a round shield Or; Crest: a Royal Crown proper.

Before the administrative unification of Warsaw in the late eighteenth century, Syrena was the official symbol of *Stara Warszawa* (Old Warsaw). In 1791, after local townships and villages became one municipal area, the newly established City of Warsaw adopted Syrena as its coat of arms. For most of the nineteenth century, the use of historical coats of arms was prohibited in all Polish cities under czarist rule, including Warsaw—seals were allowed to present only the state insignia (interestingly, very similar regulations existed in the GDR: there too, cities were ordered to use the official state symbols while historic coats of arms, such as the Berlin bear, remained at best ignored [see Siegelordnung]). After the Russian occupiers left Warsaw in 1915, the Polish authorities reestablished the historical city seal and—after Poland regained its independence in 1918—the coat of arms. In 1964, Syrenka's hair, previously tied up in a bun, was let loose and the royal crown disappeared from the top of the shield. In 1990 the Warsaw City Council ordered the return of Kwarta's 1938 design as the official coat of arms. Although the look of Syrenka transformed throughout centuries, her main attributes—the sword and the shield—prevailed, thus, "emphasizing the defensive character of the city" (Warsaw City Hall).

Figure 4. Prague Coat of Arms. Prague Information Service.

Warsaw and Prague have identical flags: each consists of two equally wide horizontal stripes, the upper one is yellow, the bottom one is red. Whereas Warsaw's city website lacks information on the origins of the flag colors, Prague's portal provides an explanation: the colors of Prague's flag derive from the city's coat of arms. Another similarity between Warsaw's and Prague's emblems is that they had represented the old towns (Old Warsaw and Prague's Old Town, respectively) before they became adopted as the coats of arms of the administratively united cities. In 1784, the municipalities of *Staré Město* (Old Town), *Nové Město* (New Town), *Malá Strana* (Lesser Town), and *Hradčany* (Castle Hill) merged into a single city, when "united Prague took over the coat of arms of Old Town as a seat of Municipality" (Prague City Hall). As in the case of Berlin and Warsaw, Prague's coat of arms changed slightly over time: today's version was created by Karel Pánek in 1991.

Prague's coat of arms (see figure 4) consists of many elaborate parts. In its center there is a red shield featuring a golden fortification with three towers and an open gate. The towers have open windows and are topped by roofs with finials. The wings of the gate are red and its lattice golden. A silver arm carrying a silver sword reaches out from the black background of the gate: a commemoration of "the successful defence of Charles Bridge against the Swedish army during the Thirty Years War" (Prague City Hall). On the shield (which can also be used separately as the small coat of arms of Prague) rest three silver helmets with golden crowns; the middle one carries a double-tailed silver lion with a golden crown and "each of the side helmets carries 12 flags of armorial towns or boroughs" (Prague City Hall). The shield is held by two double-tailed silver lions with golden crowns. The heraldic description is as follows: Shield: Gules a triple-towered castle with open portcullis Or issuant from the gateway an arm in armor maintaining (or, brandishing) a sword Argent; Crest: upon three helmets mantled Gules doubled Or coronets Or center double-tailed lion statant Argent with coronet Or dexter twelve flags of armorial boroughs sinister twelve flags of armorial boroughs; Supporters: atop a leafy branch Or two lions queue-forchy Argent crowned Or; Motto: *Praga Caput Rei Publicae* (Prague, the Capital of the Republic). As the historic coat of arms on the Old Town Hall documents, the motto used to read *Praga Caput Regni*, that is, Prague, the Capital of the Kingdom. During the socialist regime the central double-lion was removed from the coat of arms and the motto changed to *Praga Mater Urbium*, that is, Prague, Mother of Cities, thus avoiding the uncomfortable reference to the capital's royal past.

Budapest's coat of arms was created when Óbuda, Buda, and Pest merged into one city in 1873. The choice of a common symbol for the newly united municipality was a delicate matter: on the one hand, it had to relate to the heraldic traditions of Óbuda, Buda, and Pest and express the historic identities of the hitherto separate towns; on the other hand, as an official emblem of the nation's capital, it had to be simple and clear. Painter Lajos Fridrich faced the challenge and designed the coat of arms that remains in use until today (see figure 5). In the center there is a red shield divided in two by a silver ribbon symbolizing the Danube. In the upper part of the shield there is a golden castle with a single tower and a gate. The lower part of the shield also depicts a golden castle, but with two gates and three towers. The blue

Figure 5. Budapest Coat of Arms. Municipality of Budapest.

Figure 6. Budapest Flag. Municipality of Budapest.

background of the gates symbolizes Óbuda, the upper castle represents Pest, and the lower one stands for Buda. The crest is Saint Stephen's crown—a reference to the Hungarian state. The shield is held by two supporters: on the heraldic right there is a golden lion that was previously depicted in the coat of arms of Buda, on the heralding left there is a golden griffin from the coat of arms of Pest (Municipality of Budapest). Both supporters are standing on a pedestal, on which the bottom part of the shield is also resting. The heraldic description is as follows: Shield: Gules a fess wavy Argent between a single-towered castle Or with a gate Azure and a triple-towered castle Or with two gates Azure; Crest: Saint Stephen's crown proper; Supporters: on a pedestal on the dexter side a lion and on the sinister side a griffin, both Or.

The colors used in the coat of arms compose Budapest's flag, which consists of three horizontal stripes of equal width—red, yellow, and blue (looking from the top to the bottom)—with Budapest's coat of arms in the center (see figure 6). Owing to its resemblance to the Romanian national flag, the blue stripe was replaced by a green one during Admiral Horthy's regime (Municipality of Budapest). After the Second World War, the new communist authorities decided to abolish city flags altogether. Also, the coat of arms suffered alterations during socialist rule. First, in 1945, the royal crown disappeared from the top of the heraldic shield. In 1964 the Budapest city council reduced the emblem to the red shield, changed the color and shape of the castles, and, most dramatically, placed a red five-armed star in the center of the silver ribbon representing the Danube. After Hungary regained its independence in 1989, the new democratic council announced the return of Budapest's 1873 flag and coat of arms as the official municipal symbols (Municipality of Budapest).

As the above descriptions make clear, there are several similarities between the coats of arms of the discussed cities. Most parallels can be found between the heraldic symbols of Berlin and Warsaw and between those of Prague and Budapest. The coats of arms of Berlin and Warsaw are clear and simple: they do not have any supporters, mantlings, or banners. Their heraldic shields feature legendary creatures closely connected to the foundation of the cities—a bear and Syrena, respectively—and are topped with crowns. Prague's and Budapest's coats of arms are elaborate heraldic structures: both have supporters—lions and a griffin and a lion, respectively—and their shields feature castles with towers and open gates. Although in heraldic taxonomy castles or towers mean safety, in the case of Prague and Budapest they refer directly to local historic buildings.

The coats of arms and flags of Berlin, Warsaw, Prague, and Budapest changed depending on which political or national power ruled each city. Unsurprisingly, under the Soviet influence the royal elements of the coats of arms were rendered inconvenient. The crowns disappeared from the heraldic symbols of Warsaw and Budapest, and Prague's coat of arms lost not only the inscription implying the royal character of the city, but also the double lion from the crest. In addition, Budapest's coat of arms received a Soviet-inspired element: a red star placed in the very center of the heraldic shield. After the collapse of communism in 1989, the democratically elected authorities of Warsaw, Budapest, and Prague swiftly re-embraced their heraldic traditions. Berlin was a remarkable exception: since the prewar coat of arms was tainted with nazi associations, the reunited city adapted the 1954 heraldic symbol of West Berlin—a decision that may be interpreted as yet another example of the imposition of the West Berlin (and, by implication, West German) system and its symbols onto the new Berlin after 1990.

The use of municipal coats of arms is subject to strict regulations. Although the laws regarding heraldic symbols differ from city to city, they share one basic rule: coat of arms may be used only after prior approval by the city council (or its equivalent). The use of a municipal coat of arms for artistic, heraldic, scientific, and educational purposes without asking for permission is possible as long as the symbol is treated with due respect. Still, as a formal symbol strictly regulated by law, the coat of arms tends to be reserved for special occasions, and as a historical emblem, it does not always mix well with ubiquitous ultramodern imagery and, thus, may seem unappealing or simply difficult to understand for both locals and visitors. Moreover, owing to the increasing commercialization of various areas of life and the development of global tourism, cities promote themselves as brands and need to be presented in an attractive package appealing to the tastes of customers used to fast changing, colorful, and stylish designs. For these and other reasons, the municipal authorities of Berlin, Warsaw, Prague, and Budapest (as well as those of other cities such as New York, Montreal, and Cape Town, among many others) have developed city logos, which they now use not instead of, but next to, their historic coats of arms and flags.

Cities as brands

As national—and, in some cases, international—centers of culture, politics, and business, most European capitals prompt dozens of associations even among those who have never visited them. Their names instantly call to mind momentuous events (the Prague Spring of 1968), famous landmarks (the Acropolis in Athens), and specific cuisine (the Berlin *Currywurst*). They have been immortalized in pop music ("London Calling" by The Clash), film (William Wyler's *Roman Holiday*), literature (Dublin in James Joyce's *Ulysses*), painting (Ernst Ludwig Kirchner's Berlin street scenes), and photography (Robert Doisneau's pictures of Paris). They boast what Kevin Lynch defines as "high imageability," that is, they are "well formed, distinct, remarkable," and capable of evoking a strong image in any given observer (9-10). Despite their generally acknowledged uniqueness, however, in the last two decades European capitals have become increasingly alike, owing to globalization and EU-ization: chain stores offer the same products regardless of the location, international concerns provide the same services everywhere, and central business districts are created by a handful of world-famous architects (or "starchitects"). This growing uniformity of urban life prompts cities to emphasize their own identities and communicate them to current and potential residents, tourists, and investors. In other words, cities identify and market themselves as brands.

The concept of brand identity has been extended beyond its traditional role in selling consumer goods and applied to cities (see Elliott) at least since the rise of urban entrepreneurialism in the 1970s (see Harvey). According to Alina Wheeler, urban branding is hardly a new phenomenon: "Mankind has always used symbols to express fierce individuality, pride, loyalty, and ownership. The power of symbols remains elusive and mysterious. . . . Competition for recognition is as ancient as the heraldic banners on the medieval battlefield. No longer limited by physical terrain, managing perception now extends to cyberspace and beyond. As feudal domains became economic enterprises, what was once heraldry is now branding. The battle for physical territory has evolved into the competition for share of mind" (1). The newly discovered need to market cities as brands may be therefore considered simply a continuation of an old urban tradition reinvented by the corporate world: first, companies borrowed the idea of the coat of arms, processed it, and transformed it into logos and slogans; then—after "modern heraldry" started producing desired effects such as brand loyalty—city authorities were inspired to apply the modernized versions of ancient branding. Consequently, "the representation of the city is becoming closely associated with the marketing of the city. Urban representation and urban boosterism now go hand in hand" (Short and Kim 106)

As Andreas Huyssen observes, "the city is increasingly affected and structured by our culture of media images. In the move from the city as a regional or national center of production to the city as international center of communications, media, and services, the very image of the city itself becomes central to its success in a globally competitive world" (60). Dubbed "place wars" (see Haider), the fierce competition between cities has intensified owing to a number of factors such as the growth of multinational companies, the emergence of new global economic sectors, municipal governments' role in urban marketing, and competition for hosting global spectacles (e.g., the Olympic Games, the FIFA World Cup, international film festivals, and trade fairs) and international institutions, which "generate considerable economic multiplier effects" (Short and Kim 11). Creating a convincing and effective city brand is one of the most powerful tools in the interurban competition. A successful urban image can not only increase a city's chances of attracting international and state investments, but also, importantly, "help create a sense of social solidarity, civic pride and loyalty to place and even . . . a mental refuge in a world that capital treats as more and more place-less" (Harvey 14). In the face of growing standardization and cultural globalization, locality becomes a crucial asset and "difference is prized, visited, created, commodified" (Short and Kim 80). Together with the rise of global identities, local or national identities gain in importance and come to constitute a crucial part of the city image.

Next to globalization and urban entrepreneurialism, Berlin, Budapest, Prague, and Warsaw's interest in branding may be traced back to two phenomena that happened almost at the same time: the demise of communism and the progress of information technology that helped create and popularize new media. Before 1989, the noncommunist rest of the world categorized Central European capitals simply as part of the Soviet bloc; after the fall of the Wall and with the help of new technologies, especially the internet, they started focusing on restructuring and retelling their identities. In what follows, I demonstrate how Central European cities implement and execute branding, what types of urban identities they aim to communicate, and whether it is possible to distinguish any common patterns in their strategies.

In the words of Milton Glaser, the designer of the world-famous "I ♥ NY" logo: "A logo is the point of entry to the brand" (qtd. in Wheeler 4). It is not a prerequisite to a brand's success (as of 2008 Paris does not have a logo and it continues being hailed as one of the world's most fascinating cities), but it may help raise general awareness about a new or relaunched brand such as a newly independent city. As the following examples demonstrate, the creation and implementation of city logos often provokes controversy. Depending on the imagery they apply, city logos may be divided into several categories: logos featuring city names, logos featuring city landmarks, and logos featuring heraldic elements or colors. Naturally, the name of the city, that is, the brand name, appears in every city logo; some logos are even built solely around the city name, as in "I ♥ NY." Although New York has numerous internationally recognizable landmarks such as the Statue of Liberty, the Empire State Building, the Brooklyn Bridge (and, before September 2001, the World Trade Center) that it could incorporate into the logo, Glaser opted for visual simplicity. While the city acronym gives the recipients of the logo freedom to decide what New York stands for, the heart symbolizes an emotional relation with the city. Glaser's logo is indiscriminate: it may express the feelings of New Yorkers and tourists alike. Prague follows New York's example in that it structures its logo around the city name (see figure 7). Instead of embracing the emotional aspect, however, the Prague logo appeals to the intellect. The name of the city is displayed in four different language variations: Praha (Czech, Slovak), Prague (English, French), Praga (Polish, Russian, Spanish, Italian), and Prag (German, Danish, Serbo-Croatian, Turkish), which not only makes it easily apprehensible by international audiences, but also communicates several important messages about the Czech capital. First, despite slight

Figure 7. Prague Logo. Prague Information Service.

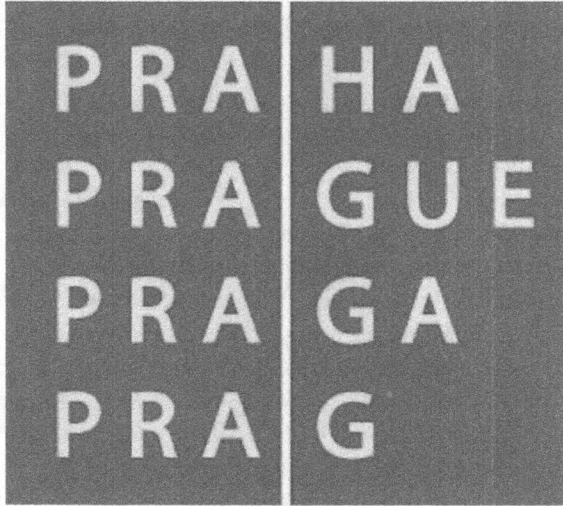

differences in the way it is named in different languages, the core of Prague's name, and—by analogy—of the city, remains constant and familiar. In Czech, the prefix "pra" means "primeval" or "ancient," thus, the white vertical line separating it from the changeable part of the word subtly emphasizes the historic character of Prague. Second, the logo points to the hospitality of the Czech capital: it welcomes visitors from various countries, promising they will feel at home regardless of the language they speak. Third, the logo communicates an image of Prague as a cosmopolitan city, comparable with New York or London in that it proudly presents its name as an internationally renowned brand.

In 2002, the Prague municipality announced a tender to develop "a new visual style of the city presentation including the new logo" (Prague City Hall). As in the case of other official city logos, the aim of the Prague logo is not to replace the coat of arms, but rather to "protect it against improper and too frequent usage. From [2003] on, the coat of arms [has been] used exclusively in official and ceremonial occasions" (Prague City Hall). The logo's complementary relation to the coat of arms is also emphasized through its colors: the Prague logo is based on the official city colors derived from the heraldic symbol. The background of the logo is bright red and the four versions of the city name are inscribed in gold block letters.

Warsaw's logo also relates to the city's coat of arms, both through its colors and content: it features Warsaw's oldest symbol, Syrenka. Her yellow hair stretches above the red shield and the red part of the slogan: a combination that calls to mind the yellow and red flag of Warsaw. Blue is not an official Warsaw color, but its presence in the logo seems more than justified since it symbolizes the Vistula. Despite her blurry shape, Syrenka is instantly recognizable to anyone familiar with the city's coat of arms, the Syrena legend, or the statues of Syrenka on the Vistula embankment and in the Old Market Square. A vast majority of Poles will promptly associate the logo with the capital; an uninformed audience, however, may have a difficulty deciphering the colorful image. In the logo, Syrenka's famous attributes—the sword and the shield—are pictured as a thick blue stripe and a red spot resembling an apple, respectively. The outline of the naked upper body makes it clear that the abstract image depicts a woman, but a hint at Syrenka's fantastic form is missing: the blue vertical stripe looks more like a long skirt than a fishtail. Interestingly, Syrenka's golden hair is loose, as it was in the coat of arms during the socialist regime. All in all, to a person unfamiliar with the legend of Syrena, the image in Warsaw's logo may look like a half-naked dancing woman waving a blue ribbon and holding a disproportionately big apple—a drunken bacchant rather than a mermaid.

The Warsaw logo (see figure 8), introduced in 2004, has several versions: with a white background and a black background, with the slogan and with the city name only, in Polish and in English. The many possible combinations allow officials to adjust the logo to specific audiences and occasions, which may be considered advantageous, but not without a serious drawback: the city is missing a universal logo that would be apprehensible to everyone. The Polish slogan says *zakochaj się w Warszawie* and has been directly translated into English as "fall in love with Warsaw," but, even though the part relating to emotions (*zakochaj się*/"fall in love") is written in red, the color customarily associated with affection, the imagery used in

Figure 8. Warsaw Logo. Warsaw City Hall.

the logo fails to explain why we should fall in love with the Polish capital. The slogan itself may be interpreted as a polite offer, an instruction, a playful proposition, a pleading, or—if we think of the sword Syrenka is holding in her right hand—even a menace. Rather than depicting a seductive mermaid, the logo calls to mind a desperate woman threatening "fall in love with Warsaw, or else . . . ."

The numerous imperfections have exposed the Warsaw logo to fierce criticism: it has been spurned for Syrenka's soggy breasts and misshaped fishtail (Bator 10), its bluriness and ambiguity (Olszewski), and the disproportionately high cost of the project (PLN 195,000) (Bator 10; Olszewski). Anna Kamińska, the chair of the jury deciding which of the thirty competitors won the bid for the capital's logo, admits that the chosen project was "not ideal," but merely better than other submitted works (Lemańska). The authors of the controversial logo, the Brand Nature Access agency, reveal that they considered depicting the Palace of Culture and Science, but eventually decided that "the Palace is a product of a completely different system and Syrenka . . . would be a better idea. We wanted her to be modern, to demonstrate that Warsaw has potential and energy, that it will be changing" (Lemańska). Settling for the Palace of Culture and Science was never really an option: the Stalinist building continues being perceived by older generations of Warsovians as an intruder, a reminder of the Soviet regime, and unrelated to anything Warsaw wants to be associated with (see, e.g., Wajda).

Unlike the logos of Prague and Warsaw, Budapest's logo seems only remotely related to its coat of arms (see figure 9). It includes red, yellow, and blue, which compose the city flag, but it also features unrelated colors such as purple, orange, and green. The colors interweave in a smooth fashion, resembling a rainbow; descending from the lightest to the darkest tone, they lend a special atmosphere to the image depicted in the logo. The Chain Bridge and a single Danube wave compose the center of the picture, the Buda Castle looms in the back, and the bottom stretch of the horizontal oval features the word "Budapest" spelled in gray block letters. The landmarks are reduced to outlines, which not only keeps the picture clear and simple, but also gives it the lightness of a sketch. The multicolored single line circling the image calls to mind a modernized version of an antique photo frame. The whole

Figure 9. Budapest Logo. Municipality of Budapest.

picture looks as if illuminated by a rising sun shining from the top left part of the oval. The Danube wave is colored with various shades of blue and green, while the Chain Bridge and the Buda Hill reflect the yellow, orange, and red tones of the sun rising, presumably, over Pest, the east part of the city, which stays out of the picture.

The Chain Bridge is a landmark generally recognizable in Hungary and abroad and, as such, a natural choice for Budapest's logo. Furthermore, whereas the Danube reminds viewers of the geographical division of the city, the bridge may be seen as a metaphor for the cultural and political unity between Buda and Pest. The Buda Castle—the historic seat of Hungarian kings since the fourteenth century—emphasizes the role of Budapest as a capital of the nation. Budapest has other famous buildings, sites, and monuments, but the selection made for the logo aspires to present an image of Budapest as a historical, picturesque, colorful city, where tradition meets modernity. Clearly, the logo continues Budapest's urban identity policy developed in the 1990s when "official narratives found the city's past references in the turn-of-the-century liberal metropolis, while at the same time, they tried to phrase Budapest as a dynamic, future-oriented city" (Polyák, "Alternative Use"). Judging by the city's informational and promotional materials, which I discuss later in this chapter, the logo is remarkably consistent with the urban identity Budapest communicates. The logo was developed and introduced not by the municipality itself, but by the capital's official tourism office (*Budapesti Turisztikai Szolgáltató*), which makes sure to include the symbol in all the materials it publishes and distributes. For obvious reasons, the repetitiveness and ubiquity of the brand identity help brands—and the cities that position themselves as brands—in their battles for a "share of mind" (Wheeler 1).

Berlin has also focused on brand recognition. Introduced in 1994, the city logo is featured in all materials issued, distributed, and supported by the municipality, starting with the city portal through all information brochures to the stamps on the mail sent by municipal offices. The sign is easily recognizable and, owing to its omnipresence, deeply embedded in the consciousness of Berliners. Importantly, although the Berlin logo has an international character and is comprehensible both by city inhabitants and by (potential) visitors, the ubiquitous image is directed predominantly at the former. Like all the cities in the region, after 1989 Berlin had to redefine its identity, however, Berlin's situation was far more complex than that of Prague, Budapest, or Warsaw: Berlin had to develop a new identity from two politically, culturally, socially, and economically different city parts that reunited in 1990 and make it possible for both East and West Berliners to identify with the reborn metropolis. The decision to use the Brandenburg Gate as the new city logo appears a thoughtful and diplomatic choice.

Whereas the landmarks such as the TV tower or the *Siegessäule* would represent only the eastern or only the western part of the city, respectively, the in-between position of the Brandenburg Gate makes it possible for all Berliners to relate to it as their common symbol. In postwar Berlin, the Brandenburg Gate was located between the Soviet and British sectors and—after the Wall was erected in 1961—in the so called "death strip" running through the city. For nearly thirty years, the Branden-

Figure 10. Berlin Logo. Presse und Informationsamt des Landes Berlin.

burg Gate was inaccessible from either side and, consequently, came to symbolize the division of Berlin and Germany. In 1987, it became the background to Ronald Reagan's famous speech, in which he called upon Mikhail Gorbachev to "open this gate" and "tear down this wall" (Ladd 22), and in 1989, it was literally turned into a stage, on which the fall of the Wall was celebrated. Furthermore, the Brandenburg Gate emphasizes the role of Berlin as the capital as it is considered, according to the 2008 Forza opinion poll, Germany's most important national monument ("Deutschlands Lieblingsmonumente" 108).

The information materials explaining the origins, design, and legal arrangements of the logo stress the role of the Brandenburg Gate as a symbol of Berlin adding, however, that "a symbol . . . does not equal a sign": "There are many possibilities to represent the pillars, the roof, and the *Quadriga*, and to combine them with the word 'Berlin.' The Berlin sign is a heavily reduced, but still unmistakable representation of the Brandenburg Gate" (Presse und Informationsamt des Landes Berlin 5). The omnipresence of the Berlin logo is facilitated by the fact that it allows for uncountable variations: the name of the city can be located either right or left, top or bottom, and it can be combined "with various slogans, backgrounds, and other elements" (Presse und Informationsamt des Landes Berlin 7). The most famous version of the logo (see figure 10) used, for example, as the domain icon of Berlin's web portal, is in Berlin's heraldic color, red, also known as Berlin red; but the logo regulations allow for the use of eight different colors specified in the palette (Presse und Informationsamt des Landes Berlin 8).

City logos are designed not only to help the city advertise itself to potential visitors and investors, but also to strengthen the local population's identification with the city. To be considered successful the logo has to meet several conditions. First, it has to be generally identifiable—which can be achieved through a simple design or a clear association with the city—and comprehensible on three different levels: within the city, nationwide, and internationally; clearly, the blurry and confusing Warsaw logo does not meet this condition. Second, the logo should be visually attractive, an interesting image to look at, a picture people may consider having on their coffee mugs or t-shirts. Although largely a matter of taste, there are some basic aesthetic rules regarding commercial symbols such as logos (see Knowles) and those have been exemplarily followed by the logos of Berlin and Prague. Third, the logo has to be memorable, either because of its outstanding design, or its ubiquity—or both, as in the case of the Berlin logo. Finally, the logo has to be synchronized with other marketing tools; or rather, since the logo remains a crucial part of any image campaign, other branding devices have to adjust to the logo. The recent city marketing campaigns in Warsaw and Berlin demonstrate how municipalities address the challenge of a coherent image building.

In 2007, the Warsaw City Council decided to apply for the title of the European Capital of Culture 2016, which will be granted by the European Union to one Polish and one Spanish city. The cities designated as European Capitals of Culture profit in numerous areas, especially in "general tourism, investments achieved for the event and the image of the city" (European Communities), hence the fierce competition. Next to Warsaw, six other Polish cities (Szczecin, Poznań, Toruń, Gdańsk, Łódź, and Lublin) applied for candidacy. In 2010, the Polish Ministry of Culture will shortlist three cities and forward their applications to the European Commission, who will then choose the winner. Apart from investments in cultural life and infrastructure, contestant cities develop marketing strategies aimed at an international audience. As the first element of its new multimedia campaign, Warsaw introduced a new logo (see figure 11).

As in the case of the city logo with Syrenka, the logo advertising Warsaw as the (potential) European Capital of Culture 2016 failed to build up enthusiasm among the residents. The logo consists of a tricolor city name spelled in block letters that come together in a form resembling a wave. The year 2016 is located in the top, while the subtitle "Europejska Stolica Kultury" (European Capital of Culture) is spelled in black block letters at the bottom of the logo. The artistic group *Twożywo* (Krzysztof Sidorek and Mariusz Libel) chose to use the colors of the Warsaw logo— the heraldic yellow and red separated with a blue stripe symbolizing the Vistula— which adds consistency to Warsaw's official branding imagery. Despite the symbolic choice of colors, however, the logo fails to prompt any direct associations: it is un-

Figure 11. Logo of Warsaw as the European Capital of Culture 2016.
Warsaw City Hall.

Figure 12. Rejected Logo of Warsaw as the European Capital of Culture 2016.

RE: WARSAW 2016
reborn by culture

clear if the vertical extensions of the letters represent the skyscrapers that abound in Warsaw's downtown, the city's general upward development, or both or neither of the two. The major part of the criticism focused precisely on the ambiguity of its imagery (see Kowalska and Szymańska). The meaning of the logo is not immediately clear to a general audience. The Twożywo designers provided the following interpretation: "In a sense, the logo relates stylistically to the golden interwar period of the city's heyday. The wavy dynamics of the logo is symbolic: it reflects the exuberant pace of the city's development, its vitality and youthfulness. The ascending letters emphasize the fact that the process of continuous development is inscribed in the city's specificity. The changeability of color stresses the coexistence of various traditions and generations" (qtd. in "Twożywo autorem logo").

The logo was introduced in May 2008. Interestingly, in 2007 the city embraced a different logo (see figure 12) and a promotional spot, but eventually dropped both as too controversial (which, incidentally, happened after a personnel change in the city promotion office). According to Warsaw's press office: "Both the previous logo and the film were controversial and failed to receive a positive reception. The initial visual communication was criticized by opinion makers and residents alike. The main reason for changing the logo was the need to establish positive symbols that would support the application for the title of the European Cultural Capital 2016" (Warsaw City Hall). Although some have appreciated it for its lightness and playfulness (see Kowalska and Szymańska), the logo designed by the artist Piotr Młodożeniec was destined to be criticized as it depicted the disputed Palace of Culture and Science.

Together with the logo, city officials rejected the slogan "reborn by culture" and the short promotion film that provoked the most outrage and opposition.

The controversial one-and-a-half-minute commercial is remarkably different from any previous materials advertising the city in that it is free from the usual obsession with Warsaw's tragic history, abandons the otherwise prevalent pathos, and shows the Polish capital in a humorous, self-ironic way. In a series of fast changing images we see examples of both high- and low-brow culture, remnants of the communist system such as milk bars and prefabricated apartments blocks, urban folklore represented by pot-bellied men fishing on the Vistula bank, street musicians and graffiti artists, and members of the Vietnamese community. Furthermore, the clip discloses that Warsaw's "biggest symbol," the Palace of Culture and Science, "was built on a frog-shaped floor plan" (Papaya Films). According to the journalists of the Warsaw edition of the daily *Gazeta Wyborcza*, the city depicted in film looks "young and dynamic . . . finally without pathos, martyrdom, and skyscrapers, which look identical everywhere in the world" (Kowalska and Szymańska). The film has been strongly criticized and ridiculed by the popular daily *Dziennik*, which bluntly describes the clip as "weird" (Bator 10). The advertising and promotion experts quoted by *Dziennik* identitfy two main downsides to the film: "First, it is unclear what the authors want to say and whom they address. Second, the film discourages foreigners from visiting the capital" (Bator 10). The newspaper's interviewees seem to reject any sort of unconventionality in communicating the image of the Polish capital and, therefore, turn their backs on some of the newest urban marketing trends.

Although Warsaw's advertising campaign for the title of the European Capital of Culture 2016 is consistent with the city logo, its first stage does not appear particularly successful: the new logo uses unclear imagery, excludes any kind of urban individuality, and largely ignores the people who create the city. Berlin's newest image campaign "*be* Berlin!" appears to be the opposite of Warsaw's endeavors to promote itself internationally: the elaborate multilayered project invites all Berliners to contribute their own ideas. Mayor Klaus Wowereit notes that whereas "many cities and countries do image campaigns . . . most of them are created by advertising experts and marketing agencies" and adds: "We do it differently" (Wowereit). He claims it is Berliners who make the city "so distinctive," and, therefore, they should also do the campaign. "People are Berlin's greatest strength, no matter where they come from"—hence the slogan: "*Sei* Berlin!" ("*be* Berlin!") (Wowereit).

Berlin's new image strategy is complementary with the city logo and includes innovative advertising techniques (see Richter) such as an interactive website, a campaign film, a radio spot, a campaign ring tone, open competitions, billboards and flyers, and postcards. The campaign was initially planned for two years: in 2008, it took place on the city level; in 2009, it was extended to the national and international levels. Consequently, the first stage of the campaign was mostly in German and the second stage partly in English. In 2008, the largest focus remained on the website, <http://www.sei.berlin.de>, which includes an elaborate explanation of the various campaign elements, the campaign film, Wowereit's launching speech, and, most im-

Figure 13. Homepage of the "be Berlin!" Campaign. Berlin Partner.

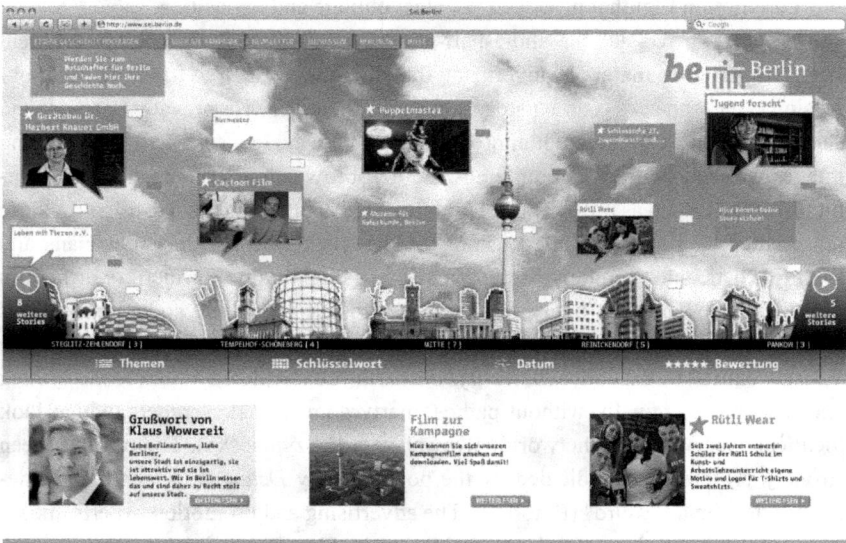

portantly, voluntary contributions from various local organizations, entrepreneurs, nonprofit associations, and private persons, among others, who take on the role of Berlin ambassadors. The individual contributions are allocated to the districts in which their authors work or live and each district is represented by its most characteristic monuments, for example, Mitte is represented by the Brandenburg Gate, the TV tower, the Red City Hall, Potsdamer Platz, and the Siegessäule; the districts of Kreuzberg (former West) and Friedrichshain (former East), combined in 2001 into one administrative unit, are represented by the *Oberbaumbrücke* (the bridge that connects them), Hermann Henselmann's socialist Frankfurter Tor in Friedrichshain, and Daniel Liebeskind's Jewish Museum in Kreuzberg (see figure 13).

Each contributor is free to invent his or her own Berlin message in the form of a three verse "*sei* . . ., *sei* . . ., *sei* Berlin" (*be* . . ., *be* . . ., *be* Berlin) in a speech balloon. The campaign took off with several slogans, which have been displayed both on the website and on billboards; they include "*sei* unikat, *sei* delikat, *sei* berlin" ("*be* unique, *be* delicate, *be* berlin"), which refers to the famous chef Tim Raue, and "*sei* straße, *sei* laufsteg, *sei* berlin" ("*be* street, *be* catwalk, *be* berlin"), which refers to the fashion line designed by the students from the troubled Rütli School in Berlin-Neukölln. Each slogan appears in a speech balloon together with a photograph of the person or people it refers to.

The launch of the image campaign in March 2008 received both praise and criticism. Whereas some marketing specialists valued the new slogan's compatibility with the already existing logo and noted its similarity to the successful "I *am*sterdam" and "I ♥ NY" logos and slogans that "look good on any t-shirt" (Zawatka-Gerlach), others criticized the slogan as relevant only in Berlin and wondered why a New Yorker or a Londoner would want to "be   Berlin" (Richter). The political opposition to the city government scorned the high cost of the enterprise. In their opinion, a city carrying a €60 billion debt was not in the position to spend €10 million on an image campaign (see Bollwahn). Friedbert Pflüger, then chairman of the CDU parliamentary group, rejected the whole idea: "Berlin does not need a new image campaign, it has a good image" and added that the city should have focused on creating more jobs and fighting poverty instead (qtd. in Richter).

According to Wowereit, Berlin needs a new image campaign for at least two reasons. First, to make Berliners aware of the great reputation their city enjoys abroad: "Wherever in the world you go and say you are from Berlin, people envy you" (Wowereit). Internationally, Berlin is perceived as "hip" and "cool", which, to Wowereit's mind, was demonstrated by Madonna and The Rolling Stones' participation in the 2008 International Film Festival Berlinale. Wowereit wants us to believe that Berlin's potential is much bigger than its present fame and therefore encourages all Berliners to share their ideas, experiences, and stories on a larger forum. Second, the campaign has been closely connected with the commemorations of the fall of the Wall: "On November 9, 2009, the whole world will be remembering the events of twenty years ago, the day the Berlin Wall opened and us Germans became the happiest people in the world. That day changed Berlin and Berlin is the symbol of that change. The world will look at Berlin. We should use this opportunity to talk about our achievements" (Wowereit). The mayor claims the campaign depicts Berlin "as one of the top cities in the area of innovation and science, competent and economically attractive," which should bring investment to a city that desperately needs it (Wowereit). While it is true that the timing of the campaign is favorable, it remains questionable whether the bankrupt city can afford such an expensive marketing strategy and whether its cost will be leveled by the potential investments.

Central European cities have realized that, as Jonathan Knowles puts it, "brands matter because of their ability to communicate meaning" (21). For a brand to succeed, however, the city has to have not only a clear understanding of the meaning it wants to communicate, but also the right tools to visualize that meaning. Jib Fowles reminds us that "the imagery must be potentially meaningful to the audience" (149) and "the symbols must be comprehensible by the many, since the advertising strategy strives to enlist multitudes, and so must be composed of familiar elements that articulate commonalities within the society. Yet by the same token, the symbols must not be so overly familiar, so banal, that they elicit indifference or even rejection from consumers" (167). As we have seen, not all the cities under discussion have managed to develop fully successful campaigns. The logos of Prague and Budapest, although remarkably different in form, seem to communicate similar meanings: both cities present themselves as historic and modern (and in the case of Prague international) at the same time. The Warsaw logo and the first stage of the city's image campaign show a city that is desperately striving to be ultramodern while paying homage to its tradition and, as a result, has problems accomplishing either. The Berlin logo and the "*be* Berlin!" campaign—despite the international and universal character of the symbols they use—advertise the city predominantly to Berliners and create an image of a friendly and fascinating city inhabited by diverse and creative people. The extent to which the official logos and advertising campaigns depict the complex identities of the cities in question remains arguable. It is clear, however, that in hiding some of their features and emphasizing others, the cities try to manipulate their image in order to create an attractive brand. To have a broader understanding of the imagery the cities use in their self-presentation, let us take a look at their promotional and informational media such as official city portals and websites, brochures, and maps of municipal tourist information offices. An analysis of the images, colors, and texts used in the cities' electronic and paper materials will help us learn more about the various means the cities use to present themselves and show whether their branding policies are consistent.

Self-representations of Central European capitals through images and text in municipal media

The internet allows municipalities to reach diverse audiences—city residents, prospective tourists, and potential investors—and choose different forms and tools to address each of them in an appealing way. Most commonly, while official city portals provide detailed and up-to-date information to all three focus groups, the websites of tourist information offices focus on promoting the city to national and international visitors. The visual (colors, symbols, photographs) and textual (introductory notes, historical notes, descriptions of recommended tours) elements of the websites are also—next to heraldry, logos, slogans, and image campaigns—part of the brand identity. Although the internet works well as a universal medium for communicating urban identities to a global public and providing specific information to those interested, it is not practical in all situations. Not everyone owns a smart phone, and some tourists need maps and brochures that they can keep with them at all times as they move around the city. More often than not, the print materials published and distributed by tourist offices include the same or similar information and images to those displayed on their websites; their design, however, tends to be different and therefore deserves a separate analysis.

City identities communicated through municipal electronic media

Interestingly, the discussed cities do not use heraldic or logo colors for their portals: the official websites of Berlin, Budapest, and Prague are composed from various shades of blue occasionally sprinkled with red elements (Berlin and Prague) and the Warsaw portal is dominated by several tones of orange. The official municipal symbols are invariably exhibited in the top left corner of the city website, the only difference is that whereas Berlin and Prague choose to display logos, Budapest and Warsaw opt for coats of arms. Another element common to the city portals—with the exception of the Berlin homepage—is the use of photographs in the header and in various sections and subsections of the websites. Owing to their top central position, the header photos are among the first images that capture the viewer's attention.

These prominently featured pictures are always easily identifiable: they feature a landmark (Prague: the Charles Bridge, the Castle Hill), its symbolic fragment (Budapest: the head of the heraldic lion from the Chain Bridge), or a city panorama (Warsaw: the downtown area with the Palace of Culture and Science surrounded by modern high-rise office buildings and hotels). Whereas Prague and Budapest emphasize their historic character, Warsaw presents itself as a business center.

The main body of each city portal is composed of various thematic sections. Of the discussed municipal websites, Warsaw's and Prague's portals have the clearest structure: they are divided into four main sections located in the center and include several minor sections below or in the right column. The Warsaw portal provides general information about the city—"The Heart of Poland" (illustrated with a night footage of the Poniatowski Bridge), "Arts and Culture" (illustrated, puzzlingly, with a picture of a businessman at a newspaper stand), "Doing Business" (with a picture of a high-rise office building), and "Sightseeing" (with a picture of a chamber in the Royal Castle). The Prague portal provides information for three main focus groups—residents, business people, and visitors—and includes the mayor's column. The photographs illustrating Prague's thematic sections seem thoughtfully selected: the residents' section, featuring a picture of a busy grocery stand, captures the city pulse and emphasizes the importance of social interactions in an urban space; the business section shows an office building under construction, which suggests an investment boom and the ongoing development of the city; the visitors' section focuses on the people rather than landmarks—it features a picture of a crowd looking up at, most likely, the *Orloj*, while the historic clock on the Old Town's City Hall remains outside the frame. Interestingly, whereas Prague's portal provides information for residents both in its Czech and English versions, the English version of Warsaw's portal omits any information for residents, implying or demanding that all the city inhabitants speak Polish (the Polish version of Warsaw's portal features an elaborate section for the residents). While it is true that Prague's expatriate community is much larger and more active than that of Warsaw (see Prague City Hall), the Polish capital increasingly attracts foreigners who decide to settle down in the city, but do not necessarily speak Polish—the Warsaw portal fails to address them in the language they are more likely to understand than Polish.

Berlin's and Budapest's portals demonstrate several similarities: they are dominated by the color blue, they consist mainly of text rather than images, the clarity of their structure is hindered by ads and announcements, and—although both feature informative sections on local politics and on Berlin and Budapest as capital cities—they lack detailed sections for residents in English. Berlin has special versions of its portal in Turkish, Polish, and Russian with detailed information regarding the situation of these minorities in Berlin as well as German-Turkish, German-Polish, and German-Russian relations, respectively. In addition, there are Chinese and Japanese editions of the Berlin portal. Next to the Hungarian and English versions, the Budapest portal is available in German and French. All foreign-language versions provide exactly the same information and none of them includes a residents' section. The Berlin portal includes the following thematic sections: "Accommodation" (with a picture of a hotel room), "Visitor's Guide" (with a picture of the *Quadriga*), "Entertainment" (with a reproduction of a painting featuring the imposters of Louis Armstrong, Elvis Presley, and Marilyn Monroe—a peculiar choice if we think of the amount of original entertainment Berlin has to offer), "Berlin Tourist Information" (which directs to the official website thereof), "Politics" (with a picture of the Red City Hall), "Berlin Capital City" (with a picture of the *Weltzeituhr* [World Time Clock] and the TV tower in the downtown area of the former East Berlin), and "Business in Berlin" (with a picture of the Adlershof scientific center). The Budapest portal includes more than a dozen thematic sections located in left- and right-side columns, the central part of the homepage features a wide stretch of latest news about cultural events, infrastructure, and tourism. The images accompanying the thematic sections have various sizes, apparently unrelated to the importance of the sections they refer to—for example, while the small horizontal picture illustrating the Local Government section depicts a green park, the relatively big and square photograph in the section informing about the hot spot places in Budapest shows an open laptop computer on a green hill. Although the images accompanying the thematic sections of Berlin's and Budapest's portals seem rather unconvincing, the content of the sections remains competent and informative.

Whereas the imagery and structure used in Warsaw's and Prague's portals differ substantially from those of Berlin's and Budapest's municipal homepages, few differences exist between the cities' official tourist information websites. Despite slightly different names (Berlin Tourist Information, Budapest Tourism Office, Prague Information Service, and Warsaw Tourist Information), the homepages serve the same aim—to provide information for prospective visitors from within the country and from abroad—and are similarly structured: each features a thick header with pictures, a logo, a slogan (when available), and flag icons enabling access to various language versions. Also, each website consists of two narrow side columns and a wider stretch in the middle. Apart from the Berlin Tourist Information homepage, which is dominated by the heraldic red and white, the websites are arranged in blue and white. In addition, Budapest's and Prague's tourist information websites have clearly visible links to the city portals in the form of the coat of arms and the city logo, respectively. The few visual differences between the four discussed homepages lie in the images used in their headers.

Although all the cities under scrutiny have official logos, only Warsaw and Budapest display them in the headers of their tourist information websites. While the red logo used by the Berlin Tourist Information looks exactly like the city logo only with the additional word "Tourism" below the word "Berlin," the logo of the Prague Information Service is remarkably different from the Prague logo: it features the name of the organization (in Czech) topped by what looks like a crown with three points. The slogan used by the Berlin Tourist Information is the adopted motto of soccer fans, overoptimistically, as it turned out, announcing Germany's participation in the finale of the FIFA World Cup 2006: *Berlin, Berlin, wir fahren nach Berlin*

("Berlin, Berlin, we are going to Berlin"). The catchy and easily recognizable phrase (although only for those with at least basic knowledge of German) meets the requirements of a successful slogan, but it may appear confusing in light of the recently introduced image campaign featuring the slogan "*be* Berlin!" Whereas the logos used by the city and the tourism office are unified and contribute to a consistent image of Berlin as a brand, the abundance of slogans seems unnecessary if not harmful.

Another difference between the individual headers is the number of country flags indicating other language versions of the website. Warsaw's official tourist website is available in Polish and English only, but such a narrow linguistic choice is the exception rather than the rule. Budapest's and Prague's tourist agencies offer their websites in six languages each: English, German, Italian, French, Spanish, and Hungarian or Czech, respectively. Berlin Tourist Information provides its services in German, English, Dutch, French, Polish, Italian, Spanish, Russian, Chinese, Japanese, and Turkish. Although a seemingly minor thing, the number of available languages in urban tourism portals is important in that it not only communicates the friendly openness of a given city to visitors from various countries and a respect for linguistic and cultural differences, but also emphasizes the city's international atmosphere.

The pictures featured in the top banners invariably depict famous landmarks. The photograph chosen by the Budapest Tourism Office for the right side of the header perfectly corresponds to the city logo located in the left side: it shows the Chain Bridge, the Danube, and the Buda Hill (see figure14). The city logo is white on a dark blue background; similarly, in the photograph, the bridge, the castle, and the embankment are illuminated and remain bright in comparison to the evening sky and the unlit parts of the hill. The combined impression of both images is romantic, perhaps even mystical, and strongly emphasizes the historical character of Budapest. The pictures displayed on Prague's tourism homepage show the Czech capital as an ancient and traditional city: the Old Town spires, the silhouette of a Czech Bridge statue in the moonlight, the Orloj, and the Saint Vitus Cathedral promise a journey in time as well as an outstanding aesthetic experience (see figure 15). The Warsaw Tourist Information website emphasizes the cultural aspects of the city; its header

Figure 14. Header of the Budapest Tourism Office Website.

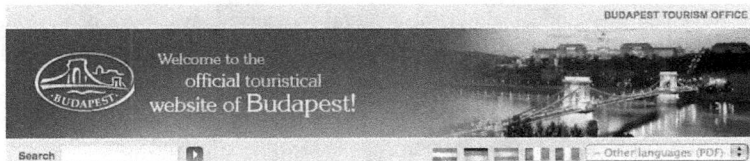

Figure 15. Header of the Prague Information Service Website.

Figure 16. Header of the Warsaw Tourist Information Website.

Figure 17. Header of the Berlin Tourist Information Website.

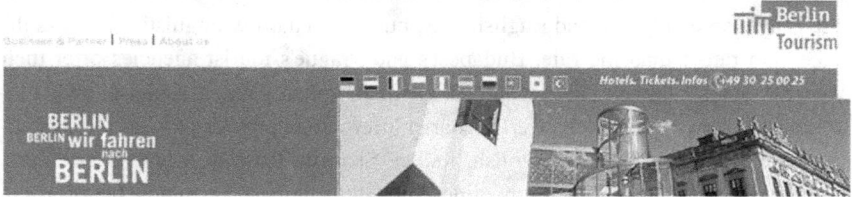

features pictures of the Palace of Culture and Science, an Old Town tower, and the statue of Frederic Chopin, informing the viewer of various sources and types of culture to be found in the Polish capital (see figure 16). Importantly, the spire of the Palace of Culture and Science appears here without the neighboring office buildings and hotels, but as a single tower illuminated against a black sky. The fluctuating images displayed in the header of the Berlin Tourist Information homepage communicate an image of a city where the traditional meets the modern and the past meets the future. The three photographs in the slide show present the newly renovated and illuminated Brandenburg Gate, the new (*I.M. Pei-Bau*) and old (*Zeughaus*) buildings of the German Historic Museum on Unter den Linden, and Reichstag visitors walking inside the glass dome (see figure 17).

Photo galleries are another important visual element of municipal and tourist information websites. More often than not, selected photographs show famous historic buildings, monuments, panoramas, street scenes, urban events, and nature. An analysis of these images helps determine which sites and situations the municipalities consider crucial for their brand identity. Also, if not above all, this is where the differences between visual self-representations of Central European capitals in electronic media are most striking. The picture galleries are divided into thematic sections in which the categories appear either too general (Budapest, Warsaw), or too detailed (Prague). The photo gallery on the Berlin portal is most convincingly structured.

The "Berlin in Pictures" part of the city's official homepage includes such diverse categories as pictures of architecture; pictures of events, city life, culture, and sights; daily updated pictures of local events; a section called BerlinImages; live web cams; virtual tours; and panorama views—each of them is, in turn, divided into subcategories. BerlinImages consists of photographs officially selected by the municipal Press and Information Office and deserves closer attention. It includes over 130 images grouped into four subsections: "Architecture and Monuments," "Culture and City Life," "Economy and Science," and "Aerial Photos" (a selection of over fifty aerial pictures of various districts, buildings, parks, and panoramas). Already the two-part

Figure 18. Memorial to the Murdered Jews of Europe, Berlin. BerlinOnline Stadtportal.

titles of the subcategories communicate some of Berlin's characteristics. First, architecture and monuments are closely interconnected in the German capital. Some of the city's newest edifices look like monuments rather than functional buildings: for example, Daniel Liebeskind's Jewish Museum, Norman Foster's Reichstag dome, and I.M. Pei's pavilion of the German Historic Museum. Similarly—as Micha Ullman's 1995 "Library," Peter Eisenman's 2005 Memorial to the Murdered Jews of Europe, and Kollhoff & Kollhoff's 1998 Berlin Wall Memorial, among many others, demonstrate—new Berlin monuments have little in common with traditional statues and plaques. Second, combining culture and city life into one subcategory is also meaningful in that it mirrors the culture-oriented character of Berlin, a city where the public space often becomes a stage and the stage takes on the role of the public space. Third, pairing economy with science acknowledges the importance of their interdependence.

The pictures in the "Architecture and Monuments" subsection show mainly government buildings (the Reichstag, the Ministry of Internal Affairs), churches (including *Gethsemanekirche*—the former East Berlin opposition center), historic sites (the Charlottenburg Palace, the Checkpoint Charlie), and monuments commemorating World War II (see figure 18) and the city division. Most photos were taken on sunny days with the exception of few night shots of the elegantly illuminated Brandenburg Gate, the *Rotes Rathaus* (Red City Hall), *Gendarmenmarkt* (see figure 19), Siegessäule, and the New Synagogue on Oranienburgerstrasse. The subsection

Figure 19. Gendarmenmarkt, Berlin. BerlinOnline Stadtportal.

Figure 20. Berlin Marathon. BerlinOnline Stadtportal.

Figure 21. Alexanderplatz, Berlin. BerlinOnline Stadtportal.

features four pictures of the Brandenburg Gate, which emphasizes the importance of the pillared structure as a symbol of Berlin and Germany. The "Culture and City Life" photos depict famous events that cyclically take place indoors (the annual Berlinale, the semiannual Long Night of the Museums) and outdoors (the Berlin Marathon—see figure 20; the Carnival of Cultures); leisure areas including parks, cafes, and squares; and cultural venues such as museums, concert halls, and theaters. The most striking aspect of these photographs is that—unlike those showing the city life of Warsaw, Budapest, and Prague—they feature random people participating in cultural events, enjoying their leisure time, socializing in cafes and on public squares (see figure 21), or simply taking a stroll. Therefore, the "Culture and City Life" section—as well as the whole photo gallery for that matter—supports the image of Berlin as a people-friendly city and is consistent with the urban identity communicated in Berlin's logo and brand campaigns.

The "Economy and Science" part of the photo gallery consists of only nine images, which—most likely accidentally—reflect the poor economic situation of the city. The pictures in the section feature international fairs (twice), Berlin's oldest shopping center (*KaDeWe*), the new train station (*Hauptbahnhof*, or *Lehrter Bahnhof*), the Molecule Men sculpture near the *Treptower* (see figure 22), the main building of the Humboldt University, and three pictures of Potsdamer Platz taken from

Figure 22. Molecule Men, Berlin. BerlinOnline Stadtportal.

Figure 23. Potsdamer Platz, Berlin. BerlinOnline Stadtportal.

various angles (see, e.g., figure 23). Judging by the photographs, Berlin's economic and scientific potential appears even less attractive than it is in real life. For example, only one of the three large and internationally renowned universities (Free, Humboldt, and Technical)—not to mention other research centers and laboratories—is displayed in the photo gallery. Also, the business aspect of the section is hardly representative of Berlin's situation: as impressive as the office buildings, hotels, and entertainment centers on Potsdamer Platz may look, the square is merely one of numerous small business centers in Berlin, incomparable in size and importance with London's City or New York's Wall Street. The value of Potsdamer Platz lies in its visual and contextual symbolism (the new modern buildings designed by starchitects have replaced what used to be no man's land) rather than in its economic power.

Business life and the city's history are the main foci of Warsaw's photo gallery (the English version of Warsaw's portal does not include a photo gallery; in what follows, I analyze the images available on the Polish version of Warsaw's portal). Four of its six sections are devoted to the city's past—"Historic Buildings," "Monuments," "War Destructions," and "Old Etchings"—which not only reflects Warsaw's preoccupation with its heritage, but also demonstrates that history is a decisive element in

Figure 24. A Busy Warsaw Street. Warsaw City Hall.

Figure 25. Castle Square, Warsaw. Warsaw City Hall.

creating and communicating the city's identity. The remaining subsections—"City Pulse" and "City Lights"—are, on the contrary, an attempt to present Warsaw's modern character. With 120 photographs, "City Pulse" is the largest and most inclusive of all six subcategories and, as the title suggests, aims to depict daily life in the Polish capital. The pictures show Warsaw as a city dominated by office buildings and shopping malls, populated by hurrying business people, and filled with cars. Judging by the official photo galleries, whereas the streets of Berlin belong to people, those of Warsaw are ruled by automobiles. With its single subway line, the Polish capital is indeed notorious for its heavy traffic; still, it is surprising that the city chooses to advertise itself with pictures of countless cars (see figure 24). In one of the photographs (see figure 25) even the meticulously renovated Old Town—Warsaw's pride and main tourist attraction—is presented from behind driving cars, as if the busy street were of primary importance and the Royal Castle merely a neat background.

Since the pictures in Warsaw's photo gallery have no descriptions, a viewer unfamiliar with the city will fail to identify most objects except for the famous land-

Figure 26. Palace of Culture and Science, Warsaw. Warsaw City Hall.

marks such as the Palace of Culture and Science and the Syrenka statues. Consequently, the dozens of office buildings, hotels, and shopping centers look even more uniform and anonymous in the photographs than they do in reality. As do most post-communist cities, Warsaw distances itself from its socialist heritage: the promotional materials completely ignore the existence of prefabricated apartment and office buildings. Following the tactics of Warsaw's urban planners, the municipal website tries to hide the gray remnants of the communist past behind new high-rise edifices made of glass and steel, which are rarely more distinctive than the prefabricated houses. In turn, Warsaw's downtown as presented in the photo gallery looks like a typical central business district distinguished from similar urban enclaves elsewhere in Europe solely by the Palace of Culture and Science (see figure 26). Still, as noted above, Warsaw hesitates to embrace Stalin's disputed gift: in the official pictures, the Palace of Culture and Science is most often depicted together with or from behind brand new office buildings and hotels.

The "City Pulse" section shows both the facades of the buildings and their interiors. There are, for example, several pictures of offices, which—despite modern furniture and equipment—apparently yield to the old-fashioned and sexist division of work: we enter a world where women are receptionists and secretaries while men are analysts and decision makers. Furthermore, the municipal portal proudly invites the viewer to the overcrowded supermarkets (figure 27) and luxuriously shiny malls, acknowledging and paying homage to the booming consumerism of post-1989 Warsaw. Since the city appears to be ruled by corporatism, traffic, and consumption, it is hardly surprising that the rare photographs of random people on the street show a dense hurrying crowd. It is worth noting that in the pictures of the crowd, the camera focuses on young heterosexual couples holding hands or hugging and therefore relates to the city slogan: in Polish, "zakochaj się w Warszawie" means both "fall in love with Warsaw" and "fall in love in Warsaw." Apart from depicting Warsaw's inhabitants, the section includes pictures of tourists, invariably in the Old Town. Clearly, "City Pulse" fails to present an attractive image of Warsaw: little can be

Figure 27. Inside of a Supermarket in Warsaw. Warsaw City Hall.

exciting about visiting a congested anonymous city where people constantly work, shop, or hurry from one place to another. In the light of Warsaw's aspiration to the title of the 2016 European Capital of Culture, the negligence of artistic, musical, and intellectual events is highly surprising (only 8 of 120 photographs are devoted to culture). Equally astonishing is the presence of several completely random pictures showing, for example, a Polish Army regiment parading on the street or a close-up of an excavator.

The "City Light" section is less chaotic and visually more attractive than "City Pulse"; it presents solely illuminated landmarks such as churches, bridges (figure 28), Old Town alleys, government buildings, the Palace of Culture and Science, and streets and the subway by night. The most striking image of the section—and of the entire photo gallery—is a picture of the Palace of Culture and Science seen from behind a Morris column. The camera focuses on the poster advertising *Good Bye, Lenin!*, a film about the fall of communism (see chapter 7). Ironically, despite the clear message directed at the former system, its elegantly lit remnant prevails.

Figure 28. Świętokrzyski Bridge, Warsaw. Warsaw City Hall.

Figure 29. Palace of Culture and Science, Warsaw. Warsaw City Hall.

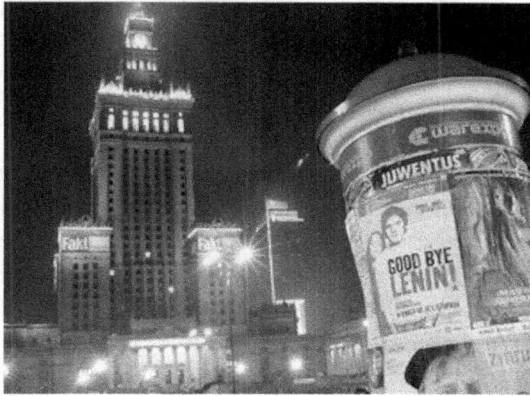

The photograph not only demonstrates that the influence of the previous colonizer is much stronger than desired and suspected, but also suggests that a new colonizing power has replaced the Soviet Union: both lower towers of the Palace feature advertisements of *Fakt*, a daily tabloid owned by the (West) German media concern Axel Springer, a symbol of Western capitalism and expansionism (figure 29).

Budapest's modest photo gallery is even more general and chaotic than Warsaw's "City Pulse." Only the aerial photographs are grouped into a clearly thematic section, namely: "Budapest from the air"; the remaining three categories—"Images from Budapest" (in two parts), "Budapest on sight", and "Budapest walk"—lack any obvious order and consistency. The first part of "Images" features random pictures of buildings (National Theater, Vigszinház Theater, Westend City Center), objects (coat of arms, an antique gramophone), parks, and the river. The Parliament, the Nyugati train station, and the Danube embankment are featured three times each, which may imply their importance, but—keeping in mind the randomness of the whole gallery—may also be accidental. The second part of "Images" focuses on the

Figure 30. Buda Castle, Budapest. Budapest portál.

Buda Hill and the bridges (the Chain Bridge, the Elisabeth Bridge), but also includes pictures of *Váci utca* (a shopping street in Pest) and Margaret Island. Many pictures in "Images" were taken on cloudy days and from unattractive angles, which implies not only poor photographic work, but also carelessness on the part of the Budapest portal staff. Even the most representative landmarks such as the Buda Castle (see figure 30), the Danube, and the bridges seem uninteresting and dull.

Most of the aerial photographs reflect little of Budapest's urban character; they mostly depict the Danube, the woods and hills surrounding the city, and village-like outskirts. The section also includes the only picture of socialist apartment buildings among the hundreds of photographs displayed on the Berlin, Budapest, Prague, and Warsaw municipal portals (see figure 31). Although prefabricated houses are widespread throughout the Central European capitals, they are absent from the visual self-representations of the cities. Remarkably, the photograph (see figure 32) was taken in winter, which emphasizes the grayness of the buildings and their surroundings.

Figure 31. Socialist Apartment Blocks, Budapest. Budapest portál.

Figure 32. A Backyard, Budapest. Budapest portál.

"Budapest on sight" consists of black-and-white and color pictures taken in the last few decades by the mayor of Budapest, Gábor Demszky. Rather than presenting an outline of the city's development, the photographs show how Budapest looked at random moments of the recent past. The section features several pictures documenting renovation and restoration works that Budapest has been undergoing after 1989 (see figure 33). Older pictures of rundown townhouses and streets are juxtaposed with newer photographs depicting their metamorphoses. The pictures imply both the mayor's inclination to romanticism and nostalgia (park benches covered with snow, antique streetcars, beautifully lit interiors of traditional coffee houses) and his interest in the neglected (dilapidated houses, alleys, and backyards). The section also includes some photographs of Budapest tourist sites and shopping centers, which, together with the abovementioned pictures, make up a random collection. Consequently, the city appears not as a beautiful historical metropolis, as its international reputation (and other municipal promotion materials) would have it, but rather as an uncanny place slowly developing its identity. Since the emotional value, which the photographs possibly possess to Demszky, is not communicated anywhere and the pictures lack description, the viewer is left pondering not only the meaning of the images, but also their content. The choice of photographs in "Budapest walk" seems equally random and—not unlike the other gallery sections—presents a fragmentary and incoherent image of the city.

Prague's photo gallery creates an image of the city as a heritage park and is only partly consistent with the identity communicated by the city logo and portal, which embrace both historic and modern aspects of the Czech capital. In most of the selected pictures, Prague looks as if time had stopped in the early twentieth century—for example, the section devoted to public transport features old-fashioned streetcars, steamboats, antique looking eco-trains and funiculars, and only one picture of the metro. While it is true that many of Prague's assets lie in the city's historic character, the photo gallery overlooks other important aspects of modern-day Prague, such as its many successful businesses and research centers.

Figure 33. A Renovated Façade with the Budapest Coat of Arms. Budapest portál.

With its fifteen sections, Prague's picture gallery appears unnecessarily detailed and lacks a clear structure. Some of its categories are geographic or historic ("Prague castle"; "Petřín Hill, Lesser Town"; "Old Town"; "Prague Ghetto"; "New Town, Vinohrady, Žižkov"; "Vyšehrad"; "Charles Bridge"), some informational ("Information centers"; "Transport"), some purely aesthetic ("Views from towers and roofs"; "Gardens, river Vltava"), and some unspecific ("People"; "Top e-cards"; "Other"). The opening section, "Well known monuments," consists of 33 pictures proving that Prague looks magical regardless of the season. The photographs feature mostly the Charles Bridge (eight images; see figures 34 and 35) and the Castle Hill (seven images) shot from various angles, in various weather conditions and times of the day, as if to say that the landmarks look different every time we look at them and that, by implication, it is impossible to get bored with Prague.

Figure 34. Charles Bridge and Castle Hill, Prague. Prague Information Service.

Figure 35. Charles Bridge and Castle Hill, Prague. Prague Information Service.

Most pictures in "Well known monuments" resemble illustrations of fairy tales rather than photographs of a real-life city (see figures 36 and 37). Similarly, the section entitled "People" fails to show Prague residents in their daily environment, but focuses on carnivals, holidays, and annual events instead. Most people depicted in the pictures wear costumes that make them look like characters in children's books (see figure 38). Whereas it is true that Prague hosts numerous festivals each year, they remain exceptions rather than a crucial part of everyday urban culture. The only image in the section that Prague residents would know from their daily life is a picture of street musicians on the Charles Bridge, a romanticized profession turned tourist attraction (see figure 39). The city's insistence on depicting folklore in its promotional materials not only intensifies the Disneyification of Prague's image, but also unnecessarily lends importance to masquerades that "caricaturize the appropriation and re-appropriation of space" (Lefebvre 21). Clearly, the Czech capital falls

Figure 36. Čertovka Canal, Prague. Prague Information Service.

Figure 37. Prague in Spring. Prague Information Service.

Figure 38. Easter Market, Prague. Prague Information Service.

Figure 39. Street Musicians, Prague. Prague Information Service.

victim of its self-imposed signification as an ancient golden city and faces the same dilemma Barthes observed in Rome: "a permanent conflict between the functional necessities of modern life and the semantic burden communicated to the city by its history" (194).

Prague's photo gallery focuses on the city's most famous sights. Apart from entire thematic sections devoted to them, the Charles Bridge and the Castle Hill are also featured in other more general categories such as "Well known monuments," "People," and "Views from towers and roofs." The overrepresentation of both land-marks raises an interesting question: which sights appear in photo galleries most of-ten and how does their presence relate to the urban identity of a given city? Whereas Prague's choice to expose the Charles Bridge and Castle Hill is hardly surprising, a minute inquiry into the other photo galleries demonstrates that the cities under discussion do not always opt for the obvious. Although the presence of the Palace of Culture and Science remains controversial, it is the most often featured (nine times) building in Warsaw's photo gallery, followed by the Świętokrzyski Bridge, which appears four times; in comparison, Syrenka is featured only twice. BerlinImages, on the other hand, focuses on the object embraced and popularized by the city logo: the Brandenburg Gate (nine times). The photo gallery also emphasizes the importance of what may be considered another symbol of reunited Berlin—Potsdamer Platz (eight times). Other recurring objects include popular landmarks of the former East Berlin: the TV tower (seven times) and the Berliner Dom (six times), and of the former West Berlin: the Siegessäule (five times). In the official photographs of Budapest, the Danube appears most often, together with the bridges or the embankment, in city panoramas, and in aerial shots. Also the other sights depicted in the city logo—the Buda Hill and the Chain Bridge—are featured several times (four and five, respectively). The abundance of pictures published in municipal electronic media results in unclear, incomplete, or contradictory messages about the city. For example, while the Prague logo represents a historical but at the same time international and modern city, its photo gallery presents exclusively historic landmarks, people in traditional costumes, and old-fashioned means of transport. Similarly, Budapest's photo gallery shows random pictures that present the city in an unflattering light, while the logo represents the historic beauty of the city.

City identities communicated through municipal print media

The promotional print materials distributed by the cities' tourist agencies feature the same or similar pictures to those included in the official photo galleries. Even the photographs that are not identical to those used on the websites usually depict the same or similar landmarks and situations. Therefore, instead of analyzing the same pictures again, I propose to take a closer look at the design and images used on the covers of selected promotional and informational materials: city maps, city guides, and city tourist cards. The Budapest, Prague, and Warsaw tourist information offices are (co)financed by city authorities and distribute their print materials free of charge. Berlin Tourist Information (Berlin Tourismus Marketing GmbH) is a private company owned by hotels, airports, international fairs, banks, and the State of Berlin and is commissioned with the worldwide promotion of Berlin; their print materials are not given away for free, but can be purchased at selected stores and online. Visitors are likely to carry these information tools with them at all times and may take them back home as souvenirs. Like the municipal and tourist service websites, these print publications are available in several language versions. The main importance of the maps, guides, and city cards lies in their (passive) mobility: they are carried by various people to various places and circulate the images and messages the given city wants to communicate. Since the materials have no specific target group, the images they use have to be clear, attractive, and understandable to a general audience and, ideally, remain consistent with the city identity.

The cover of the city map published and sold by the Berlin Tourist Information is perfectly consistent with the city's image campaign: it uses the heraldic colors, includes the tourist information logo with the Brandenburg Gate, and quotes the website, <http://www.visitberlin.de>. Furthermore, the cover features a piece of the Berlin city map showing only the area around the Brandenburg Gate, that is, the Pariser Platz and a stretch of Unter den Linden in the east and *Platz des 18. März* and a stretch of Straße des 17. Juni in the west—with a thick red line marking the former east-west border; the Brandenburg Gate and the nearby Reichstag are marked as pictograms. The bright and easily recognizable colors, the twice-repeated representation of the Brandenburg Gate, and the word "Berlin" written white on red make it clear which city the unfolded map will present.

The city map distributed by the Budapest Tourism Office lacks any sort of cover or other visual packaging and, when folded (and because of its size it has to be folded), looks like a random newspaper page. Both sides of the city map feature advertisements of the Budapest Tourism Office, Memento Park, various sightseeing tours, and escort agencies, among others. The city logo appears in the disclaimer, but is hardly visible among colorful ads that surround it. Clearly, the Budapest map is not only inconsistent with the city's brand identity, but completely ignores it. Whereas its visual aspect leaves much to be desired, the map may well serve its main purpose, that is, to be a functional source of information to Budapest visitors: apart from the general city map on one side, it also includes more detailed maps of Buda and Pest, a public transport map, and a small map of the Budapest area.

In many ways, the cover of the Warsaw city map resembles that of Berlin: it uses the Warsaw flag colors and features the city logo, the website of the municipal tourist information <http://www.warsawtour.pl>, and the word "Warsaw" spelled white on red. The cover also includes a list of information to be found inside: tourist attractions, culture, eating out, sport and recreation, shopping, and practical information. The back cover looks exactly like Warsaw's flag and features the addresses of the tourist information offices and their websites. However, a poorly staged photograph that fills out most of the front page spoils the otherwise thoughtful cover design: the picture shows two young women and a young man smiling and talking to each other while looking at the Warsaw city map, which they are holding in front of them. In the background, we see the façade of the Wilanów Palace—one of the important landmarks located outside the city center. The image is obviously photomontaged: it does not take an expert to figure out that the picture of the people was taken in a studio and then pasted onto a photo of Wilanów. The result is artificial and, thus, unconvincing and highly unattractive. The city map cover is not an exception: montaged photos appear in various types of print materials issued by the Warsaw Tourist Information, both on the covers and in the text.

The picture on the cover of the Prague city map (front and back) presents, unsurprisingly, the Charles Bridge and Castle Hill. The cover also features the city logo, the tourist information logo, the world heritage logo, the word "Prague" in large red letters on a white background, and a list of information items to be found in the publication: Prague historical reserve, national cultural monuments, important buildings and monuments, and basic tourist information. Like the city map of Berlin, the cover of the Prague map is clearly and easily identifiable with the Czech capital. "Historical Monuments and Culture" is a city guide published and distributed by the Prague Information Service. It has the same format as and is visually similar to the Prague city map; the main difference between their covers lies in the color of the word "Prague" displayed at the top of each publication: it is red in the city map and yellow in the city guide (both yellow and red are Prague's heraldic colors). The front and back covers of the city map are fragments of the same picture showing the Old Town with Petřín Hill (front) and Castle Hill (back). The back cover also features the city logo, the world heritage logo, and a picture of the coat of arms sculpted in the façade of the Old Town City Hall. The covers of the Prague city map and city guide not only embrace and incorporate city symbols (the logos, the heraldic colors), but also focus on the capital's historic beauty and, consequently, remain consistent with Prague's brand identity. The openness and international character of Prague are not directly expressed on the covers, but are communicated by the various languages the publications are available in.

Despite a different format, the city guide published by Berlin Tourist Information is very similar to the Berlin city map: it has the same red-and-white cover design and the same logo in the top right corner of the front page. Also, the cover incorporates the slogan of Berlin Tourist Information (*Berlin, Berlin, wir fahren nach Berlin*). The middle part of the front page features a picture of the I.M. Pei-Bau: the elegant glass interior of the building represents Berlin's relationship with modern architecture and communicates an image of the city as a modern metropolis. Therefore, the city guide is consistent not only with the content and look of the tourist information website, but also with the overall image of Berlin as a brand.

"Warsaw in short" is a booklet-size city guide designed similarly to Warsaw's city map; it includes the city heraldic colors, the city logo, the tourist information website, and a list of information sections included in the guide: museums, shops, events, hotels, restaurants, tourist routes, and practical information. It comes as a relief that the photograph chosen for the cover is not a montage, but a more natural-looking street scene: it shows a couple sitting in an outdoor café on a busy boulevard, where renovated facades of historic houses are visible in the back from behind green trees. The spontaneity, visual attractiveness, and urban flair missing in most other official pictures of Warsaw are successfully captured on the cover of the city guide.

The front cover of the Budapest city guide is colorful and visually responds to the city logo. The top part of the page features the phrase "city of senses" in sixteen languages, which would normally signal the international character and openness of the Hungarian capital, but the association has been spoiled by careless translations, a few of which contain mistakes. The cover photo depicts the Danube by night with the illuminated embankment, the Parliament, Buda Hill, and the Chain Bridge visible in the back. Right in the middle of the picture there is a large image of a compass, which seems rather irrelevant. The lower half of the cover features the word "Buda-pest" spelled in colorful letters ranging from pink to orange on a vertically striped background. A white sign below the city name spells "city guide." The front cover of the Budapest city guide appears more aggressive in comparison with the other publications. The back cover is a full-page advertisement of Memento Park featuring a dark gray statue of a Soviet fighter; the background of the ad is "communist red" sprinkled with highly symbolic words, names, and dates such as "dictatorship," "Lenin," "1956," "Red Army," "revolution," "KGB," "Marx and Engels," and "1989"

Apart from city maps and city guides, municipal tourist services issue city cards: paid devices that usually include, among others, free public transport for a few days and numerous discounts in local museums, restaurants, bars, theaters, stores, and various types of city tours. With the exception of the Berlin Welcome Card, which has the form of a regular subway ticket, city cards are the size of a credit card and include basic information (date, name of the card holder) and images (city logo or pictures of landmarks). City cards deserve attention because—owing to their small size and multiple use possibility—they belong to the most frequently used (and looked at) products of municipal tourist offices. The only image featured in the Budapest Card is the colorful city logo on a white background; consequently, the card is not only easily identifiable, but also popularizes the official visual symbol of the Hungarian capital as a brand. The Prague Card consists of more visual elements: the city logo in the top right corner and three square pictures of famous landmarks (the Bridge Towers, the Saint Vitus Cathedral, and the Old City Hall with the Orloj) in the top left corner are located on a photograph that fills up the whole card and depicts the Charles Bridge with Castle Hill. Here again the message is clear and consistent with the official tourist and image policies. The Warsaw Tourist Card resembles the Prague Card in that it consists of several colorful pictures featuring old (or rather rebuilt or renovated) Warsaw buildings. Clearly, its imagery and the message it contains differ remarkably from the Warsaw identity presented in other media, especially the internet. Whereas the latter depict Warsaw as a business and shopping center dominated by cars and grim historical monuments, the Warsaw Tourist Card implies the Polish capital is an old, colorful, and picturesque town. The message conveyed by the Warsaw card is not unattractive, but rather distant both from the city image communicated elsewhere and from reality.

More often than not, the image of the city presented in the municipal print materials is consistent with the image of the city communicated in electronic media. City maps, city guides, and city cards incorporate heraldic colors, city logos or slogans, and pictures of famous landmarks and, thus, strengthen their presence and meanings in the viewer's mind. The print materials used by the Berlin and Prague tourist offices are most consistent with the cities' image and brand campaigns. The Budapest city map and city guide are visually unattractive and only remotely connected to the city's identity communicated on the homepage, but the city tourist card, which features only the city logo, fully embraces Budapest's official symbol. The print materials distributed by the Warsaw Tourist Office use the heraldic colors and the city logo, but their choice of photographs is usually unfortunate and either spoils the otherwise positive effect, or is completely inconsistent with the image of Warsaw presented in other municipal media.

Communication of city identities through text in municipal media

So far, we have seen how the Central European capitals present themselves through images, the identities they seek to communicate therewith, and whether the visual devices they implement are consistent with one another. Next to images, text is another important means of communicating the city's (official) identity. As in the case of images, the texts featured on the municipal websites are often the same or similar to those published in the print materials, but owing to larger space and lower publishing costs, the electronic texts tend to include more detailed and diverse information. I look at four types of texts that, in my opinion, most clearly communicate the cities' identities: introductions or general information texts, historical texts, texts describing the modern-day city, and lists of recommended sightseeing tours (the latter is present in all the municipal electronic media under scrutiny except in those of Prague: neither the Prague municipal portal nor the tourist service homepage recommend any specific tours).

An introduction is likely to be the first text a website visitor encounters; therefore, it includes most general information about the city, lists its attributes, and attempts to present it in the most favorable light. A historical sketch provides more than mere historical dates and facts: it informs the reader about the city's attitude toward its past and shows which historical events are considered noteworthy and which tend to be ignored. Similarly, texts describing the contemporary city not only list modern-day political, economic, and architectural achievements, but also make it clear which recent developments the city considers worth mentioning. Lastly, the recommended sightseeing tours suggest which parts of the city in particular deserve a visit and, in turn, manifest how the city would like to be perceived by its visitors. In what follows, I quote from the texts published on municipal portals and municipal tourist service websites of Berlin, Budapest, Prague, and Warsaw.

In "General Information" on the Budapest tourist website we read that the Hungarian capital is "one of the most beautiful cities in the world"—a phenomenon that dates back to the city's origin: the geographic beauty of the Danube valley and the protective function of the hills were the decisive factors for early settlements in the area. Further, we learn that as early as the late nineteenth century Budapest developed into a "world capital" and that it boasts "a rich and fascinating history." The importance of the Danube is strongly emphasized: the river "flows majestically through the center of the modern city" and Budapest itself is "rightly known as the Queen of the Danube" (which implies the Hungarian capital is more beautiful or important than Vienna). The text stresses the "unique value of [the city's] tradition" as well as its "magic and charm." Consequently, and despite the quoted adjective "modern," the image of Budapest presented in the introduction is that of a historical city rich in beauty and tradition.

The historical text published on the municipal portal emphasizes the role of Budapest as the capital of Hungary: "perhaps no other capital has played such a dominant role in the life of a nation." Undeniably, as discussed in chapter 3, Budapest is the biggest city in Hungary, home to every fifth Hungarian and the political, business, and cultural center of the country. Despite "innumerable" destructions, Budapest "has always risen again, evolving and becoming ever bigger and more colorful." The implicit resemblance to a phoenix underlines the "magic" character of the capital praised on the municipal tourist website. The city portal defines Budapest not only as the nation's capital, but also as an international city: "besides the citizens of many nations, more and more foreigners choose to make Budapest their home," "it is, from head to toe, a European city"; moreover, it is "growing into a true 'world city.'" Nonetheless, despite its claimed importance inside and outside the country, the capital is far from being flawless. Budapest is "in places opulent, in other places dingy," which, however, makes it only more "exciting." The city portal boasts about the ongoing rebuilding of "ruined and neglected edifices" and clearly points at how these developments are financed: "the economic boom in the years after the recent political changes has given these labors a powerful boost." The presentation of Budapest as a constantly developing ("renews and transforms itself from day to day"), "exciting, bustling city" where "the past and the present live together" is consistent with the message incorporated in the city logo.

The city portal features a list of (invariably historical) sights worth visiting: the Parliament, the Buda Castle, the Matthias Church, the Fishermen's Bastion, the Chain Bridge, Heroes' Square, the Opera House, St. Stephen's Basilica, the Synagogue in Dohany Street, the Danube Embankment, the Hungarian National Museum, the Széchenyi and Gellért Baths, the Museum of Fine Arts, the Zoo, the Citadel, and Margaret Island. The tourist information website mentions several possible walks—most of which include the aforementioned landmarks—and other apparently attractive activities such as bathing and shopping; other suggested tours are: Jewish Budapest, traveling by number 2 tram, socialist realism (based solely on a visit to Memento Park and the 1950s People's Stadium), tours through the local examples of art nouveau and Bauhaus architecture, and unusual (meaning historical) means of transport. The image of Budapest communicated through the recommended sights and tours is that of a historic city that boasts different architectural styles and is the political and cultural center of the country. Contemporary aspects of the city are completely absent from the tourist offerings and the newest past is either ignored or—as in the case of the socialist period—presented in the form of a heritage park.

The introduction on the Prague Tourist Service website is similar to that of the Budapest tourist website: not only does it describe Prague as "one of the most beautiful cities in the world," but it also lists the city's many attributes such as "golden," "hundred-spired," "the crown of the world," and "a stone dream." Further, the text emphasizes the role of the river, the Vltava, along which the historical core of the city is located, and boasts about Prague's "unique collection of historical monuments." Also, the list of important historical dates published on the municipal tourist portal demonstrates the richness and length of Prague's history; however, it does not neglect the more recent events—the postwar dates include 1945 ("the Prague upris-ing, liberation of Prague by Soviet army"), 1948 ("the February putsch"), and 1968 ("Prague Spring") followed by 1989 ("so-called velvet revolution, Václav Havel elected the president"), 1993 ("formation of the independent Czech Republic" after the split of Czechoslovakia and "Václav Havel elected the first president of the Re-public"), 1999 ("the Czech Republic has become a member of NATO"), 2004 (entry to the EU), and 2007 (integration into the Schengen Area). The above choice of dates demonstrates several important phenomena: the importance of Václav Havel (his name is mentioned twice) as one of the nation's most prominent figures, the impor-tance of Prague as the capital city of Czechoslovakia and then the Czech Republic, and the pride at being a member of international political and economic organiza-tions such as the EU and NATO. Prague presents itself here on a few levels: as the most important city in the Czech Republic, as one of the EU or European capitals, and as one of the world capitals.

Whereas Prague's tourist service website lists only some of the most crucial dates, the historic section on the Prague municipal portal gives a relatively elaborate account of the city's past divided into thematic sections. Importantly, the histori-cal sketch completely omits the post-1989 period and, instead, brings the last two decades down to a single sentence: "a new chapter in the thousands years history of Prague began." The socialist period has been designated a separate section that focuses mostly on urbanism, architecture, and infrastructure and, hence, escapes the otherwise possibly uncomfortable political analysis. The sensitive attitude towards the most recent past is explained by "the distance in time from the period 1948 to 1989 [which] is not long enough for us to be able to objectively assess the city de-velopment of that time. The majority of people that live in Prague still remember the socialist period and everyone has a different perspective. It is difficult to write about those forty years without an ideological and political evaluation of events."

Although most recent events are absent from the historical description, the municipal website features an account of Prague's newest accomplishments. In the section for residents we learn, for example, that Prague is not only the tourist center of the Czech Republic ("about 50 percent of all tourist activities take place directly in the capital"), but also, in certain aspects, the most popular destination in the re-gion: "in the field of congress tourism it has surpassed even Vienna, and its cultural life does not lag behind." As in the case of Budapest, the comparison with Vienna is meaningful for many reasons, especially because of the former colonial relations be-tween Prague (and Budapest) and the capital of the Habsburg Empire. Furthermore, Prague is presented as the most successful capital of the new EU member states: "the capital produces approximately 25 percent of national volume of GDP and it is the only region from the new EU countries that significantly exceeds the union average." Thus, Prague is not only the leading city in its own country and in Central Europe, but also an equal player among the West European cities. Owing to its central loca-tion, Prague has become an important transport junction in the Czech Republic and in Europe; the texts makes it clear, however, that parts of the infrastructure such as highways and railways still require renovation and improvement.

The overall image of Prague produced in the analyzed texts is that of a beautiful historical city that consciously takes advantage of its tourist attractiveness and uses thus earned money to introduce improvements in other areas such as infrastructure. Also, the national, regional, and international importance of Prague and its reputation as a model Central European city are strongly emphasized. Prague's self-presentation is in many ways similar to that of Budapest, except that it provides more information attesting to its modern character.

Interestingly, and in contrast to the above cases, the short introduction to the "Berlin Capital City" section of the city portal is free of historical and visual descriptions; instead, it focuses on the nature of modern-day Berlin as a "dynamic, cosmopolitan, creative," and tolerant ("allowing for every kind of lifestyle") city. Berlin's vitality and attractiveness derives predominantly from its special geographic, cultural, and political position: "East meets West in the metropolis at the heart of a changing Europe." Again, as in the case of Budapest and Prague (and we notice it again when discussing Warsaw), Berlin presents itself as a city between west and east; however, its Central Europeanness is not communicated as an "in-between peripheral" (see chapter 2) but rather as an "in-between central": "at the heart of changing Europe" implies a leading position in the region and a potential to transform the hitherto peripheral character of Berlin (and Central Europe) into an equal partner of the West. This potential is also communicated in the description of the German capital as "a city of opportunities" in "all areas, like entertainment, recreation, economy, science and academic life."

"Change" is a word that most often surfaces in the descriptions of Berlin. Perhaps for this reason both past and future are treated as part of the same story of continuous transformation and belong to the same section, "City History and Future." "Eventful" history renders Berlin special among other cities: "almost no other metropolis has experienced such frequent, radical change transforming the face of the city." Despite "darker eras" (a clear euphemism for twentieth century totalitarianisms), "the formerly divided city has succeeded in becoming a vibrant metropolis in the heart of Europe." Berlin's history is divided into nine subsections describing the city as a medieval trading center, the electors' residence, the royal capital, the imperial capital, the cosmopolitan city of the Weimar Republic, the capital of nazi Germany, after the end of World War II, during the fall of the Wall and the reunification, and as a reunited city, that is, "the new Berlin." Importantly, the postwar period is discussed in detail regarding both parts of the city.

The section devoted to present and future developments looks back at the city's history through its architecture, claiming that it is the best mirror of past times. Apparently, Berlin is currently experiencing another crucial period: "to the numerous [architectural] layers an additional [one] is now being added: that of Berlin becoming the Nation's Capital." Similarly, the tourist service website presents Berlin's history as a phenomenon whose traces are detectable everywhere: "History has left an indelible mark on Berlin. It is not only the city's memorials which evoke images of bygone days. Berlin's streets and squares also tell the tale of its unique, turbulent history." One of the most meaningful examples illustrating Berlin's relation to its "eventful" and "unique" past and its communication is the emphasis put on the 2006 FIFA World Cup: it is listed in the important historical dates, right after the first parliamentary session in the rebuilt Reichstag (1999) and the opening of the Chancellor's Office (2001). The World Cup finale took place in the newly renovated (2004) stadium (in)famous for hosting the 1936 Olympic Games. Thus, the remnant of a "darker era" of Berlin's and Germany's history is given a new meaning and incorporated into the city's future rather than kept in a heritage park.

Both the city portal and the tourist information website recommend numerous ways (by bus, by boat, by car, by plane) to visit Berlin. Apart from countless links to professional city tour guides and companies, the municipal homepage suggests six walking routes: a government precinct tour, a Wall tour, a museum tour from Alexanderplatz to Pariser Platz, a walk from Adenauerplatz to Wittenberg Platz, and one around the Royal Palace. The first fours tours explore both east and west parts of the city, the fifth one is a walk through the former West Berlin, and the last one takes place in what used to be the center of East Berlin. As in the texts about the German capital discussed above, the list of recommended tours communicates a strong emphasis on a just and balanced portrayal of both hitherto separated parts of the city.

The introductory text of the Warsaw portal resembles that of Berlin: it also focuses on contemporary times rather than—like those of Budapest and Prague—the city's past; however, whereas Berlin emphasizes the characteristics that are bound to appeal predominantly to its residents and visitors (tolerant, "dynamic, cosmopolitan, creative"), the Polish capital emphasizes its business potential as if the text were directed solely at prospective investors:

> In Warsaw, you can see the most clearly how the city is taking full advantage of the tremendous and unique opportunities arising from the emergence of a free market and the development of democracy. Poland's capital is one of the fastest growing cities in Europe. The investment boom is visible everywhere you look. The city has become one big construction and renovation site. The office and commercial buildings commissioned in recent years accommodate hundreds of business, research institutions, banks, and international organisations. Scores of new ones are going up in Warsaw, and the demand for high-class office space is still enormous. Keys have been handed to nearly 20,000 new flats and luxury apartments. The underground line is currently being extended, and the construction of a waste treatment plant is in progress. Each year sees the opening of new hypermarkets and shopping centres. Industrial facilities in the automotive, electronics, and food-processing sectors have been undergoing refurbishment. (Warsaw City Hall)

Together with the header showing high-rise office buildings encircling the Palace of Culture and Science, the introduction creates the impression of an advertisement of investment possibilities in a newly created business center. As in the photographs discussed above, Warsaw presents itself as a city of corporate work and consumerism, which may appeal to potential investors, but will hardly interest private visitors. Nevertheless, towards the end of the introductory text we read: "We are pleased to invite you to Warsaw, the city that is also attractive in cultural and tourist terms." We further learn that several events of international importance take place in Warsaw and that the city boasts numerous theaters, cinemas, concert halls, and other attractions.

Warsaw's history is mentioned in the last paragraph of the introduction and, as in the case of Berlin, is connected to ongoing developments. The Polish capital is "changing rapidly from a drab city into a modern metropolis, as young as the people who live here, and becoming more beautiful by the day." Apparently, the text is an attempt to improve Warsaw's reputation of an ugly gray city by drawing a comparison to the young and attractive people who inhabit it. Despite the claimed focus on the present, the list of important historical dates suggests that the city is still deeply preoccupied with its past. Most recent events are completely ignored and the only postwar dates mentioned in the list are: "1945-1989, Poland lived under socialism"; "1981, beginnings of Solidarity movement which contributed to the fall of communism"; and "1989, free, democratic elections marked the end of the communist regime." The crucial message communicated here is the emphasis on the role of Warsaw as the capital of free and democratic Poland.

While the municipal portal presents Warsaw as an investors' paradise and a proud capital city, the tourist information website, despite a very poor English translation, manages to present a more diverse (and, thus, inevitably more attractive) image of the city. Already at the beginning of the introduction we learn that Warsaw is an "unusual city" that "fascinates visitors with history, climate [meaning, presumably, the cultural atmosphere not the weather conditions], monuments" and "intrigues with its multifaceted culture"—a result of Western and Eastern European influences. Like Berlin, Warsaw is described as "dynamic," which is manifested in the constant "changeability of its image" and "abundance of contrasts." Further, Warsaw presents itself as an "international" and "European" city. The numerous adjectives, metaphors, and comparisons used in the introduction may at times appear contradictory, but even so, they succeed in communicating Warsaw's complex nature.

Warsaw's most recent history is even more neglected on the tourist information website than on the municipal portal. The last quoted date is 1945 ("the process of rebuilding Warsaw started immediately") followed directly by "today the capital city of Poland, which was to be erased from the map of Europe, is reborn and throbbing with life." The recommended sightseeing tours partly fill the historical gap in that they include a route titled "Social realism in Warsaw," which leads through residential neighborhoods built in the 1940s and 1950s (Mariensztat, Muranów, and MDM) and the Palace of Culture and Science. The other listed tours are: Old Town and New Town; the Royal Route; historic squares; places related to Polish martyrdom and struggle; Warsaw of Chopin; Jewish Warsaw; and the district of Praga. The recommended tours suggest that—like Budapest and Prague—Warsaw prefers to be perceived as a historical city, which is strikingly inconsistent with the urban identity communicated in the introductory texts.

The above quoted passages and phrases demonstrate that all four cities often use the same or similar words or whole sentences in their self-presentational texts. Naturally, all describe themselves as European and strongly emphasize their importance as capitals. They boast about ongoing changes, renovations, developments, and transformations—all of which imply vitality and progress. Also, like any other city in the world, each of the Central European capitals considers itself "unique" (or "unusual," as does Warsaw). Most similarities in the choice of words can be found between Budapest and Prague and between Berlin and Warsaw. The former present themselves as the most beautiful cities in the world that have played a special role in their nations' histories; the latter define themselves as metropolises located between west and east, modern, and—above all—constantly changing.

The images and texts used in municipal media represent these cities on three levels: as independent cities, nations' capitals, and (Central) European metropolises. Invariably, it is the city's dominant role within the country and the region that is most strongly influenced. Berlin, Budapest, Prague, and Warsaw want to be perceived as historically interesting and internationally successful. The emphasis on a city's history stresses its importance for the whole nation, since the capital has often played a defining role in its country's past. A city's international character also partly relates to its history, but is mostly linked to contemporary times and current political, economic, and cultural alliances. My analysis of urban self-representations demonstrates that Central European cities have difficulty communicating their manifold identities and, although they declare to cherish both traditional and modern features, they are prone to concentrate on one and neglect the other. Budapest and Prague emphasize their historical beauty and heritage, while Warsaw and Berlin present themselves as modern and continually changing. Budapest's and, especially, Prague's focus on their golden age creates a drawback: as Rem Koolhaas observes, "as [the past] becomes more abused, it becomes less significant—to the point where its diminishing handouts become insulting. This thinning is exacerbated by the constantly increasing mass of tourists, an avalanche that, in a perpetual quest for 'character,' grinds successful identities down to meaningless dust" (1248). Berlin and Warsaw's emphasis on their constantly developing urban identities may be strategically smarter as it helps them avoid being pigeonholed.

My analysis of images and texts communicated through municipal electronic and print media hints at the cities' (post)colonial condition. As is characteristic of postcolonial cultures (see chapter 2), Budapest, Prague, and Warsaw put heavy emphasis on both their national heritage and regained economic and political independence. Arguably, re-embracing national or local cultures can be seen as a worldwide phenomenon developed in reaction to cultural globalization; however, pride at a newly established autonomy and rejection of the colonial heritage manifest themselves as a postcolonial particularity. The socialist past of Central European cities is hardly ever thematized in their municipal media; instead, the cities choose to turn to their golden age (Budapest, Prague) or focus on contemporary times (Warsaw). Also, all of these capitals consciously stress the long and fascinating histories that they boast, thus implying that the four decades of Soviet colonial rule were nothing but a short unpleasant incident, not worthy of mention. The period of socialism is absent (Warsaw) or limited to few remarks (Budapest, Prague) in the historical sketches and lists of important dates. Similarly, with few remarkable exceptions (the Palace of Culture and Science in Warsaw; prefabricated apartment blocks and the Freedom Monument on Gellért Hill in Budapest), photo galleries mostly refrain from showing remnants of communist times. In comparison, Berlin appears as a model example when it comes to a respectful and objective treatment of the most recent past. The history of divided Berlin as well as the post-1989 period are described in detail and illustrated with numerous photographs. Further, the photo gallery features pictures of landmarks created during communist times—such as the TV tower, the World Time Clock, and Karl-Marx-Allee, among others—and emphasizes their role as landmarks of reunited Berlin rather than exotic items from a heritage park.

Selected photographs and words published in municipal media also point towards the extent to which Central European capitals have been Westernized. The Warsaw photo gallery stresses the importance of modern office buildings, hotels, and shopping centers and, therefore, communicates the city's openness to foreign (mostly Western or global) investments. The portals of Budapest and Prague feature only a few images of new buildings, but all of them strongly emphasize the capitals' international or Western character: for example, the West End Business Center in Budapest is depicted together with a flag of the European Union (the name of the building may also suggest that Budapest is the place where the West ends). Similarly, in the texts published on the municipal portal, Prague stresses its membership in the EU and NATO and its role as the leading congress center in the region. Berlin is an important exception: although the city homepage addresses potential investors, the photo gallery presents it as the reunited nation's capital rather than a thriving business center.

One of the most important conclusions of the above analysis is the existence of similarities between Berlin and Warsaw and between Budapest and Prague with regards to their self-representations in municipal media. Interestingly, these similarities can be traced back to the cities' coats of arms. The heraldic symbols of Budapest and Prague have a traditional and elaborate character and feature gated castles or fortifications. The coats of arms of Berlin and Warsaw are clear and simple and their shields feature legendary creatures: a bear and a mermaid, respectively. As for the contemporary urban identities communicated through images and texts, Prague and—to a lesser extent—Budapest opt for rather defined identities as historical cities, while Warsaw and especially Berlin escape pigeonholing by presenting themselves as ever changing. Although some critics may consider an elusive urban identity a serious drawback, I agree with Koolhaas who argues against semantic oversimplifications: "The stronger identity, the more it imprisons, the more it resists expansion, interpretation, renewal, contradiction" (1248). As I demonstrate in the following chapters, similarities between Budapest and Prague and between Berlin and Warsaw extend beyond their self-representations in municipal media.

Chapter Five

Disposable and Usable Pasts, New Architecture, and Their Impact on Urban Identity

Although today's cultures of European metropolises have been shaped by centuries of turbulent histories, their most recent past provokes the most public interest and controversy. Unsurprisingly then, in Central European cities memories and material remnants of socialist regimes remain particularly difficult to address and incorporate into the new democratic present. After 1989, city authorities have chosen to emphasize some pasts and neglect others and, thus, (re)write their own versions of urban history. Importantly, as capital cities, Berlin, Budapest, Prague, and Warsaw represent not only their local heritage, but also that of a whole nation; their identities are of crucial importance to the country's image and, as such, especially valuable. An urban identity is a complex construct and may be approached from various perspectives (see chapter 2). In the 1970s, philosophers, architects, and literary critics popularized a discourse of the city as text; the 1990s witnessed a clear shift to a discourse of the city as image—a perspective encouraged by politicians and developers striving "to increase revenue from mass tourism, conventions, and office or commercial rental" (Huyssen 50). The focus on the city as image seems dominant in Central Europe, where after 1989 metropolises have faced the challenge of (re)defining their urban identities and making themselves visually attractive for potential investors and visitors.

As Andreas Huyssen is right to note, "especially since 1989, the issues of memory and forgetting have emerged as dominant concerns in postcommunist countries" (15). In what follows I look into which elements of Central European cities' pasts have been remembered and which have been forgotten. Predictably, many material remnants of socialist regimes have been destroyed or hidden from the public eye. My interest lies not only in which buildings and monuments had to go, but also in why and how they disappeared. The partial erasure of communist reminders in post-1989 Berlin, Budapest, Prague, and Warsaw has been executed in various ways depending on local conditions of the moment, but it is possible to distinguish trends in how these cities have dealt with their recent past. Next, I move on to discuss which urban or national pasts have been considered worthy of commemoration. In

120

the growing absence of traces of the socialist past, the focus had to be shifted to other historical periods: the cities have often chosen to focus on the times perceived as their golden age, "their reference points, which, in the identity-seeking climate of crisis periods, are perpetually instanced by politicians" (Polyák, "Heritage as Argument"). This trend has been particularly visible in new street names, buildings chosen for renovation and reconstruction, and some monuments. Also, the collapse of socialist regimes put an end to decades of silencing or misrepresenting uncomfortable pasts, especially the Second World War and the Holocaust, ethnic cleansings and expulsions, and people's revolutions violently repressed by communist authorities. Consequently, after 1989, European capitals have witnessed an emergence of countless monuments, plaques, and museums.

Since urban identities are shaped not only by cities' treatments of their pasts, but also by their attitudes toward current and prospective developments, the last part of the chapter focuses on how Berlin, Budapest, Prague, and Warsaw imagine themselves in the future. The aestheticization of urban space and consequent shift of attention from content to form have had a remarkable affect on urban planning and architecture. In my analysis of the buildings constructed in Central European capitals after 1989, I focus mostly on downtown areas as the most representative and recognizable parts of the cities. In addition, I distinguish three main groups of buildings depending on the sector they represent—government, culture, and (global) capital—and inquire into what architectural and urban planning trends, if any, the cities have in common.

A number of academic publications have proven particularly beneficiary and inspiring for my analysis of new urban developments in Central Europe. In what follows I repeatedly refer to or quote from Andreas Huyssen's *Present Pasts: Urban Palimpsests and the Politics of Memory* (2003), *Transformation of Cities in Central and Eastern Europe: Towards Globalization* (2005) edited by F.E. Ian Hamilton, Kaliopa Dimitrovska Andrews, and Nataša Pichler-Milanović, and *The Post-Socialist City: Urban Form and Space Transformations in Central and Eastern Europe After Socialism* (2007) edited by Kiril Stanilov. I also make extensive use of newspaper articles and interviews (found mostly in online editions of Central European newspapers and magazines), which allows me to demonstrate how post-1989 urban transformations have been communicated and commented on in local and national media. Another reason to turn to daily media is that many of the issues I discuss in this chapter have yet to be thoroughly analyzed in scholarship. My third source of information includes the websites of various institutions (museums, foundations, ministries, etc.) which are directly involved in urban development in Central European capitals.

Disposable pasts and their erasure from urban space

The momentuous events that took place in Central European capitals in 1989 abounded in symbolic gestures of bidding farewell to the communist past: cheering crowds dismantled statues of communist heroes as an act of long awaited revenge on the hated system, street name signs devoted to Soviet politicians and generals were torn off the posts, and the doors and windows of secret police and communist party headquarters yielded under the pressure of justice seeking crowds. While it is true that some of these gestures—such as the dismantling of the Felix Dzerzhinsky statue in Warsaw in November 1989 and the storming of the Stasi Headquarters in Berlin in January 1990—were spontaneous and inspired by the enthusiastic atmosphere of the first months of the transition, the majority of the breaking-with-the-communist-past actions were executed by the new city or state authorities, far from the media spotlight and not rarely without consulting or even against the will of city residents.

The socialist past was uncomfortable baggage for both the new political elites and the humiliated societies. The material remnants of the previous system, which vanished in the first years following the 1989 revolutions, were destroyed or hidden away for a number of reasons. First, many residents of (East) Berlin, Budapest, Prague, and Warsaw were simply embarrassed by omnipresent red stars, communist memorials, and statues of Soviet revolutionaries. According to architectural historian Zdenek Lukes, "people felt something like shame connected with those symbols from this era" (qtd. in Velinger) and supported their destruction. Second, some of the communist symbols were of poor artistic quality and generally (although secretly) criticized for their gray concrete drabness. Naturally, dismantling the politically loaded eye-sores had been impossible under the socialist regime. It remains questionable, however, whether it was (democratic) artistic taste or merely a different set of political principles that triumphed over the outdated ideological guidelines in 1989. It would only be realistic to assume that new municipal and state elites used the aesthetic argument as one of the possible excuses to get rid of the inconvenient symbols of the most recent past. Third, as Huyssen argues, the post-1989 treatment of the socialist heritage was "a pure strategy of power and humiliation, a final burst of Cold War ideology, pursued via a politics of signs, much of it wholly unnecessary" (54). Huyssen's explanation supports my claim that Central European capitals are (post)colonial cities: the new colonizer in the region has been both global capital and Western culture; in the case of Berlin, it was West Germany that executed the most influence over the reunited city.

Despite the relative freedom with which new democratic authorities removed the remnants of the previous regime from view, much of the socialist architecture proved impossible to destroy for practical and cultural reasons. The prefabricated apartment buildings in the outer city districts had been losing popularity as early as the 1980s, especially in Budapest and Warsaw, where increasingly more people were allowed to build family houses in the suburbs (see Murawski). In the 1990s, socialist apartment blocks experienced an exodus of their residents followed by a ghettoization of whole neighborhoods (see Tosics, "City Development"). Despite the declining living conditions, razing prefabricated apartment blocks has never been a serious option because of the tremendous economic and social costs such enterprise would entail. Similarly, prefabricated office and hotel buildings in downtown areas have been renovated rather than demolished and continue to exist in the urban landscape as reminders of the communist system. Moreover, some architectural objects of the bygone era have been embraced by the post-1989 popular culture, aesthetically rehabilitated, and reevaluated as "cool." In Berlin, for example, many newcomers from West Germany found East German architecture exciting and exotic and, consequently, the GDR became the new German pop (Cammann 285-86). Again, the West took on a decisive role in shaping the new aesthetic canon of Central European cities.

While many prefabricated houses and office buildings in Central European capitals escaped razing because of their allegedly exotic qualities or the estimated unprofitability of their demolition, a number of socialist statues and memorials also survived the 1989 system changes, though for political rather than economic reasons. It is not always possible to discern what rules, if any, were applied in the cities' memorial policy. More often than not, if a socialist statue managed to survive, it was simply because it was overlooked in the general frenzy of the transition period (Benning), or—and this was especially true of Berlin—because community protest groups and activists prevented its demolition (Huyssen 54). In the case of postwar Soviet memorials in Berlin, such as those in Treptower Park and Tiergarten, their preservation and maintenance were secured during the international negotiations preceding Germany's reunification (Ladd 194).

Clearly, the system change did not mean a complete eradication of the socialist past: its remnants are still to be found, sometimes in abundance, in Central European cities even two decades after the fall of the Wall. It is important to emphasize, however, that in post-1989 Berlin, Budapest, Prague, and Warsaw, treatment of the communist past has been dominated by "a culture of spatial erasure and temporal oblivion" (Polyák, "Heritage as Argument") and that the forgetting and erasing have taken on various forms and intensity. Below, I discuss the most popular methods of hiding or effacing the remnants of socialism that range from subtle (surrounding of communist landmarks with tall buildings) to obvious (renaming of streets, squares, metro stations; giving old communist buildings new names and functions) to irreversible and, thus, most controversial (razing of socialist buildings and monuments).

The changing of street names was a particularly widespread method of urban memory engineering in and right after 1989, probably because it was relatively easy to execute and allowed for immediate substitutes: whereas demolished monuments and buildings had to wait for months or even years for their replacements, streets instantly acquired new names (see Verheyen). The practice of street renaming was hardly a new phenomenon in the postwar history of Central European cities. During the first years after the end of the Second World War, hundreds of streets in Berlin, Budapest, Prague, and Warsaw received new names, often commemorating the Red Army and the battles it had won, Soviet heroes, and local communist activists. The next large-scale wave of street renaming took place in the late fifties and early sixties as part of the de-Stalinization process, when streets and squares previously devoted to Joseph Stalin received more ideologically comfortable names, for example, Stalinallee in Berlin was renamed Karl-Marx-Allee in 1961. Importantly, during the revolutions of 1956 and 1968, Budapest and Prague, respectively, witnessed acts of enthusiastic and spontaneous, but, as it soon turned out, temporary removal of Soviet imposed street names (Schmidl and Ritter 56). The changing of street names that accompanied the demise of the Soviet empire started in Budapest even before 1989: the first changed street name, "one which marks the beginning of the postcommunist era was the renaming of Dimitrov Square to Church Square . . . on 3 June 1987" (Palonen).

As in Budapest, in Berlin, Prague, and Warsaw, many of the renamed streets were not necessarily "ultra-left," but "broadly speaking leftist or anti-fascist, and formed the communist canon of communist party members which the new power holders decanonized" (Palonen). The power aspect is particularly significant here: in the first years after the democratic revolutions of 1989, it was the new political elites rather than the newly liberated urban societies who decided on which street names had to go and how they would be replaced. Additionally, the street renaming in (East) Berlin may be seen as a (post)colonial practice since the new street names were "imposed" by West German politicians (Huyssen 54). Huyssen is convinced that much of the "often petty" street renaming was "wholly unnecessary" and only intensified the "political fallout in an East German population that felt increasingly deprived of its life history and of its memories of four decades of separate development" (54). While the German capital witnessed protests against some of the changes imposed on the former East Berlin city text (Jordan 54), the residents of Budapest, Prague, and Warsaw seemed—at least in the first years of the transformation—rather content with what they perceived as liberating anti-Soviet developments.

The choice of new street names in Central European capitals was greatly influenced by what political parties happened to be in power in the city and state governments at the time and the renaming process was often chaotic and lacked a bigger plan. In Berlin, many streets were given back their "presocialist" names, some of which were "decidedly antisocialist" (Huyssen 54), while others received neutral city names: for example, *Leninallee* became *Landsberger Allee*, *Dimitroffstrasse* became *Danziger Strasse*, and, similarly, the subway station *Dimitroffstrasse* was named *Eberswalder Strasse* (see Umbenennungen; Georgi Dimitrov, 1882-1949, was a Bulgarian communist; Alt-Landsberg and Eberswalde are towns in Brandenburg). In Budapest, the removal of street names related to the communist past invited a "reintroduction of other pasts," namely the "golden era" of the late nineteenth century, which, in the first half of the 1990s, was seen as "the most neutral period in the Hungarian past to return to" (Palonen). Consequently, *Lenin körút* (Lenin Ring Road) reverted to *Teréz körút* (after Habsburg Empress Maria Theresa) and *Népköztársaság útja* (People's Republic Avenue) regained its 1885 name of *Andrássy út* (after the nineteenth-century prime minister Gyula Andrássy); the latter changed its name several times after the Second World War: *Sztálin út* (Stalin Street) 1950-56, *Magyar ifjúság útja* (Street of Hungarian Youth) 1956-57, and *Népköztársaság útja* 1957-90 (Esbenshade 72). As the Hungarian right wing parties gained more support and power in the mid-1990s, the interwar period became increasingly popular as the main inspiration for Budapest street names (see Palonen). Interestingly, "instead of being removed, the old [street] signs were left standing above the new, marked merely by a red diagonal slash. They remain 'under erasure' in the Derridean sense, neither truly there nor fully absent, the presence of an absence, memory markers of a most ambiguous, yet eerily appropriate, kind" (Esbenshade 72-73).

Warsaw's city text also experienced a return to the interwar period and to more recent pasts that had no chance to be commemorated under the socialist regime. Consequently, *ulica Marcelego Nowotki* was renamed *ulica Generała Władysława Andersa*, *aleja Karola Świerczewskiego* became *aleja "Solidarności"* (Marceli Nowotko, 1893-1942, was a Polish communist politician; Karol Świerczewski, 1897-1947, was a Polish general in the Red Army; Władysław Anders, 1892-1970, was general in the Polish Army before and during World War II and later member of the Polish government in exile in London). Furthermore, the avenue devoted to the October Revolution (*aleja Rewolucji Październikowej*) received a new patron, Cardinal Stefan Wyszyński, also known as the Primate of the Millennium (*aleja Prymasa Tysiąclecia*). Interestingly, in Prague, the street devoted to the October Revolution was renamed to commemorate the Velvet Revolution, but the difference in the name was hardly visible as it changed from *7 listopadu* (according to the Gregorian calendar, the Bolshevik Revolution started on 7 November 1917) to *Listopadová*. While some of the street renaming practices pointed at the sense of irony of Prague's new decision makers—*Pětiletký ulice* (Street of the Five-Year Plan) changed to *Československého exhilu* (Street of the Czech Exiles) and *Náměstí Krasnoarmějců* (Square of Red Army Soldiers) is now *Náměstí Jana Palacha* (Jan Palach Square)—others verged on paranoia: even the slightest associations with the Soviet regime had to go, for example, *Rudý vrch* (Red Hill) became *Strmý vrch* (Steep Hill) (see Podzimková).

Despite local differences, all the changes in city texts produce the same effect: general confusion. It takes years before city inhabitants get used to the new street names, if at all. In the 1990s, while older generations continued using the old street names, younger residents and newcomers quickly embraced the new names, which irrevocably led to misunderstandings and disorientation. Although a nuisance for many, the subsequent space confusion was not unfunny. Unsurprisingly then, a city visitor asking for directions to a nonexistent street is a recurrent figure in post-1989 films and novels staged in Central European capitals (see chapters 6 and 7).

Next to street names, the new functions given to some of the most famous socialist buildings have also contributed to the reputation of Berlin, Budapest, Prague, and Warsaw as urban palimpsests: metropolises whose city texts have been constantly reimagined and rewritten, where the same edifices play diametrically different roles under various political regimes. As the examples below demonstrate, historical irony became particularly widespread in Central Europe after 1989. In 1991, the building where the Polish United Workers' Party (*Polska Zjednoczona Partia Robotnicza*, or *PZPR*) once had its headquarters was transformed into the seat of the newly established Warsaw Stock Exchange. Despite the decidedly non- (or even anti)communist character of its post-1989 function, many (especially older) residents of Warsaw kept calling the building by its former name, that is, *Dom Partii* (House of the Party) or *Biały Dom* (White House). Since 2000, when the stock exchange relocated to the newly constructed *Centrum Giełdowe* (Stock Exchange Center) at 4 Książęca Street, the 1952 building has housed the offices of financial and banking companies. The building of the Czechoslovak Federal Assembly near Wenceslas Square, one of the very few examples of socialist realist architecture in central Prague, became home to Radio Free Europe in 1995, when the broadcaster moved from Munich to Prague on Václav Havel's invitation. Interestingly, the monumental building was created as an extension of the old Prague stock exchange—the 1935 modernist structure is still visible from below the glass and steel overhang added in 1966-72 (Kohout, Šlapeta, and Templ 43). The symbolically loaded building changed its function once again in 2006 when it was handed over to the neighboring National Gallery.

Quite another trend in the treatment of the past was the museumization of important socialist buildings. The headquarters of the Ministry of State Security in Berlin-Lichtenberg was turned into the Stasi Museum as early as 1990, shortly after the building had been stormed by crowds seeking information and justice (see Stasi Museum). Among other rooms, visitors have access to the offices of Erich Mielke, GDR's last minister of state security. Also, the former Stasi prison in Berlin-Hohenschönhausen was preserved as a historical document and transformed into a memorial in 1994; "since the vast majority of the buildings, equipment and furniture and fittings have survived intact, the Memorial provides a very authentic picture of prison conditions in the GDR" (Stiftung Gedenkstätte Berlin-Hohenschönhausen). Preserving the prison and opening it to the public not only makes it possible to learn about recent history in the place where it actually happened, but also commemorates the victims of the GDR regime and renders Berlin-Hohenschönhausen valuable both as a museum and a memorial. Although seemingly based on a similar concept, that is, using a former site of crime for education and commemoration purposes, the *Terror Háza* (House of Terror) in Budapest fails to repeat the success of the Berlin-Hohenschönhausen Memorial for many reasons, primarily because it gives a biased and historically incorrect perspective on the totalitarian institutions formerly located in the house (see Marsovszky).

The nineteenth-century building at 60 Andrássy út is infamous for "what has always been its invisible part to the public: the underground prison cells" (Rév 285). Before 1945, the villa known as the "House of Faith" was the seat of the Arrow-Cross Party. After the end of the war, the communist authorities—"partly for symbolic reasons" (Rév 279)—started using the building as the headquarters of their secret police. Consequently, "where Jews and Communists had been tortured and killed before 1945, their torturers and interrogators were tortured and interrogated" (Rév 279). These were soon to be replaced by "the political opponents of the emerging Stalinist political system, critics of its oppressive measures, innocent scapegoats," and other victims of Stalinist show trials (Rév 279). When the museum opened in 2002, its initiators and curators claimed to commemorate victims of both fascist and communist regimes; however, as István Rév is right to note, "out of the twenty-seven rooms of the House of Terror dedicated to the double history of terror, two and a half are devoted to the history of the Arrow-Cross times" (285). Clearly, the palimpsest nature of the building has been dealt with selectively: while the exhibition focuses on the crimes of the communist regime, it downplays the scope of the Arrow-Cross crimes and Hungary's collaboration with Hitler.

Although obsessed with monuments (Huyssen 31), Berlin has also shown pragmatism in relation to its history: some of the buildings constructed under the nazi regime were used during the GDR and then recycled again by reunited Germany. The most prominent example is the 1936 building of the former Reichsluftwaffeministerium at 97 Wilhelmstrasse, which—having suffered astonishingly little damage during the bombings of Berlin—was used immediately after the war as the headquarters of the Soviet military administration and served several functions under the GDR regime: first as the seat of the *Volkskammer* (People's Chamber), where the GDR constitution was signed in 1949, then as the Haus der Ministerien. On 16 June 1953, crowds of East Berlin workers gathered in front of the building and demanded economic reforms: their protests escalated to a brutally repressed revolution and ignited mass emigration from the GDR (see chapter 3). In 1990, the *Treuhand* privatization agency moved in and in 1992 the building was renamed *Detlev-Rohwedder-Haus* after the former Treuhand director murdered by RAF terrorists in 1991. Ten years after the fall of the Wall, the former Haus der Ministerien became the seat of the Federal Ministry of Finance (see Bundesministerium der Finanzen). Similarly, the *Haus am Werderschen Markt*, built in 1935 as an extension of the Reichsbank and home to the Central Committee of the SED party in the GDR, was transformed into the Federal Foreign Office in 1995 (see Auswärtiges Amt). Although "attempts have been made to find ways of sanitizing the [nazi] past through refurbishment (e.g. opening them up to more light and removing material and design intended to 'humble,' 'browbeat' or intimidate visitors)," Allan Cochrane remarks that "in practice, the outcome remains ambiguous and uncertain—these are still spaces of power and retain some of the heaviness associated with that, even if the explicit symbols of nazism (as well as communism, since these buildings were also used by the East German regime) have been removed, more open space has been created and new furniture inserted" (7-8).

Karen E. Till argues that East Berlin buildings "were quickly closed or renovated because they were perceived as a threat to the legitimacy of a new Germany. . . . These sites were understood by Western officials as places of GDR memory that promoted Eastern values, pride, and truths" ("Re-Imagining" 273). The treatment of socialist buildings in reunited Berlin has had a remarkably (post)colonial character; still, it is important to differentiate between the various intensities of those practices: assigning new functions and names to old buildings seems mild—if, at times, paradoxical or ironic—when compared to the more dramatic razing practices. The most obvious example of destroying remnants of the previous regime is the dismantling of the Berlin Wall. International media reports turned the fall of the Wall into a collective experience: the videos and pictures that traveled across the world

showed cheering crowds tearing down the concrete slabs—some covered with graffiti, some purely gray—with whatever sharp objects they could lay their hands on.
Despite the ensuing impression that the Wall was spontaneously dismantled by city
residents, the actual destruction of all border installations around West Berlin took
two years and several political decisions to complete; the official dismantling works
did not even start until June 1990. Right after the collapse of the socialist regime,
the destruction of the Wall seemed the most natural thing to do not only because the
concrete structure symbolized the Cold War and Germany's postwar division, but
also because keeping it in the reunited city would be simply impractical. Only few
observers argued in favor of keeping part of the border installations in place for the
sake of future generations (Klausmeier and Schmidt 11).

Today, the Berlin municipality, city visitors, and some residents seem to re-
gret the thoroughness with which the Wall was torn down, even if, presumably, for
various reasons (Klausmeier and Schmidt 11; Tangen). Searching for remnants of
the Wall became an urban obsession, a quest for contemporary historians, and a
highlight of thematic guided tours. It turns out that despite the seemingly minute
destruction of the border installations, hundreds of remnants can be still found in
Berlin today, some kept on purpose, other simply forgotten: they range from soli-
tary concrete slabs covered with graffiti to random watchtowers and lampposts to
desolate and rusty distribution boxes (see Klausmeier und Schmidt). Despite their
remarkable quantity, traces of the Wall remain mostly overlooked or undecipher-
able to a layman's eye. Surprisingly, it took the city a decade to realize the necessity
of commemorating the former division. Among dozens of memorials, a museum,
artistic installations, and exhibitions, which will be discussed below, possibly the
most important attempt to revive the memory of the Wall was the creation in 1999
of a twenty-kilometer long stretch of a double-row cobble-stoned line built into the
streets and sidewalks, where the inner city border used to run. The subtle yet clear
outline serves as a tip not only to those Berlin visitors who try to understand the topography of the former city division, but also to older generations of Berliners, who,
among the constantly changing urban landscape, may not be able to remember where
the Wall used to stand. Immersed in streets, intersections, sidewalks, curbs, and bike
paths, the line becomes part of the city body without posing any inconvenience for
the residents.

Whereas tearing down the Wall was generally applauded, the decision to de-
molish the Palast der Republik aroused controversy and resulted in several years of
protests, petitions, uncertainty, and, above all, chaos. The concrete and steel cube
with an orange glass façade was opened in 1976 as, primarily, the seat of the GDR
parliament, but due to its diverse functions quickly became one of the most popular
buildings in East Berlin. The Palast der Republik hosted a theater, concert halls, dis-
cotheques, restaurants, day care centers, stores, and a bowling alley and was visited
by 15,000 people a day (Bündnis für den Palast), some even called it their "second
home" (Tangen). Clearly, the political function of the Palace seemed secondary to
its role as a meeting point and an entertainment center and the multifunctionality

of the building emphasized its uniqueness: "perhaps nowhere else in the world did a parliament share quarters with a bowling alley" (Ladd 59). After the collapse of the communist regime, construction inspectors discovered that the building was contaminated with asbestos and ordered it closed. For years, the sealed Palace remained "in many eyes the symbolic legacy of a poisonous state" (Ladd 59), while others missed its socialist-day attractions. The year 1993 marked the beginning of a never-ending dispute between those advocating the preservation of the Palace as a crucial element of Berlin's complex history and those in favor of its demolition and the rebuilding of the Hohenzollern castle (Stadtschloss), seriously damaged during the Second World War and then destroyed by the East German regime in 1950. In other words, "the empty GDR showpiece and the ghost of its baroque predecessor were competing for the same site" (Ladd 59). Since both options found devoted followers and opponents, the heated discussion continued for over a dozen years. As if irrespective of the ongoing debate, between 1998 and 2003, the asbestos was removed at the cost of DM 105 million (Aldenhoven) and in the summer of 2003 local architects, artists, and activists started using the Palace as a temporary art space (see Bündnis für den Palast). Despite the popularity of the new cultural activities taking place in the decontaminated Palace, in November 2003 the Bundestag voted to tear the building down and—after taking into consideration protest statements and petitions issued by various nongovernment organizations, intellectuals, artists, urban planners, and some of the left-wing and green parties (*Linke*, *PDS*, and *Bündnis 90/Die Grünen*)—reconfirmed its decision in January 2006, after which demolition works commenced (Senatsverwaltung für Stadtentwicklung, "Rückbau"). For technical reasons, the Palace had to be deconstructed piece by piece rather than simply torn down; ironically, it has taken longer to destroy it than it took to build it.

Deciding on a new use for *Schloßplatz* (Castle Square, known as *Marx-Engels-Platz* between 1951 and 1994) produced as much controversy as the demolition of the Palast der Republik. After years of debates that failed to result in a consensus, in 2000 the federal and municipal governments established an international committee of experts "Historische Mitte Berlin," whose main task was to analyze the development plans submitted by architects, activists, politicians, institutions, and associations and to decide on the most favorable project for Schloßplatz (Senatsverwaltung für Stadtentwicklung, "Rückbau"). The committee's recommendations were officially presented in 2002 and included razing the Palast der Republik, a return to the historical ground plan of the area, the creation of a cultural and scientific center *Humboldt-Forum*, and the reconstruction of the baroque façades and the courtyard of the Stadtschloss (Senatsverwaltung für Stadtentwicklung, "Rückbau"). Despite countless critical responses to the committee's suggestions, the Bundestag voted in favor of the proposal. The rebuilding of the Stadtschloss was planned to start in 2010 and be finished by 2013, with a cost estimated at €480 million (Kilb and Wefing); however, in 2010, the construction of the disputed edifice was postponed indefinitely owing to the world economic crises. Apart from its high cost, the decision to reconstruct the baroque edifice appears questionable on other grounds ranging from simplified if not untrue observations that the need for the castle disappeared together with the monarchy in 1918, to a critique of the original building's dubiously attractive architecture, to the fact that the majority of Berlin tourists are more interested in the city's Cold War history than its Prussian past and, by implication, would prefer to visit the authentic Palast der Republik rather than the artificial and Disneyfied Stadtschloss (Knöfel, Kronsbein, and Sontheimer).

Whereas the demolition of the Berlin Wall became an international historical and media event and the deconstruction of the Palast der Republik triggered a decade-long nationwide debate involving politicians, architects, urban planners, activists, and artists, the destruction of valuable examples of socialist architecture in Warsaw took place with little to no media exposure. While large socialist edifices like the Palace of Culture and Science escaped razing, a number of small buildings such as cinemas and supermarkets were torn down despite protests of local communities, architects, and activists. Three of the destroyed movie theaters—*Kino Moskwa* (1948), *Kino Praha* (1948-49), and *Kino Skarpa* (1956-60)—were widely acknowledged relics of postwar architecture, rich in symbolism, and popular among the city residents (Pinkas and Kozak). Kino Moskwa possessed a particularly iconic quality primarily because of Chris Niedenthal's famous photograph showing a tank parked in front of the cinema in December 1981, right after the introduction of martial law in Poland: the large neon sign on top of the building reads *Moskwa* while the billboard stretched above the pillared entrance advertises Francis Ford Coppola's *Apocalypse Now*. In the 1990s, despite its good technical condition, Kino Moskwa proved less attractive to new investors than the plot it stood on and, consequently, in 1996 the building was razed and soon replaced by a Silver Screen multiplex cinema. Similarly, Kino Praha was torn down in 2005 to give way to a new movie theater *Nove Kino Praha* (Pinkas and Kozak). Where Kino Skarpa stood until early 2008, a luxurious condominium has been built (Kozak). The official reasons for demolishing Warsaw's postwar cinemas were purely economic, not ideological or aesthetic, as was the case with many socialist buildings in Berlin. Since the futures of Praha, Moskwa, and Skarpa were decided solely by the free market, the protesters pointing at the cultural, historic, and architectural values of the cinemas used arguments irrelevant to the interested investors and, therefore, were doomed to fail in their attempts to save the buildings.

Clearly, while some socialist buildings had to disappear after 1989 for ideological reasons, the fate of others was sealed solely by the awkwardly implemented capitalist system. The destruction of communist monuments, however, was decisively ideological: the new political authorities—especially those on the right side of the political scene—viewed socialist monuments in strictly ideological terms and (dis)regarded them as propaganda tools of the previous regime (Benning). Their removal in the months during and right after the collapse of Moscow-controlled regimes received substantial social support. After the wave of general revolutionary enthusiasm subsided and empty pedestals grew in numbers, residents of Central European capitals started questioning some of the razing practices. The prompt destruction of the monuments commemorating feared Soviet leaders such as Lenin and Dzerzhinsky produced various responses: while the residents of Budapest, Prague, and Warsaw generally welcomed the disappearance of the reminders of Kremlin's influence, in Berlin some struggled to preserve socialist monuments as part of the urban environment.

The removal of Dzerzhinsky's statue in Warsaw in November 1989 was enthusiastically greeted by the gathered crowd and the photographs documenting the event are among the most popular images to symbolize the fall of the largely unwanted regime. Similarly, the demolition of the Lenin monument in Berlin in 1989 "was certainly the best-publicised case of post-revolution iconoclasm. This highly symbolic event is remembered to this day in the city's collective memory and was alluded to, for example, in the final sequence of the feature film *Good-Bye, Lenin!*" (see Sigel; on the GDR symbols in post-1989 film see chapter 7). Unlike in the case of the Dzerzynski statue, however, the Lenin monument in Berlin-Friedrichshain found supporters among local residents, politicians, and artists. The promptly established community initiative "Lenindenkmal" protested for weeks against the razing of the monument, but only managed to postpone it for a few days (Strauss). A decade later, commentators and some of the involved parties noticed that the demolition may have been unnecessary and added that it would have been unlikely to take place ten years after the fall of the Wall (Strauss). The implication that it was the post-1989 political and social chaos that was to blame for removing the Lenin monuments and others is at best questionable, especially in the light of the aforementioned decision in 2006 to raze the Palast der Republik.

Importantly, the residents who protested against or criticized the removal of socialist monuments in Central European cities did not defend the ideology behind the statues, but rather their significance for the urban environment. Interviewed in 2001, a former member of the Lenindenkmal initiative remarked: "The monument belonged to the housing complex on Lenin Square. It did not bother anyone" (Strauss). Where the Lenin monument used to stand, today there is an assembly of fourteen large rocks and fountains—an intentionally neutral *ersatz* that continues to be seen as alien by those who can still remember the previous look of the square (Strauss). The changes in the urban landscape also puzzled Budapest residents, who complained about the suddenly missing elements in their surrounding. Unlike in Berlin, however, the removal of the statues depicting Soviet leaders did not trigger protests in Hungary's capital—it was the destruction of less obviously socialist monuments that aroused criticism (see Benning; Palonen). Budapest residents seem to have little understanding for the disappearance of the statues "that did not deserve it," as was the case of the bronze sculpture by Imre Varga showing "a group of people dressed in the 1920s style who walk pass a man giving a speech, the only statue, where women appear as women, a critical work" (Benning). The small park in Buda, where Varga's monument used to stand, has been described as now "bleak and deserted" (Benning). Apparently, the feeling of void, so prevalent in post-1989 Berlin (see Huyssen) and Warsaw (see Bartoszewicz), was also detectable in Buda-

pest, where "the former sites of the sculptures are often still marked by empty pedestals, and by their absence looming in the memories of people who had grown used
to them" (Esbenshade 72). Socialist statues were removed from Prague as well, but
the city, particularly the city center, remains a high-density area of a historic (even
if commercialized) character (Polyák, "Coherent Fragmentation") and, as such, has
resisted the postsocialist urban void.

In Berlin, Prague, and Warsaw, the general public rarely knows the where-
abouts of the removed statues or their remnants, which, more often than not, disappeared from the city right after they were dismantled (see Strauss). Budapest, with
its Statue Park in the XXII district, is a remarkable exception. Established in 1993
by the municipal authorities and designed by the Hungarian architect Ákos Eleőd,
the Statue Park is an open-air assembly of unwanted socialist monuments. Aside
from attracting foreign visitors hungry for the socialist heritage, otherwise largely
invisible in the city, the Statue Park serves another important function: it enabled the
Budapest right-wing government to make "a political leap from the radical removals
to the third way of civilized removals" (see Palonen). In her article on Budapest's
city text Emilia Palonen argues that the Statue Park "constructs the distinction between us and them"—whereby "them" means "the past or the socialist"—and excludes "them" into "a 'zoo' that could be visited." When detached from their urban
surrounding, the monuments—some of which (Lenin, Marx and Engels, Béla Kun)
had been regarded as everyday reminders of the socialist regime—were rendered
innocuous. It is one of history's many ironies that the statues that were formerly
seen as communist propaganda (but also part of the urban environment) became the
source of strictly capitalist profit-making when exhibited in the Statue Park: "the
art of power in the time of the market art" (*Machtkunst im Zeitalter von Marktkunst*
[Benning]).

Whereas statues and small buildings could be demolished at a relatively low
financial cost, the removal of larger structures such as prefabricated apartment houses and office buildings has been in most cases—with the notable exception of the
Palast der Republik in Berlin—considered too expensive to execute. Also, some early socialist or Stalinist buildings have been classified as cultural heritage and, thus,
saved from demolition. While the *Zuckerbäckerstil* (wedding-cake style) buildings
on Karl-Marx-Allee in Berlin, previously the object of ridicule or embarrassment,
have quite unanimously become part of the post-1989 German pop (Cammann 285),
the Palace of Culture and Science in Warsaw continues to arouse controversy. Hardly any other building in Poland's capital has produced such extreme responses or en-
gaged the public in such heated discussions involving decision makers and respected
figures from the world of art and entertainment (see Wajda). Razing the Palace of
Culture and Science has never been a serious option; instead, there have been numerous attempts to hide it among other tall buildings and, thus, degrade its role as a
landmark and the most outstanding element of the Warsaw skyline.

Since the early 1990s, urban planners have been presenting various projects
for the vastly undeveloped area around the Palace of Culture and Science, but none

of them have been carried out, mostly due to political shifts in the municipality (Bartoszewicz). The proposal to create a boulevard circling the Palace and surrounded by new buildings in three different heights was replaced by a project to build a crown of skyscrapers around the Stalinist high-rise, each at a minimum height of 200 meters and separated by a row of lower-rise buildings, which, in turn, gave way to a few other development plans that survived only on paper (Bartoszewicz). As of 2010, the future of the Palace's immediate vicinity remains unclear. Remarkably, the first plans for *Plac Defilad*—the immense square, on which the Palace of Culture and Science is located—were ready and accepted in 1992, as was the case with the development proposal for the (re)creation of Potsdamer Platz in Berlin; whereas the latter was swiftly completed, the former continues to be changed or postponed (Bartoszewicz). Regardless of the urban plans accepted or rejected by the municipality, the highly attractive plots around Plac Defilad have drawn numerous investors. Consequently, the area around the Palace of Culture and Science has been changing dramatically and chaotically over the last two decades while the municipality chronically lacks a consistent vision for the most central part of the city. In an attempt to optimize their profits, national and foreign developers decide on the uncompromisingly vertical development of Warsaw's downtown. Since the municipality issues permits for the construction of skyscrapers, we may assume that it approves of the upward trend.

While the decision of the Warsaw authorities to hide the Palace of Culture and Science behind tall office buildings may be influenced by financial rather than ideological factors, some public figures have been advocating the disappearance of the Stalinist edifice for what they considered aesthetic and cultural reasons. One of the loudest voices in the debate belongs to Andrzej Wajda, who claims to be personally offended by the Palace's presence. In his open letter published in the biggest Polish daily, *Gazeta Wyborcza*, the world-famous film director mockingly calls the Palace "the temple of Joseph Stalin" and warningly suggests that "works of architecture are the most important symbol of what the sovereigns want to tell their subordinates." Wajda demands "more courage" and adds that the Palace "has to disappear among other high-rise buildings so that, surrounded by them, it is no longer a symbol of those gruesome times, but rather an example of the 1950s Soviet architecture astray on the Vistula" (Wajda). Crowded with skyscrapers, the new Warsaw skyline envisioned by the filmmaker would resemble Manhattan and not "the village of Warszawa with Joseph Stalin's church" (Wajda). Also minister of foreign affairs Radek Sikorski would like the Polish capital to look like New York City and suggests the Palace be razed and replaced with an enormous lawn with a pond in the middle, a Warsaw version of Central Park (qtd. in "Minister Sikorski").

The desire to get rid of the Palace of Culture and Science has been motivated by two forces: the embarrassment at and, in turn, rejection of the Soviet-imposed heritage on the one hand and the aspiration to transform Warsaw into a Western(like) metropolis on the other hand. In his commentary to Wajda's letter, Krzysztof Nawratek dismisses the proposal to copy the forms existing in the United States as "infantile" and characteristic of the Polish elites who "not only accept the imitational capitalism of the periphery that is being created in Poland, but are simply numbed by their fascination for it" ("Wajda"). The "in-between peripheral" position of Central European cities and their (post)colonial nature are acknowledged in Nawratek's critique, even if not expressed in these specific words. Nawratek interprets Wajda's appeal as merely a shift of directions in the center-periphery relations from east to west: "We are no longer to follow the example of the Big Brother from Moscow, but that of the Bigger Brother from New York" ("Wajda").

As some of the photographs published on Warsaw's official websites demonstrate, the attempts to hide the Palace of Culture and Science among modern skyscrapers have been partly successful. Still, the landmark position of the Stalinist high-rise remains not only unshaken, but also increasingly popular, especially among foreign tourists who come to Warsaw in search of the city's communist past (see Kowalska). Just like Berlin's TV tower, the Palace has become an important inspiration for designers: its outline has been reproduced on t-shirts, mugs, calendars, and other types of souvenirs and has become an internationally known symbol of Warsaw, probably even more recognizable than the capital's official symbol, Syrenka. Both the Palace of Culture and Science in Warsaw and the TV tower in Berlin are more popular among city visitors and residents than among urban planners and decision makers. The new development plans for Alexanderplatz—the central square neighboring the TV tower—foresee a construction of several high-rise office buildings, similar to those towering over Potsdamer Platz. (East) Berlin architect Bruno Frierl criticizes the plans as "stupid and dangerous . . . from the point of view of German unification . . . It's occupation and not unification" (qtd. in Harris). Hans Kollhoff, the (West) German architect responsible for the new development plan for Alexanderplatz, dismisses the above accusations on what he claims to be aesthetic grounds: "the TV tower can be respected as a DDR monument in East Berlin, but it cannot be respected by any means as a great piece of architecture" (qtd. in Harris). Kollhoff's judgmental stance implies that one of the city's most important architects is uninterested in the cultural implications of his designs and remains oblivious to the impact the hiding of the TV tower may have on Berlin's urban identity (Kollhoff has also authored the Kollhoff Tower on Potsdamer Platz, 1999; the Leibnizkolonnaden in Charlottenburg, 2001; the Europäisches Haus on Pariser Platz, 1999; and many more).

Taking into account the political, social, and cultural chaos Central European capitals were experiencing in and right after 1989, it is hardly surprising that decisions regarding the city text and body often lacked logic and strategy. While the destruction of some architectural remnants of the communist regime was ordered, others were allowed to stay, or were even assigned new important functions. The treatment of the socialist past has been largely unpredictable and differed depending on which parties were in charge of the local and national governments. Next to political and economic reasons, cultural and historical traditions have been determining the fate of socialist monuments and buildings, albeit to a far lesser extent: for example, Marx and Engels statues and street names were removed from Budapest and Warsaw, but remain part of Berlin's urban landscape both in the east and the west. Last but not least, community initiatives advocating a preservation of parts of the socialist heritage, even if well organized like those in Berlin, have been largely unsuccessful in achieving their aims. In the German capital the treatment of the recent past has triggered the most controversies and debates and has been often re-garded—by East Berliners, but also by international observers—as a (post)colonial practice with the Federal Republic of Germany being the new colonizer (see Huyssen; Harris; Strauss). Although voices criticizing the ubiquitous and uncontrollable influences of Western and global capital and politics can be heard also in Buda-pest, Prague, and Warsaw, they remain moderate, especially when compared to the prevailing and outspoken hatred towards the former colonizer. Ironically, although hardly surprisingly, the (Soviet) empire, whose signs gradually disappear from the urban landscape, strikes back in the language used by Central European city inhabit-ants. Even when physically removed, some of the socialist monuments and street names continue to exist not only in residents' memory, but also in their mental city maps. In Budapest, people keep naming Steinmetz or Osztapenkó as meeting points (see Benning; Miklós Steinmetz was a Hungarian-born captain in the Red Army; Ilja Afanaszjevics Osztapenkó was a Ukrainian-born captain in the Red Army—both took part in the Soviet "liberation" of Budapest in December 1944) even though the statues of the Red Army soldiers were removed from their locations on *Vörös Hadsereg útja* (Red Army Road, today *Üllői út*) and *Budaőrsi út*, respectively, and taken away to the Statue Park. In Prague, years after the monumental statue of Stalin had been destroyed in 1962 and replaced by a gigantic metronome in 1991, older residents keep using the Soviet dictator's name to describe the viewing point on the edge of the Letná Park (see Szczygieł, *Gottland*). Apparently, decades after having been forced into oblivion, the "disposable data" (Huyssen 18) continues to influence urban identities of Central European capitals.

Usable pasts and their commemoration in urban space

The disappearance of the remnants of the socialist past has been accompanied by intense commemoration practices verging, especially in the 1990s, on memorial obsessions (Huyssen 52). New monuments, plaques, street names, and museums appeared almost as quickly as the old "disposable" ones were forced out from the urban landscape. Berlin, Budapest, Prague, and Warsaw set on transforming their identities and chose new memory policies, among other tools, to achieve their goals. Importantly, being not only major Central European urban centers, but also capitals, the cities strive to commemorate both local and national (and in some cases inter-national) histories. It is no wonder then that the new urban memory strategies are strongly politicized and vary depending on which parties happen to be in power on the city or state levels. Despite local differences, it is possible to distinguish two main trends common to the cities. First, the most recent past has been commemo-rated only to a limited extent, primarily because of the proximity of these events and the difficulty of reaching consensus on how the era of Soviet-imposed communism should be judged, if at all. The monuments and museums devoted to the postwar decades either pay long-due tributes to the victims of the socialist regimes (especially the victims of the collapsed people's revolutions of 1953 in Berlin, 1956 in Budapest, and 1968 in Prague) or take on a Disneyesque form and aim at entertaining the viewer. Second, after 1989, Central European cities bade farewell to the Soviet-imposed reading of the Second World War and started, painstakingly, revising their pasts. Although countless war memorials had been built in Central Europe during the socialist regime, many of them misinterpreted, belied, or ignored the facts. The fall of communism and the subsequent withdrawal of the Soviet Army created a new opportunity to come to terms with the atrocities of World War II (see Judt). In what follows I discuss the ways in which different pasts have been commemorated in Central European capitals after 1989 and how the new monuments and museums have influenced urban identities and landscapes.

Among all four capitals, the socialist past is most visible in the urban landscape of Berlin. Apart from the relatively large—when compared to Budapest, Prague, and Warsaw—number of socialist buildings, monuments, and street names that survived the (post-)1989 system changes, Berlin has become home to several monuments and museums that focus on hitherto silenced aspects of the city's complex postwar history. The emergence of memorials devoted to (East) Berlin's socialist decades was prompted by the reunification of 1989 and remained "in line with the general memorial obsessions of the 1990s" (Huyssen 52). These new memorials focus primarily on the uprising of 17 June 1953, the Wall, the Stasi, and their many victims.

The demonstrations of East Berlin workers were commemorated in West Berlin as early as four days after the brutally repressed events: *Charlottenburger Chaussee* was renamed Straße des 17. Juni. It took nearly five decades to honor the victims of the uprising in the part of town where the protests actually took place. On 17 June 2000, right in front of the former Haus der Ministerien on the corner of Wilhelmstrasse and Leipziger Strasse, a new memorial for the victims of the 1953 workers' demonstrations was unveiled. Created by the Berlin artist Wolfgang Rüppel, the artwork is an enlarged photograph embedded in the ground and covered with glass. The picture shows the now legendary Stalinallee workers (see chapter 3) marching forward with their arms linked. Since it is incorporated into the pavement, the monument could have been easily overseen if not for the colorful mural on the façade of the ministry building that Rüppel's piece corresponds to both in its proportion and motif (Schomaker). Max Linger's propaganda wall painting depicts a crowd of workers cheerfully praising socialism. Remarkably, the mural was unveiled in January 1953, only a few months before the East Berlin workers' rebellion. In the words of Germany's former finance minister Hans Eichel, the artworks "juxtapose the real and virtual socialism" and present a poignant combination (qtd. in Schomaker).

Similarly, the victims of the Wall had been commemorated in West Berlin already during the city's division, but it was only after the collapse of the socialist regime that more elaborate Wall memorials were erected. Although the Wall has almost completely disappeared from the urban landscape, it is still possible to find original parts of the border installations scattered in the city. The most famous and longest (1.3 km) stretch of the Wall has been preserved in the (eastern) district of Friedrichshain. In February 1990, over a hundred international artists were invited to cover the gray concrete slabs between the Oberbaumbrücke and the Ostbahnhof with their own interpretations of the then ongoing system change. The result, known as the East Side Gallery, may (and does) appear confusing to some tourists, who tend to think the graffiti and murals had been painted already during the city's division (as was often the case of the border installations facing West Berlin, but would have been impossible in East Berlin as that part of the Wall was constantly watched by guards). The Gallery's exposure to changeable weather conditions, traffic, and vandalism has resulted in serious damage of both the artworks and the concrete slabs. A thorough renovation that was completed in 2009, just in time for the twentieth anniversary of the fall of the Wall. Although widely known and not unpopular with city visitors, the East Side Gallery has a major drawback: its location. Situated far from major tourist attractions such as the Brandenburg Gate, Potsdamer Platz, and Kurfürstendamm, the longest preserved stretch of the Wall fails to receive due recognition as one of the city's symbols, which it would most likely have, had it been located downtown. Arguably, keeping a 1.3-kilometer long remnant of the Wall in the very center of the city would have been impossible for economic and political reasons. The fact is, however, that the most elaborate memorials devoted to the Wall are located outside the downtown area.

On the tenth anniversary of the fall of the Wall, the former division of the city was commemorated in three different ways in *Bernauer Strasse*. Back in August 1961, the street witnessed some of the most dramatic and symbolic scenes from the first chapter of the city's division: the houses on Bernauer Strasse were located in the Soviet sector, but the street was already part of the district of Wedding administered by the French; when the Wall was built on 13 August 1961, the apartment buildings became part of the border installations with ground- and first-floor windows forcefully bricked up. Archival photographs and films document the escapes of desperate residents jumping out of the windows as well as the subsequent demolition of the borderland houses by East German soldiers. Today, Bernauer Strasse is home to the Berlin Wall Memorial (1998), the Berlin Wall Documentation Center (1999), and the Chapel of Reconciliation (2000).

The Berlin Wall Memorial, designed by Kollhoff & Kollhoff, incorporates part of the border installations that survived in Bernauer Strasse. It consists of two concrete walls separated by the death strip and limited on both ends by large steel walls that are polished and smooth as mirrors on the inside (symbolizing infinity), but rusty on the outside and, as such, reminiscent of the backwardness of the "iron curtain" reality. It was only after years of debates on the "appropriate form and design of commemoration" that the Kollhoff design was accepted as the winning project and even then it continued to arouse dispute: "The memorial is dedicated to 'the memory of the division of the city from August 13, 1961 to November 9, 1989,' but following vehement protest from people who had been personally affected by these events and from victim associations, the inscription on the memorial plaque was extended to include the words 'in memory of the victims of the communist tyranny'" (Gedenkstätte Berliner Mauer). Owing to its size, the Berlin Wall Memorial can be seen in its entirety only from above—an opportunity that the upper terrace of the neighboring Documentation Center conveniently provides. Since it features an elaborate permanent exhibition and "provides historical information and educates the public" (Gedenkstätte Berliner Mauer), the Documentation Center may be considered a Berlin Wall museum, however, the name *Mauermuseum* (Wall Museum) is reserved for the private museum also known as the House at Checkpoint Charlie. The third element of the Bernauer Strasse ensemble, the Chapel of Reconciliation, was built in 2000 in place of the 1894 Evangelical church that—located in the death strip and considered "Wall property"—had been blown up in 1985 during the renovation of the border installations. Parts of the old staircase and the altarpiece have been incorporated into the chapel while the original church bells hang on the scaffolding outside.

Not far from the Bernauer Strasse ensemble, on *Invalidenstrasse*, there is another memorial devoted to the former border: it is entitled *Sinkende Mauer* (Sinking Wall) has the form of a tilted rectangular block of concrete disappearing in the ground calling to mind an iceberg or, more adequately, the Titanic. The latter association is prompted by the cascades of water flowing down the top edge of the concrete wall. Interestingly, the 1997 monument was also built in place of a church (*Gnadekirche*) razed during the Wall construction works in 1967. Although both Invalidenstrasse and Bernauer Strasse are streets in Berlin's central district of Mitte, they are relatively far from other tourist attractions and, hence, do not attract as many visitors as they may have, had they been located closer to the Reichstag or the Checkpoint Charlie.

Most museums dedicated to the city's former division and the socialist regime focus on the victims of the Wall (e.g., the Berlin Wall Documentation Center, the House at Checkpoint Charlie) or the GDR secret police (e.g., the Memorial Berlin-Hohenschönhausen, the Stasi Museum) and, thus, fail to document other aspects of life in East Berlin. Apart from the city (*Märkisches Museum*) and historical (*Deutsches Historisches Museum*) museums that occasionally feature exhibitions on various themes from Berlin's postwar past, the newest attempt at approaching East Berlin's reality—although not exclusively, but rather as part of a larger East German culture—has been the establishment of the DDR Museum at 1 Karl-Liebknecht-Strasse, right across the river from the cathedral (Berliner Dom) and across the street from where the Palast der Republik used to stand. Advertised as "one of the most interactive museums in Europe" (DDR-Museum), the exhibition aims first and foremost at entertaining visitors by presenting well-known GDR products such as the *Trabi*, the Plattenbauten, FDJ uniforms, and the Wall, among many others. The concept and form of the museum are based solely on stereotypes about East Berlin and the GDR. Although on its website the DDR Museum claims to allow for "a hands-on experience of history" and an "opportunity to experience the GDR everyday life yourself" (DDR-Museum), it resembles a theme park or a toy store rather than a competent historical exhibition.

Despite its strongly anticommunist policy after 1989 (especially under mayor Lech Kaczyński, 2002-2005; later, 2005-2010, Poland's president), Warsaw has seen only two major monuments devoted to the victims of the communist regime, both focusing on the first postwar decade: the Memorial to the Martyrs of the Communist Terror in Poland 1944-1956 (1993) in Warsaw-Ursynów and the Memorial to the Victims of Stalinism (2001) in Warsaw-Praga. The former, located near the cemetery on Wałbrzyska Street where *Urząd Bezpieczeństwa* (*UB*, or Office of Security, as the communist secret police in postwar Poland was called) dumped the bodies of their victims, is an ensemble of large rocks with torn prison bars sticking out from one of them and a 10-meter tall iron cross in the back. Both the openly (Catholic) Christian symbolism and the choice of materials (stone and iron) follow the Polish tradition of monuments commemorating victims of communism (e.g., the Memorial to June 1956 Events in Poznań, the Memorial to the Dead Shipyard Workers in Gdańsk, the Memorial to the Victims of Communism in Rzeszów). The Warsaw Memorial to the Victims of Stalinism has been heavily criticized as the "ugliest monument in recent years" and dubbed a "bugaboo from Praga" (Urzykowski and Majewski). It depicts a man captured between two gigantic walls, his arms are stretched apart—which lends his figure the shape of a cross and corresponds to the cross hanging around his neck—and his head slightly tilted forward as if from exhaustion; from one of his wrists hang prison chains while the other hand is resting on the bars sticking out from the wall. The monument is located on Namysłowska Street, previously home to the infamous "Toledo" prison where between 1944 and 1956 the UB and the NKVD interrogated, tortured, and kept soldiers of the Polish Home Army and members of independence and conspiracy organizations. Presumably, the monument aims at presenting a victim of the communist regime breaking away from the prison. To many locals, however, the statue resembles a drunkard trying to keep balance by holding on to the walls or a criminal waiting for his victim in a dark alley (Urzykowski and Majewski).

Warsaw's awkwardness in commemorating its postwar past has also been visible in the difficulties, uncertainties, and delays surrounding the establishment of the Museum of Communism. The idea of creating a museum that would (re)present "the paralyzing power of [the communist] system, its duration and disintegration" came from filmmaker Andrzej Wajda, satirist Jerzy Kawalerowicz, and architect Czesław Bielecki, who in the late 1990s started the SocLand Foundation and put together a traveling exhibition on communism in Poland. Their hope that the collection would find its home in the basements of the Palace of Culture and Science—or "Stalin's Palace," in Wajda's words—had been shattered many times for various reasons ranging from architectural to financial to political. In the summer of 2008, the City of Warsaw re-embraced SocLand's idea, but not without emphasizing that "locating [the museum] under the Palace is unfeasible as it would necessitate drilling through the fundament, which is technically very difficult. Besides the Palace is a historical building" (Warsaw's mayor Hanna Gronkiewicz-Waltz qtd. in Urzykowski, "Muzeum Komunizmu"). At the conference titled "Memory After Communism," Poland's former president and Nobel Peace Prize Laureate Lech Wałęsa noticed that the museum would make sense only if it showed how the collapse of communism had been made possible: "if you merely want to hang Soviet uniforms there then you may as well skip the whole idea altogether" (qtd. in Urzykowski, "Muzeum Komunizmu"). Agreement was reached in the concept of a museum which will be prepared by a team of young historians who will try to interweave important political events with everyday life in communist Poland (Urzykowski, "Muzeum Komunizmu"). However, it remains unclear when and where the museum will be established.

Similarly, as of 2009 Budapest does not have a museum thematizing the city's communist past except for the already discussed outdoor Statue Park. The heavily criticized Terror Háza (2002) may be only partly considered a museum devoted to some of the most violent aspects of communism. Although its curators claim to focus on the crimes of both the nationalist and communist regimes, the museum is preoccupied almost exclusively with the latter (see Rév; Marsovszky). The inner architecture and dramaturgy of the Terror Háza rely on dark walls, low ceilings, strong lights, tunnel-like passages, and other devices designed to make the visitor feel trapped and watched. Probably the most powerful part of the museum is its basement, where the reconstructed prison cells are located: "besides the simple cells [the museum] also installed disciplinary cells as well as death and execution cells," that is, karcers, fox holes, treatment rooms, and water cells, among other things (Terror Háza). More than any other part of the exhibition, the cellars of the Terror Háza come close to the initial intention of the museum founders to create "a monument to the memory of those held captive, tortured, and killed in this building" (Terror Háza)—although, importantly, primarily to the victims of the communist political police who moved to the building at 60 Andrássy út in January 1945 rather that to those killed and tortured in the same basement by the Arrow Cross regime. Similarly, the Memorial to the Persecuted on *Dózsa György tér* in Buda is devoted only to those imprisoned, tortured, and killed by communists in 1944-90; the 1996 monument has the form of a concrete prison cell topped by barbwire with a single man sitting inside with hands on his ears and staring at his shoes as if to avoid the reflection in the mirror positioned in front of him.

The reburial of Imre Nagy in June 1989 triggered the system change in Hungary and marked the beginning of new commemoration practices in Budapest. Finally able to address its biggest postwar trauma, in the 1990s and 2000s Budapest experienced an abundance of monuments and plaques devoted to the failed revolution of 1956. The city's preoccupation with the events of 1956 verges on obsession similar to Berlin's focus on commemorating the victims of World War II (see Huyssen). The dozens of 1956 memorials scattered around the city may be divided into two main groups: those that remind viewers of singular participants of the revolution and those that commemorate the rebellion as a whole. The former include, among others, the

1996 sculpture of Imre Nagy on a bridge on *Vértanúk tere* (Martyrs' Square), the highly dramatic monuments of Péter Mansfeld depicting the young revolutionary hero imprisoned (2004) and during his famous escape (2007), and the 2006 busts of Anna Kéthly and Zoltán Tóth. Unsurprisingly, most 1956 monuments were unveiled on the fortieth and fiftieth anniversaries of the revolution. Apart from the Nagy statue, in 1996, Budapest's Fifth District welcomed three other monuments devoted to the events of 1956: a plaque dedicated to the *Forradalmi Karhatalmi Bizottság* (Revolutionary Committee of Public Security Forces) that depicts a fighter standing on a tank and features the inscription, "Pro Libertate: Remember October 1956"; an abstract monument on *Kossuth Lajos tér* resembling a large heavy shadow; and an art installation on the façade of one of the government buildings reminding of the bullets shot on 25 October 1956. Other important 1956 memorials include the tall obelisk-like monument erected in Tabán Park on the fortieth anniversary of the revolution; the 2006 gigantic memorial on *Ötvenhatosok tere* (1956ers Square) exactly where the Stalin statue was famously torn down by the crowd on 23 October 1956; and the 2007 Angel Statue depicting an angel kneeling on what at first looks like a grave, but is actually a flag fallen on the ground, reminiscent of the flags carried by participants of the 1956 street fights.

Whereas the commemoration of 1956 is "one of the most important themes in [Budapest's] new city-text" (Palonen), the Prague Spring has been only modestly remembered in the urban landscape of the Czech capital. The best known and most centrally located memorial devoted to the victims of the 1968 Warsaw Pact intervention is the monument of Jan Palach and Jan Zajíc—the young students who in January and February 1969, respectively, committed suicide by self-immolation as a protest against the Soviet occupation of Czechoslovakia. The memorial was unveiled in 2000 right in front of the National Museum on Wenceslas Square, where Jan Palach had set himself on fire: it resembles a half-burned wooden cross immersed in the pavement. In downtown Prague there are two more monuments devoted to the crimes of the postwar regime: the Memorial to the Victims of Communism (2002) and the Memorial to the Victims of Collectivization (2004). The former, located at the foot of the Petřín Hill, presents seven bronze sculptures descending a long concrete staircase, whereby the front sculpture depicts a thin and exhausted man and the remaining six have cracks in their bodies or miss limbs or heads as if they were literally falling apart step by step. A bronze inscription in the stairway lists the estimated numbers of "the victims of communism 1948-1989: 205,486 arrested, 248 executed, 4,500 died in prison, 327 shot while trying to escape." The memorial has been fiercely criticized because of its arguably kitschy form and failure to represent women-victims of communism and repeatedly destroyed through graffiti, glue tape, and even homemade bomb attacks (see Blažek). The Memorial to the Victims of Collectivization has been free of controversy. Situated near the Ministry of Agriculture in Těšnov, it resembles a bunch of cereal stems tied together with barbwire and is devoted to those who suffered from Soviet-imposed collectivization in 1948-1960.

Apart from the memorials commemorating the victims of the Soviet-imposed regime, the city has also paid tribute to the Velvet Revolution. As early as 1991, a monument titled *Nike '89* was unveiled in the quiet park Chotkovy Sady between Castle Hill and Letna Park. The artwork is a modern version of the Greek goddess of peace; smooth, golden, and without any formal or aesthetic relation to its surroundings. The November 17 Memorial also has a remarkably simple and clear design: it features a board with the date 17.11.1989 inscribed in golden letters and with several hands showing the V for victory sign on top. Located in the arches of the building called *Kaňkův dům* on *Národní třídě*, the bronze relief is decorated with flowers every year on the anniversary of the students' protests that triggered the peaceful revolution in Prague in 1989. Interestingly, whereas the memorials commemorating the victims of communism are not only elaborate in form and size, but also situated in strategic tourist spots such as Wenceslas Square and the Petřín Hill, the monuments devoted to the Velvet Revolution are modest and hidden rather than exposed to the crowds.

Just like in Berlin, it was a private investor and not the city that built a museum of communism in Prague. Remarkably, "it took an American businessman to make it happen" (Krosnar) and, as if that were not ironic enough, the museum is situated in Prague's main shopping district, above a McDonald's restaurant and next to a casino. The museum creator, Glenn Spicker, claims his venue is directed at the people, who have little to no knowledge of the communist regime: "The younger generation has not been told the whole story by their parents because everyone's too busy living a new life" (qtd. in Krosnar). Possibly, partly because of the target group and partly because of the newest global trends in museum building (the DDR Museum in Berlin, the Museum of Warsaw Uprising, the Terror House in Budapest, to name only few), Prague's Museum of Communism is an interactive multimedia exhibition that focuses on providing entertainment rather than a thorough analysis of historical facts. The exhibition was designed by Czech-born filmmaker Jan Kaplan, who decided to depict the communist regime (from which he had fled to England in 1968) in the form of a "three-act tragedy: 'the dream, reality and nightmare'" (Krosnar). Although acknowledged as "an important step toward helping the country come to terms with its past" (Krosnar), the museum has been criticized both for its scarce space, which makes its squeezing in of four decades of dictatorship impossible, and its "strangely amateur feel": "Busts of party heroes are collected in one corner haphazardly and without explanation, like knick-knacks in a grandmother's attic" (Kulish).

Clearly, as of yet, none of the Central European capitals have succeeded in creating a fully competent and insightful museum thematizing the decades of the communist regime. In June 2008, a group of famous Central European politicians, who helped facilitate and administer the system change of 1989, published an open letter in the *Süddeutsche Zeitung* advocating "the establishment of a Cold War Museum in Berlin to lastingly safeguard the memory of the division of Europe and its liberation" (Bartoszewski et al.). The Polish diplomats and former ministers Władysław Bartoszewski and Bronisław Geremek, (West) Germany's former minister of foreign affairs Hans-Dietrich Genscher, the former Czech president Václav Havel, and the former Hungarian prime minister Miklós Németh, among others, called upon the German government and the Berlin Senate to safeguard a plot of land in the vicinity of the Checkpoint Charlie, which they consider the perfect location for the proposed Cold War museum. Although Berlin already has the Allied Museum in Zehlendorf and the German-Russian Museum in Karlshorst, they present two different sides of history rather than a more objective and inclusive evaluation of the past (see Bartoszewski et al.). The signatories of the appeal note that as a result of the rapid post-1989 changes the experiences of the Cold War tend to be forgotten and the generation born after 1989 has no personal memories of the division of the continent—even Berlin visitors have difficulties finding the traces of the Wall (see Bartoszewski et al.). It remains questionable whether the Berlin Senate and the German government will allow for the establishment of yet another costly museum in a city overcrowded with memorials.

In *Present Pasts,* Andreas Huyssen recalls Robert Musil's observation that "there is nothing as invisible as a monument" and concludes that the "memorial-crazed" Berlin clearly opts for invisibility: "The more monuments there are, the more the past becomes invisible, and the easier it is to forget: redemption, thus, through forgetting" (Huyssen 32). Musil's and Huyssen's remarks add important questions to the debate on the viability of memorials everywhere. It is important to remember, however, that after 1989, Berlin—as well as other Central European cities—had no chance but to rethink their commemoration practices. Despite the fact that the Second World War and the Holocaust were designed and administered largely in and from Berlin, in the postwar decades the city built few monuments related to its nazi past. Aside from the Soviet war memorials and a few monuments devoted to the communist victims of Hitler's regime in East Berlin (the most famous being the Ernst Thälmann monument devoted to the communist party leader killed in Buchenwald in 1944), there were only three other memorials in (West) Berlin that attempted to thematize some of the aspects of World War II: the German Resistance Memorial on *Stauffenbergstrasse* (1953); the Topography of Terror (1987) on the grounds of the former Gestapo headquarters and right behind the Berlin Wall on *Niederkirchnerstrasse* (formerly the infamous *Prinz-Albrecht-Strasse* synonymous with the nazi regime); and the information center in the House of the Wannsee Conference (initiated in 1987, but opened five years later), where the "Final Solution" was officially agreed upon in January 1942. As German historian Götz Aly was right to observe in 2005, "Berlin's so-called memorial landscape [left] all the central questions unanswered"; he criticized not only the lack of thematic and organizational connection between the museums of terror, resistance, and persecution, but also their "mustiness and hostility to innovation," stating bluntly that "they have become museums to themselves" (Aly).

The Memorial to the Murdered Jews of Europe (also known as the Holocaust Memorial) that opened on the sixtieth anniversary of the end of the Second World War started a new trend in the commemoration practices in Berlin. The idea for the memorial surfaced as early as 1988, but it was not until the reunification and the re-location of the federal government to Berlin that the project became "the subject of a fundamental debate concerning German people's historical self-awareness at the end of the 20th century" (Stiftung Denkmal). The unprecedented dispute aroused count-less controversies and went on for over a decade before the Bundestag was able to pass a resolution giving a green light to the construction of the memorial. The resolu-tion not only designated the location of the memorial in the very center of the emerg-ing government district, but also specified its form and role. The Bundestag chose Peter Eisenman's monumental design as the winning project, but stressed that the memorial "cannot replace the historical sites of terror where atrocities were commit-ted" (Stiftung Denkmal). Furthermore, the resolution explicates what the parliament intends to achieve with the memorial, namely to "honour the murdered victims, keep alive the memory of these inconceivable events in German history, and admonish all future generations never again to violate human rights, to defend the democratic constitutional state at all times, to secure equality before the law for all people and to resist all forms of dictatorship and regimes based on violence" (Stiftung Denkmal). Whereas the intentions behind the project have been clearly expressed, the memorial itself continues to arouse controversy, confusion, and criticism.

Spread over 19,000 square meters (or the size of two Bundesliga football fields, as it is often explained in Berlin guide books), the Memorial to the Murdered Jews of Europe consists of 2,711 concrete slabs that vary in height and angle. Nei-ther the number nor the shape of the stelae intentionally possess any symbolic value because, in the words of the architect, "the enormity and scale of the horror of the Holocaust is such that any attempt to represent it by traditional means is inevitably inadequate." Instead, the memorial "attempts to present a new idea of memory as distinct from nostalgia" (Eisenman qtd. in Stiftung Denkmal). Whereas the inten-tion behind the memorial may be unclear to those unfamiliar with its political and artistic background, the Information Center located underneath the concrete field provides thorough information on the history of the Holocaust. The underground museum consists of several rooms that correspond architecturally to the memorial and incorporate various audiovisual techniques to convey the complex themes of the exhibition. Importantly, the museum relies on academic texts and original letters and photographs as well as video and audio recordings of testimonies by Holocaust survivors.

Unlike the pre-1989 memorials criticized by Aly for a "lack of themat-ic and organizational connection," the Holocaust Memorial aims at remain-ing "connected to other memorial centres and institutions within and beyond Berlin" (Stiftung Denkmal). In fact, the Foundation Memorial to the Murdered Jews of Europe cooperates closely with the organizations behind other monu-ments and museums such as the Topography of Terror, the Centrum Judaicum, the House of the Wannsee Conference, the Jewish Museum, and the Sachsen-hausen Museum. Furthermore, the foundation has been entrusted with the su-pervision of the Memorial to the Homosexuals Persecuted under the National

Socialist Regime (2008) and, together with the Topography of Terror, the "Gray Buses" Memorial devoted to the victims of the nazi-imposed "euthanasia" (2006-2008). Sadly, the size of the Holocaust Memorial and the hidden location of the Homosexuals Memorial among the trees in Tiergarten render both monuments difficult to protect from anti-Semitic and homophobic attacks and sheer vandalism. In August 2008, three months after the Homosexuals Memorial was unveiled, unknown offenders smashed the viewing window that is part of the cube-shaped artwork and through which visitors normally can see the film showing two kissing men. Survivors, gay activists, and Berlin's (openly gay) mayor Klaus Wowereit voiced their concern over the incident.

In *Structure of Memory: Understanding Urban Change in Berlin and Beyond* (2006), Jennifer A. Jordan enumerates the reasons for Berlin's post-1989 interest in monuments reminding people of the nazi crimes: "because someone took up the cause, because land was available, because the land was publicly owned, because it could be politically difficult *not* to build a memorial at a certain point, because enough people supported its construction, because it resonated" (94). Clearly, Jordan sees the memorials as a natural consequence of the new political and social situation in Berlin. One of the first remarkable monuments to appear in the city after 1989 was the Book Burning Memorial on Bebelplatz that opened in 1995. Designed by Israeli artist Micha Ullman, the memorial is located precisely on the square where on 10 May 1933, members of the SA and the SS, together with students and professors of the nearby Humboldt University, burned thousands of books by authors considered "un-German" such as Sigmund Freud, Heinrich Mann, Karl Marx, and Kurt Tucholsky. The major part of Ullman's artwork is underground and can be seen through a glass plate incorporated into the cobbled-stoned square: the inside of the memorial shows empty, brightly lit bookshelves. The second part of the memorial is located several meters away and consists solely of a bronze plate immersed in the pavement with a quotation from Heinrich Heine (dated 1821) prophetically pronouncing "Dort, wo man Bücher verbrennt, verbrennt man am Ende auch Menschen" (Where they burn books, they will also, in the end, burn human beings). Up to date, Ullman's underground library remains one of Berlin's most subtle memorials and does not yield to the trend observed by Huyssen: "the notion of the monument as memorial or commemorative public event has witnessed a triumphal return" (31).

In Warsaw, many World War II monuments had been built already under the socialist regime, including the Warsaw Ghetto Uprising Memorials (1946 and 1948), the Nike Monument to the Heroes of Warsaw (1964), the Little Insurgent's Monument (1983), the Umschlagplatz Monument (1988), and the Warsaw Uprising Monument (1989). Still, because of the Soviet-imposed interpretations of history that were in force throughout the postwar decades, certain events and organizations of the Second World War, such as the Polish anti-Soviet partisan movement, the Battle of Monte Cassino, and the deportations of Polish civilians and soldiers to Russia, were allowed to be commemorated only after 1989. Remarkably, the Monument to the Fallen and the Murdered in the East (*Pomnik Poległym i Pomordowanym na*

Wschodzie) was one of the first war memorials to open in Warsaw after the fall of the socialist regime. The monumental bronze structure includes railway tracks and a train carriage (reminiscent of those the Soviets used for deportations) filled with religious symbols, predominantly Roman-Catholic crosses, but also some Orthodox Christian crosses, Stars of David, and Islamic crescents, which recall the multiethnic and multireligious character of the former East Poland. The tracks are inscribed with the names of the cities and towns from which Polish citizens were forced out (such as Grodno, Wilno, Białystok, Brześć, and Pińsk) as well as the names of the Siberian deportation and labor camps where they were delivered (such as Krasnoyarsk, Yakutsk, and Irkutsk). Symbolically, the monument was unveiled on 17 September 1995, the anniversary of the Soviet invasion on Poland, which had not been spoken of under the socialist regime.

Another tragic event that had been mostly ignored or downplayed by the local and state authorities before 1989 was the Warsaw Uprising of 1944. The enthusiastic patriotic rebellion against German occupiers led to the murder of an enormous part of the young Polish intelligentsia and to the destruction of nearly the whole city. While the Warsaw insurgents and civilians alike were slaughtered by the German troops, the Red Army remained on the other bank of the Vistula, waiting for the city and its people to perish (see Davies). Naturally then, the Soviet-imposed regime was not keen on commemorating the uprising in the postwar decades. After 1989, dozens of monuments, plaques, and street names devoted to the uprising appeared in the city. Moreover, each anniversary of the uprising is elaborately commemorated in Warsaw and the rest of the country. In many ways, Warsaw's preoccupation—if not obsession—with the event calls to mind Budapest's commemoration of the 1956 revolution in that both capitals focus on the heroism and suffering of their residents as an integral aspect of their urban identities.

The Warsaw Uprising became particularly celebrated under mayor Lech Kaczyński, who pronounced that "commemorating the events of the summer of 1944 and restoring them to their proper place in Poland's history is our duty and obligation towards the insurgents," but also "a family celebration" for himself, since he comes "from a family with strong Home Army traditions" (Kaczyński's father Rajmunt fought in the uprising) (qtd. in Warsaw Rising Museum). The Warsaw Rising Museum opened on the sixtieth anniversary of the insurrection; its goal is to conduct teaching and research and to "integrate veterans' and military circles and educate youth in the spirit of patriotism and respect for national traditions" (Warsaw Rising Museum; the Polish name of the institution, *Muzeum Powstania Warszawskiego*, is officially translated into English as Warsaw Rising Museum). The patriotic education and commemoration of the victims dominate the concept of the exhibition, which focuses on the determination, idealism, and suffering of the insurgents and Warsaw civilians alike. Like most aforementioned museums, the Warsaw Rising Museum relies to a great extent on multimedia techniques and oral history. The museum is integrated with the city: apart from constant cooperation with schools, historical institutes, and veteran associations, it initiates various entertainment and educational mass events for the residents of Warsaw.

The opening of the Warsaw Rising Museum in 2004 was part of the elaborate commemorations of the sixtieth anniversary of the insurrection. Along with numerous new plaques and statues, concerts, historical enactments, and speeches, an important event rich in symbolism was the renaming of the *Kopiec Czerniakowski* (Czerniakowski Mound). The mound in the district of Mokotów was created from the rubble and ashes of destroyed Warsaw: fragments of buildings, bricks, roof tiles—some of them most likely containing human remains—were piled up together in 1946-50 in an attempt to create a pantheon for those who died during the uprising (Warsaw City Hall). For decades, the mound remained neglected, and it was not until 1994 that Home Army veterans initiated a monument on the top of the hill, a 15-meter tall symbol of "Fighting Poland," the so-called *kotwica*, or anchor. In 2004, when the mound was renamed in honor of the Warsaw Uprising, 400 steps and 40 landings (symbolizing the year 1944) were added to make it easier for visitors to climb uphill.

Whereas outside of Poland the Warsaw Uprising of 1944 is often confused with the Warsaw Ghetto Uprising of 1943, in the Warsaw urban landscape the differences between the two are clearly marked and commemorated through separate memorials. The Warsaw Ghetto Uprising Memorials (1946 and 1948) were among the first to appear in postwar Warsaw. After 1989, a few other monuments related to the Holocaust have been built, including the Żegota Monument (1995) and another Janusz Korczak Memorial (2006) (*Żegota* is the code name for underground Polish organization *Rada Pomocy Żydom* / Council to Aid Jews, 1942-45; Janusz Korczak's real name was Henryk Goldszmit, 1877-1942, a pediatrician, pedagogue, and orphanage director in the Warsaw Ghetto, killed in Treblinka together with "his" children; memorials devoted to Korczak were built in Warsaw and in other Polish cities already before 1989). Also, the Museum of the History of Polish Jews is scheduled to open on the site of the former Warsaw Ghetto in 2011. The "multimedia narrative museum and cultural center," as its creators describe it, "will be a unique institution," because to date there is no other museum that focuses on the history of Polish Jews (Museum of the History of Polish Jews). The museum, which expects to draw 450,000 visitors a year, is directed primarily at Jewish visitors from Israel, the United States, and Europe as well as Polish visitors, who "will discover that the history of Poland is not complete without a history of Polish Jews" (Museum of the History of Polish Jews). The curators ambitiously aim at demonstrating that "being a Jew in Poland was not limited to being a Holocaust victim" (Museum of the History of Polish Jews).

The Museum of the History of Polish Jews is likely to resemble—both when it comes to the content and form of the planned exhibition—the Jewish Museum in Berlin located in Daniel Libeskind's world famous building. The exhibition on the history of German Jews opened on 11 September 2001 and had to be immediately closed for a few days in fear of terrorist attacks. The building takes the form of a zig-zag and is based on two linear structures: "The first line is a winding one with several kinks while the second line cuts through the whole building. At the intersections of these lines are empty spaces—'Voids'—which rise vertically from the ground floor of the building up to the roof. Libeskind imagines the continuation of both lines throughout the city of Berlin and beyond" (Jewish Museum Berlin). The voids refer to "that which can never be exhibited when it comes to Jewish Berlin history: humanity reduced to ashes" (Libeskind qtd. in Jewish Museum Berlin). These aspects of history that can be represented are exhibited along three axes: the Axis of Emigration that leads outside the building to the Garden of Exile, the Axis of the Holocaust that ends in the Holocaust Tower, and the Axis of Continuity that leads to the exhibition. Whereas the exhibition itself tells the history of German Jews in a rather conventional way, Libeskind's architecture, his use of light and air, the surprising angles of the walls, and the heaviness and lightness of the used materials create an opportunity to "sense" the fate of German Jews and learn about it through empathy and imagination rather than through curatorial texts. Andreas Huyssen is among many to praise the Jewish Museum for its uniqueness and insightful consideration of Berlin's urban landscape and history: "Libeskind's museum is the only project in the current Berlin building boom that explicitly articulates issues of national and local history in ways pertinent to post-unification Germany" (71).

Like the Jewish Museum in Berlin, where Libeskind's zinc-coated building is an extension of the eighteenth-century *Collegienhaus*, the Holocaust Memorial Center in Budapest is a combination of classical and contemporary architecture. Inaugurated in 2004, the museum building consists of the renovated Páva Synagogue and the adjoining new wing designed by István Mányi. Another similarity with the Jewish Museum in Berlin lies in the symbolism of Mányi's design: "the building's asymmetrical outline, the dislocated walls, and the descending stairs in the exhibition halls, all symbolize the distorted and twisted time of the Holocaust" (Holocaust Memorial Center). Moreover, the place itself is rich in historical meanings, since the synagogue served as an internment camp in 1944-45 (see Holocaust Memorial Center). Next to the permanent exhibition, titled "From Deprivation of Rights to Genocide," the Holocaust Memorial Center houses a memorial to the victims of the Holocaust in Hungary: the names of the victims are engraved in the eight-meter tall glass wall surrounding the courtyard. In 2007, the glass Tower of Lost Communities was added to the memorial complex: it lists the names of all 1441 settlements, where, "owing to the deportations, the Jewish communities have ceased to exist" (Holocaust Memorial Center).

Apart from the Holocaust Memorial Center, Holocaust victims have been commemorated in Budapest through monuments. The poignantly symbolic 2005 memorial called "Shoes on the Danube Bank" depicts, as its name suggests, shoes stranded along the riverbank in Pest, south of the Parliament. Gyula Pauer's artwork is a tribute to the victims shot into the Danube by Arrow Cross militiamen in 1944-45. The Raoul Wallenberg Memorial Park near the famous Great Synagogue on Dohány Street—where, during the war, some of the architects of the Holocaust (including Adolf Eichmann) had their offices, in which they planned and administered the transportation and killing of over 400,000 Hungarian Jews—is home to several monuments devoted to both the Holocaust victims and the rescuers of the Jews. The park is named after the Swedish diplomat who saved tens of thousands of Budapest Jews from extermination. The most spectacular monument in the square is the "Tree of Life" created by Imre Varga: each of the five thousand metal leaves on the willow tree is engraved with a name of a Holocaust victim. At the center of the memorial there is a granite slab with two long vertical holes in the shape of Biblical tablets, which call to mind a missing Decalogue. Also, one of the walls surrounding the park has been covered with dozens of small square plaques commemorating the victims by name. The monument to the rescuers consists of five granite boards: the black horizontal table in the middle is devoted to Raoul Wallenberg and other prominent rescuers such as Carl Lutz and Per Anger, and the surrounding red vertical slabs feature the names of some of the Hungarians who rescued Jews during the war. Carl Lutz has been commemorated individually elsewhere in Budapest, at the entrance to the former Jewish Ghetto (1991), in the park adjacent to the US Embassy (2006), and as a memorial room in the so-called Glass House (2005; *Üvegház*, or Glass House, was an industrial building and one of the secret houses where Lutz helped hide the Jews during the war). The first memorial is the most elaborate: it depicts an angel-like golden figure situated high on the wall, as if leaning out from the window, throwing a long scarf to a thin person lying on the pavement and reaching an arm out for help. The inscription accompanying Tamás Szabó's monument reads, "Whoever saves a life is considered as if he has saved an entire world (*Talmud*). In memory of those who in 1944 under the leadership of the Swiss Consul Carl Lutz (1895-1975) rescued thousands from National Socialist persecution." The monument near the US-American Embassy has the shape of an open book laid out on a pedestal with the portrait of Lutz engraved on one page and an inscription on the other page praising Lutz for his courage, adding that the Swiss diplomat "honorably represented the interests of the United States and other countries between 1942-1945."

In Prague, Holocaust victims are commemorated in the Pinkas Synagogue in Josefov. The names of the 77,297 Jews from Moravia and Bohemia killed in the Holocaust are inscribed on the interior walls of the temple and arranged by the towns and villages they came from. Although created in the 1950s, the memorial was closed in 1968 owing to the poor state of the building (see Jewish Museum in Prague). Neglected for decades, the Pinkas Synagogue was renovated after the fall of communism and reopened in 1996. Compared to those of the other Central European capitals, most war memorials built in Prague after 1989 are relatively small and unobtrusive, but the Monument to the Legionary of the Second World War in Dejvice and the Monument to the Second Resistance in Klárov are remarkable exceptions. The former is a tall wavy column in *Vítězne náměstí* (Victory Square), unveiled in 2004 and devoted to the Czechoslovak soldiers who fought on foreign fronts. Fifteen of the tiles that cover the square hide ashes from the military cemeteries, where the bodies of Czechoslovak soldiers had been buried. The latter depicts a gigantic Czechoslovak flag, torn and shattered, but still holding on to the tilted pole; the dates on the pedestal read 1938-1945. Inaugurated in 2006, the memorial to World War II resistance fighters is located near a busy Lesser Town intersection and has become an important part of Prague's urban landscape and a geographic and cultural reference point. The Czechoslovak twentieth-century resistance movements against the country's many occupiers have also been commemorated in Nusle in the form of a fountain monument at the foot of a small park. As its name and the dates on the pedestal clarify, the memorial (*Památník I., II. a III. odboje*) is devoted to the first, second, and third Czechoslovak resistance movements active in Prague in 1914-1918, 1939-1945, and 1948-1989. The monument is located on *náměstí Generála Kutlvašra* (General Kutlvašr Square*)*—named after the leader of the Prague rebellion against the German occupation (May 5-8, 1945), who was imprisoned in 1949 by the Soviet-imposed regime and released only in 1960—and well integrated into its surrounding: it resembles an elegant entrance to the adjacent park rather than a war memorial.

Whereas the contemporary urban landscapes of Berlin, Warsaw, and, to a lesser extent, Budapest are dominated by monuments related to World War II, a different phenomenon may be observed in post-1989 Prague. Although the Czech capital does have dozens of plaques, busts, and monuments devoted to various aspects and events of the Second World War, they are not as visible—and certainly not as visually attractive—as the humorous statues by David Černý that can be found in the most unexpected places in the Golden City. In his thought-provoking works, Černý vivisects the Czech(oslovak) culture and history, makes fun of it, and—sometimes literally—turns it upside down. The artist became widely known in 1991, when he covered a Soviet tank memorial standing in Smíchov with pink paint (Szczygieł, "Wkurzacz czeski"). The artistic performance was spurned as sheer vandalism and the army repainted the tank green, which outraged several center- and right-wing MPs, who painted the tank pink; the army repainted the tank green again and put it in a museum, but then, after high-ranking NATO officials expressed their interest in seeing the by-then famous Soviet tank, themselves put a coat of pink paint on it (Szczygieł, "Wkurzacz czeski"). What is of special interest here is not exactly Černý's decision to paint the tank pink, but the reactions it provoked. The color changes and the accompanying disputes illustrate the political and cultural chaos of the years following the collapse of communism in Prague and elsewhere in Central Europe.

Although probably best known for his sculptures of faceless babies with oversized heads crawling up the Žižkov Television Tower (*Mininka*, 2000), Černý has authored numerous politically and culturally loaded artworks. In 1990, he created a bronze statue of a golden Trabant on four legs and with testicles: since 2001, the artwork titled *Quo Vadis* has been displayed in the garden of the German Embassy, where it reminds viewers of the thousands of East Germans seeking refuge in the West German Embassy in the summer of 1989 (Szczygieł, "Wkurzacz czeski"). Černý's 1999 *Kůň* (Horse), located in the Lucerna Palace in Wenceslas Square, is inspired by one of Prague's most prominent symbols, the equestrian statue of Saint Wenceslas standing at the top of the same square. Whereas the historical monument of the Czech patron saint is serious and noble, Černý's Wenceslas sits on the stomach of his dead horse hanging from the ceiling. The artist himself sees his work as a commentary on the Czech mentality: "someone is hanging upside down, but in the Czech Republic everyone pretends that nothing has happened, we close our eyes" (qtd. in Szczygieł, "Wkurzacz czeski"). Even more provocatively, Černý celebrated the 2004 enlargement of the European Union by creating a statue depicting two men urinating into a pool in the shape of the map of the Czech Republic. The artwork is interactive: it is possible to send a text message to the phone number displayed near the fountain with a word or a sentence, which will then, after a few minutes, be written in the water by the stream from the moveable penises.

Prague's tolerance for Černý's provocative ways of thematizing Czech history and culture is exceptional for a Central European capital. In Budapest and Warsaw Černý's works would have been most likely considered unacceptable as blasphemous and offensive and completely banned from the public space. The urban memories of the Hungarian and Polish capitals have a decidedly patriotic nature. Next to the memorials devoted to the 1956 revolution and the Warsaw Uprising, respectively, in the last two decades both capitals have witnessed the emergence of monuments commemorating some of the events and public figures of the interwar period that for ideological reasons had received little or no attention before 1989. Consequently, the dozens of statues and plaques in the streets and squares of Budapest and Warsaw remind viewers of interwar politicians, military officers, priests, and artists, some of whom were (in)famous for being openly nationalistic or anti-Semitic. For example, the statue of Roman Dmowski (1864-1939) was unveiled to fierce protests on the part of left-wing organizations and renowned intellectuals such as Marek Edelman (the only surviving leader of the Warsaw Ghetto Uprising) and Maria Janion (literary scholar and feminist) who dismissed the leader of the *Endecja* (National Democratic Party) as an anti-Semite and nationalist ("Pomnik Dmowskiego"). The initiators and supporters of the statue praise Dmowski as one of the founding fathers of the independent and democratic Poland ("Pomnik Dmowskiego"). Consequently, the monument continues to produce extreme reactions: on the one hand, it has been repeatedly vandalized by left-wing radicals and on the other hand, representatives of right-wing organizations regularly lay wreathes and light candles at the foot of the statue. Just as in the case of Černý's pink tank, the controversy surrounding the Dmowski statue reveals some of the political and cultural divisions characterizing post-1989 Central European societies.

After the fall of communism, each of the cities has chosen a different focus point for their memory policies. In Berlin, World War II and some of the nazi crimes have been re-evaluated and their victims commemorated on a—literally—monumental scale. In Budapest, the 1956 revolution has been remembered in dozens of memorials and street names and each anniversary of the anti-Soviet rebellion is elaborately celebrated in the city. In Warsaw, statues, plaques, and festivities commemorating the Warsaw Uprising prevail. Prague, on the contrary, seems to lack a clear focus: some of its post-1989 monuments are devoted to World War II, some to the victims of the socialist regime, some to the Velvet Revolution, and some to national heroes, but none of these pasts appears as dominant. Instead, the Czech capital boasts a collection of surprising and unconventional statues by artist David Černý that comment on Czech history, culture, and mentality. Aside from local differences, however, after 1989, each of the Central European capitals has experienced similar developments when it comes to commemorating their histories. First, a number of memorials have been devoted to the victims of the socialist regimes; second, the memories of the Second World War have been freed from a Soviet-imposed reading, which has allowed for a new understanding of the tragic events and, in turn, their commemoration; and third, the previously downplayed historical importance of some national heroes has been newly recognized and celebrated with statues and busts (e.g., Tomáš and Jan Masaryk in Prague, Józef Piłsudski in Warsaw). Clearly, when it comes to expressing their urban memories through monuments, Central European capitals remain preoccupied with the twentieth century. By contrast, post-1989 architecture and particularly urban planning are partly inspired by the late nineteenth century, or the so-called *Gründerzeit*, when Central European cities were changing under the influence of industrial developments.

Imagining the futures of Central European metropolises

In order to understand the nature and scope of the recent transformations of their urban landscapes, it is important to remember how Central European capitals looked in and shortly after 1989. Substantially destroyed during World War II, Warsaw, Berlin, and Budapest still showed signs of air raids, street battles, and expulsions. With few exceptions—such as the Old Town in Warsaw and the *Nicolaiviertel* in Berlin that resemble film sets rather than real-life neighborhoods—more elaborate renovations did not start until the mid-1980s and even then affected only small parts of the cities (Ladd 43-44). Moreover, certain (mostly central) parts of Warsaw and Berlin had been completely destroyed through bombs or subsequent razing and rebuilt in a decidedly socialist fashion, which completely changed the spatial layout. Consequently, the historical urban structure had been—largely irretrievably—abandoned and socialist spatial plans reshaped not only parts of city landscapes, but also entire networks of urban interactions. Since hardly any money flowed into the modernization of prewar buildings, many of them, often with no indoor toilets and no proper heating, decayed and gradually turned into slums (Musil, "City Development" 39). Compared to nineteenth-century working class tenements (like those in Berlin's Prenzlauer Berg and in parts of Pest), the 1970s and 1980s prefabricated apartment blocks seemed state-of-the-art dwellings and attracted the residents of the dilapidated Mietskasernen, which, in turn, led to an even greater depopulation and decline of historical neighborhoods (Häußermann, Holm, and Zunzer 52-54; Musil, "City Development" 39-40).

After the fall of the Wall, attempts have been made to revive city centers and to re-establish functional urban networks and structures. The revitalization and aesthetization of city centers has been connected to "the manipulation of city images and marketing" (Short and Kim 89-90) and has contributed to the transformation of historic downtown areas into glitzy simulacra (see Jameson, *Geopolitical Aesthetic*; Soja). Importantly, the post-1989 architectural and spatial plans have been partly inspired by the cities' golden age—this has been especially true of Berlin where new developments in the downtown districts have been tied to nineteenth-century patterns, introducing a conservative vision for the historic center: the so-called *Planwerk Innenstadt* (see Senatsverwaltung für Stadtentwicklung Berlin). Based on what Hans Stimmann (Berlin's chief urbanist of the 1990s) defined as "critical reconstruction"—and what more progressive architects rejected as Prussianism—the new aesthetic concept for the historic center has accelerated "the retreat into the building of simulacra of the past" (Cochrane 10). A walk down Unter den Linden has come to resemble a journey through a film studio, with mock-up buildings filling in the post-Wall void: the Bertelsmann headquarters, Schinkel's Bauakademie, and Hotel Adlon—all recreated from the scratch as exact copies of pre-1914 Berlin buildings that no longer exist—will soon be joined by the Stadtschloss. These developments have been interpreted as Berlin's aspiration towards being a "normal" European city (see Cochrane; Till, *New Berlin*) whereby "the 'normality' being reconstructed . . . draws directly on the language and strategies of neoliberalism" (Cochrane 20).

Apart from the renovation or rebuilding of whole neighborhoods, some of the most urgent post-1989 investments in Central European cities included the replacement or (re)construction of the infrastructure. The long-awaited completion of Warsaw's metro line, the re-establishment of inner-city public transport between the former West and East Berlin, and the renovation and construction of bridges in Berlin, Budapest, Prague, and Warsaw are only some examples of the thorough construction works that the infrastructure of Central European cities had to undergo. Some of the renovation and construction works, especially in the early 1990s, were largely encouraged or necessitated by Western enterprises that were moving their offices and factories to Central Europe and needed good infrastructure (see, e.g., Stanilov, "Taking Stock"). The presence of international (mostly Western) companies has manifested itself in other ways. In Budapest and Prague, foreign enterprises made use of already existing buildings: owing to their attractive central location or picturesque views over the river, many of the dilapidated historic houses have been transformed into offices. The scale of the developments has been immense and permanently changed whole neighborhoods from residential to commercial (Sýkora, "Office Development" 130; Musil, "Prague Returns to Europe" 299-300). In Berlin and Warsaw, some of the old palaces, townhouses, or apartment buildings were also adapted for corporate purposes; however, in the German and Polish capitals it has been more common to build completely new office buildings in an attempt to create modern business districts at Potsdamer Platz and around the Palace of Culture and Science, respectively.

The end of communism famously triggered euphoria among Central European societies. Aside from the new forms of entertainment served by the media, the urban entertainment and cultural sectors bloomed: new bars, clubs, restaurants, cinemas, theaters, and museums opened on a daily basis, and some of them closed only to make room for new ones. As Stefan Arndt, the producer of the German blockbuster film *Good Bye, Lenin!* (2003), put it: "Everything was changing so fast. If you tried to go to the same bar you had visited the previous week, it wasn't there anymore. Instead, one floor above or below (often in the basement), there would be a new place, even cooler than the old one" ("Interview mit Produzent Stefan Arndt"). In other words, the supply of entertainment and culture in Central Europe has finally started meeting the demand (at the same time, however, many theater companies, cinemas, publishing houses, and other cultural institutions had to close down because, with state subsidies cut, they proved unprofitable or incapable of competing in the new realities of the market economy). Similar changes have been observed in the political sector. Now that more than a single party was actually allowed to exist, the setting up of offices for foundations, youth organizations, and other groups was needed in order to accommodate them in the capitals. In addition, new ministries, parliamentary groups, and embassies had to establish their headquarters or representative offices in the most prominent locations available. The political sector has contributed to the construction boom, particularly in Berlin, where the whole government district had to be (re)created from scratch.

The transformations of urban landscapes were not limited to central districts, but affected the whole cities. In the 1990s, suburbanization was one of the most widespread trends in Central European capitals, particularly in Budapest, Prague, and Warsaw. Those who could afford to leave the decaying prefabricated apartment buildings often opted for a family house in the suburbs, part of the "American dream" that was becoming increasingly popular in Central Europe (partly owing to the US-American television shows aired on national and local channels). Moving to the suburbs was a clear message: "I have made it" (Murawski 94). The popularization and affordability of cars as well as the emergence of hypermarkets and malls on the outskirts of the cities both helped facilitate and were influenced by the suburbanization process (Dimitrovska Andrews 157). By the early 2000s, however, the exodus to the suburbs reversed and a new—although already known from Western metropolises such as New York City and London—phenomena started: downtown development and gentrification.

The following section focuses on how post-1989 architecture and urban planning influenced the landscapes of Berlin, Budapest, Prague, and Warsaw and how the cities communicated their postcommunist—and, I argue, (post)colonial—identities through new buildings. I look specifically at the most representative architecture located in central areas. As researchers from the Ghent Urban Studies Team notice, "the late-capitalist downtown is almost exclusively geared to three functions: consumption, finance, and the symbolic economy," whereby the latter comprises "tourism, entertainment, culture, sports, the media and fashion industries, and an amalgamation of services logistically underpinning these activities" (GUST 98). I propose to add politics as the fourth sector prominently represented by high-profile buildings. Whereas cultural and political buildings such as museums, libraries, concert halls, ministries, and court houses help shape and communicate (intended) national or local identities, the new (often foreign owned) office buildings, hotels, and shopping centers shape the cities' image and reputation as global players. Below, I discuss some of the most viable examples of post-1989 architectural developments in Berlin, Budapest, Prague, and Warsaw, the meanings they communicate, and the impact they have on Central European urbanities.

Although new construction works in Central European capitals were obviously triggered first and foremost by the collapse of communism, it is important to note that they have coincided with global changes in architecture and urbanism such as the rise and fall of starchitects, the development of the tourist city, and the emergence of the generic city. As Nezar AlSayyad is right to observe, contemporary urban phenomena are interconnected and often occur as a chain reaction: "as urban governments turn cities into centres of consumption, their particular innovations—downtown stadia, festival marketplace, shopping and restaurant complexes—soon circulate and are imitated by other cities" (125). Although they do not belong to the group of trendsetting global players, Central European capitals are substantially affected by the changes taking place in megacities. One of these trends has been the construction of airports, shopping malls, and office buildings that appear "equally exciting—or unexciting—everywhere" (Koolhaas 1250) and, thus, render cities generic. According to Rem Koolhaas who coined the term, "the generic city . . . is nothing but a reflection of present need and present ability. It is the city without history" (1250). The Dutch architect claims that both the new cities that have sprung up in the deserts of the Arabian Peninsula and some of Europe's historic metropolises may be described as generic: "sometimes an old, singular city"—Koolhaas mentions Barcelona and Paris—"by oversimplifying its identity, turns Generic. It becomes transparent, like a logo" (1250). Arguably, as I demonstrate in chapter 4, the Disneyfied center of Prague could also fall under this category. Even if they possess some features characteristic of the generic city, however, Central European capitals are too obsessed with their histories and memories to turn entirely generic. When it comes to global trends, in Central Europe the tourist city (see, e.g., Hoffman, Fainstein, and Judd) seems to have caught on more than the generic city. As an "increasingly important sector of the city's economy" (Häußermann and Colomb 201), urban tourism is one of the main factors behind the construction boom in Berlin, Budapest, Prague, and Warsaw. Facing fierce interurban competition, cities constantly attempt to introduce new attractions to lure more tourists. As David Harvey notes, "many of the innovations and investments designed to make particular cities more attractive as cultural and consumer centers have quickly been imitated elsewhere, thus rendering any competitive advantage within a system of cities ephemeral. . . . The result is a stimulating if often destructive maelstrom of urban-based cultural, political, production and consumption innovations" (12). This widespread tendency is also true of post-1989 Central European metropolises.

In Berlin, more so than in other capitals in the region, the political sector has been responsible for much of the construction boom. Since the Bundestag decided in 1991 that Berlin would become the seat of the government of reunited Germany, dozens of new buildings had to be built to house ministries, parliamentary offices, press agencies, representative offices of the federal states, party headquarters, party foundations, and many other organizations. The most prominent government buildings have been grouped north of the Reichstag along the Spree (the so-called *Spreebogen*) and include the *Bundeskanzleramt* (Chancellor's Office—2001), the *Paul-Löbe-Haus* (2000) with the offices of MPs and parliamentary commissions, and the *Marie-Elisabeth-Lüders-Haus* (2003), home to the parliamentary library, archives, and other offices (Paul Löbe 1875-1967, was a social democrat and the Bundestag President during the Weimar Republic; Marie-Elisabeth Lüders 1878-1966, was a liberal politician and advocate for women's rights). Both the location and the architecture of the ensemble also known as the *Band des Bundes* are permeated with symbolism. Built on the grounds that were formerly divided between the west and the east, the new government and parliamentary buildings strike viewers as particularly airy and light despite their colossal dimensions and the concrete used for their construction. The large sheets of glass that reflect both the neighboring buildings and the Spree waves, the tall and slim pillars, the bright colors of the outside walls, and the elegant bridges that connect the buildings over the river increase the impression of lightness and, additionally, counterbalance the heaviness of the neighboring late nineteenth-century Reichstag building. Clearly, the Band des Bundes designed by Charlotte Frank and Axel Schultes aims at presenting the image of Germany as a transparent and people-friendly democracy, in which everyone can have a look at the work of the administrative and legislative authorities. Furthermore, the naming of the parliamentary buildings after respected Weimar Republic democrats expresses Germany's wish to re-embrace a democratic system after decades of nazi and communist regimes.

The transparency principle and the re-evaluation of Germany's history were also important factors behind the Reichstag renovation plan. In 1994-99, Paul Wallot's 1894 building was almost completely emptied and restructured according to the design of British architect Norman Foster. The most historically loaded elements of the edifice—including the Soviet soldiers' graffiti from May 1945 and the balcony from which Philipp Scheidemann gave the famous speech establishing a democratic German state in November 1918—have been preserved. Foster's impressive glass dome with a viewing platform is not only a work of art, but also an example of state-of-the-art technology. The structure allows visitors to admire the panorama of the city and look below into the plenary chamber. The Bundestag press materials describe the latter attraction as representative of "far-reaching transparency" and "a further symbolic element of [the Bundestag's] commitment, inscribed in large letters above the main portal of the west side of the building, 'Dem deutschen Volke' (To the German People)" (Deutscher Bundestag 25). Furthermore, the mirrored cone in the center of the cupola and several technological devices in the adjacent parliamentary buildings possess numerous ecological functions and express another important element of modern Germany's image as an ecologically conscious and environmentally friendly country.

In the immediate vicinity of the Band des Bundes several other new buildings have been constructed to support the work of the parliament and the government: the *Jakob-Kaiser-Haus* (named after another Weimar Republic politician) with offices for parliamentarians, fractions, and the Bundestag administration; a futuristic kindergarten for children of the MPs and administration employees; and the *Bundes-Pressekonferenz* buildings, where, aside from the correspondents' offices, press conferences are held. Most ministries are also centrally situated, but, with the notable exception of the colossal Interior Ministry (1992-94) on the Spree, they most often moved into already existing buildings after those had been renovated or extended. Another interesting group of brand new political buildings are the *Landesvertretungen* (permanent representations of the federal states) located in the former death strip between the Brandenburg Gate and Potsdamer Platz. Five cubic constructions on *Allee in den Ministergärten* house the offices and conference rooms of Rheinland-Pfalz, Niedersachsen and Schleswig-Holstein, Saarland, Brandenburg and Mecklenburg-Vorpommern, and Hessen. Although designed by various architects, similar heights and shapes turn the buildings into an aesthetically consistent ensemble. Here too, large windows and partly glass façades serve the transparency principle. Furthermore, the Landesvertretungen are located in the back of the former Reich and nazi government quarter on Wilhelmstrasse and symbolize an attempt at a new democratic beginning.

Although mostly centrally located, Berlin's government and parliamentary buildings are still scattered around a few downtown districts; the same is true of the other Central European capitals. Budapest had an ambitious plan to group all thirty-three ministries together under one roof—only the prime minister's office would have a separate seat in the former Ministry of Agriculture across the Parliament. The idea to centralize the ministerial offices and, as it was argued, improve efficiency and save time spent on traveling between separate buildings first appeared in the late 1990s, but it was not until 2007 that the government agreed on a project and a budget for the new government quarter (see Design Build Network). The winning project by Peter Janesch from Hungary and Keno Kuma from Japan was unanimously chosen by the international jury: Daniel Libeskind, Hans Stimmann, and Josep Acebillo Marin (Barcelona's chief architect), who praised it for environmental awareness (see Design Build Network). Estimated at €567 million, the cost of the investment proved too high, however, and the government suspended the project in its planning phase as early as January 2008 (see Hodgson).

Other new important buildings from the political sector include party headquarters, political foundation headquarters, and embassies, the latter aspiring to express the national identities of the countries they represent rather than their guest countries and cities. After 1989 new embassies have been built in all the capitals (the Dutch Embassies belong to the finest works of modern architecture in Berlin, Budapest, and Warsaw), with a particularly large number in Berlin. Although they differ greatly in architectural designs and aesthetic concepts, most new embassies in Berlin, like other political buildings in the city, rely predominantly on concrete and glass as the building materials. Still, neither the long windows of Christian de Portz-amparc's French Embassy nor the sharply carved void of Koolhaas's Dutch Embassy seem to be as ardently focused on allowing for transparency as the post-1989 German political buildings in Berlin.

Culture, education, and entertainment comprise another sector that has had a remarkable impact on the construction boom after the fall of communism. This development has coincided with another global trend, namely, the increased public and private investment in cultural capital as a means of city promotion (Short and Kim 90). "Culture draws tourists" and is considered an important economic asset (GUST 99). In Central Europe, the emergence of new museums, research institutes, libraries, and academies has been mostly facilitated by public money; private investors have been more active in the field of leisure and entertainment. The attempt to revive cultural capital in Central European cities did not necessarily mean creating new venues from scratch, but also, if not predominantly, renovating, extending, or incorporating already existing ones. The amalgamation of historical edifices with modern constructions or the thorough, often environmentally friendly, modernization of classical buildings have been a widespread phenomena in the urban landscapes of Central Europe. Some of the most prominent examples of this trend include the Jewish Museum and the German Historical Museum in Berlin; the modern extension of the Páva Synagogue in Budapest; and the Kampa Museum, the Langhans Palace, the Academy of Fine Arts, and the DAX Center in Prague. Whereas keeping historical buildings in place clearly points at the cultural heritage Central European capitals take pride in, the post-1989 modernization, renovation, or extension works help present the cities as modern and progressive, which perfectly corresponds to the urban identities the local authorities communicate through their logos and image campaigns (see chapter 4).

Among the brand new cultural centers in the region, Budapest's 2005 Palace of the Arts (*Művészetek Palotája*) is particularly prominent. This "conglomeration of cultural buildings," as the Palace's creators describe it on the homepage, features the Béla Bartók National Concert Hall, the Festival Theater, the Ludwig Museum of Contemporary Arts, the Glass Hall, the Auditorium, and the Blue Hall and has "no precedent in 20th century Hungarian architecture" (Palace of Arts Budapest). Although relatively far from Budapest's historical centers, the Palace's location is considered one of its many advantages. Located right on the Danube in the part of Pest called Ferencváros, between the Petőfi Bridge and the Lágymányosi Bridge, the cultural complex is part of the so-called Millennium City Center—a development project aimed at creating a new modern center for Hungary's capital that would include residential and office buildings, stores, a convention center, and cultural venues. Another advantage of the Palace's location is the impressive panorama of Buda that can be seen from every level of the enormous glass lobby. The Palace of Arts is promoted as one of the most prestigious cultural centers in Budapest and in Hungary and, indeed, the whole region: "unparalleled in Central Europe," the building boasts "world class acoustics" from New York and "one of the best [stages] in the world."

The exhibition rooms meet "all the most modern expectations of museum technology" (Palace of Arts Budapest). Clearly, the Palace of Arts aspires for recognition as a worldwide renowned cultural center. Although the national or local character of the Palace is hardly visible through Gábor Zoboki's architecture, it has been celebrated, for example, by naming the National Concert Hall after one of Hungary's greatest composers and by the choice of presented theater plays, concerts, and works of art.

A similar attempt—known as *Mediaspree*—to (re)develop the river bank for corporate, media, and cultural purposes have been made in Berlin; however, the initiative failed after the May 2008 referendum in which the residents of the most affected district, Kreuzberg-Friedrichshain—fearing gentrification and the loss of the free access to the river—voted against the new investments. The voting was preceded by countless demonstrations, art performances, and educational and cultural activities organized mainly by protesters grouped in the community initiative "Mediaspree versenken" (to sink the Mediaspree), started by architect Carsten Joost. Still, although the protests have successfully put most new developments on hold, several buildings on the Spree had been completed in the late 1990s and the 2000s. While some of them respect their surroundings and fit their designs in accordingly (e.g., the Radialsystem V, the MTV Central Europe Headquarters, the Oberbaum-City), others—such as, most notably, the O2 World indoor arena for sports, music, and other events—ignore the urban landscape around them and, therefore, provoke the most criticism.

The above observations are not to suggest, however, that only the extensions and modernized reconstructions of old buildings stay in tune with their neighborhoods or seek to express (desired) local or national identities through their architecture. Aside from several exceptions, the new cultural, educational, and entertainment buildings in Central European capitals generally attempt to aesthetically correspond to their surroundings. The 1999 University Library in Warsaw, for example, connects to its immediate vicinity and the nearby Vistula through its shape and colors as well as its roof garden. Designed by Marek Budzyński (the author of the impressive Supreme Court building in Warsaw, 1999), the library's green façade and ivy-covered walls call to mind the colors of the river and its surrounding flora. Technologically advanced, ecologically friendly, and sustainable, the University Library is among the most modern buildings in the capital. The lush garden covering its roof and spreading onto one of its sides turns the exterior of the building into a popular leisure area for students, Warsaw residents, and visitors—a rarity in a city notorious for its lack of attractive public spaces. Similarly, the new Philological Library of the Free University in Berlin combines aesthetic and functional qualities with concern for the environment. The 2005 building designed by Norman Foster relies on natural energies. Whereas the exterior of the library calls to mind the Reichstag cupola, the interior resembles the wavy architecture of the modernist Shell building on the Landwehrkanal (1932) and relates to both new and older local architecture. Although Foster's creation stands out as the most prominent on the campus, it does not dominate the surrounding buildings, but rather completes them as the chief organ of the whole body: soon after its completion the library received a nickname, "the Berlin Brain."

Glass, the construction material so enthusiastically used in Berlin's political buildings, has also been important part of the city's post-1989 cultural buildings. Whereas in most cases the use of glass for a library, a museum (German Museum of Technology, 2003), or a gallery (Contemporary Fine Arts, 2007) can be explained as an aesthetic or ecological preference or simply an international trend, in the case of the 2005 Academy of Arts (*Akademie der Künste*) the glass façade takes on a symbolic meaning, just like the transparent walls of the parliamentary buildings. Located near the Brandenburg Gate, the Academy of Arts stands out on Pariser Platz precisely because of its untypical façade: while all the surrounding buildings, including Hotel Adlon, Frank Gehry's DZ-Bank and Christian de Portzamparc's French Embassy, followed Planwerk Innenstadt's strict rules regarding the choice of construction materials, the height, and the window percentage (below fifty), the façade of the Academy of Arts is an enormous wall of glass. Berlin's senator for construction allowed for the exception from the rule only after several alterations of the project had been submitted. Although it is not mentioned in the senator's official statement (see Senatsverwaltung für Stadtentwicklung Berlin, "Änderungsverfahren"), glass as a symbol of transparency is of particular importance here because of the shady history of the building's predecessor. Before and during the war, Hitler's chief architect Albert Speer had his offices in the old Academy of Arts on Pariser Platz and was frequently visited by the Führer, whose Chancellery was located within walking distance, on the other side of the neighboring Ministerial Gardens, where the Holocaust Memorial is today.

Still, aside from its symbolical and cultural meanings, glass is primarily considered a modern and visually attractive construction material and has been generously used in post-1989 Central European capitals and elsewhere in the world. The opening of the hitherto centralized and Soviet-dependent markets to global capital has drawn foreign investors to Central Europe. Since socialist office space was, for the most part, poorly designed and lacked what the Western companies considered basic infrastructure and since, especially in the early 1990s, the demand for offices was much greater than the supply, (international) developers started building new offices that would meet international (meaning Western) standards (see Sýkora, "Office Development"). Importantly, while foreign investors were interested exclusively in centrally located office space, which they considered particularly prestigious and economically safe, domestic companies, familiar with the "urban ecology" of Central European cities, "could squeeze in segments where they were not directly outbid by stronger foreign capital" (Sýkora, "Office Development" 120-21). Consequently, not only did the downtown areas of Berlin, Budapest, Prague, and Warsaw become instantly commercialized, but they were also Westernized and globalized. New subsidiaries, representative offices, and regional headquarters of foreign companies dominated the architecture and the entire urban lifestyle in the center including the emergence of bistros and restaurants specializing in business lunches and dinners as well as chain stores selling coffee to go. By the 2000s, several central business districts (CBD)—styled, to a large extent, after London's City, New York's Wall Street, and Frankfurt's *Bankviertel*—emerged in Central European capitals, including Potsdamer Platz and parts of Friedrichstrasse in Berlin, the area around the Palace of Culture and Science as well as parts of Mokotów in Warsaw, parts of Smíchov and Pankrác in Prague, and the Millennium City Center in Budapest.

Despite globalization-induced changes in business and finance sectors, the importance of "the CBD remains a key form of centrality" (Sassen, "Locating Cities" 13). Also, as Sassen observes, the last few decades brought about "a new architecture of centrality that represented and housed new forms of economic power—that is, the hyperspace of international business; witness the corporate towers, corporate hotels, and world-class airports that have constituted a new geography of the built environment of centrality" (Sassen, "New Centrality" 208-09). Post-1989 Central European CBDs share many similarities with one another as well as with CBDs in other parts of the world. The new office buildings, hotels, and shopping malls appear uniform: they are made of the same materials, often designed by the same architects, and built by the same construction companies. Another thing they have in common are their English names: the Twin Towers, the Sony Center, and the Bahn Tower in Berlin; the Duna Tower, the West End, and the Capital Square in Budapest; the Danube House, the Nil House, and the rest of the River City Prague; the Warsaw Financial Center, and the Warsaw Trade Center, to name only a few.

When compared to their counterparts in global cities, the Central European CBDs are relatively small-scale. Among them, Warsaw has the largest number of high-rise buildings. Although the 231-meter tall Palace of Culture and Science remains the tallest building in the Polish capital, it is gradually being surrounded by other high-rises: the Warsaw Trade Tower (208 m), the Rondo 1-B (159 m), the Warsaw Financial Center (144 m), and the TP S.A. Tower (122 m). Warsaw's vertical obsession results both from Manhattan-inspired ambitions and an urge to hide the Stalinist edifice. In comparison, although Prague is known as "the city of a hundred spires," its buildings hardly ever exceed 100 meters; the tallest post-1989 building in Prague is the 80-meter tall Lighthouse Vltava Waterfront Tower in Holešovice. Even the most famous construction site of the 1990s, Potsdamer Platz, did not produce any skyscrapers: the Bahn Tower is 94 meters tall. In Budapest, St. Stephen's Basilica and the Parliament remain the tallest buildings, while the modern Duna Tower is only 64 meters tall. The height of buildings is determined by specific laws that differ from city to city. As these examples demonstrate, Warsaw's regulations regarding new architecture are much more liberal than those in the other Central European capitals.

Other prominent investments in and around CBDs, often (re)defining whole neighborhoods, include hotels and shopping centers. Although some international hotel chains had been present in Central European capitals before 1989, it was not until the fall of the Wall that these cities experienced a surge of InterContinentals, Hiltons, Sheratons, and Westins. The new hotels are particularly tall in Warsaw; in

Budapest, Berlin, and Prague their height is more moderate and adjusted to the surroundings. Although modern and uniform structures of glass and concrete remain
popular, a new trend has been observed since the late 1990s, namely, the re-emer-
gence of historical hotels such as the Adlon in Berlin and the Grand in Prague. In
many of these cases it is an international hotel corporation that buys an old hotel and
finances the renovation works, adding a famous historical object to its offer. When
it comes to shopping centers, two main developments can be distinguished: while
the shopping malls in the outskirts and noncentral districts are designed according to the laws of international uniformity (i.e., cubic structured resembling small
airports), those located downtown often impress viewers with their architecture and
technologies, such as the *Galerie Lafayette* in Berlin, the *Zlatý Anděl* (Golden Angel) in Prague, and the *Złote Tarasy* (Golden Terraces) in Warsaw. These and other
developments clearly demonstrate that Central European cities have been attaching
increasing importance to their downtown areas, often at the cost of neglecting other
districts. Berlin's new shopping mall, *Alexa,* is a notable exception: its enormous,
windowless, and nondescript pink structure violates the already aesthetically chal-
lenged Alexanderplatz on which it is located.

Huyssen notes that "in the move from the city as a regional or national center of production to the city as international center of communications, media, and
services, the very image of the city itself becomes central to its success in a globally
competitive world" (60). Since "visibility equals success" (Huyssen 60), Berlin, Budapest, Prague, and Warsaw strive to stand out both among their neighbors and in the
global arena. Aside from their urban images communicated in and through the media
(see chapter 4), these capitals increasingly concentrate on the aesthetic side of their
centers, trying to make them visually attractive and interesting first to prospective
visitors and investors and only then to residents. Huyssen's observations on the architectural developments in Berlin may as well be applied to Budapest, Prague, and
Warsaw: "The major concern with developing and rebuilding key sites in the heart
of Berlin seems to be image rather than usage, attractiveness for tourists and official
visitors rather than heterogeneous living space for Berlin's inhabitants, erasure of
memory rather than its imaginative preservation. The new architecture is to enhance
the desired image of Berlin as capital and global metropolis of the twenty-first century, as a hub between Eastern and Western Europe, and as a center of corporate
presence, however limited that presence may in the end turn out to be" (60).

In an attempt to increase their global competitiveness, importance, and recognition, Central European capitals readily approve of investors inviting world-famous architects—dubbed, somewhat sarcastically, starchitects—to build landmark
structures and help elevate the cities to international fame. Some of the starchitects
who have worked in Central European cities after 1989 include David Chipperfield
(Parkside Apartments, 2004; Contemporary Fine Arts, 2007; the reconstruction of
the Neues Museum, 2009—all in Berlin), Norman Foster (the Reichstag restoration,
1999, and the Free University Philological Library, 2005, in Berlin and the Metropolitan Building in Warsaw, 2003), Frank Gehry (the DZ-Bank in Berlin, 2000,

and the Dancing House in Prague, 1995), Helmut Jahn (the Sony Center, 2000; the Neues Kanzler Eck, 2001—both in Berlin), Rem Koolhaas (the Dutch Embassy in Berlin, 2003), Daniel Libeskind (the Jewish Museum in Berlin, 1999 and the Złota 44 Building in Warsaw, 2008-), Jean Nouvel (Galerie Lafayette in Berlin, 1995, and the Zlatý Anděl in Prague, 2001), Renzo Piano (Potsdamer Platz in Berlin, 2000), and I.M. Pei (the extension of the German Historical Museum in Berlin, 2003).

The cities that invite starchitects to work for them clearly hope for the so-called "Bilbao effect": Frank Gehry's Guggenheim Museum in Bilbao has not only attracted millions of visitors ever since it was created in 1997, but also, importantly, "in its first three years . . . helped generate about $500 million in economic activity and about $100 million in new taxes" (Rybczynski). Paradoxically, however, the buildings designed by a handful of signature architects to attract crowds of international visitors "have made cities around the world look similar" (Short and Kim 76) and therefore less attractive to tourists looking for "authentic" urban experiences. The architecture critic Witold Rybczynski notes several other problems concerning such "show-dog architecture": first, starchitects have built their reputation "almost entirely by participating in competitions"; second, their architecture is "unlikely to pay much attention to its surroundings"; and third, "the 'wow factor' may excite the visitor and the journalist, but it is a shaky foundation on which to build lasting value" (Rybczynski). Although Rybczynski foresaw an eventual surfeit in starchitecture as early as 2002, as of 2009, Central European capitals still seemed to linger under the spell of famous names.

Undoubtedly, the postsocialist architectural and spatial transformations of Central European cities have been substantially driven by globalization and, I argue, possess a strongly (post)colonial character. Soviet(-imposed) ideology has been replaced by the free market as the main force behind urban developments. One of the most poignant examples illustrating how promptly the old (Soviet) colonizer was replaced by the new one (Western or global capital) and what type of unexpected hybrid situations this development has created is Huyssen's description of the historically loaded Checkpoint Charlie in Berlin "being turned into an American business center watched over, temporarily, by a towering photographic cutout of Philip Johnson and a shrunken, gilded Statue of Liberty placed atop the former East German watchtower" (53).

To conclude, the post-1989 urban identities of Central European capitals are being (re)shaped both by the cities' obsession with history and by their often uncritical willingness to absorb new, mostly corporate-driven, architecture. The remnants of the socialist past such as prefabricated apartment and office buildings continue to exist side by side with newly renovated nineteenth-century tenement houses and modern office buildings, creating a fragmented and aesthetically diverse urban landscape. The inescapable juxtaposition of pre- and post-1989 elements creates surprising and ambivalently symbolic combinations such as the monumental McDonald's restaurant overlooking the neighboring Palace of Cultures and Science in Warsaw. Interestingly, as my analysis demonstrates, recent urban transformations in Central

Europe have been substantially determined by the scale of the destruction caused by World War II. Whereas Budapest and Prague were able to keep large parts of their urban landscapes intact and preserve many elements of their long urban histories, Berlin and Warsaw had to be thoroughly rebuilt and, given the political situation, followed a Soviet-imposed image of what a city should look like. Berlin and Warsaw, then, had to reinvent themselves in 1945 and then again in 1989, which has lead to spatial confusion, countless architectural and aesthetic hybrids, palimpsests, and a specific obsession with cultural heritage and its commemoration. All these and other aspects of the newly (re)discovered urban identities have been communicated in works of literature and film, which I discuss in detail in the following chapters.

Chapter Six

Post-1989 Literary Representations of Berlin and Warsaw

Literature has proven to be important in the analysis of urban cultures for a number of reasons. First, the development of the modern city has had a tremendous impact on literary forms from Charles Baudelaire's writings on Paris to James Joyce's portrayal of Dublin to Bret Easton Ellis' Los Angeles and New York novels, to name only few obvious examples. Since the experience of modernity and the urban experience are nearly synonymous (see, e.g. Berman, *All That Is Solid*; Simmel), writers compelled to express the condition of contemporary men and women have been naturally drawn to cities. Second, the city has been compared to a poem (see, e.g., Barthes) and the act of walking through the city has been likened to the act of writing (see de Certeau), which suggests that literature offers itself as a forum for a description and interpretation of urban phenomena. Third, as Roland Barthes notes, in order to deliver an all encompassing analysis of urban cultures, "the most important thing is not so much to multiply investigations or functional studies of the city as to multiply the readings of the city, of which, unfortunately, till now, only the writers have given us some examples" (201). Arguably, the city appears most fascinating and inspiring in its moments of social upheaval and transition.

Whereas, undeniably, all Central European capitals have been in many different ways affected by post-1989 transformations, the previous chapters demonstrate that changes in urban landscapes, societies, and cultures have been particularly substantial and widespread in Berlin and Warsaw. The exceptional position of these two cities derives partly from the fact that their urban identities are shaped predominantly by the historical events of the twentieth century (the terror and destruction of the Second World War and the postwar urban reconstruction conducted in compliance with the Soviet regime), while Budapest and Prague define themselves largely through the architectural and cultural achievements of their golden age, that is, the late nineteenth century and the early twentieth century, when the metropolises were part of the Habsburg empire. The impact of post-1989 transformations on the urban landscape has been powerful in Berlin and Warsaw because of the cities' characteristic voids and the countless new urban planning opportunities they entailed. Unsurprisingly, the significant changes the German and Polish capitals have experienced since the fall of communism have proven inspirational for various artists both from within and from outside the region, resulting in countless works of literature, film, visual and performing arts, and music. In this chapter, I discuss how Berlin and Warsaw have been represented in contemporary literature, and in the next chapter I focus on the cities' post-1989 film portrayals. I have chosen to analyze those selected works that, in my opinion, most extensively thematize the (post)colonial urban reality.

Despite the number and variety of aspects of urban life present in literary representations of Berlin and Warsaw, it is possible to distinguish several recurring themes. Contemporary authors have been particularly conscious of economic transformations and how they affect the residents: capitalism, consumerism, and globalization or Westernization have been repeatedly criticized in post-1989 novels both in (post)colonial and other contexts. Similarly, the social transformations resulting from the new economic system, such as polarization, new class divisions, and disparities between the winners and the losers in these momentuous changes are prominently featured in contemporary works of literature set in Berlin and Warsaw. Both cities attract newcomers and their magnetism has been conveyed in literature although, arguably, more so in the case of the novels set in Berlin than those that take place in Warsaw. Clearly, the ambivalent literary portrayals of both cities relate only partly, if at all, to the official images of Berlin and Warsaw communicated through municipal media as discussed in chapter 4.

As for the theoretical framework of this chapter, the empiric and systemic theories as well as Steven Tötösy de Zepetnek's comparative cultural studies appear particularly well equipped to analyze the literary representations of Central European urbanities. As discussed in chapter 2, literature is one of many types of media and remains in close relation not only to other print media such as newspapers, magazines, and journals, but also to electronic audiovisual media such as television, film, and the internet. After 1989, Central European literatures have been increasingly interweaving and overlapping with film, television, and the new media—partly because of post-1989 economic and social changes and partly because of worldwide technological progress and globalization. Siegfried J. Schmidt's empirical study of literature is not interested in literature in the traditional or hermeneutic sense, but rather in "social system 'literature'" ("Empirical Study of Literature" 141), that is, the psychological, social, cultural, political, and other contexts in which literature exists. Similarly, comparative cultural studies focuses on the study of culture both in parts (e.g., literature, film, television, the internet) and as a whole, "in relation to other forms of human expression and activity and in relation to other disciplines in the humanities and social sciences" (Tötösy de Zepetnek, "Constructivism and Comparative Cultural Studies" 8). Furthermore, since Central European urban cultures may—and, I argue, should—be considered (post)colonial, a postcolonial analysis of their literary representations is both viable and necessary.

Post-1989 economic order and its impact on the city

One of the most widespread phenomena resulting directly from the introduction of the market economy in 1989 and 1990 has been the prevalence and ubiquity of US-American-style malls. Unknown under the Soviet-imposed regimes, multipurpose shopping centers that opened in (the former East) Berlin and Warsaw in the 1990s were at first perceived mainly as outposts of the West and, thus, a status symbol for those who frequented them. Very soon, however, they became commonplace and generally regarded as inherent in—even if not necessarily considerate of—the urban landscape. A humorous description of a Berlin shopping mall can be found in Wladimir Kaminer's collection of short stories titled *Schönhauser Allee* (2001). Wladimir and Juri are immigrants from the former Soviet Union who have made post-1989 Berlin their home; one day they decide to visit the *Schönhauser Arkaden*—the new shopping center located on the title street—in order to investigate whether capitalism has a human face. "Juri claimed one couldn't get anything for free in capitalism, everything had its price and for this reason cynicism has been celebrated as the only correct attitude toward life. I objected and said it is exactly in capitalism that everything is for free and this is why young people here are so romantic and dreamy" (Kaminer 27). Their mock research turns out successful: "Both of us ended up loaded with all possible things. Juri had a big yellow balloon, a box of crayons, five paper plates, a lollipop, and a Shiseido anti-wrinkle cream tester. I managed to capture about 200 gram of *Mettwurst*, a green balloon, five *Kabinett mild* cigarettes, an Escada perfume tester, and a half-warm pretzel" (Kaminer 27). On the surface then, capitalism appears harmless or even people-friendly and, thus, dramatically different from what Wladimir and Juri learned about it in their Soviet schools. Clearly, Kaminer laughs both at the contempt for capitalism he grew up with and at the boundless devotion to consumerism he experiences in post-1989 Berlin. Juggling stereotypes and seemingly naïve observations, the author of *Schönhauser Allee* presents a satire on contemporary urban society obsessed with shopping and entertainment.

Kaminer returns to the Schönhauser Arkaden several times in his collection. At one point, Wladimir assumes that thousands of people could live there for a hundred years and they would never need anything from the outside world, to which he adds: "Actually, many already live here—in any case, one sees the same faces here all the time" (Kaminer 63). The author criticizes Berliners' consumerism, but also acknowledges the bigger framework and the purposefully addictive nature of the ubiquitous "new gigantic shopping centers" where people "learn the consumption pleasures of the future" (Kaminer 63). The malls lure visitors with the promise of achieving a state of absolute fulfillment, a sort of consumerist paradise, where "everything for everyone" (*alles für alle*) is the house rule (Kaminer 63). Kaminer reminds us that apart from their numbing impact on consumers, the new shopping centers root out small retailers and, thus, affect neighborhood structures and urban landscapes. Still, on Schönhauser Alle one finds time and again "courageous shop owners who enter the hopeless fight against big corporations" (Kaminer 38). Although their attempts to survive in a market dominated by international corporate giants are undeniably doomed, in Prenzlauer Berg small entrepreneurs continue their quest to make a living in hard economic conditions: interestingly, they are all immigrants who have a limited knowledge of German, cannot rely on state support, and are forced to start their own businesses in order to survive. In Kaminer's short stories, the shop owners from the former Yugoslavia and Vietnam are both warriors and jesters.

Whereas Kaminer adds a humorous tone to the debate about growing consumerism and the dubious nature of the malls, Ulrich Peltzer takes a more serious stance. His 2007 novel *Teil der Lösung* (Part of the Solution) starts at Potsdamer Platz. After the fall of the Wall, the city focused on rebuilding the square and giving it back the glamour, style, and liveliness it possessed during the Weimar Republic. Instead of becoming Berlin's cultural and social center, however, Potsdamer Platz turned into one of the city's malls. Peltzer's narrator laments what the square has become and notes that it looked more impressive and interesting while it was still under construction. "Later it all changed and all you could see was a flaunty downtown district created in record time, shopping malls and hotels next to corporate administration centers, and underground parking lots connected to the shopping areas with soundless elevators" (Peltzer 14). Additionally, ubiquitous surveillance cameras and security guards have rendered Potsdamer Platz devoid of any properties of public space. As a matter of fact, together with its rise from the ashes, the legendary square has ceased to belong to Berliners: "This is no public space," a security guard tells a group of performers, "These are private premises" (Peltzer 16).

Although dominated by corporate property and culture, the Potsdamer Platz is still financially accessible to many Berliners and tourists alike. The same cannot be said of the new upscale shopping centers on Friedrichstrasse such as Galeries Lafayette and Quartier 206. The latter is described by Peltzer as a temple of excess: "Moschino, Louis Vuitton, Commes des Garcons, Yohji Yamamoto, Dries van Noten, Etro, Celine, Strenesse, Donna Karan, the foundations and window edges were made of black marble and identical golden letters spelled the names of the companies whose products you could get here, or simply admire . . . Three floors, three galleries, a lavish areaway, stairways and escalators intertwined like in Maurits Escher's pictures. In the basement there was an open café with a grand piano where a pianist dressed in suit and tie sat from morning till night and tickled away" (Peltzer 287-88). This "sophisticated dramaturgy" (288), acquirable only to the rich, is strongly guarded by security personnel and countless cameras that register the movements and sounds of all visitors. In *Teil der Lösung*, Peltzer repeatedly criticizes not only the gradual disappearance of public space, but also the ubiquity of both state and corporate surveillance in Berlin. More literary descriptions and criticism of the impeding commercialization of the urban space and prevalent consumerism may be found, for example, in Kathrin Röggla (*Irres Wetter*) and Andre Kubiczek (*Die Guten und die Bösen*).

Next to the emergence of countless shopping malls and the impeding commercialization of urban space, the introduction of capitalism in 1989 and 1990 has affected the work culture of Berlin and Warsaw residents. Under the socialist regime, the most common office hours in Warsaw were 7 am to 3 pm (and they hardly ever extended to overtime), leaving white-collar workers whole afternoons to spend with their families. The main meal of the day (*obiad*) would take place about four o'clock when both the children released from school and the adults who just finished work could sit together at the table. With the arrival of Western-style companies, the popular Anglo-Saxon work model was introduced and most office workers and their families had to adapt to 9-to-5 jobs. The seemingly trivial change has influenced various areas of life of Warsaw's residents, including their eating habits. The midday meal, formerly associated with home or family, has shifted both in time (usual lunch hours in Warsaw are noon to 2 pm) and in space (from the kitchen table to a canteen or a business lunch restaurant) and has contributed to the growing uniformization of urban life. These changes are mirrored in several scenes of Krzysztof Varga's 2007 apocalyptic novel *Nagrobek z lastryko* (Terrazzo Tombstone).

Set in Warsaw of the future, the story repeatedly returns to contemporary times—that is, the first decade of the twenty-first century—and to the city already immersed in Western corporate standards. In one of the scenes, the narrator's grandfather, Piotr Paweł, a white-collar worker in one of Warsaw's high-rise office buildings, enters the cafeteria and looks around at "the tables where the corporate Warsaw is sitting and humming: colleagues from his office, strangers from the office below, and strangers from the office above. Even the plates with 19,99 lunch menu are more diverse because you can have them in green, orange, or yellow. And you can have spaghetti, lasagna, or chicken salad, so there is choice" (Varga, *Nagrobek* 80). Varga points not only at the banality of corporate life and the repetitiveness of everyday rituals, but also at the limitedness of real choices hidden under the pretence of colorful variety. Further, the author thematizes the prevalent urban haste resulting from deadlines at work and at home (which is a popular phenomenon in Warsaw, among many other metropolises, but largely absent in Berlin), the constant rush that lies at the bottom of failed relationships and countless disorders: "After all, time is most important. It is better to resign from having a meal altogether rather than to lose time, better to lose some weight in result of not eating a meal, even if lunch in this cafeteria is low in calories, fat, flour, and carbs" (80-81). In *Nagrobek*, all passages thematizing the Western- or global-style corporate culture and its participants are satirical.

A critique of the many ways in which globalization affects Central European capitals can be also found in Röggla's *Irres Wetter* (Strange Weather, 2000). The Austrian author based in Berlin takes a sarcastic stance both when it comes to these phenomena and the terminology used to describe them. In the late 1990s, next to *Wendegewinner* (winners of the *Wende*, or the 1989-1990 transformations—for more on the term "Wende" see, e.g., Reimann 22-26), *Globalisierungsgewinner* (winners of globalization) became another word to describe those few who have managed to profit from the new socioeconomic situation. Although they represent various professions, Globalisierungsgewinner tend to frequent the same places such as international airports, designer boutiques, and trendy restaurants. Röggla's narrator encounters them at Hackesche Höfe in Mitte: a complex of interconnected court-yards in the former Jewish neighborhood; neglected during the city division and completely renewed after the fall of the Wall, the yards are now home to restaurants, bars, theaters, and designer boutiques. The presence of Globalisierungsgewinner in the largely poor city strikes the narrator as unbelievable: "yes, *globalisierungsge-winner*: you would never think so, but they actually exist, right here among us. you can touch them, you can talk to them, sometimes they even respond" (Röggla 43; original spelling without capital letters). The rare occurrence of Globalisierungsge-winner in Berlin not only lends them the status of an endangered species, but also makes it clear that most Berliners have not been able to fully adapt to the recent transformations.

Wende-winners and Wende-losers in urban space

The division of urban societies into winners and losers of post-1989 transformations is one of the most widespread themes in contemporary novels set in Berlin and War-saw. The relatively few characters identified as winners are mostly representatives of the new media, politics, and—especially in the case of Warsaw—big international corporations, that is, part of the new establishment. Interestingly, their literary rep-resentations usually suggest that Wende-winners have profited from the economic and social transformations only on the surface, while inside they tend to be insecure, cynical, decadent, or emotionally and morally crippled. The literary portrayals of urban Wende-losers are much more common than those of Wende-winners and may be subdivided into three categories: the ordinary unsuccessful people, the pathologi-cal underdogs, and—a relatively new phenomenon—the well-educated precariate.

    The contemporary novels set in Berlin and Warsaw repeatedly criticize or ridi-cule those who have managed to take advantage of the post-1989 economic situa-tion. An arguably small part of the urban societies, the media, political, and business establishment, is presented in literature as greedy, vain, and not particularly smart. Furthermore, the Wende-winners are often associated with Western culture and capi-tal—either because they represent it (West Germans in the former East Berlin), or because they are enthusiastically devoted to it (Polish businesspeople in Warsaw) and are portrayed as ruthless and taking advantage of the less fortunate fellow city residents. In *Die Guten und die Bösen* (The Good and the Evil, 2004), Kubiczek juxtaposes the Westerners, who came to Berlin after the fall of the Wall, with those who had lived in the city before, particularly the former East Berliners. One of Ku-biczek's protagonists, Zampano Dunkel, a forty-something West German, comes to the reunited city for a job interview and meets his future wife Nadine on his "first visit *over there*": "he decided against booking a hotel room in the Western *City* and went to the East with an ethnologist's curiosity. . . . At first he thought the hotel he ended up at was called AST, but then he noticed that the other neon letters were dam-aged" (24-25). Zampano's hotel is located on Kastanienallee, one of the main streets in Prenzlauer Berg, still run down in the early 1990s, but nicknamed Castingallee by the mid-2000s because of the many outdoor cafes and hip designer boutiques. Back in the first years following the demise of communism, Kastanienallee as well as other centrally located parts of the former East Berlin were home to "dozens of half-legal and illegal clubs in musty basements and wrecked factories" (Kubiczek 26). Immersed in the avant-garde milieu of the new Berlin, Nadine earns her living as a part-time receptionist at the dilapidated hotel where Zampano encounters her and instantly falls in love: "in the West, he has not seen such a natural and fresh woman in a long time" (Kubiczek 26; Kubiczek uses the word "unverbraucht," which also translates into English as unused or unconsumed).

To Zampano, Nadine is a fascinating Other, an East Berlin princess, irresist-ible owing to her affiliation with a world hitherto unknown to the West German busi-nessman. Clearly, Zampano's sinister personality is suggested already through his name, which refers to the protagonist of Federico Fellini's *La Strada* (1954) played by Anthony Quinn—a violent alpha male, who buys Gelsomina (Giulietta Masina) from her impoverished family, and after repeated instances of abuse, abandons her. Furthermore, in Kubiczek's novel, Zampano's last name is Dunkel, which means "dark," and, thus, encourages the reader to anticipate the West German to be abso-lutely evil. Importantly, to Nadine, Zampano is also an Other: different from the men she knows from underground clubs and illegal bars, Zampano impresses her with his West German exoticism and also, undoubtedly, with his money and career. Al-though Nadine's comfortable life in Charlottenburg is obviously far from Gelsomi-na's doomed fate, Fellini's Zampano and Kubiczek's Zampano are similar in that they both buy their women. If we take the comparison one step further, it becomes clear that in *Die Guten und die Bösen* Zampano stands for the strong and powerful West Germany who buys the poor, but somehow oddly attractive East Germany. Kubic-zek's humorous and exaggerated play on cultural associations and symbols reveals some of the truths about the relationships between the former East Berliners and the West Germans who are often identified and represented in contemporary literature as Wende-losers and Wende-winners, respectively.

Whereas Kubiczek portrays the Wende-winners as seemingly powerful and frightening, but in fact laughable, the novels set in Warsaw tend to present them as downright pathetic or detestable. In Dorota Masłowska's satire on Warsaw and its society, *Paw królowej* (The Queen's Peacock), the reader is confronted with the dual, often conflicting nature of the local establishment. Received to large critical acclaim and distinguished with a Nike (Poland's highest literary prize), the 2005 novel strips the media and business elites—as well as, importantly, the intellectual circles—of their attractive packaging and demolishes the myths about Warsaw's Wende-win-ners. *Paw królowej*'s narrator—and the author's namesake—acknowledges the role and meaning of Warsaw as Poland's business, media, political, and cultural center that continues to fascinate people in provincial towns and villages. The novel is writ-ten in slang and heavily stylized, at times resembling a hip-hop song, which renders translation particularly difficult. The author laughs at the virtual world of media and the public image of celebrities that has little to do with reality. One of the protago-nists, Stanisław Retro, a pop singer and idol of teenage girls, is undergoing a serious breakdown when his career slows down and popularity decreases. Addicted to fame, Stanisław is ready to sacrifice everything including his mental integrity to make his way back to the tabloid front pages. In the unstable world of celebrity fame, where everything, even—or rather, especially—private life is for sale, success lasts only as long as there are interested buyers.

Apart from the glossy magazines and celebrity banquets, Masłowska is also critical of Warsaw's intellectual and artistic circles, which she describes as vain, arrogant, and lacking substance: "nothing is happening, but turn on the camera, we will camerize you and you will camerize us camerizing you and standing around and saying nothing to each other" (Masłowska, *Paw królowej* 14). Partly reminiscent of Andy Warhol's Factory, partly of a high school party, the art gathering caricaturized by Masłowska does not strike the reader as specific to Warsaw, as such happen-ings look similar in most cities around the world; what is important, however, is that the author includes the real names of places, artists, and curators and therefore adds authenticity to the portrayal of Warsaw artistic elites. Significantly, Sławomir Sierakowski, one of Warsaw's most prominent young intellectuals, appears in *Paw królowej* in a recurring scene, in which he expresses his surprise at the conditions in which the narrator and her family live. Visiting (fictional?) Dorota Masłowska's apartment in a run down part of Praga, Sierakowski exclaims in shock: "you live here?!" (Masłowska, *Paw królowej* 45).

Next to the caricatural portrayals of Wende-winners, a large part of Masłowska's novel concentrates on the working and unemployed poor inhabiting the dilapidated tenement houses in Praga. Interested in the exaggerated rather than in the average, the author forces the reader to look closely at dysfunctional relationships, alcohol and drug abuse, and other pathological behavior she observes among those who have not been able to learn how to profit from the post-1989 changes. In *Paw królowej*, drunkards sleep in gateways and on the pavement during the day and get into violent fights at night, but the police are reluctant to intervene and remain oblivious to the fate of Praga residents. The narrator's neighbors "rake through a strange avalanche of garbage" in the backyard (Masłowska, *Paw królowej* 12), alcohol stores abound, "fa-ther killed mother while the son was only holding her" (Masłowska, *Paw królowej* 19), loud screams echo in gateways, and the whole micro world of Praga is presented as apocalyptic and dystopian.

Inka Parei's *Schattenboxerin* (The Shadow Wrestler), published a decade af-ter the fall of the Wall, also thematizes the fate of the people living on the edge of society—and also on the edge of town—excluded from everyday life of the city describing itself as vibrant, diverse, and modern. Unlike Masłowska, however, who satirically examines the grotesque and absurd, Parei opts for sheer realism and de-votes an entire chapter to the description of living conditions of the former East Berlin factory workers made redundant after the collapse of communism. März, who as a child emigrated to West Germany with his mother, comes back to Berlin to search for his father. His only clue is a photograph of his father standing in front of an old Gründerzeit factory. Together with the novel's main protagonist, Hell, März arrives at the scene known from the picture and is amazed at how little has changed over the years, as if the economic and social transformations never reached this part of Berlin. Soon they discover, however, that the whole traditionally working-class neighborhood has deteriorated badly: "Many houses are empty. The windows are nailed up with crossed bars, the doors walled up" (Parei 135) and the people are left with no work and grim perspectives. Near a supermarket, Hell and März encounter a few people carrying their shopping items in black briefcases, "the type of briefcases, in which working men carry thermos jugs and sandwiches, but these people do not work, they look poor, aimless, and tired" (Parei 136). März's father turns out to be unemployed: he has succumbed to alcoholism, and lives in a backyard of a dilapidated Mietskaserne, where garbage piles up to the second floor and babies cry all day (Parei 137-39). After he sees his father's deeply wrinkled face, empty eyes, and trembling hands embracing a bottle, März runs away in terror and embarrassment. Without saying a word, he throws a stack of Deutschmarks into the mailbox marked with his father's name and hurries away to the next tram stop to escape the scene.

Aside from descriptions of urban pathologies, post-1989 novels set in Berlin and Warsaw include more moderate portraits of Wende-losers. Jens Sparschuh's novel *Zimmerspringbrunnen* (Tabletop Fountain, 1995)—filmed by Peter Timm in 2001 (see chapter 7)—tells the story of Hinrich Lobek, an East Berliner who loses his job after the fall of the Wall and is unable to find a new one for another half decade. Unlike his wife, Hinrich fails to adjust to the post-1989 social, cultural, and economic situation. Instead, he grows bitter and thinks of himself as "the last Mohican" of East Berlin (Sparschuh 39). The constant changes in the city render him insecure and—to a comical effect—suspicious. "Even the address changed from one day to the next. One morning Friday [the dog] and I went for a walk and something was different. Then I noticed: secretly, overnight so to speak, we were moved out from our street. It had a different name now" (Sparschuh 38). Clearly upset, Hinrich continues his walk and whistles an old *Pionier* song to calm his nerves: "Everywhere you look new houses are being built . . ." (Sparschuh 29). Annoyed rather than excited about the new urban transformations, Hinrich expresses repeatedly his contempt for all post-1989 Western influences and complains that even the *Schrippen*—as Berliners call their bread rolls—taste and look different in reunited Berlin, like "imported windbags" (Sparschuh 39). The Wende has also changed Julia, Hinirch's wife, who now looks younger, more serious, and increasingly impatient with her husband's attitude. To Hinrich's dismay, one day over breakfast Julia tells him: "It is always convenient to place yourself on the side of the losers—then you're morally a winner!" (Sparschuh 39). Hinrich ends up thinking about her statement for months to come, but does not draw any conclusions.

Next to the "average" Wende-losers, who fail to swiftly adjust to post-1989 transformations, but somehow—often with the help of family and friends—manage to continue to function within the society, and the "pathological" Wende-losers, who are completely unable to come to terms with the new postcommunist social and economic order, in the last few years another group of urban losers emerges in contemporary novels set in Berlin and Warsaw: the educated poor. Importantly, their indigent condition is a result of the impending globalization processes on the one hand and the decline of the European postwar welfare state model on the other hand and, thus, only indirectly related to the post-1989 changes in Central Europe. Some of the most poignant portrayals of the modern "intelligentsia precariat" may be found in Ulrich Peltzer's *Teil der Lösung*, a multilayered novel about Berlin free-lancers, academics, and students intertwined with reflections on terrorism, the police state, and late capitalism.

Peltzer's protagonist, Christian, is a freelance journalist in his mid-thirties. Unable to find a magazine that would buy his elaborate story on the Italian terrorist movements of the late 1970s, he makes his (very modest) living on random restaurant and art reviews. Unable to pay the rent, he lives permanently-temporarily in his ex-girlfriend's disheveled Prenzlauer Berg apartment awaiting a complete renovation. Together with other freelancers, Christian shares an office space in one of Mitte's backyards and struggles to pay his monthly rent there as well. Despite his education, skills, and experience, the prospects for his career look fairly bleak. This does not make him exceptional among his friends: they all struggle to survive on a very basic level (defined, of course, by European standards). Christian's long-time friend Jakob is one of the very few from their social circle who is a salaried employee, but even his job as an assistant professor in the humanities department of Humboldt University pays barely enough for him to support himself and his family. Nele, Jakob's highly talented student with whom Christian falls in love, stays afloat thanks to her job as an archivist and—partly for financial, party for ideological reasons—by restricting her expenses to the few basic necessities. Also, Christian's acquaintances and colleagues from galleries, publishing houses, and the media live on tight budgets and happily frequent openings and parties where wine and beer are free. Although it is true that most bohemians and academics in humanities have never been well paid, what is so special about the described situation is its scope and frequency. In Berlin, the phenomenon of the "intelligentsia precariat" has become particularly widespread in the 2000s and inspired numerous academic and artistic responses, most notably René Pollesch's play *Tod eines Praktikanten* (Death of an Intern) that had its premiere at Volksbühne im Prater in 2007, the same year Peltzer's *Teil der Lösung* was published.

More often than not, Wende-winners and Wende-losers inhabit different parts of urban space and their paths rarely intersect. Still, since Berlin and Warsaw are relatively diverse cities—although, arguably, the former more so than the latter—the division lines are not clear and predictable, but rather vary depending on current social and economic developments. Prenzlauer Berg, for example, which used to be the enclave of East Berlin dissidents, artists, and intellectuals, turned in the 1990s into a haven for squatters and young independent artists from all over the world and in the 2000s further evolved into a clean bourgeois neighborhood for young families (mostly newcomers from western parts of Germany). Gentrification and other post-1989 urban developments in Berlin and Warsaw are described at length in contemporary prose and will be discussed below. What is also important and deserves mentioning here are the nuanced relations and borders between Wende-winners and Wende-losers. In some novels, those who appear to profit from the economic and social transformations are often portrayed as scheming, demoralized, or weak. In Tomasz Piątek's famous literary study of addiction *Heroina* (Heroin, 2002), drug addicts are not runaways, the homeless, or prostitutes, but young successful people, representatives of the budding middle class of post-1989 Warsaw. Although they occupy brand new computerized offices, suburban villas, and renovated downtown apartments, they are also well familiar with the city's backstage and underbelly: "The most beautiful thing is that hiding places emerge no matter where I go. About every ten meters there is a gate. Or an abandoned garage. Or a narrow overgrown path between two fences. Or an unguarded parking lot where I am completely invisible if I squat between the cars. . . . I didn't use to see all these places. They seemed to belong to no one. Now I know they are mine. I feel so good in each one of them that I could stay there forever" (Piątek 5).

Literary portrayals of post-1989 urban space

The changeability of the post-1989 urban space is a recurring theme in contemporary novels set in Berlin and Warsaw. Even if the renaming of the streets, constant renovations, and gentrification are not always discussed at length, they are clearly present. The changes in the postcommunist city text portrayed in new fiction are either seen as intrusive and disconcerting (as in the above quoted excerpt from Sparschuh's *Zimmerspringbrunnen*), or mocked as purely absurd as in Krzysztof Varga's collection *45 pomysłów na powieść* (45 Ideas for a Novel, 1998), in which he talks about Warsaw as a city that "looks much better today than it used to . . . although it is hard to believe it " (Varga, *45 pomysłów* 86) because it is still gray, chaotic, and unattractive (Varga, *45 pomysłów* 98). To Varga, the renaming of the streets follows a simple logic of exchanging the old for the new and is in sync with the character of most post-1989 urban transformations. "And so the street that yesterday was still named Hydrangea is Cosmic today, and the former Ancient Street has turned into Bright Future Street. It is hard not to get lost on the intersection of Mahogany and Eucalyptus when the street signs clearly inform you that it is actually Gnosis crossing New Age. And the square where I used to meet with girls as a teenager is no longer Marco Polo Square but Steven Spielberg Square" (Varga, *45 pomysłów* 86-87). The wholesale and often unreflective street renaming disrupts private memories of urban life before and after 1989 and leads to a creation of hybrid universes composed of real and imagined recollections.

Although at first generally desired and much needed, the renovation of old houses and the emergence of privately owned stores, restaurants, and bars have decidedly changed whole neighborhoods and, consequently, seriously interfered with their traditional character and demographics. Many of the former residents of Prenzlauer Berg have been forced to move to cheaper districts and their apartments and businesses have been taken over by newcomers from the West who are attracted to Berlin because of its uniqueness, but—paradoxically—do everything to render it similar to affluent and uniform West German towns. Wladimir Kaminer, who arrived in Prenzlauer Berg in the early 1990s, perceives gentrification as the inescapable arrival of a new era: "The 21st century is making itself visible on our street. A couple of years ago you could hardly spot it in the neighborhood. The main local attractions featured two and a half squatted houses, a movie theater, and a planetarium. . . . Already a copy store was considered an excessively progressive institution. But times have changed. Now our neighborhood is peppered with gourmet restaurants and fitness clubs, first contact doctors retrain themselves to psychoanalysts, the movie theater turned into a multiplex, in which you can watch ten films simultaneously, and many snack bars [*Imbissbuden*] have been replaced by internet cafes" (137).

Whereas Kaminer describes the post-1989 urban developments in Berlin in an ironic and humorous way, Inka Parei's literary account of gentrification is somber and dramatic. *Schattenboxerin*'s protagonist, Hell, is one of the last tenants of an old Mietskaserne in Mitte. She lives in a cold apartment in the side wing, with no bathroom and a shared toilet located in the staircase. "Before the beginning of winter, the last of the few remaining tenants had moved out, mostly somewhere near their relatives, to the Plattenbauten with central heating and garbage chutes, out to Marzahn or Hellersdorf" (Parei 7; Marzahn and Hellersdorf are districts in the former East Berlin dominated by large prefabricated housing complexes from the 1980s). Although the building is only beginning to be rebuilt, its fate—just like that of its former tenants—is clearly sealed. "It has been unlikely from the start that this dilapidated house would be simply forgotten while all the others have been successively renovated. It was foreseeable that I would not be able to hole up here forever with no rent contract, unknown to any administration, and unregistered" (Parei 9). Judging by the descriptions of the neighborhood, its houses and cafes, Parei's story is most likely taking place in the mid-1990s. Although the time is never specified, we learn that the district is inhabited by poor artists and students and the food prices in local bistros are still affordable to construction workers. At the same time, however, the first signs of gentrification are already visible: the same construction workers who have breakfast in newly emerged cafes are renovating the neighborhood Mietskasernen, in which they will be very unlikely able to afford the rent.

Peltzer and Kubiczek describe the same neighborhood about a decade later (in 2007 and 2004, respectively). In *Teil der Lösung*, the moderately priced cafes and bars in Mitte and in Prenzlauer Berg are extinct, the rents belong to the highest in Berlin, and convenience stores have been replaced by trendy art galleries. Kubiczek laments the loss of everyday normalcy in Mitte—(the former East) Berlin's downtown borough that has fallen "into the hands of yuppies, educated bourgeoisie, and their rank and file, who have turned the ground floors of whole blocks of houses into tapas bars rarely punctuated with stores, in which you could buy nothing but shimmering silver espresso machines" (*Die Guten* 191). This open contempt for gentrification and its culprits is widespread in post-1989 Berlin novels and varies only in form and intensity, but rarely in meaning. All of these authors are unanimously critical in their evaluation of recent urban developments. The image of Berlin as a city in constant flux is acknowledged by the local authors as true; however, unlike the municipal media, contemporary literature does not make it clear whether the changes are for the better. As Kathrin Röggla notes, a talk about the post-1989 transformations often proves to be little more than just a random collection of empty slogans: "this here is a real landscape of surprise (overbooked)! . . . a transient mood prevails! a store today will be a bar tomorrow. and the day after tomorrow—an office . . . every single thing in flux" (99). Also, the general progress hyped by the city authorities appears suspicious and—according to one of Kubiczek's characters—reminiscent of colonial practices. On entering the district of Mitte, Dr. Schwarzhaupt, an assistant professor at the Institute for African Studies at Humboldt University, engages himself in an inner monologue and angrily complains about "an imperialism that came to East Berlin and the rest of [the GDR] not with weapons, but with optimistic chatter and a good mood" (Kubiczek 164). Although clearly exaggerated, Schwarzhaupt is not merely comical, but also tragic in that, unlike other characters of *Die Guten und die Bösen*, he appears to have a broader understanding of the ongoing changes, but realizes he is unable to stop them from happening.

The transformations of Warsaw's landscapes have been discussed at length by, among others, Krzysztof Varga (*45 pomysłów na powieść, Nagrobek z lastryko*), Jerzy Pilch (*Miasto utrapienia*), and, probably most articulately, by Dorota Masłowska (*Paw królowej, Między nami dobrze jest*). In her 2005 novel, the author devotes much attention to the desolate condition of large parts of Praga, but—despite their hopelessness—values them more than the newly emerged housing estates for the rich(er). To the narrator, the dirty and not exactly safe streets of Praga appear more authentic than the residential oases: "Praga is my district and Okrzei is my street . . . I will not live with dickheads in a gated community" (Masłowska, *Paw królowej* 12). Importantly, whereas in *Paw królowej* those who are better off choose to live in brand new houses in the safer newly developed parts of Praga, in the 2008 play *Między nami dobrze jest* (It Is Going Well between Us) the rich are more aggressive and unscrupulously take over the living space of the poor. The second act starts with a description of an "elegant, stylish, fresh" (Masłowska, *Między nami* 42) man moving into a small studio apartment previously occupied by (the ghosts of?) a family of mother, daughter, and grandmother. Located in a prewar building, the apartment is attractive only because it is old—a rarity in the city nearly completely destroyed during World War II. The man moves in together with a "neat Ikea workers team" who deliver cardboard boxes of furniture and decoration (Masłowska, *Między nami* 42). The man is a successful screenwriter and representative of *bobos*—the bourgeois bohemian (see Brooks) the author blames for gentrification and its many disastrous effects. With his laptop, a bottle of expensive wine, and an unshaken belief in his own importance, the screenwriter is a caricature of the class of creative (or "creative") professionals, to which Actor and TV Host (who appear later in the play) also belong. To Masłowska, gentrification in Warsaw is closely connected with commercialization, "Ikeaization," and, therefore, uniformity.

The continuous transformations of urban life and landscapes are hardly perceived as positive in post-1989 literature—at best, they are presented as ambivalent, but are mostly associated with the negative influences of the Western or global capital and politics. Consequently, in contemporary novels, Berlin and Warsaw appear as (post)colonial cities that are still awkwardly developing their identities, whereby—next to these Western or global influences—the cultural heritage of years of Soviet-imposed communism continues to prove important. As the examples of Berlin's and Warsaw's urbanities demonstrate, Western and Eastern (post-Soviet) influences are not mutually exclusive: instead, they continuously intersect, resulting in mostly unexpected cultural hybrids and, thus, contribute to the eclectic character of both capitals. As Varga notes, Warsaw always "changes according to the directives of its subsequent architects"; these urban developments are not necessarily for the better and sometimes they change hardly anything at all: "instead of new houses, cardboard effigies were erected—at first glossy and pastel, but the rain and air pollution would soon render them pale, gray, and ugly, and once again they would have to be replaced by completely new ones. It all resembled a gigantic mockup, or inflatable tanks and planes of a great invasion army" (*45 pomysłów* 51). The concrete grayness of the communist period is replaced by the cardboard box grayness of the post-1989 era; therefore, the uniformity largely associated with the Soviet-imposed political and economic system prevails even after its demise.

Next to changeability and gentrification, other aspects of post-1989 Central European urban space discussed in literature include architectural eclecticism, the ubiquity of prefabricated buildings, and the void. Naturally, a coexistence of various architectural styles is typical for cities with long histories. What makes Berlin and Warsaw particularly interesting, however, is that the historic traces written in their urban landscapes are often interrupted or unreadable and many seemingly historic buildings are not what they appear to be. In Varga's opinion, Warsaw's architectural eclecticism seems inauthentic, especially when compared to cities with better preserved urban landscapes such as Budapest. In Warsaw, "everything is fake and forged, even houses pretend to be old and they are so good at pretending that many actually believe it"; in this "fake city . . . there are no real narrow alleys, there are only fake narrow alleys" (Varga, *Bildungsroman* 47). The author refers to the Old Town that was entirely destroyed during and after the Warsaw Uprising and—in accordance with old etchings, paintings, and urban plans that had survived the war— rebuilt from scratch in the late 1940s and early 1950s. Although impressively reconstructed, the Old Town still resembles a mockup rather than a real neighborhood and attracts mostly international tourists and school groups, but not regular Warsaw residents. The fake old buildings in Varga's *Bildungsroman* contrast with the genuinely prewar tenement house that provides the setting for Masłowska's *Między nami dobrze jest*. To make sure that no one confuses the abodes for a pile of garbage, the author reassures us that "this despairing mess is indeed a beautiful old prewar apartment" only that it has not been renovated "more or less since the war" (Masłowska, *Między nami* 40-41). Importantly, Masłowska points at the fate of many historical and mostly centrally located tenement buildings in Central European cities that were neglected after the war (see chapter 3) and after 1989 transformed into offices by and for Western or global capital, or, alternatively, renovated by the emerging class of bobos. Regardless of whether it is corporations or affluent private residents who purchase apartments in the old houses, the effect is always the same: the old tenants have to leave since they cannot afford the higher rents and costs of living in the gentrified neighborhood.

While prewar housing gained in attractiveness after 1989, the prefabricated apartment buildings have experienced an exodus. Before the fall of the Wall, the Plattenbauten were considered more attractive than the Mietskasernen because they were new and equipped with central heating and indoor bathrooms (see chapter 3). Apparently, in the decades following the end of the war, living in old buildings with shared outdoor bathrooms and tiled ovens was not particularly appealing to people seeking at least basic comfort (see Sparschuh). The thorough renovations of prewar tenement houses in Berlin and Warsaw have immediately increased their desirability (and market prices) and the few remaining drawbacks seem to possess a romantic quality. Kaminer's narrator, who grew up in a prefabricated apartment block on the outskirts of Moscow, is excited to "discover old buildings [*Altbauten*]" in Berlin and together with his wife, who also spent all her childhood and youth in a Soviet Plattenbau, become "the biggest fans" of the nineteenth-century Mietskasernen (Kaminer 169). Wladimir's parents, however, have problems understanding their love for old houses. "When my father comes over and sees the holes under the windowsill, the wooden floors eaten by bark beetles, and the flaking plaster on the facade, his eyes turn very round. 'Why are you doing this to yourselves? And for so much money at that? You could get a supernice apartment in a new building [*Neubauwohnung*] in Karow-Nord for a much lower price,' he always says" (Kaminer 169; Karow-Nord is the north-east district of the former East Berlin dominated by apartment blocks built with prefabricated parts).

Finding an affordable prewar apartment is easier in Berlin than in Warsaw, first, because of the scale of war destruction, which was much bigger in the Polish capital, and second, because Berlin—despite all optimistic expectations following the fall of the Wall—remains an underpopulated city. Consequently, many Warsaw residents are forced to stay in their Plattenbauten simply because they have no other place to go, as the few centrally located prewar houses are being turned into offices, galleries, and hotels and buying a house in the suburbs means not only large expenses, but also long commuting hours. Varga describes inhabitants of one communist housing block from the perspective of a neighboring prefabricated building; therefore, what the narrator sees may as well be a mirror reflection: "Or maybe it's really better not to leave? Maybe it's better to stay here, on this balcony, to smoke a cigarette and embrace a glass with the other hand, to look at the group of high-rises on the hill, and to move the knight across the squares of lit windows. Every minute one of them goes off, someone goes to bed with the hope of a relaxing sleep, but first they open the window to air the room and look out at the houses located across the wide street connecting the peripherial settlements with the city center" (*45 pomysłów* 77). Even a decade or two after the demise of the Soviet-imposed system, communist aesthetics and living conditions continue to determine many people's lives and, when juxtaposed with the brand-new Western-inspired shopping malls, multiplexes, and office buildings, create a schizophrenic situation. Clearly, although immersed in capitalism and democracy, Warsaw residents continue to live under the influence of the Soviet-imposed system.

Another effect the postwar decades continue to have on Warsaw and especially Berlin is the presence of the void. Large open spaces, abandoned buildings, forgotten alleys, and wide empty streets abound in post-1989 prose. In Berlin, the void is ubiquitous not only on the outskirts of the city (see Stasiuk) and along the S-Bahn lines (see Parei), but also, as Röggla notes, in the centrally located districts: "along the empty department stores on friedrichstrasse, across the whole investment waste land . . . brand new silence, i suppose. after all, you don't enter these planets voluntarily. in this day and age you should consider yourself lucky if architects take into consideration 'the local needs' . . . everything gone to serve the capital city, deserted squares. . ." (40). Interestingly, the void Röggla describes is not related to a complete absence of buildings, but rather to the desertedness of the renovated areas in downtown Berlin: the office houses, hotels, and stores aimed first and foremost at potential investors rather than residents. Consequently, at night, the whole central part of the city resembles an abandoned town rather than a dynamic metropolis. In Warsaw, the void is present mostly along the Vistula. Unlike in most cities intersected by rivers, the Warsaw waterfront is not integrated into urban life and resembles a no man's land rather than a recreational or entertainment area. In *Paw królowej*, the Vistula bank on the Praga side is a shady setting for late night meetings of the bored local police and a grotesque backdrop for dates that pretend to be romantic, but are in fact unspeakably sad. Masłowska juxtaposes the contemporary condition of the riverbanks with the memories of its prewar glory as expressed by Dejected Old Lady In A Wheelchair in *Między nami dobrze jest* and reminds us once again that neither urban landscape nor urban life have fully recovered from the Second World War and the succeeding decades of Soviet-imposed rule. As in Berlin, the void prevalent in Warsaw is a direct result of the city's twentieth-century history.

Rather than being homogeneous entities, Berlin and Warsaw consist of a number of individuated districts and dozens of neighborhoods, so it is hardly surprising that certain city areas attract authors' attention more than others and that many post-1989 novels play nearly entirely in single boroughs rather than across the city. More often than not, writers choose to focus on the districts they live in: Masłowska writes about Praga, Varga about Mokotów, Kaminer and Kubiczek about Prenzlauer Berg, Peltzer about Kreuzberg, and Katja Lange-Müller about Wedding. Although most of the authors notice both the positive and the negative aspects of their neighborhoods, they fail to escape a certain degree of sentimentality and favoritism in their descriptions. Even Masłowska's apocalyptic visions of Praga include nearly loving declarations of loyalty and devotion. Although the narrator describes Praga as a "bad district starting with the letter pee" (Masłowska, *Paw królowej* 33), she has no intention of moving to a different place. Throughout the book, she uses the real names of streets, stores, churches, sometimes even people, and, thus, helps the reader (familiar with the borough) to visualize the setting of the novel. In a sense, *Paw królowej* may be seen as a—slightly off-key and decidedly disturbing—hymn sung to and about Praga and its people. The author makes it a point to acknowledge on the last page that the book was "written, illustrated, and printed in Praga" (Masłowska, *Paw królowej*). Krzysztof Varga's descriptions of Mokotów are fragmentary and resemble a recurring dream rather than a linear urban story. In *Nagrobek z lastyko*, the author imagines the district in the future, destroyed together with the rest of the city, but still homely enough for the narrator to linger there. Interestingly, whereas Masłowska chooses the grotesque and exaggeration and Varga resorts to time travel and dreamy imagery, Kaminer describes his neighborhood in Prenzlauer Berg with an almost documentary precision: reading his short stories several years after they were published, the reader is not only reminded of how those streets, houses, and people used to look, but also what has changed since. Peltzer's descriptions of Nele's and Jakob's walks through Kreuzberg strike one as realistic and detailed and allow the reader to walk along foot to foot with the protagonists.

Whether or not the focus is on an individual district or on the cities as cultural and geographic entities, post-1989 novels recognize the importance of history and its substantial influence on contemporary Berlin and Warsaw. Particularly the events of the twentieth century continue to affect the urban landscapes and mentalities of the residents. In *Nagrobek z lastryko*, for example, Piotr Paweł is haunted by recurring dreams, in which various Warsaw war monuments come to murder him. "About three in the morning, when no one except grandpa could see it, Four Sleepers stepped down from the pedestal in Praga and—without lifting up their chins or throwing away the burp guns—commenced their walk to Mokotów and although a walk from Praga to Mokotów would normally take hours, they would arrive at Piotr Paweł's bed already a few minutes later and without saying a word and still not lifting up their heads, with faces hidden in the shadow of their four-cornered caps and helmets, they would lift up their firearms and—since they were stone burp-guns and could not be used for shooting—smash grandpa's head with the gun butts as easily as if it were a watermelon" (Varga, *Nagrobek* 100; Four Sleepers Monument/*Pomnik Czterech Śpiących* is a nickname given to the Monument of the Brotherhood of Arms/*Pomnik Braterstwa Broni* erected in 1945 in Praga, the first monument in postwar Warsaw devoted to the Polish-Soviet brotherhood of arms). Aside from the Four Sleepers, other monuments tormenting Piotr Paweł in his sleep include the Memorial to the Sappers (*Pomnik Chwała Saperom*), the Memorial to the Thousand Years of the Polish Cavalry (*Pomnik Tysiąclecia Jazdy Polskiej*), the Monument of the Armed Action of the Polish Diaspora in the USA (*Pomnik Czynu Zbrojnego Polonii*

Amerykańskiej), the Monument of the Warsaw Uprising (*Pomnik Powstania Warsza-wskiego*), and the Monument of the Little Insurgent (*Pomnik Małego Powstańca*). Night after night, Piotr Paweł's head is chopped off, his limbs twisted and torn apart, and his body set on fire by the familiar bronze and stone statues. Clearly, Varga laughs not only at the Polish tendency to linger in the country's—officially only heroic—past, but also, if not predominantly, at the ubiquity of war memorials in the Warsaw landscape that continue to obsessively remind the residents of twentieth-century atrocities and the sacrifice and suffering of their forefathers. As Masłowska demonstrates in *Między nami dobrze jest*, the traumas of the Second World War and, particularly, the Warsaw Uprising are passed on from one generation to the next and constitute an important element of the local urban memory.

Kaminer looks at the history of Berlin from a highly personal perspective and discusses it in the context of various waves of Russian immigration, which always took place in moments particularly decisive for the city. When Russians escaped to the west in the first years of the Soviet terror, they often sought refuge in Berlin, which itself was in torment as the capital of the Weimar Republic. An even larger and violent influx of Russians into the city took place at the end of the Second World War, when the Red Army "liberated" Berlin. The third wave came with the fall of the Wall: "we haven't had so many Russians in Berlin since 1945," says "a gentlewoman as old as Schönhauser Allee itself" and Wladimir's neighbor in one of Kaminer's short stories (115). "As [Gorbachev] drove down Schönhauser Allee in 1989, the rooftops in the whole neighborhood were crowded with curious locals, everyone wanted to wave to the first Soviet General Secretary with a human face. Gorbachev friendly waved back: 'Life punishes those who come too late.' The excited locals nearly fell down the roofs straight into the arms of the secret police. They thought Gorbachev meant them and that they should quickly reunite with the West. But that was a mistake. Gorbachev's words were not directed at the Germans, but at the Russians. . . . 'Come to Europe,' Gorbachev invited his fellow countrymen, 'it is nice here!'" (Kaminer 115-16). Kaminer's interpretation of the 1989 events is characteristically humorous and purposefully oversimplified, but it is nevertheless true that the last twentieth-century wave of Russian immigrants—of which Kaminer himself was part—has influenced the social, economic, and cultural life in individual districts (particularly Prenzlauer Berg and Charlottenburg) as well as in the city as a whole (see, e.g., Bottà).

As demonstrated through the excitement of the Russian—but also Vietnam-ese, Turkish, and South American—immigrants portrayed by Kaminer, Berlin continues to attract and become home to ever new people of various backgrounds. Next to economic or political immigrants, other large groups of Berlin newcomers in the 1990s and 2000s have included students, international artists, and West Germans (mostly managerial staff, politicians, entrepreneurs, and children of rich parents). Whereas students are characteristic of any city with universities and colleges includ-ing Warsaw (see Varga, *45 pomysłów*; Pilch, *Miasto utrapienia*), the remaining two groups are specific to Berlin. The relatively cheap rents and large spaces, the general enthusiasm for and impressive turnouts at art events, and the highly inspiring history render Berlin particularly attractive for artists, especially the young or "undiscovered" ones who cannot afford a studio in New York or London. New galleries emerge and disappear in various neighborhoods, but as Kaminer is right to acknowledge, galleries are often harbingers of gentrification: "When the house was renovated two years ago, the first business to appear on the ground floor was a bakery, then a small pizzeria, then a shoe store with great bargains. Then the place stayed empty for some time until a chic gallery with international contacts moved in there. Quite in the spirit of modern times" (110-11). Importantly, whereas the official municipal media hype the art(ist)-friendly character of Berlin as entirely positive and contributing to the city's hipness and cultural variety, post-1989 novels point out its side effects such as gentrification, but also the boosting numbers of unemployed artists (see Peltzer), which are only natural since the supply of art substantially exceeds the demand.

West German newcomers to Berlin in post-1989 novels are often presented in negative terms or ridiculed: naïve and lost in what appears to them as an exotic world (see Timm), ruthlessly taking advantage of their better material situation (see Kubiczek), and focused only on making money (see Peltzer) or attending to their business (see Timm). Still, it is not only the Wessis who execute their powerful influence on the reunited city—Berlin also changes them and not necessarily for the better. In Uwe Timm's 1996 novel *Johannisnacht* (Midsummer Night), we find an exaggerated portrait of Kubin, a businessman from Hamburg who came to Berlin after the fall of the Wall, worked for the privatization agency Treuhand for four years, and then established himself as a corporate consultant. When the narrator meets his old friend in his spacious and unbelievably cheap—at least for someone coming from Munich—(East) Berlin apartment, he notices right away that Kubin has not only gained weight, but also looks "tired, gray, unhealthy" (Timm 13) and his behavior shows signs of manic depression. "The rest of the evening he complained about Berlin and Berliners, especially about their efforts at being always quick-witted and funny. In other words, the *Berliner Schnauze* was getting on his nerves" (20). Interestingly, the native West Berliners, that is, those that had lived in the city before the fall of the Wall, are hardly ever caricaturized in the novels that take place in post-1989 Berlin—with the notable exception of Sven Regener's *Herr Lehmann* (*Berlin Blues*, 2001), which, however, ends on the night of November 9, 1989, and does not thematize the post-Wende reality. The overall negative or exaggerated portraits of Westerners suggest that even a decade or two after the reunification West Germans living in the former East Berlin continue to be perceived as intruders, exploiters, or colonizers. In the 1990s, works of fiction set in Berlin often elaborated on the differences between the west and east as differences "between the soul and the capital, between originality and sickness, substance and appearance. . . between primitive people and degenerated civilization. . . . Irony, indifference, and consumption in the West. Ideals, earnestness, and soul in the East" (Radisch 17). Nevertheless, as time passes, the main division lines within the society of reunited Berlin—in real life as in literature—run not along the former Wall, or between the Wessis and the Ossis, but rather between the rich and the poor and the better and more poorly developed boroughs (see Peltzer).

The literary portrayals of Berlin and Warsaw demonstrate that both cities are (post) colonial spaces: while large parts of their urban landscapes—and partly also their residents' mentality—continue being shaped by the Soviet colonial system, the capitals have become increasingly influenced by a new center of power (Western or global capital and culture). Literary descriptions of Berlin and Warsaw streets, neighborhoods, and places of work and leisure make it clear that the collision of different ideologies, economies, mentalities, and aesthetics has led to a hybridization of urban space and intensified the confusion of urban life. In the selected novels and short stories, the cities tend to be presented from an insider's perspective: the narrator is familiar with various aspects of post-1989 urban life and voices strong and often emotional opinions about the recent transformations. A visitor's perspective is rare and one-dimensional: the city portrayals sketched by newcomers have fewer subtleties and appear black-and-white in comparison to the city descriptions narrated by insiders. Regardless of the applied perspective and narration, contemporary novels and short stories set in Berlin and Warsaw make it clear that political and economic transformations continue to affect both the local societies and the urban landscapes in multilayered ways. Most striking, perhaps, is that the literary representations of the cities offer strongly critical interpretations of post-1989 changes: growing consumerism, impeding and often embarrassingly uncritical Westernization, social polarization and injustice, and the poor living conditions of large parts of the urban population are the recurring themes of recent literary works set in Berlin and Warsaw. It is hardly an exaggeration to say that the literary representations of contemporary Berlin and Warsaw are permeated with disappointment with the recent past and skepticism about the future.

Chapter Seven

Central European Cities in Post-1989 Film

The city has been a major film inspiration at least since Fritz Lang's 1927 *Metropolis*. Fascinated by the city's rhythm, diversity, modernity, and countless other properties, filmmakers have been trying to capture the elusive urban condition for nearly a century now (Berman, *On the Town*; Highmore). Cinematic portrayals of urban life are important sources of information about the city not only because film, as Walter Benjamin argues, is a medium best equipped to capture urbanity (see, e.g., "Work of Art"), but also because it can be seen as a mirror in which (urban) society looks at itself (see, e.g., Kracauer). The intrinsic relationship between film and the city has been analyzed and elaborated on by countless scholars; some of the recent academic publications worth mentioning include Nezar AlSayyad's *Cinematic Urbanism: A History of the Modern From Reel To Real* (2006), Stephen Barber's *Projected Cities: Cinema and Urban Space* (2002), and Mark Shiel's and Tony Fitzmaurice's edited volume *Cinema and the City: Film and Urban Societies in a Global Context* (2001). These and other analyses leave no doubt that the city proves to be especially inspirational in times of social and cultural change, of which it is not only witness, but also object. Unsurprisingly then, postcommunist transformations in Central European cities have prompted a production of numerous feature, documentary, experimental, and short films. Cinematic representations of post-1989 Central European capitals correspond closely to or complement literary representations of the cities: some of the themes (such as polarization, growing consumerism, the Westernization and globalization of urban space) occurring in the novels discussed in the previous chapter can be also observed in works of film.

Aside from interweaving with the issues thematized in literature, post-1989 film portrayals of Central European cities relate to other topics discussed in my book, that is, the newest history, the official images of Central European cities as communicated through municipal media, and the transformations of and in urban landscapes and city texts. The films in question offer their own interpretations of urban changes and, most importantly, insight into some of the phenomena neglected or underrepresented in literature and new media. In what follows I examine how the newest history of Central European capitals and their post-1989 urban space have been evaluated and represented in film. Further, I discuss some of the themes that have been particularly widespread in the contemporary cinema of the region: the newcomer to the city, the (Western) foreigner, and the juxtaposition between winners and losers in the new socioeconomic system.

Newest history of Central European cities as portrayed in post-1989 film

The most recent history of Central European cities has been represented in film in three main ways: through partial re-enactment of the 1989 events, through juxtaposition of the urban life before and after 1989, and, most subtly, through historic allusions communicated in dialogues or through historic sites rich in symbolism. Remarkably, most films elaborately thematizing post-1989 events started emerging only a decade after the fall of the Wall. One of the reasons for this delay was the widespread confusion and ambiguous approach towards the recent past prevalent in the societies of Central European cities in general and in the German capital in particular. The reunification of East and West Berlin took place amidst numerous controversies, and a general disappointment with the changes gradually replaced the initial euphoria. Once communism collapsed, West Berlin lost its special status as an island (*die Insel*), which meant not only a reduction of state subsidies, but also an outflow of creative communities to the cheaper districts of Mitte and Prenzlauer Berg, the new Bohemian enclaves that dethroned the western districts of Kreuzberg and Schöneberg. At the same time, thousands of East Berliners headed the opposite direction in search of better-paid jobs they were hoping to find in West German cities. Those who stayed were soon confronted with the rising costs of living boosted by the new neighbors who had just moved in from Stuttgart or Hamburg (see, e.g., Holm). The longing for pre-1989 Berlin lingered on both sides of the scar left by the Wall, hence, nostalgia was far greater than the memory of the absurdities and injustice that reigned during the division of the city. Even a decade after the fall of the Wall, the city's history remained problematic and prompted overtly cautious artistic responses. Instead of entering a dialog with the prevalent nostalgia, filmmakers largely yielded to sentimentalism and turned their films into fairy-tale-like monuments of pre-1989 Berlin.

One of the most elaborate descriptions of the events preceding and succeeding the fall of the Wall can be found in *Good Bye, Lenin!* (2003). Alex Kerner (Daniel Brühl), the main protagonist of Wolfgang Becker's blockbuster, comes of age when his country is on the decline. On the evening of 7 October 1989, on the 40th anniversary of the GDR, Alex joins the huge crowd of protesters demanding the opening of the borders. At the same time, his mother, an ardent supporter of socialism, is on her way to the official celebration at the Palast der Republik. At the sight of the NVA soldiers brutally dispersing the demonstration and pushing her son into a van, Alex's mother experiences a severe shock, subsequently falling into a coma. Comatose, she remains completely unaware of the revolutionary changes taking place during those critical months. Not only does she sleep through the fall of the Wall, but also through East Berlin's opening to the market economy. When she regains her consciousness eight months later, the world she knew has ceased to exist. Doctors warn the family that Christiane's heart would not survive any additional stress. In order to protect his mother from another major shock, Alex reconstructs the world of East Berlin: he replaces brand-new Ikea shelves with old mirror-finish furniture, tries to get hold of typical—and now nearly extinct—GDR groceries, and even prepares fake television programs. The desperate attempt to save the dying world emphasizes the absurdities of the previous system. *Good Bye, Lenin!* makes fun of nostalgia, however, tenderly rather than cynically.

Even if Alex's quest is destined to fail, the viewer wishes him luck. Alex's friends, family, and colleagues, but also complete strangers, try to help him in his hopeless mission. Not only the buildings and objects that constituted the old East Berlin, but also the people who not so long ago inhabited it change or simply leave. Coca-Cola and Ikea advertisements replace East German propaganda posters. The film features a number of symbolic yet humorous scenes commenting about the sudden commercialization of urban space, like the one in which a Coca-Cola truck drives down Unter den Linden past the deserted *Neue Wache* where the East German soldiers used to keep guard, or when a zeppelin with a cigarette advertisement banner spelling "Test the West" flies behind the TV tower. Supermarkets filled with Western products emerge where co-operative stores used to be located and—to Alex's dismay—most typical East German brands such as *Spreewälder Gurken* and *Mocca Fix Gold* are impossible to find. Thousands of people move to the West and leave all their belongings behind; those who stay have only two options: to join the rapidly growing unemployed or to adapt to the capitalist mentality, as does Ariane, Alex's sister, who starts working at Burger King.

Whereas *Good Bye, Lenin!* shows some of the pre- and post-1989 political, social, and cultural developments through the eyes of an East Berliner, Leander Haußmann's 2003 film adaptation of Sven Regener's novel *Herr Lehmann* (translated into English as *Berlin Blues*) focuses on the western side of the city. The action of the film takes place in the fall of 1989, mainly in the rundown district of Kreuzberg inhabited by artists, students, Turkish Gastarbeiter, and draft dodgers (the protagonist, Frank Lehmann, moves to West Berlin from West Germany in the early 1980s to evade obligatory army service). *Herr Lehmann* tells a story of young people who live in Kreuzberg, surrounded from three sides by the concrete border, and who are uninterested in anything that takes place outside their district. Mr. Lehmann (Christian Ulmen), as his friends choose to call him, is a bartender, therefore, the action takes place at night in smoky bars and on badly lit streets. Since all the buildings are gray or covered with graffiti, the Wall ideally fits into its surroundings and its presence is anything but irritating.

Mr. Lehmann turns 30 on 9 November 1989. He is sitting in a bar and watching the fall of the Wall on television. The breakthrough event has no sobering effect either on Lehmann or his fellow beer drinkers. To Kreuzbergers, East Berlin seems as far away as the bourgeois Charlottenburg or the upper-middle-class Grunewald. "Now they all are going to come over here," someone remarks, but the comment triggers no panic or anger. Just as we expect Mr. Lehmann and his fellow drinkers to linger in the Kreuzberg lethargy, the birthday boy suddenly gets up and exits the bar. He sets out to meet the neighbors from the east. Greeting the joyful crowds, Mr. Lehmann introduces himself as Frank: this is the first time in the film we hear his first name. Until now, the protagonist's immaturity has been disguised by the prefix "Mister" mockingly added to his last name. The fall of the Wall seems to help Mr. Lehmann understand the inevitability of changes and the necessity of action.

Although in both films the opening of Berlin's inner border is presented as a meaningful event happily greeted by large crowds on both sides of the Wall, in *Good Bye, Lenin!* and *Herr Lehmann* the universal joy is overshadowed by personal problems: Alex mourns his mother's medical condition and Mr. Lehmann is lovesick after the breakup from Katrin. Although 9 November 1989 has come to symbolize the collapse of communism, the reunification of Germany, and the rebirth of united Europe, instead of glorifying the fall of the Wall and its universal meanings, both Haußmann and Becker decide to present it as an individual and strongly subjective experience, ambivalent rather than purely positive. Similarly, in Hannes Stöhr's 2001 film *Berlin is in Germany* (the original title is in English), the main protagonist Martin Schulz (Jörg Schüttauf) learns about the opening of the borders in a GDR prison where he had been recently placed after accidentally killing his neighbor. Although it stands for freedom, the historic event fails to affect Martin in any way: he is sentenced to spend another decade behind bars. Clearly, none of the films portray the fall of the Wall as an entirely beneficial phenomenon, but present the November night from a strongly subjective perspective—ambivalent rather than enthusiastic, skeptical rather than hopeful. A decade after the opening of Berlin's inner border, Haußmann, Becker, and Stöhr perceive the event no longer as hopeful and excited onlookers, but with the knowledge of subsequent disappointments and misunderstandings.

Skepticism also permeates the portrayal of the Velvet Revolution presented in Academy Award-winning *Kolja* (*Kolya*, 1996). Another in the series of works from the Svěrák father and son film tandem, *Kolja* tells the story of the middle-aged concert cellist František Louka (Zdenek Svěrák), tricked into taking care of a Russian boy whose mother leaves for West Germany. The action takes place in Prague in the year preceding the democratic revolution. In one of the last scenes—a reenactment of the November street demonstrations that led to the collapse of the communist regime in Czechoslovakia—Louka recognizes two secret police officers who repeatedly interrogated him in the past: overnight they have changed fronts and become part of the crowd demanding democratic reforms and, thus, as Louka sarcastically observes, remain on the side of the winners. The subsequent corruption of democratic values and the opportunism of the political elites are visible as early as in the midst of the peaceful revolution, among enthusiastic cheers and idealistic slogans. Here too, the personal perspective proves more viable than historical objectivity. Louka's experiences and observations speak against a black-and-white understanding of the

Cold War division and its demise. The Svěráks demonstrate that not all Soviets or Russians are evil just as not all Czechoslovak democrats are virtuous.

The re-evaluation of the 1989 events in Budapest lies at the basis of Ferenc Török's *Moszkva tér* (Moscow Square, 2001). Named after the busy traffic and meeting point in Buda, the film tells a story of a group of high school seniors officially preparing for their final exams and in reality keeping themselves busy with partying. The political transformations Hungary undergoes in the spring of 1989 pass unnoticed as the main character Petya (Gábor Karalyos) and his friends focus on little pleasures such as driving around the city in a sports car (the father of one of the boys is a wealthy man), drinking alcohol, smoking cigarettes, watching porn, falling in love, and (illegally) earning their first money. While his grandmother is excitedly watching a live transmission from Imre Nagy's reburial, Petya turns up the volume on his stereo and listens to pop music. To the 18-year-olds in Török's film, Nagy's name does not ring a bell; what worries them is how the political transformations are going to affect the validity of their final exams taken under the still socialist regime. In his 2008 book about Budapest and Hungary *Gulasz z turula* (Turul Goulash), Krzysztof Varga remarks that if a sequel to *Moszkva tér* were filmed today, "none of the characters would dare not to know Nagy's name or not to respond emotionally to news about, say, Ferenc Gyurcsány or Viktor Orbán's death. For today Hungarians live in a political reality show, in some kind of national Big Brother, in a distorted reality . . . in which everyday life has become politicalness" (Varga, *Gulasz* 119-120) (Ferenc Gyurcsány was Hungary's prime minister in 2004-2009 and leader of MSZP/Hungary's Social Democratic Party; Viktor Orbán, the leader of Fidesz/Hungary's Christian Democratic Party, was Hungary's prime minister in 1998-2002 and was reelected in 2010).

What the above film representations of the 1989 events have in common is not only their skeptical and critical character and their focus on the personal rather than the historical perspective, but also the implementation of archival films and footages into the main body of the feature film. The street demonstrations in Berlin and Prague, the surge of the Wall and the subsequent parties, and the celebrations surrounding Imre Nagy's reburial were all crowded events—their full re-enactment would have been possible only with a Hollywood budget, if at all; therefore, the film directors opted for a partial re-enactment (*Herr Lehmann*; *Good Bye, Lenin!*; and *Kolja*) or relied solely on excerpts from television or newspaper coverage (*Berlin is in Germany* and *Moszkva tér*). Moreover, the implementation of documentary materials lends an authentic feel to the films and increases their sentimental character: the part of the audience old enough to have lived through the events of 1989 is also likely to remember the archival footage and, possibly, promptly recall what they were doing while watching or listening to the transmissions.

Whereas ambivalence surmounts enthusiasm in the film representations or partial re-enactments of the democratic revolutions, the parts juxtaposing pre- and post-1989 realities in Central European capitals range from sentimental portrayals of the time before the fall of the Wall (Leander Haußmann's *Sonnenallee*, 1999;

Dani Levy's *Alles auf Zucker!*, 2004; *Herr Lehmann*) to critical assessments of the political and social transformations (Władysław Pasikowski's *Psy*, 1992, and *Psy 2*, 1994; Andreas Dresen's *Sommer vorm Balkon*, 2005) to hopeful prognoses on a post-1989 future (Krzysztof Kieślowski's *Three Colors: White*, 1994; *Berlin is in Germany*). Despite its candy-sweet colors, Haußmann's *Sonnenallee* (*Sun Alley*) strikes the viewer as particularly black and white. Taking place in the 1970s, when the title street was still divided by the Wall (its shorter stretch was located in East Berlin, the longer one in West Berlin), the film tells the story of a group of East Berlin high school students who live next to a border crossing where they are closely watched by border guards, the NVA, the Stasi, teachers, parents, groups of foreigners in tourist buses, and West Berliners standing on viewing towers. Almost all characters and events are exaggerated, which creates the intended comical effect. West Berliners are portrayed as cunning, cowardly, and stupid, while East Berliners are likable and their shortcomings seem funny rather than irritating. The apartments on Sonnenallee with their mirror-finish furniture, brownish wallpapers, and the awkward presence of state-designated tenants from Saxony are as GDR-like as it gets. Haußmann created a heritage park of East Berlin, packed it with comical goofballs and likable teenagers, added a hit soundtrack, and achieved commercial success. In *Sonnenallee*, West Berlin functions as an unknown place behind the Wall, colorful, but hostile. Both city parts seem accidentally attached, as if a united Berlin were never meant to exist.

In his portrayal of Berlin a decade after reunification, Hannes Stöhr lets the viewer (re)discover the post-1989 changes of the urban landscape and urban life through the eyes of Martin, who has known the new Berlin only from television before he gets released from prison in 2000. Although *Berlin is in Germany* includes portraits of *typische Wendeverlierer*, or typical transformation losers, it also presents success stories and, thus, provides "a nuanced picture of eastern Germans since the Wende, demonstrating that many were able to find their feet" (Evans 71). Whereas Peter (Tom Jahn), the friend Martin saves from committing suicide, represents "the western stereotype of the *Jammerossi* ["whiny Eastie" from *jammern*—to whine, to lament; and *Ossi*—Eastie], for whom the new Germany has been one disaster after another" (Evans 71), Martin's ex-wife Manuela (Julia Jäger) and his Cuban friend Enrique (Oscar Martinez) have managed to make a decent living after the collapse of the GDR, and readily offer their help and guidance to Martin. It is impossible not to notice that the most genuine and friendly people sympathetic to Martin's plight are either (former) East Berliners or foreigners—"a fact all the more intriguing since Stöhr himself is a Wessi" (Evans 73); however, the new German state embodied by the probation officer appears to be on Martin's side as well. Despite initial confusion and problems with understanding the new reality as well as Berlin's changeable landscapes, Martin is determined to adjust to the reunited city—partly for the sake of his son, partly for his own.

Aside from partial re-enactments of real-life events and comparisons of urban life before and after 1989, the newest history of Central European cities represented in film has also been communicated through portrayals of symbolical buildings and monuments as well as allusive dialogues. Probably the most emblematic film representation of the departure of communism is the scene in *Good Bye, Lenin!* when Alex's mother, ignorant of the ongoing transformations, sneaks out of her prefabricated apartment building into the street and sees Lenin's gigantic monument being towed away by a helicopter—a perfect illustration of Karl Marx's famous statement: "all that is solid melts into air." In *Kolja*, the Soviet troops pose a constant reminder of the 1968 Warsaw Pact intervention in Prague. Lying in bed at night, Kolja and Louka listen to military trucks passing by the window of Louka's downtown apartment: "Kolja (in Russian): Are they ours? Louka (in Czech): Yes, yours. Kolja (in Russian): Are they going to Moscow? Louka (in Czech): No, they're here for good. They just go back and forth. Kolja (in Russian): Do they live here? Louka (in Czech): Unfortunately. Kolja (in Russian, after a short pause): Like me. (Sigh)." Clearly, at that point, Louka refuses to believe that the democratic developments taking place in Central Europe could put an end to the Soviet occupation of Czechoslovakia. Louka perceives the Soviet troops as intruders, but is able to differentiate between the oppressive system and the defenseless Russian boy; Louka's mother is less tolerant and demands the child leaves her house once she discovers Kolja is Russian and not Yugoslavian as Louka introduced him. Aside from Prague residents' general (although quiet) contempt of for everything Soviet, the Svěráks show other signs of Soviet presence in the city such as the Moskevská (today Anděl) metro station with murals and mosaics depicting—to Kolja's unconcealed joy—the Red Square.

The complex and complicated relationships with the former Soviet occupier are also echoed in Márta Mészáros' 1999 film *Córy szczęścia* (Daughters of Luck). After her husband loses his job, Natasza (Olga Drozdova), an English teacher from the Russian province, comes to Warsaw with her teenage daughter Masza (Masza Petraniuk) to sell clothes and other goods on the *Stadion Dziesięciolecia* (the Tenth Anniversary Stadium opened on June 22, 1955, eleven years after the June Manifesto that laid out the basis for the communist Poland; turned into a bazaar in 1989-2007, the demolition of the stadium commenced in 2008 and it is to be replaced by a modern sports venue in time for the 2012 European Football Cup). When they get off their train in Warsaw's Central Station, the nearby Palace of Culture and Science not only presents a symbolic background, but is also the main subject of a short conversation with the women's Polish contact, Janek (Olaf Lubaszenko), who points at the Stalinist building and sarcastically remarks: "just like home." Later in film, after Natasza has become a luxurious prostitute, Janek takes her to the Palace and says: "This is where you will be working now. Do you recognize it? It's a gift from your nation to my nation." Moreover, while Natasza is selling her body to (mostly Western) clients on the 56th floor of the Palace, her patron Robert (Jan Nowicki) and Masza are attending Tchaikovsky's *Eugene Onegin* in the theater located on the ground floor. Here, Warsaw's most recognizable edifice provides not only the geographic center to the film, but also illustrates the complicated historical and cultural relationships between the former colonized and the former colonizer. In *Córy szczęścia* and *Kolja*, among other films, confrontation with individuals associated with the former oppressor reveals interesting facts about the formerly colonized society. Although Natasza, Masza, and Kolja are portrayed as completely helpless and dependent on the goodwill of the people they encounter in their respective host countries, they continue being perceived as representatives of a hostile power and, thus, a threat. The decades-long distrust and fear of the Soviet Union persist even after the communist empire is gone. Contemporary filmmakers reveal the ridiculousness of this prevailing paranoia and demonstrate that the former colonizer has become more vulnerable than the former colonized.

As in the case of recent works of literature, post-1989 films set in the Polish capital are permeated with memories of the Warsaw Uprising. In Dariusz Gajewski's *Warszawa* (Warsaw, 2003), a film about the many faces of the Polish capital at the beginning of the twenty-first century, a veteran resistance fighter walks around the city in search of people and houses that no longer exist. His mental map of Warsaw has little to no relation to the urban landscape of today. Since nearly the whole city was destroyed by the Germans in 1944, the old man's walk resembles a journey through an imaginary land of the dead or a ghost town. Permanently confused and mocked or misunderstood by the people he meets on his way, the veteran points at the street corners and squares where some of the street fights took place. One of the most poignant moments of his walk takes place at the Warsaw Uprising Monument on Krasinskis Square where the former insurgent confronts an unemployed man stealing flowers from the memorial site. What could otherwise be considered sheer profanity appears a sad necessity in the context of post-1989 economic transformations.

In *Warszawa*, the memories of the uprising are presented as inevitable, important, and defining for the city, but also as an unbearable burden. The party girl Malina (Katarzyna Bujakiewicz) lives in an apartment overlooking the Warsaw Uprising Monument: "Nice view, eh? I have an uprising here every day. Where this house is standing there used to be a hospital, in the basements. Actually, my house is a grave. About a thousand people are in the foundation." Malina's mocking attitude towards the rebellion that has been nearly unanimously glorified after 1989 breaks a taboo in that it demonstrates the mental and physical burden the Warsaw Uprising continues to execute on the city residents. Also, Gajewski's film shows how the events of 1944 irrevocably influence Polish-German relationships: the obnoxious and shady German businessman Karl (Jack Recknitz), with a smirk on his face, tells Wiktoria (Dominika Ostałowska) that his father fought in the Warsaw Uprising and "judging by his stories, nothing has really changed here," to which Wiktoria replies that her grandfather also took part in the rebellion. Clearly, there is no need to specify which sides Karl's father and Wiktoria's grandfather fought on. In *Warszawa*, the German-Polish animosities, mutual contempt, and distrust thrive despite the peaceful and officially friendly relationships between both countries. In a city obsessed with its war past and, simultaneously, focused on achieving a quick economic success, the German is an ambiguous figure: an intruder and a villain on the one hand and an important business partner and a link to the rest of the Western world on the other hand.

The film portrayals of the newest history of Central European capitals show numerous similarities. The 1989 events have been (re)evaluated mostly a decade or a dozen years later, which shows that filmmakers needed time to process and understand the democratic revolutions and their meaning for the future of the cities. Naturally, their assessments of 1989 have been strongly influenced by the succeeding—and often disappointing—developments; hence, the film portrayals of the street demonstrations in Budapest and Prague and the removal of the inner-city border in Berlin are skeptical rather than enthusiastic. Although some film directors (Hauß-mann, Becker) opt for the idealization and sentimentalization of the pre-1989 period, many of the new films reject a black-and-white understanding of the transformation and offer a more nuanced portrayal of the changes in urban societies and landscapes (*Berlin is in Germany*; *Sommer vorm Balkon*; *Three Colors: White*; among many others). The post-1989 film also demonstrates how Soviet influences continue to define Central European cities: irrevocably changed under the communist regime, parts of the urban landscapes of Berlin and Warsaw (as well as, albeit to a smaller extent, Budapest and Prague) are constant reminders of the former occupier and colonizer. The (post)colonial urban condition of Central European capitals is presented on film as something exotic and shameful, foreign and familiar at the same time. The remnants of the communist system strike the viewer as morbid or absurd, but at least well known, whereas the new influences of Western or global capital are often pictured as colorful, but hostile.

Film portrayals versus official images of Central European cities after 1989

History plays a crucial role in recent film representations of Central European capitals whereby the events directly preceding or succeeding the revolutions of 1989 as well as—especially in the case of Warsaw—the Second World War receive far more attention than a more distant past. When contemporary times are thematized, the focus is often on the cities' failed attempts to catch up with the West (*Zimmerspring-brunnen*, 2001; *Dzień świra*, 2002) and when a success story is presented, it tends to involve the moral collapse of the protagonists (*Amok*, 1998; *Billboard*, 1998). The official images of Central European capitals as modern and successful urban centers are not only repeatedly questioned in film, but often juxtaposed with portraits of impoverished districts, run down buildings, polarized societies, and all other urban phenomena that municipal marketing specialists obviously prefer not to communicate. In what follows I demonstrate how the film portrayals of Warsaw and Berlin differ from their representations in and through the municipal media (see chapter 4).

As of 2009, Warsaw has two official logos: the city logo with Syrenka that—according to the municipal authorities—symbolizes both the city's ancient history and its modern character and the logo for the 2016 European Capital of Culture, which aims at presenting Warsaw as a twenty-first century metropolis. Although it clearly aspires to being acknowledged as an attractive modern city of international importance, post-1989 Warsaw is more often than not portrayed as backward and provincial in film. The decaying prefabricated apartment blocks evolving into violence infested ghettos (*Cześć, Tereska*, 2000), the dilapidated family houses hidden among concrete high-rise buildings (*Three Colors: White*, 1994), and the traditionally neglected working district of Praga (*Rezerwat*, 2007) convey that there is much more to Warsaw's landscape than merely the glamorous skyline presented in the municipal print and online information materials. Although the ghettoization and dysfunctionality of run down neighborhoods are widespread urban pathologies and, at various times, can be observed in both Western (New York, Paris, Madrid) and Eastern (Moscow, St. Petersburg) metropolises, Warsaw's urban problems—as presented in film—have a particularly provincial character.

Although office buildings and hotels in Warsaw are much taller than in any other Central European city, they only marginally emphasize the intended metropolitan image of the Polish capital. In post-1989 cinema, the glamour Warsaw aspires to strikes the viewer as fake: striving to adapt to the newly introduced capitalist reality, Warsaw businesspeople lack both the urban style, manners, and knowledge of their counterparts in Western cities and the unimaginable fortunes of the Moscow oligarchs. In comparison to Oliver Stone's *Wall Street* (1987) and Mary Harron's *American Psycho* (2000), the film representations of Warsaw's world of stock exchange, business, and the young rich—for example, Natalia Koryncka-Gruz's *Amok*, Łukasz Zadrzyński's *Billboard*, and Mariusz Treliński's *Egoiści* (Egoists, 2000)—strike the viewer as amateurish and sad if not purely embarrassing since the protagonists appear convinced they have reached the top both when it comes to their professional or financial success and hedonistic lifestyles. Without a clearly communicated identity of its own, Warsaw in post-1989 film calls to mind a poor copy of New York, London, or Moscow rather than a city of century-long traditions and unique character.

Another striking feature of Warsaw's landscape presented in film is its architectural hybridity and cultural in-betweenness. Although after 1989 Warsaw has experienced Westernization both from within and from the outside, it is still to a large extent defined by the remnants of the Soviet regime and the destruction in World War II and, thus, essentially (post)colonial. The shiny glass façades of office buildings capture reflections of both gray prefabricated apartment blocks and the few turn of the century buildings that survived the air raids. Modern downtown buildings often open to crooked sidewalks where small retailers sell fruit, clothes, electronic gadgets, among many other things, either at makeshift tin stands or straight from the trunks of their cars—such pictures are especially popular in the films staged in Warsaw of the 1990s, during the first years of the economic transition (*Three Colors: White*; *Amok*; *Córy szczęścia*). Architectural and cultural eclecticism is also visible in the combination of Western-style advertisement and still very socialist design of many residential and commerce buildings—this trend was also particularly widespread in the first decade after 1989. Furthermore, Warsaw's adoration of and attempts to copy the Western corporate culture have resulted in another aesthetic phenomenon, namely the ubiquity of outdoor advertising: countless buildings both downtown and in the outer districts of the city are partly, or, in some cases, completely covered with billboards, neon lights, or advertising sheets, which may be seen not only as an intrusion into the urban landscape, but also as a violation of the space of the people who live or work in the these buildings (*Billboard*; *Warszawa*; *Dzień świra*).

While both Warsaw logos are colorful and modern in shape, film representations of the city prefer to focus on its grayness, architectural and cultural chaos, and backwardness. Also the century-long traditions Syrenka embodies in the city logo are hardly communicated in film, which refers mostly to Warsaw's twentieth-century heritage, particularly the Second World War and the post-1989 transformations. Similarly, Berlin in contemporary film appears as a city defined by the turbulent twentieth century, not as the former Prussian capital.

Naturally, the Brandenburg Gate in Berlin's omnipresent logo (chapter 4) symbolizes not the Prussian construction, but rather Germany's reunification. Presented in the municipal media as a stable element uniting two previously separated parts of the cities (and the nation), the neoclassicist structure is rarely featured in post-1989 film: we see it nearly exclusively as a background to some of the re-enactments of the fall of the Wall (*Good Bye, Lenin!*; *Berlin is in Germany*; *Herr Lehmann*). While the Brandenburg Gate is not a particularly popular film set (possibly because it may be difficult to acquire a filming permit on the square that is home to both the French and the US Embassies and is located in the immediate vicinity of the Reichstag), Berlin's reunification is one of the most popular themes in film. Still, whereas the municipal marketing specialists optimistically prefer to communicate it as a completed task, filmmakers perceive the reunification as a constant work in progress. Next to the films that present the attempts at re-integration of the previously divided city in black-and-white terms with unlucky, but good-hearted Ossis on the one hand and successful, but cunning or obnoxious Wessis on the other hand (*Good Bye, Lenin!*; *Sonnenallee*; and, partly, *Berlin is in Germany*), there are also some films that try to thematize the ambiguities and complexities of coming to terms with post-1989 in Berlin. In Andreas Dresen's *Sommer vorm Balkon* (*Summer in Berlin*, 2005), for example, the main protagonist Katrin (Inka Friedrich), an unemployed, alcohol-abusing single mother who lives in a small ground-floor apartment in a rundown Prenzlauer Berg building, has all characteristics of a typische Wendeverlierer—we are genuinely surprised to find out she comes from the former West Germany and came to (East) Berlin only because of her then husband. Although it may be easier for many to believe that the Western or Eastern origin fully determines one's post-1989 fate, Andreas Dresen reminds of the obvious existence of other factors such as sheer luck, entrepreneurial skills, family situation, and personality.

Similarly, in Dani Levy's *Alles auf Zucker!* (*Go for Zucker!*), the newly reunited brothers Jackie (Henry Hübchen) and Samuel (Udo Samel) differ from each other not only as an Ossi and a Wessi, but also as a secular Jew and an Orthodox Jew and, simply, as two independent human beings. Levy not only mocks the stereotypes about Easterners and Westerners so prevalent in post-1989 Germany, but also ridicules all kinds of generalizations. While he describes himself as a typische

Wendeverlierer, Jackie Zucker calls Samuel and his family frankfurters ("ihr Frankfurter Würstchen") and blames them for all his failures. The Zuckermanns' mother
left East Berlin shortly before the Wall was built: she took the younger Samuel with
her and wanted to come back for 14-year-old Jack, but failed to do so because of the
newly introduced border installations. Soon after he was abandoned, Jack changed
his name to Zucker and became a devoted atheist; Samuel reverted to religion and
disapproved of his older brother, whom he liked to compare to Stalin. Forty years
after they were separated, Jackie and Samuel are forced to meet and deal with their
mother's last will. To do so, they need to work out a number of compromises and
learn how to respect each other's differences. Clearly, in a humorous way, the fate of
the Zuckermann brothers—forcefully separated and forcefully reunited—refers to
the history of Germany in the second part of the twentieth century.

     As the differences between the former West Berlin and the former East Ber-
lin—and between their residents—gradually disappear, in the most recent films
about the city, urban society is polarized not along the east-west line, but rather
according to class divisions. In *Sommer vorm Balkon*, as well as in Eoin Moore's
Im Schwitzkasten (In the Sweatbox, 2005), Bern Böhlich's *Du bist nicht allein* (You
Are Not Alone, 2007), and Detlev Buck's *Knallhart* (*Tough Enough*, 2007) it matters
little if the unemployed and (thus) insecure and depressed Berliners come from the
west or the east—the films portray those who suffer as a result of the poor economy
and the impeding collapse of the welfare state. Also, whereas in the 1990s the differences between the urban landscapes of the former West and East Berlin were
still remarkable, in the 2000s the hitherto separated parts of the city have become
increasingly similar thorough renovation projects, improvements in infrastructure,
and, importantly, similar if not identical stores such as chain supermarkets, boutiques, and coffee shops. Although the protagonists of Böchlich's film live in a prefabricated apartment block in the former east, they may as well have been residing
in its Western counterpart, for example, Gropiusstadt in Neukölln, known for its
relatively cheap housing. Similarly, Katrin from *Sommer vorm Balkon* may have
been living in one of Kreuzberg Mietskasernen surrounded, like her house in Prenzlauer Berg, by corner bars and filled with vibrant night life. Clearly, whereas the
east-west division has lost on importance in the 2000s, the newest film productions
demonstrate that both the city and its residents remain fragmented or separated along
economic, social, and cultural lines.

Representations of post-1989 urban space in film

Walter Prigge's observation that "the architecture of the city appears in film not as
a stage . . . but as an object" (83) strikes as particularly true in the case of post-
1989 Central European film, in which urban landscapes, buildings, and infrastructure serve as important sources of inspiration and sometimes take on the role of
characters rather than that of mise-en-scène. The changes in city text as well as the
new architectural and urban developments discussed in the previous chapters have

been repeatedly interpreted and represented in film. Since Berlin and Warsaw show similarities in their post-1989 urban landscapes, it is hardly surprising that representations in film of the new urban spaces share a number of themes and motifs, among them postcommunist buildings as palimpsests or symbols, the fate of prefabricated apartment blocks, the renaming of streets, constant renovation and construction works, the void, and "in-betweenness." In the following discussion of these selected themes and motifs, I demonstrate how the contemporary urban landscapes of Berlin and Warsaw have been represented and commented on in film.

Regardless of their aesthetic value, the tallest buildings in the city are likely to become landmarks. In the case of Berlin and Warsaw, the tallest structures—the TV tower and the Palace of Culture and Science, respectively—were erected under the communist regime and soon became the most recognizable buildings in these cities. After 1989, they continue to serve as symbols of Berlin and Warsaw, but are also constant reminders of the bygone era. The TV tower is particularly visible in *Good Bye, Lenin!*. Even the protagonist's name is closely connected to Alexanderplatz, East Berlin's main square located in the direct vicinity of the TV tower. In one of the most symbolic moments in the film, Alex is standing on the rooftop of a prefabricated apartment building and angrily throws handfuls of already useless East German money in the direction of the TV tower. Remarkably, in *Berlin is in Germany*, Peter, the self-proclaimed victim of the reunification, threatens to commit suicide while staring at the TV tower. Clearly, the protagonists associate the tall structure with the collapsed GDR and, thus, by implication, with all their personal and professional misfortunes, difficulties, and failures triggered by the system change. Far from being a mere scapegoat, however, the TV tower is also prominently featured in the already mentioned zeppelin scene in *Good Bye, Lenin!*, where its silver ball is shining in the cloudless sky and the bright sun renders the usually gray body of the tower snow white. It is also portrayed as home-like in at least two scenes in *Berlin is in Germany*: first, when Martin comes back to Berlin after eleven years in prison and sees the TV tower from the train window and second, when Martin looks out of his cheap hotel window, sees the TV tower surrounded by prefabricated houses, and smiles. Furthermore, it is in the restaurant located in the tower's silver ball where Martin goes to revise Berlin's new street names for his taxi driver test—not only does it offer an aerial view of the city, but it is also one of the few well-known and constant spots in the rapidly changing urban environment.

Similarly, film portrayals of the Palace of Culture and Science convey miscellaneous meanings ranging from nostalgic to ambivalent to dismissive. The office Karol (Zbigniew Zamachowski) rents out in *Three Colors: White* overlooks one of the Palace's enormous walls and points at one of many post-1989 urban paradoxes in Warsaw: on the one hand, the Palace is repeatedly scathed for its Stalinist origin and questionable aesthetics; on the other hand, its central position in the city proves magnetic to small and big business interested in the most prominent location for their offices. Owing to its height and easily recognizable shape, the Palace is also featured in numerous shots depicting newcomers entering the city center, particularly those arriving at the nearby Central Station (*Warszawa*; *Córy szczęścia*): in these scenes—as well as in those presenting the city's panorama both by day and by night (*Egoiści*; *Córy szczęścia*; *Amok*)—the Palace acts primarily as a symbol of Warsaw rather than a reminder of the communist regime. The building's Stalinist design and its communist past are most elaborately commented on in *Córy szczęścia*, where large parts of the plot take place in the Palace, and Mészáros comments on the new, often contrasting uses of the edifice. The fact that Natasza works as a prostitute in a luxurious brothel located in the "gift of her nation to the Polish nation" depicts not only the ironic nature of history, but also the Palace's changeable fate and its ongoing relevance.

Other palimpsest buildings featured in post-1989 films about Warsaw include the former communist party headquarters (*Amok*) and the Tenth Anniversary Stadium (*Córy szczęścia*; *Billboard*). Although the Warsaw Stock Exchange moved to the building of the Central Committee of the Polish United Workers Party as early as 1991 (and remained there until 2000), the edifice continues to be called the House of the Party (*Dom Partii*). Although its previous function is not discussed in *Amok* (the original title), the building's communist past is clearly communicated through its monumental exterior and interior. In Natalia Koryncka-Gruz's film, the seat of the Warsaw Stock Exchange serves as one of the main settings: its halls and rooms are filled with men in suits focused on their careers, just like under the communist regime, although the brokers probably wear better suits and shoes than the communist party officials. The House of the Party is portrayed in *Amok* as drenched in adrenaline and greed, a trap for young ambitious men such as the journalist Maciek (Rafał Maćkowiak), who falls under the spell of the opportunities the stock exchange promises: seemingly easy and quick money. Furthermore, the film portrayal of the building thematizes the post-1989 transfer of real power from party to financial elites.

Both *Córy szczęścia* and *Billboard* depict the Tenth Anniversary Stadium as a place dominated by illegal trade, human trafficking, and other crimes. In Mészáros' film, the former communist sports venue is a meeting point and working place of illegal immigrants from the former Soviet Union, Africa, and Asia, fully dependent on and constantly threatened by the local mafia. The Poles who appear at the stadium are either scheming criminals who take advantage of the immigrants, or simply poor people who cannot afford shopping at other markets. Also, some of the trailers at the *Jarmark Europa* (Europe Bazaar) are makeshift brothels: whereas Western clients go to luxurious prostitutes at the Palace of Culture and Science, Polish men find cheaper erotic services—provided by Eastern European women—at the former stadium. Jarmark Europa is the background to much more serious prostitution-related crimes in *Billboard*, a story about Kuba (Rafał Maćkowiak), a casting director from an advertising agency who discovers that his favorite Russian model has been brutally raped and murdered. Compared with Kuba's comfortable apartment and his modern office, the former stadium appears desolate and threatening, especially in the late afternoon, when it is nearly completely deserted and covered with abandoned plastic bags, papers, and half-torn announcements in Russian pinned onto wooden stands. Designed to accommodate cheering crowds, the Tenth Anniversary Stadium experienced a dramatic decline in the 1990s when it became synonymous for crime, dirt, and illegal immigrants, and has been represented as such in film.

Aside from portraying the new functions of communist buildings, post-1989 film also comments on the changes in city text, particularly the ubiquitous renaming of the streets. In *Berlin is in Germany*, Martin needs to learn the topography of reunited Berlin in order to take a taxi driver test; to his confusion, many (East Berlin) street names he remembers from 1989 have disappeared from the map and have been replaced with new ones: *Dimitroffstrasse* became *Danzigerstrasse*, *Helmut Just Strasse* is *Behmstrasse*, *Leninplatz* is now *Platz der Vereinten Nationen*, *Willi Bredel Strasse* is *Schivelbeinerstrasse*, and so on. Interestingly, rather than discussing the ideological reasons behind the renaming of the street, Martin complains about the simple everyday life inconveniences it has caused. Since the new city text is only partly readable to him, it becomes Martin's quest to learn how to decipher it.

The renaming of Warsaw's streets is commented on in *Warszawa* in the scene in which Father (Sławomir Orzechowski) is looking for his daughter and has problems finding her house not only become so many pedestrians he asks for directions turn out to be newcomers and, thus, like himself, unfamiliar with Warsaw, but also, if not primarily, because many streets have been renamed. The phenomenon is referred to most humorously in Marek Koterski's 2002 *Dzień świra* (The Day of the Wacko), when Adaś Miauczyński (Marek Konrad) encounters a small group of demonstrators—some of them carry signs spelling "yes," others hold on to signs saying "no," all seven of them are surrounded by police forces—passing a street corner where one street is called *ulica Lewicy* (Street of the Left) and the other *ulica Prawicy* (Street of the Right). Clearly, Koterski mocks the widespread practices of renaming the streets according to ideological preferences of the political elites who happen to be in power at a given moment.

Although large parts of both city text and urban landscape have been entirely transformed after 1989, some elements that defined Central European cities under the communist regime prevail or have developed into new urban phenomena. Despite the fact that they exist also in Western European cities, prefabricated tenement blocks are predominantly associated with the former "East bloc." In post-1989 film, concrete apartment buildings are presented as relics of the communist system, breeding grounds of violence and urban pathologies, and a dysfunctional environment in which to live. To the protagonist of Rober Gliński's 2000 social drama *Cześć, Tereska* (*Hi, Tereska*), the prefabricated high-rise building, where she spends her childhood and comes of age in the 1990s, is the only home she knows. The drab concrete blocks portrayed in the first minutes of the film strike the viewer as unfriendly and gray and are juxtaposed with Tereska's white First Communion dress. The protagonist is watching other children throw stones and sand at each other in the playground, when suddenly a random rock breaks the glass door behind which she is standing and hits her on the head. Although the injury is probably an accident rather than an intentional attack, it shows clearly that even children's games are not entirely innocent and can be perilous in Tereska's neighborhood: the scene serves as a prelude to the protagonist's somewhat accidental downfall into pathology and crime. Lacking any sort of cultural or sports facilities, the prefabricated tenement buildings in *Cześć, Tereska* provide little entertainment for its residents; consequently, the youth end up hanging around the dilapidated playground and waste land between the apartment blocks where they drink cheap alcohol, smoke cigarettes, bully small children, and have their first experiences of both sex and crime. Even if sitting around on broken benches appears unexciting, Tereska finds it better than staying in her small apartment with drunk, abusive parents, constant money problems, and a spoiled younger sister.

The (in)famously difficult living conditions in prefabricated houses are criticized and mocked at length in *Dzień świra*, where the protagonist suffers both physically and mentally every day when he tries to write poetry and is disturbed by an upstairs neighbor listening to Chopin at full blast, a downstairs neighbor practicing karate, the housekeeper mowing the lawn with what looks like an electric shaver, a child going up and down the stairs with roller skates on, and countless other sounds. Adaś Miauczyński considers himself a sensitive and sophisticated intellectual, sees his existence in the concrete box as deeply unjust, and constantly tries to distance himself from his neighbors, whom he labels as uneducated working class with no understanding for poetry and subtlety. Miauczyński's frustration with his environment and life results in obsessive compulsive disorder, which further complicates his relationships with the outside world. The presented collection of behaviors and phenomena that characterize existence in a neighborhood composed of prefabricated high-rise buildings is clearly exaggerated and intentionally comical, however, it is based on real-life patters. Koterski criticizes the prevalent lack of respect for the private space and the neglect of the public space as leftovers from the previous system and, partly, a typically Polish phenomenon. In one of the most poignant and symbolic scenes, all residents of Adaś's building go out to their small balconies at night and say a prayer in unison, in which they beg God to make life difficult for their neighbors: "destroy that son of a bitch, my fellow countryman neighbor, that enemy, that reptile. May someone break into his garage, may his wife cheat on him, may they burn his shop, may they hit him on the head with a brick, may his daughter hook up with a black guy, and may he suffer altogether, may he have AIDS and cancer—this is a Polish prayer" (Koterski). Although Koterski sees envy and ignominy as typically Polish faults widespread also outside prefabricated apartment blocks, he demonstrates that they thrive most among the concrete apartment buildings with thin walls and brutally limited privacy.

Whereas *Dzień świra* takes on a tragicomic approach and comments on the dysfunctionality of the settlements designed and built under the communist regime in a humorous way, Marek Bukowski's *blok.pl* (2001) adapts surrealist aesthetics and apocalyptic imagery. Although it is never made explicit, the film takes place in one of Warsaw's many districts filled with prefabricated apartment buildings, *osiedle Bernardyńska*. None of the characters ever seem to leave the neighborhood; their lives revolve around and in the concrete blocks. Importantly, the communist idea of a self-sufficient housing estate is rendered by first experiences of uncontrollable capitalism: Henryk (Jerzy Łapiński), an ardent worshipper of the European Union, who owns a shop and a bistro, is a caricature of a Central European businessman—provincial, scheming, and ignorant. Henryk's unquestionably high position within the local community alludes to how hopeless and confused the other residents must be. Although all characters are exaggerated, they represent various types that normally inhabit prefabricated apartment blocks: bullies with shaved heads and thick necks who spend their days in the basement gym, dolled-up homegirls in tight jeans, big and poor families thrown into small apartments, computer freaks who never leave their rooms, and young drug addicts mentally distanced from their surrounding, among many others. The community as well as the dilapidated blocks it inhabits seem to be on a verge of a total collapse and, eventually, get destroyed once the devil—whom we see speeding in a red sports car in various sequences throughout the film—arrives in the neighborhood.

In *Du bist nicht allein*, the residents of the prefabricated apartment building in an eastern district of Berlin are poor, unemployed, and miserable, but Bern Böhlich is far from presenting apocalyptic visions: he prefers—like Koterski—to describe life in Plattenbauten through a tragicomedy. The characters portrayed in the 2007 film manage to stay optimistic and energetic despite the bleak perspectives on making a better living. In one of the first scenes we see Hans Moll (Axel Prahl) on his balcony overlooking other concrete blocks separated with patches of greenery: in an attempt to add some of nature's vitality and beauty to his dull apartment, Hans is painting colorful landscapes on the balcony walls. Later, when he falls in love with his new neighbor, Jewgenia (Katerina Medvedeva), Hans brings her Mrs. Moll's (Katharina Thalbach) tallest pot plant to decorate and enliven the empty apartment. After many years of unemployment, Mrs. Moll starts working as a security guard and—although she is underpaid and has to work night shifts—sees it as a great opportunity not only for herself and her family, but also for her environment. Consequently, Mrs. Moll becomes more interested in what is happening in and around the Plattenbauten settlement: one day, for example, she finds Jewgenia's rebellious daughter begging for money in the street and brings her back home.

Despite its visual drabness and the miserable situation of its residents, the prefabricated apartment building portrayed in *Du bist nicht allein* does not strike the viewer as entirely hopeless. Unlike the aforementioned films about Warsaw, Böhlich shows that genuine and deep relationships between people who inhabit the concrete blocks are not impossible. In *Good Bye, Lenin!*, the Plattenbau where Alex lives is homey and friendly to the point of disbelief: neighbors seem always happy to have a chat, check on each other casually, and are ready to help. The house radiates a feeling of a small-town neighborhood rather than that of a gray high-rise building located in the very center of a metropolis undergoing serious economic and social changes. Aside from the small size of the apartments, the usual shortcomings of prefabricated blocks (as represented, in an exaggerated form, in *Dzień świra*) are completely omitted here. *Good Bye, Lenin!* also features portrayals of old Mietskasernen abandoned by East Berliners moving to the West in search of a better life: these, unlike the Plattenbauten, are largely deserted and disheveled, but cheap (or even completely free) and somehow charming and, thus, attractive to young people such as Alex and his girlfriend Lara (Chulpan Khamatova).

With dozens of functional prefabricated housing settlements located around the city and whole neighborhoods of Mietskasernen undergoing gradual renovation, there have been few investments in residential developments in post-1989 Berlin. The reputation of world's biggest construction site the city gained in the 1990s was related primarily to the removal of the Wall and new architectural concepts for the former borderland, the urgent need to create professional working space for new corporate and political organizations moving into town, the construction of the new government district, and countless renovations, including those of infrastructure. Although films about post-1989 Berlin are inevitably permeated with images of construction sites, they rarely make it clear whether the depicted works aim to produce residential or office buildings. The hundreds of cranes towering over the otherwise largely horizontal city are depicted often in the films created in the late 1990s and the early 2000s: *Das Leben ist eine Baustelle* (Life is a Construction Site, 1997); *Lola Rennt* (*Run, Lola, Run*, 1998); *Berlin is in Germany*, 2001; *Zimmerspringbrunnen*, 2001, whereby only two of the listed films show how the ongoing construction works influence the everyday lives of Berliners. In Tom Tykwer's *Lola Rennt*, the main protagonist runs through the city punctuated by construction sites, which affects her already hectic route. Lola (Franka Potente) has twenty minutes to save her boyfriend, who threatens to rob a supermarket if she fails to help him arrange 100,000 Deutschmarks: Manni (Moritz Bleibtreu) lost the moneybag his boss expects to collect at noon. Lola has to hurry. Inspired by Krzysztof Kieślowski's *Przypadek* (*Blind Chance*, 1987), Tykwer tells three versions of Lola's and Manni's story: in the first version, Lola is shot dead by the police, but refuses to die and magically turns back the time to 11.40 a.m.; in the second version, Manni is deadly hit by an emergency car; in the third version, the couple not only manages to survive, but also acquires an extra 100,000 *Deutschmarks*. Among other problems she encounters on her way, infrastructure and construction works make Lola's run even more difficult than it already is. In many ways—also owing to the use of animation techniques—*Lola Rennt* resembles a computer game, in which the construction site is one of many types of obstacles. Similarly, in Peter Timm's *Zimmerspringbrunnen*, Berlin's construction boom is presented as a negative phenomenon rather than a sign of the city's development. While Hinrich Lobeck (Götz Schubert)—yet another "typical Wende-loser" to appear in post-1989 film—continues to be unemployed, his wife Julia (Simone Solga) finds a job as one of the architects working on Berlin's largest construction site: Potsdamer Platz. Since most of Julia's colleagues (particularly those higher in rank) are West German, Hinrich is quick to associate the new developments with the Western colonization of the former East Berlin's space, economy, culture, and—inevitably, once Julia leaves him—private lives of East Berliners. Whereas in Tykwer's blockbuster construction sites are merely everyday nuisance, in Timm's film they take on a more symbolic meaning as described by Andreas Huyssen (chapter 5).

Although construction sites rarely appear in post-1989 films about Warsaw, they are repeatedly alluded to in dialogue as well as through chosen locations. Presented mostly as positive phenomena related to Warsaw's economic success, the end products of construction developments featured in film include high-rise office buildings (*Billboard*), new housing estates (*Warszawa*; *Kiler*, 1997), and suburban villas (*Egoiści*; *Córy szczęścia*; *Kiler*), all of which communicate the social status of the portrayed characters. In all the films, the new office and residential space is occupied mostly by the winners of post-1989 transformations: business and media professionals, successful artists, politicians, and gangsters. Importantly, in *Plac Zbawiciela* (*Saviour Square*, 2006), Joanna Kos-Krauze and Krzysztof Krauze present quite different—and possibly more commonplace—aspects of the construction boom, namely the struggle of an average Warsaw resident to find an affordable and attractive apartment. Beata (Jowita Budnik) and Bartek (Arkadiusz Janiczek) are a young married couple with two children, who invest all their savings, take loans, and receive a substantial sum from Bartek's mother Teresa (Ewa Wencel) to buy their first own apartment on the outskirts of the city. The drama starts when the developer announces bankruptcy and it becomes clear that not only has the couple—as well as dozens of other people—lost all the money invested in the project, but they are also heavily in debt and in no position to pay it back. The financial disaster affects the personal lives of the involved and leads to an unpredictable tragedy. Abandoned by her husband and constantly abused by Teresa—in whose apartment on Plac Zbawiciela she is forced to live—Beata attempts to poison herself and her children; in the courtroom, Bartek takes the blame on himself and asks the judge to be punished for the intended crime. The film that starts as a simple tale about purchasing an apartment and ends like a Greek tragedy is based on a true story.

Despite the ongoing construction works and architectural developments, the post-1989 urban landscapes of Berlin and—to a lesser extent—Warsaw still contain large areas of indefinable, often completely empty space. The Berlin void discussed at length by Andreas Huyssen (see chapter 5) is particularly present in Michael Klier's *Ostkreuz* (1991) and Tom Tykwer's *Lola Rennt* (1998). Although the title of the former refers to the area of the Ostkreuz S-Bahn station in the eastern district of Fridrichshain where the north-south and east-west lines meet, the protagonists live in a West Berlin refugee camp. Apparently, the title has a symbolic rather than a geographic meaning and implies that "Berlin has become a crossroads, both literal and metaphorical, as communism collapses across the continent" (Evans 64). The phrase "no-man's-land" seems particularly fitting as in *Ostkreuz* nothing belongs to no one, everything is stolen, borrowed or makeshift. Klier's Berlin of the first Wende years consists of large spaces inhabited by garbage and the wind. The shapeless landscape surrounded by gray Plattenbauten and disheveled Mietskasernen provides the sole background for the peregrinations of the East German teenager Elfie (Laura Tonke) and her new acquaintance, Dariusz (Mirosław Baka), a petty criminal from

Poland. The couple drifts about with no particular aim and only occasionally stops in bars where representatives of the unwanted Central Europe—well known from Andrzej Stasiuk's novels—meet. Interestingly, in his 2007 book titled *Dojczland*, Stasiuk names Ostkreuz one of the very few places in Germany that do not disgust him ("Dojczland" is the Polish phonetic spelling of the German word "Deutschland"; the Polish name for Germany is "Niemcy"):

> I like Ostkreuz and I hope they will never renovate it; I hope the black steel, the red brick, the leaking roof, and the scrappy vendor stand on the platform will remain there forever. Whenever I have some free time in Berlin, I buy a *tageskarte* and visit subway lines, stations, and transfer points. I know I should finally go see a museum, a gallery, a monument, but I never get to do it. Instead on *Museumsinsel* I invariably end up at Ostkreuz to catch, say, the S5 and go to Strausberg. Oh, that gradual vanishing, that lowness and greenness. Behind the window, the countryside emerges: horses, cows, goats, fallow, thickets, nettle, the infinite suburbs, and inside, in the car—a post-Soviet design, almost like in Kishinev. Thugs, fake chains, bleached hags, golden teeth, black roots, zits on thick necks, no one smiles, they growl something to each other, everything becomes provincial and PGR-like. The youngsters have shaved heads and their ears stick out; in their loose nylon trousers extending to the floor, they look just like the kids back home, as if we were approaching Białystok, Minsk, or a Moscow rat hole. One loves Berlin for this. (Stasiuk 59)

In *Lola Rennt*, space is just as vague and in-between as time. For those who know Berlin, Lola's hectic route makes little sense. She leaves her parents' apartment in Mitte, not far from the Charite Hospital, and in the next scene we see her running from Kreuzberg to Friedrichshain over the Oberbaumbrücke. Other stages of her run are equally accidental and dispersed. Naturally, we may assume that Tykwer simply filmed in those locations where he was given permission. Still, it is hard not to notice that the chaotic portrait of Berlin as a city glued together from random pieces adequately mirrors the character of the German capital. Like in *Ostkreuz*, it is difficult to tell the west from the east, however, *Lola Rennt* features some of Berlin's most famous streets and squares. Apart from the construction sites she passes on her way, Lola runs along Friedrichstrasse and crosses Gendarmenmarkt in Mitte: both oddly deserted despite their central location and the fact that the action takes place presumably shortly before noon.

The director of *Lola Rennt* has repeatedly commented on the Berlin void and its meaning in the film. Although Tykwer claims that his story "could take place in any major city of the world," he quickly adds that "Berlin is the perfect match, because Lola is someone who is running between times and Berlin itself is a city between eras. The whole center of town is a construction site" (qtd. in Winters 17). Tykwer portrays the side of Berlin that is arguably most difficult to define: a city caught up in "a fascinating synthetic stage between modernity and decomposition.

No other city is as synthetic and lively as Berlin. Gigantic gray streets without any greenery, devoid of people, ghostly—almost like in a film studio. Here you can feel detached from the world and devoured by a huge metropolis at the same time" (Tykwer, "Anything Runs").

Although deserted streets are a rare view in the center of Warsaw, particularly on a working day, the void is a familiar phenomenon in the Polish capital, prevalent especially in the outer districts dominated by prefabricated housing as well as along the river. With few exceptions, the banks of the Vistula are completely undeveloped and call to mind a no man's land. The emptiness is striking particularly in *Córy szczęścia* and *Amok*, when the protagonists cross the river: no matter if they travel by train or go by foot, the view of the river the characters see from the Warsaw bridges is equally desolate, depressing, and simply surprising when compared with the busy downtown. Natasza and Masza cross the river twice a day: on their way to the Tenth Anniversary Stadium in the district of Praga and on the way back to the cheap motel located on a boat on the left riverbank. Every time they walk toward the center, they see the silhouette of the vertical downtown, however, in the immediate vicinity of their work and temporary home—that is, on both ends of the bridge—Warsaw loses its metropolitan character. In *Amok*, the deserted banks of the Vistula serve as a border separating the richer and more representative part of Warsaw from Praga Północ. Although he appears to be earning well at the Stock Exchange, Max (Mirosław Baka) continues to live in the right-bank district traditionally infamous for its small, dilapidated houses and social pathologies. When he looks out of the train window, the desolate and uncanny riverbanks seem to be mirroring his dark and unfathomable soul. Similar to Berlin's deserted and indefinable urban spaces portrayed in *Ostkreuz* and *Lola Rennt*, the Warsaw void in *Córy szczęścia* and *Amok* takes on symbolic meanings that relate both to the city and the lives of its residents.

The post-1989 Central European urban space has been prominently featured in film together with its most distinguished characteristics, developments, and phenomena. The changeable nature of urban landscapes, city text, and urban palimpsests as well as the new architectural and economic developments of the metropolises have been re-enacted or represented in film. Consequently, cinematic portrayals of Berlin and Warsaw provide important commentaries on recent changes in urban space and the people who use it.

Post-1989 archetypes in film representations of Central European cities

The recent transformations of Central European capitals are often implicitly represented in film through a portrayal of the post-1989 fate of the people inhabiting the urban space. As demonstrated in most of the films discussed above—*Du bist nicht allein*; *Berlin is in Germany*; *Zimmerspringbrunnen*; *Warszawa*; *Cześć, Tereska*; and *Dzień świra*, among others—the typische Wendeverlierer is a particularly popular archetype usually introduced to tell the story of economic, social, and cultural changes, presumably because of the comical potential the figure of a loser possesses. Although the Wende had its share in bringing many careers and relationships to an end, it has also produced impressive success stories and, consequently, the type of a Wendegewinner—the winner of the post-1989 transformations. In what follows, I propose to discuss film representations of both losers and winners of the system change as well as the other recurring archetypes, namely the newcomer and the Westerner.

Strikingly although unsurprisingly, the economic and social gap between the winners and the losers of the Wende is so large that the two groups hardly ever interact in the city. Whereas the former drive fancy cars, work in air-conditioned, spacious, and elegantly designed offices, and live in equally spacious and elegant homes (Filip in *Egoiści*, Flo and Maik in *Was tun, wenn's brennt*, 2001), the former freeze at bus stops, ride overcrowded trams, have no work or move from one badly paid job to the next, and live in small apartments (Hinrich in *Zimmerspringbrunnen*, Peter in *Berlin is in Germany*, Tereska's family in *Cześć, Tereska*, Beata in *Plac Zbawiciela*, to name only a few). More often than not, the winners and the losers live in completely different districts and there is little chance their ways will ever cross. Filip (Jan Frycz) in *Egoiści* lives outside the city and Kuba in *Billboard* owns an apartment in one of the few renovated turn-of-the-century buildings in downtown Warsaw—both could afford either, however, they choose what better suits their life-styles. The Wende-losers, on the contrary, have next to no choice when it comes to determining their addresses and are simply forced to accept the only option they can afford, which more often than not means a small apartment in a prefabricated block (*Dzień świra*; *Cześć, Tereska*; *Berlin is in Germany*; *Du bist nicht allein*) or living on the mercy of one's family (*Alles auf Zucker!*; *Plac Zbawiciela*).

The only thing winners and losers of the post-1989 transformations seem to have in common is their susceptibility to various types of addictions. The latter turn mostly to alcohol as the cheapest and most easily available drug: they drink at home (Katrin in *Sommer vorm Balkon*, Tereska's father in *Cześć, Tereska*), at cemeteries, playgrounds, and other random outdoor places (Tereska in *Cześć, Tereska*), or sit around in cheap bars (Katrin in *Sommer vorm Balkon*, Dariusz in *Ostkreuz*, Peter in *Berlin is in Germany*). They drink to forget about their failures such as unemployment and broken families, but also—as is true in the case of Tereska and her peers—simply because everyone around does. The Wende-winners (over)use drugs, sex, and alcohol out of sheer boredom (Anka and Ilona in *Egoiści*), because of peer pressure turned ad-diction (Młody in *Egoiści*, Maik in *Was tun, wenn's brennt*), to fight the stress related to professional and private life (Smutny and his friends in *Egoiści*), and in an attempt to fill up the emotional gap (Filip in *Egoiści*, Robert in *Córy szczęścia*). Clearly, even those described as Wende-winners turn out to be emotional losers: the success they achieve turns out to be superficial and meaningless in the end. In post-1989 film, it is not the rich and beautiful, who are the real winners of the transformations, but rather those who manage to oscillate between the two extremities: people like Manuela and Enrique in *Berlin is in Germany*, Jackie Zucker's daughter Jana (Anja Francke) in

Alles auf Zucker!, and Alex in *Good Bye, Lenin!*—(former East) Berliners who succeed to adapt to the new economic and social situation without losing integrity.

Next to Wende-winners and Wende-losers, another recurring stereotype in film representations of Central European cities is the newcomer. Although the newcomer theme is widespread in international works of film and literature depicting city life and not exclusively characteristic of post-1989 Central European film, it is important to discuss it here since filmmakers use the archetype to achieve a certain distance in their commentary and a fresher look on the recent urban developments. Most often a young person, the newcomer arrives in the city to escape the provincialism of the small town or village he or she comes from or is determined to achieve the professional success only a metropolis is able to guarantee. Paweł (Łukasz Garlicki) in *Warszawa* comes to the Polish capital with a fistful of banknotes embezzled from his estranged father, whom he sees right after being released from a provincial orphanage; he has only one acquaintance, upon whom—clearly despite his expectations—he cannot count, and a single plastic bag, in which he carries his belongings. Despite his miserable situation, Paweł appears to be hopeful and optimistic about the future, possibly because he is freshly infatuated with the girl he met on the train. Initially, Klara (Agnieszka Grochowska) ignores the stranger, but after it turns out that her lover, for whom she moves to Warsaw, has no intention of leaving his wife and family, she is more interested in befriending Paweł when they accidentally run into each other on a street. Although they have come to the city for various reasons, both feel equally lost, disappointed, cold (the action takes place on a snowy winter day), but, at the same time, are filled with hope and dreams typical to all newcomers. In their eyes, Warsaw is a concrete jungle inhabited by heartless people, a hostile place where everyday life is a constant struggle and one is judged solely by their wealth, but they also see it as a land of opportunities and a city with a (Second World War) history they feel proud of.

Since *Warszawa* depicts only one day in the lives of Klara, Paweł, and the other characters, we are left wondering what happens to them next. In the case of mother and daughter in *Córy szczęścia*, we know for certain how different their fates turn out to be from what they expected. When they arrive at Warsaw's Central Station, they are filled with hope and excitement; they also have a plan: they want to work selling clothes at the Tenth Anniversary Stadium, earn as much money and possible, and go back to their family in Russia. At the end of the film, Natasza is working as a luxurious prostitute and her teenage daughter Masza starts a relationship with Robert and runs away with him. While Natasza's dream is shattered, Masza's has evolved during her stay in Warsaw and she is ready to chase it. Similarly, the women's perceptions of the Polish capital are strikingly different: whereas Natasza is full of contempt for the city and its residents, Masza learns Polish and takes advantage of what Warsaw has to offer. Importantly, mother and daughter climb the economic (and partly social) ladder starting with the despicable Europe Bazaar through the bright and spacious apartment in a brand new building and ending in Robert's impressive villa and, thus, have a rare chance of becoming familiar with various aspects of the city.

Interestingly, many of the newcomers portrayed in post-1989 Berlin film arrive in the city not to chase their dreams, but rather because they have been forced there by other circumstances. Teenage Elfie has little choice but to follow her mother to a West Berlin shelter for East German refugees. Eager to get out of the container camp, Elfie is set on earning enough money to move to a Plattenbau apartment. Despite her young age, she takes on random jobs (some of them clearly illegal) in an attempt to earn a better life for herself and her mother. The mother, however, has no intention of making West Berlin her home: she takes the first opportunity to depart for West Germany with her current lover, even at the cost of leaving Elfie behind. Although her situation seems miserable, the girl does not give up, but continues her struggle to survive in the hostile environment. Despite the repulsiveness of the city and its residents, Elfie manages to find happiness: she starts taking care of a homeless boy named Edmund (Stefan Cammann) and finds meaning and joy in the newly discovered feeling. Consequently, she is strong enough to face everyday challenges and create a home for herself and her new companion. Although they live in an abandoned building with no windows and fight the cold by stuffing up their shoes with old newspapers, Elfie's life energy remains unshaken. *Ostkreuz* serves as a reminder that whereas many people came to Berlin during the Wende in search of adventures and excitement, there were also others, more skeptical about the transformations and focused predominantly on mere survival rather than experiencing historical moments.

Similarly, in Wolfgang Eissler's *Berlin am Meer* (*Berlin by the Sea*, 2008) we see the city through the eyes of a skeptical newcomer. Mavie (Anna Brüggermann) is a young student from Bavaria, who comes to Berlin for an internship with the government. Unlike her brother and his friends who take pride in living in what they consider the coolest place on the planet, Mavie refuses to fall under the charm of the Berlin party scene. She criticizes her new roommates for not getting any work done, falling into addictions, and wasting their talents. Although their parents believe they are still students and keep sending them money, Tom (Robert Stadlober) and Malte (Axel Schreiber) have long dropped out and try to establish themselves as DJs. Also Mavie's brother Mitsch (Clausius Franz) stopped going to medical school and spends his days in bed with his girlfriend instead. Mavie as an outsider and a newcomer manages to present a fresh—and highly unpopular—perspective on Berlin and the lifestyle of its residents. Although she recognizes the attractiveness of the urban space and its multifarious functions and has warm feelings for her new friends, Mavie sees the prevalent—if not obligatory—coolness as mundane and irritating.

While taking on a newcomer's perspective helps recognize otherwise overlooked features and facts about the city, the stereotypical portrayal of the Western foreigner in new Central European cinema discloses the region's fear of a new colonization. More often than not the Westerner is presented as an appalling figure who (mis)uses the economically and culturally vulnerable Central Europeans: this violation and abusiveness are most symbolically thematized in the film portraits of Western foreigners as sexual perverts. Natasza's clients in *Warszawa* are nearly always rich foreigners with most unexpected erotic fantasies. In *Billboard*, it is a Westerner who orders sex tapes depicting brutal rape and murder scenes, in which he himself participates as the perpetrator. Judging from the post-1989 films, West Europeans (mostly West Germans) and US-Americans are not only the main reason why prostitution exists in the region—and, hence, are seen as exploiters of women and children—but are also involved in other shady types of business. Karl in *Warszawa* is presented as appalling both visually and through his behavior. When we first encounter him in his hotel room, he opens the door wearing only his boxer shorts and socks, his beer belly sticking out, and greets Wiktoria and Andrzej (Lech Mackiewicz) with a grunt. Arrogant and obnoxious in everything he does, Karl intentionally says disrespectful things about Warsaw, its history and residents, and is openly unhappy about having to do business in the Polish capital. Karl's character has been composed solely of the many prejudices about Germans that exist in the Polish society, but—despite the obvious exaggeration—he is definitely not a comical figure: his presence in the film is not intended to act against stereotypes, but rather to reconfirm them.

The portrait of the Westerner in post-1989 film about Berlin is not exactly positive either, but it contains much more irony, humor, and distance than the overtly serious although caricatural representations of the Western foreigner in the Polish cinema. In the new Berlin films, the Westerner is more often than not a West German: clumsy, not particularly smart, and mostly incapable of understanding the specific situation in the reunited city. Jackie Zucker's family from Frankfurt (*Alles auf Zucker!*) and Mr. Lehmann's parents from Bremen (*Herr Lehmann*) are some of the most comical film representations of West Germans visiting the strange land that is Berlin. Partially paralyzed with fear of the historically loaded space, they ask questions and make statements that sound naïve if not simply ridiculous to anyone well familiar with Berlin and produce the intended comical effect. Samuel not only compares his atheist brother to Stalin, but also confuses *Staatseigentum* (state ownership) with *Staatssicherheit* (state police), which enrages Jack and leads to yet another argument between the estranged brothers.

Post-1989 films set in Central European cities show a remarkable inclination to stereotypical representations of certain types of characters. Although the portrayals of Wende-losers are much more common than those of Wende-winners, which may suggest a negative evaluation of social and economic transformations, it is important to remember that the majority of Central Europeans exist between these two extremities and appear to be the only ones to fully profit from the Wende. The newcomer is presented as a dreamer and idealist in Warsaw films and a skeptical and sharp observer in Berlin films. The differences between the film representations of these two cities are also striking when it comes to the portrayal of the Westerner who tends to be an appalling pervert or an obnoxious schemer in the films set in the Polish capital and a comical even if irritating figure in the new films about Berlin.

As in the case of literary portrayals of post-1989 Berlin and Warsaw, the (post)colonial character of Central European capitals has been captured in film mainly through the juxtaposition of the remnants of the Soviet-imposed system and the invasion of the Western culture and capital. Since in most films under scrutiny urban landscape serves as an object rather than merely mise-en-scène, the viewer is forced to pay attention to architectural hybrids, palimpsests, and the void that characterize a (post)colonial space. Furthermore, the films discussed in this chapter provide an insight into some of the phenomena of the post-1989 urban changes in Central Europe underrepresented in other media, such as the archetypes of the newcomer and the Westerner and detailed portrayals of the ever-changing urban space. Whereas the fall of the Wall and other 1989 events are represented in film mainly through the implementation of archival footage, the years of economic, social, and cultural transformations are portrayed either through re-enactment and juxtaposition of the pre- and postcommunist reality, or through historical allusions expressed in dialogues and featured monuments. Since they were created over a decade after the actual events and, hence, with the knowledge of the disappointments that succeeded the fall of the Wall, the film portrayals of post-1989 transformations are characterized by skepticism rather than enthusiasm. The film representations of urban space are far from the glossy and colorful images of the city communicated through the municipal media: Central European filmmakers show urban phenomena uncomfortable to city promoters such as the void, the neglected prefabricated apartment blocks, and the politically motivated changes in and of urban space and city text.

Conclusion

In this book I develop and apply a definition of the (post)colonial city, which proves itself to be particularly useful in an interdisciplinary analysis of Central European capital cities after 1989. I do not mean to suggest that other theoretical approaches to Central European cities that perceive these metropolises as primarily postcommunist, postsocialist, or postmodern have lost their practicability. Rather, I propose that an application of a (post)colonial perspective yields new viable opportunities for further research and analysis of Central European cultures in general and the urban cultures of this region in particular.

According to the definition I develop in chapter 3, Berlin, Budapest, Prague, and Warsaw are (post)colonial cities because their politics, cultures, societies, and economies have been shaped by two centers of power: the first is the Soviet Union as the former colonizer, whose influence remains visible predominantly in architecture, infrastructure, social relations, and mentalities; the second is Western culture and Western or global capital as the current colonizer, whose impact extends over virtually all spheres of urban life. Central European cities are characterized by political, cultural, social, and economic tensions resulting from the condition of being postcolonial and colonial at the same time. Furthermore, the cities under scrutiny are "in-between" not only because they exist between the west and the east, but also because they are torn between the Soviet colonial past and the Western or global colonial present. These cities are not exclusively postcolonial or solely colonial: they are "in-between" these two predicaments and, hence, are best described as (post) colonial. The (post)colonial and "in-between peripheral" identities and locations of the Central European capitals complement each other and their analysis provides a timely and relevant perspective on the transformation processes that have shaped and continue to shape the region after 1989.

If we accept—as Edward W. Said and Gayatri Chakravorty Spivak, among others, argue—that the Soviet Union was a colonial power, then the cultures that remained under its occupation or economic, political, and ideological influence can be described as colonized. In chapter 3 I provide various examples illustrating the colonial condition of Central European capitals in the years 1945-1989. Naturally, Moscow's colonial rule was not consistently powerful throughout that time: particularly brutal in its first phase (Sovietization), it waned in the 1980s together with

211

Gorbachev's perestroika and glasnost. Nevertheless, the four decades of Soviet influences irrevocably transformed Central European metropolises and remain partly visible today. The renaming of streets and squares in compliance with the official communist ideology, the demolition of the architectural remnants of the previous "imperialist" systems, the creation of Moscow-controlled political apparatus and secret services, the enforcement of the centrally planned economy, and the suppression of all ideological opposition are only some of the proofs of the colonial nature of the Soviet rule. It is only logical to conclude then that together with the collapse of communism in 1989 and the official retreat of the Soviet colonizer, Central Europe automatically became postcolonial. At the same time, another important process was underway, namely the colonization through Western or global culture, capital, and politics. We can therefore speak of a new form of colonization that commenced in Central Europe in 1989 and which, in an arguably milder form, prevails to this day.

The democratic reforms introduced in Central European capitals in and after 1989 were shaped largely along well-established Western patterns. Whereas the political developments were inspired or extorted by the European Union and can therefore be called EU-ization, the economic and cultural transformation—especially in the first years after the demise of communism—followed the US-American path (Americanization). Catching up with the West became one of the main goals of municipal and state governments and the most common way of achieving it was through the adaptation of Western standards in virtually all areas of life starting with politics through business to entertainment. US-style malls, chain stores, and fast food restaurants influence not only the consumption patterns of city residents, but also the look and functions of whole districts. Although mallification of urban space is hardly an exclusively Central European phenomenon, it is particularly striking when juxtaposed with the previous scarcity or absence of Western-style commercial space in these cities. State ownership decreased rapidly and the newly privatized companies often fell under foreign (mostly Western) ownership that introduced their own modes of management, production, and marketing. This often unconditional implementation of late capitalism onto Central European ground has affected both corporate and private areas of urban life and resulted in pauperization and polarization of urban societies. Arguably, some of the post-1989 ongoing changes in Central European metropolises such as gentrification and commercialization of downtown areas have been part of globalization and, as such, observable also in other cities across the world. However, the special condition of Central European capitals results from the juxtaposition of these new developments with the remnants of the Soviet-imposed system, which leads to creation of urban hybrids, palimpsests, and prevailing confusion.

Unsurprisingly, city and state authorities prefer to present Berlin, Budapest, Prague, and Warsaw as independent metropolises boasting impressive histories and international importance rather than former colonies of the Soviet Union that currently remain under colonial influence of the Western culture and Western or global capital. City logos, slogans, image campaigns, and other urban marketing tools implemented by Central European metropolises have been developed in order to communicate a very similar message, namely to present the cities as both historical and modern. As I demonstrate in chapter 4, Central European capitals are prone to focus on one aspect of their urban identities and neglect the other. As a result, Budapest and Prague emphasize their historical beauty and heritage, while Warsaw and—to a large extent—Berlin present themselves as modern and continually changing. Judging by their official websites and urban marketing materials, municipal authorities treat their history and contemporary times selectively and, more often than not, ignore the socialist period and limit the presentation of the post-1989 era to the accounts of economic progress and new international political alliances.

The municipal media of Central European capitals focus entirely on the discourse of urban representations known as "the positive portrayal of a city" (Short and Kim 97), which is aimed at attracting investors and visitors, while influencing local politics and, as such, is closely connected with urban marketing. The other kind of urban representation—"the identification of the shadow"—tends to be contained and controlled in official imagery and, therefore, "works through silence" (Short and Kim 97). Keeping the above in mind, I propose that by ignoring their (post)colonial condition Central European cities only confirm its existence. This shadow side of the city—mostly more complex than the positive portrayal—is frequently represented in literature and film. The momentous changes Central European capitals have been experiencing ever since the fall of communism have proven inspirational for various writers and filmmakers from inside and outside the region. Contemporary authors have been particularly conscious of economic changes in the cities and how they affect the residents: capitalism, consumerism, and globalization or Westernization have been repeatedly criticized in post-1989 novels both in (post)colonial and other contexts. Similarly, the social transformations resulting from the new economic system such as polarization of the society, new class divisions, and disparities between Wende-winners and Wende-losers are prominently featured in contemporary works of literature set in Berlin and Warsaw. Post-1989 film representations of Central European cities relate to the newest history and the transformations of and in the urban landscapes and city texts. The films I analyze in chapter 7 offer their own interpretations of the urban changes and, most importantly, an insight into some of the phenomena neglected or underrepresented in literature, new media, and historical accounts of the recent transformations. The ambivalent literary and film portrayals of Central European capitals hardly ever overlap with the official images of Berlin and Warsaw communicated in and through municipal media.

Central European cities' preoccupation with history on the one hand and their often uncritical willingness to absorb Western (often corporate-driven) culture on the other hand are also clearly mirrored in new architecture and memorials. The remnants of the socialist past such as prefabricated apartment and office buildings continue to exist side by side with newly renovated nineteenth-century tenement houses and modern office buildings, thus, creating a fragmented and aesthetically diverse urban landscape. The inescapable juxtaposition of the pre- and post-1989 elements—and thus, by implication, postcolonial and new colonial features—creates surprising and ambivalently symbolic combinations. Undeniably, all Central European capitals have been in many different ways affected by post-1989 transformations; however, the changes in and of urban landscapes, societies, and cultures have been particularly substantial in Berlin and Warsaw. As I observe in chapter 5, this phenomenon has been determined by the scale of war destruction: whereas Budapest and Prague were able to keep large parts of their urban landscapes intact and, thus, preserve many elements of their long urban histories, Berlin and Warsaw had to be thoroughly rebuilt and, given the political situation, were forced to follow the Soviet-imposed image of what a city should look like. Therefore, Berlin and Warsaw had to reinvent themselves in 1945 and then again in 1989, which has lead to spatial confusion, countless aesthetic hybrids, palimpsests, and specific obsession with cultural heritage and its commemoration. Furthermore, post-1989 architectural and spatial transformations of Central European cities have been driven by globalization and, I argue, possess a strongly (post)colonial character: the Soviet(-imposed) ideology has been replaced by the free market as the main ideology behind urban developments.

The development and implementation of the definition of the (post)colonial city, which, I believe, is the most innovative and, thus, most interesting aspect of my book, prove the relevance of theory and its application in general. The theories discussed in chapter 2 and repeatedly put in practice in the subsequent chapters provide a basis for an interdisciplinary analysis of Central European urban cultures and, thus, enable a thorough and many-sided understanding of post-1989 urban identities. Steven Tötösy de Zepetnek's comparative cultural studies offers a set of methods and tools to look at urbanities as larger complex systems. Since cities are multilayered and constantly changing organisms, an urban identity remains an open-ended concept, a metaphor rather than an analytical category. Through the application of comparative cultural studies, urbanities may—and I argue, should—be perceived as cultural, social, and historical constructs that continue to change together with political, social, and economic developments. Also, postcolonial theories are particularly significant with regards to political and cultural changes in Central Europe as they help to understand the impact of two cultural centers on the region: the former colonizing power (the Soviet Union) and the current colonizer (Western culture and Western or global capital). Lastly, since urban cultures are the main object of my study, selected concepts from the field of urban studies, such as urban image, urban identity, and urban representation, have proven beneficial for my work.

I do hope that my analyses and the results of the analyses would, perhaps, penetrate some levels of decision making in the political and administrative leadership of city governments encouraging reflective and inclusive thinking and practice, thus fulfilling one of the several postulates of comparative cultural studies: namely the social relevance of the framework in the study of the humanities and social sciences.

Works Cited

Aldenhoven, Claudia. "Gesundheit: Dicke Luft?" *Tagesspiegel.de* (10 February 2002): <http://www.tagesspiegel.de/zeitung/Sonntag;art2566,1990725>.

Al Sayyad, Nezar. *Cinematic Urbanism: A History of the Modern From Reel To Real*. London: Routledge, 2006.

Alles auf Zucker! Dir. Dani Levy. Berlin: X-Filme Creative Pool, 2004.

Aly, Götz. "The Woes of Berlin's Memorials." Trans. John Lambert and Lucy Powell. *Süddeutsche Zeitung* (1 March 2005). *singandsight.com* (2009): <http://www.signandsight.com/features/67.html>.

American Psycho. Dir. Mary Harron. New York: Am Psycho Productions, 2000.

Amok. Dir. Natalia Koryncka-Gruz. Warszawa: Agencja Produkcji Filmowej, 1998.

Andruchowycz, Jurij. *Ostatnie terytorium. Eseje o Ukrainie*. Trans. Ola Hnatiuk, Katarzyna Kotyńska, and Lidia Stefanowska. Wołowiec: Czarne, 2002.

Artmann, H.C., Péter Esterházy, Danilo Kiš, György Konrád, Edward Limonov, Claudio Magris, Czesław Miłosz, Paul-Eerik Rummo, Miklós Mészöly, and Adam Michnik. "The Budapest Roundtable." *Cross Currents* 10 (1991): 17-30.

Ash, Timothy Garton. *We The People: The Revolution of '89 Witnessed in Warsaw, Budapest, Berlin and Prague*. Cambridge: Granta, 1990.

Ashcroft, Bill, Gareth Griffiths, and Helen Tiffin. *The Empire Writes Back: Theory and Practice in Post-Colonial Literatures*. London: Routledge, 1989.

Auswärtiges Amt. "Das Haus am Werderschen Markt: Von der Reichsbank zum Auswärtigen Amt." Berlin: Auswärtiges Amt, 1999.

Barber, Stephen. *Projected Cities: Cinema and Urban Space*. London: Reaktion Books, 2002.

Barthes, Roland. "Semiology and Urbanism." 1967. *The Semiotic Challenge*. Trans. Richard Howard. Berkeley: U of California P, 1994. 191-201.

Bartoszewicz, Dariusz. "Dzikie pola strasza w centrum solicy." *Wyborcza.pl* (4 February 2008): <http://wyborcza.pl/1,87647,4896128.html>.

Bartoszewski, Władysław. "Aufruf zur Gründung eines 'Museum des Kalten Krieges—Teilung und Befreiung Europas'." *Süddeutsche Zeitung* (16 June 2008): <http://www.stiftung-aufarbeitung.de/downloads/pdf/2008/Aufruf.pdf>.

Bator, Bartosz. "Kapuściana reklama stolicy wywołała burzę." *Dziennik* (14 November 2007): 10.

Benjamin, Walter. *Charles Baudelaire: A Lyric Poet in the Era of High Capitalism.* Trans. Harry Zohn. London: Verso, 1973.

Benjamin, Walter. "Work of Art in the Age of Mechanical Reproduction." 1935. *Illuminations.* By Walter Benjamin. Trans. Harry Zohn. New York: Schocken, 1969. 217-52.

Benning, Maria. "Gnadenbrot für Lenin." *Die Zeit* 40 (1998): <http://www.zeit. de/1998/40/Gnadenbrot_fuer_Lenin>.

Berlin am Meer. Dir. Wolfgang Eissler. Berlin: Alin Filmproduktion, 2008.

Berlin is in Germany. Dir. Hannes Stöhr. Berlin: Deutsche Film- und Fernsehakademie Berlin, 2001.

BerlinOnline Stadtportal. *The Official City Portal of Berlin* (2008): <http://www. berlin.de/english/>.

Berlin Partner. be *Berlin—Die Hauptstadtkampagne* (2008): <http://www.sei.berlin. de>.

Berlin Tourismus Marketing. *Berlin Tourist Information* (2008): <http://www.visit-berlin.de>.

Berman, Marshall. *On the Town: One Hundred Years of Spectacle in Times Square.* New York: Random House, 2006.

Berman, Marshall. *All That Is Solid Melts Into Air: The Experience of Modernity.* New York: Penguin, 1982.

Bhabha, Homi K. *The Location of Culture.* London: Routledge, 1994.

Billboard. Dir. Łukasz Zadrzyński. Warszawa: Agencja Produkcji Filmowej, 1998.

Bishop, Ryan, John Phillips, and Wei-Wei Yeo, eds. *Postcolonial Urbanism: Southeast Asian Cities and Global Processes.* London: Routledge, 2003.

Bishop, Ryan, John Phillips, and Wei-Wei Yeo. "Perpetuating Cities: Excepting Globalization and the Southeast Asia Supplement." *Postcolonial Urbanism: Southeast Asian Cities and Global Processes.* Ed. Ryan Bishop, John Phillips, and Wei-Wei Yeo. London: Routledge, 2003. 1-34.

Blažek, Petr. "Pomník obětem komunismu." *Totalita.cz* (1998-2008): <http://www. totalita.cz/pomnik/pomnik_praha_001.php>.

blok.pl. Dir. Marek Bukowski. Warszawa: Maat Studio, 2001.

Blumsztajn, Seweryn. "Siedem grzechów Warszawy." *Gazeta.pl Warszawa* (16 February 2007): <http://miasta.gazeta.pl/warszawa/1,34862,3925286.html>.

Blunt, Alison, and Cheryl McEwan, eds. *Postcolonial Geographies.* London: continuum, 2002.

Bollwahn, Barbara. "Neue Image-Kampagne. Berlin ist eine Sprechblase." *Spiegel Online* (11 March 2008): <http://www.spiegel.de/kultur/gesell-schaft/0,1518,540821,00.html>.

Bottà, Giacomo. "Interculturalism and New Russians in Berlin." *CLCWeb: Comparative Literature and Culture* 8.2 (2006): <http://docs.lib.purdue.edu/clc-web/vol8/iss2/5>.

Boyer, M. Christine. *The City of Collective Memory: Its Historical Imagery and Architectural Entertainments.* Cambridge: MIT P, 1994.

Bradshaw, Michael J. "Foreign Direct Investment and Economic Transformation in Central and Eastern Europe." *Foreign Direct Investment and Regional Development in East Central Europe and the former Soviet Union.* Ed. David Turnock. Burlington: Ashgate, 2005. 3-20.

Brooks, David. *Bobos in Paradise: The New Upper Class And How They Got There.* New York: Simon & Schuster, 2000.

Buck-Morss, Susan. *The Dialectics of Seeing: Walter Benjamin and the Arcades Project.* Cambridge: MIT P, 1991.

Budapest Tourism Office. *Budapest Tourism Office—Official Website of Budapest* (2008): <http://www.budapestinfo.hu/en>.

Bundesministerium der Finanzen. "Das Detlev-Rohwedder-Haus." Berlin: Bundesministerium der Finanzen, 2005.

Bündnis für den Palast. "Informationen zum Palast der Republik." (2005): <http://www.palastbuendnis.de/pages/info/info_chronik.html>.

Capello, Ernesto B. "The Postcolonial City as Universal Nostalgia." *City* 10.2 (2006): 125-47.

CLCWeb: Comparative Literature and Culture: <http://docs.lib.purdue.edu/clcweb/>.

Cochrane, Allan. "Making Up Meanings in a Capital City: Power, Memory and Monuments in Berlin." *European Urban and Regional Studies* 13.1 (2006): 5-24.

Cochrane, Allan and Andrew Jonas. "Re-imagining Berlin: World City, National Capital or Ordinary Place?" *European Urban and Regional Studies* 6.2 (1999): 145-64.

Córy szczęścia. Dir. Márta Mészáros. Warszawa: Agencja Produkcji Filmowej, 1999.

Cronin, Anne M. and Kevin Hetherington, eds. *Consuming the Entrepreneurial City: Image, Memory, Spectacle.* New York: Routledge, 2008.

Cześć, Tereska. Dir. Robert Gliński. Warszawa: Propaganda Film, 2001.

Das Leben ist eine Baustelle. Dir. Wolfgang Becker. Berlin: X-Filme Creative Pool, 1997.

Davies, Norman. *Europe at War, 1939-1945: No Simple Victory.* London: Macmillan, 2006.

Design Build Network. "New Government Buildings, Budapest, Hungary." *designbuild-network.com* (2008): <http://www.designbuild-network.com/projects/budapest-government/>.

Deutscher Bundestag. "Insights: A Tour of Berlin's Parliamentary Quarter." Berlin: Deutscher Bundestag, 2006.

"Deutschlands Lieblingsmonumente." *Cicero* 6 (2008): 108.

Dimitrovska Andrews, Kaliopa. "Mastering the Post-Socialist City: Impacts on Planning the Built Environment." *Transformation of Cities in Central and Eastern Europe: Towards Globalization.* Ed. F.E. Ian Hamilton, Kaliopa Dimitrovska Andrews, and Nataša Pichler-Milanović. New York: United Nations UP, 2005. 153-86.

Döblin, Alfred. *Berlin-Alexanderplatz.* 1929. München: dtv, 1996.

Du bist nicht allein. Dir. Bern Böhlich. Berlin: Rundfunk Berlin-Brandenburg, 2007.

Dujisin, Zoltan. "Global Tourism Swallowing Prague." *Kommunikation Global* 7.2 (2007): 9-10. <http://www.global-perspectives.info/download/2007/pdf/ausgabe_02_07.pdf>.

Dzień świra. Dir. Marek Koterski. Warszawa: Agencja Produkcji Filmowej, 2002.

Egoiści. Dir. Mariusz Treliński. Warszawa: Agencja Produkcji Filmowej, 2000.

Ellger, Christoph, ed. *Budapest und Bukarest. Systemwechsel und stadträumliche Transformation*. Spec. issue of *METAR: Manuskripte zur Empirischen und Theoretischen und Angewandten Regionalforschung* 36 (1999).

Elliott, Stuart. "A City Seeks to Sell Itself." *NYTimes.com* (10 December 2004): <http://www.nytimes.com/2004/12/10/business/media/10adco.html>.

Esbenshade, Richard S. "Remembering to Forget: Memory, History, National Identity in Postwar East-Central Europe." *Representations* 4.9 (1995): 72-96.

Esterházy, Péter. "A Reading Session with Péter Esterházy at the 1998 Frankfurt Book Fair" (1998): <http://www.frankfurt.matav.hu/angol/esterhazy.htm>.

European Communities. "European Capitals of Culture." (1995-2008): <http://ec.europa.eu/culture/our-programmes-and-actions/doc457_en.htm>.

Even-Zohar, Itamar. *Polysystem Studies*. Spec. issue of *Poetics Today* 11.1 (1990).

Foerster, Heinz von. *Wissen und Gewissen. Versuch einer Brücke*. Frankfurt: Suhrkamp, 1993.

Fowles, Jib. *Advertising and Popular Culture*. Thousand Oaks: Sage Publications, 1996.

Gedenkstätte Berliner Mauer (2008): <http://www.berliner-mauer-dokumentation-szentrum.de/>.

Geter, Marek. "Straty ludzkie i materialne w Powstaniu Warszawskim." *Biuletyn Instytutu Pamięci Narodowej* 8-9 (2004): <http://www.powstanie.pl/index.php?ktory=27&class=text>.

Ghent Urban Studies Team, ed. *The Urban Condition: Space, Community, and Self in the Contemporary Metropolis*. Rotterdam: 010 Publishers, 1999.

Good Bye, Lenin! Dir. Wolfgang Becker. Berlin: X-Filme Creative Pool, 2003.

Haider, Donald. "Place Wars: New Realities of the 1990s." *Economic Development Quarterly* 6.2 (1992): 127-34.

Hamilton, F.E. Ian, Kaliopa Dimitrovska Andrews, and Nataša Pichler-Milanović, eds. *Transformation of cities in Central and Eastern Europe: Towards Globalization*. New York: United Nations UP, 2005.

Hanssen, Beatrice, ed. *Walter Benjamin and the Arcades Project*. London: Continuum, 2006.

Hardt, Michael and Antonio Negri. *Empire*. Cambridge: Harvard UP, 2000.

Harris, Emily. "Old East Berlin Fades Away Amid Renovations." *NPR Morning Edition* (27 October 2006): <http://www.npr.org/templates/story/story.php?storyId=6389848>.

Harvey, David. "From Managerialism to Entrepreneurialism: The Transformation in Urban Governance in Late Capitalism." *Geografiska Annaler* 71 B (1989): 3-17.

Häußermann, Hartmut, and Andreas Kapphan. "Berlin: From Divided to Fragmented City." *Transformation of Cities in Central and Eastern Europe: Towards Globalization.* Ed. F.E. Ian Hamilton, Kaliopa Dimitrovska Andrews, and Nataša Pichler-Milanović. New York: United Nations UP, 2005. 189-222.

Häußermann, Hartmut, and Claire Colomb. "The New Berlin: Marketing the City of Dreams." *Cities and Visitors: Regulating People, Markets, and City Space.* Ed. Lily M. Hoffman, Susan S. Fainstein, and Dennis R. Judd. Oxford: Blackwell, 2003. 200-18.

Häußermann, Hartmut, Andrej Holm, and Daniela Zunzer. *Stadterneuerung in der Berliner Republik: Modernisierung in Berlin-Prenzlauer Berg.* Opladen: Leske+Budrich, 2002.

Herr Lehmann. Dir. Leander Haußmann. Berlin: Boje Buck Produktion, 2003.

Highmore, Ben. *Cityscapes: Cultural Readings in the Material and Symbolic City.* New York: Palgrave Macmillan, 2005.

Hodgson, Robert. "Government Quarter Crumbling." *The Budapest Times* (14 January 2008): <http://www.budapesttimes.hu/content/view/4217/26/>.

Hoffman, Lily M., Susan S. Fainstein, and Dennis R. Judd, eds. *Cities and Visitors: Regulating People, Markets, and City Space.* Oxford: Blackwell, 2003.

Hoffmann-Axthelm, Dieter. "Das Einkaufszentrum." *Mythos Metropole.* Ed. Gotthard Fuchs, Bernhard Moltmann, and Walter Prigge. Frankfurt: Suhrkamp, 1995. 63-72.

Holm, Andrej. *Die Restrukturierung des Raumes: Stadterneuerung der 90er Jahre in Ostberlin. Interessen und Machtverhältnisse.* Bielefeld: transcript, 2006.

Holocaust Memorial Center (2008): <http://www.hdke.hu/>.

Huyssen, Andreas. *Present Pasts: Urban Palimpsests and the Politics of Memory.* Stanford: Stanford UP, 2003.

Im Schwitzkasten. Dir. Eoin Moore. Berlin: Moneypenny Filmproduktion, 2005.

"Interview mit Produzent Stefan Arndt." *Good Bye, Lenin!*—Ein Film von Wolfgang Becker. (2005): <http://www.good-bye-lenin.de/int-arndt.php>.

Jameson, Fredric. *The Geopolitical Aesthetic: Cinema and Space in the World System.* Bloomington: Indiana UP, 1992.

Jameson, Fredric. *Postmodernism; or, The Cultural Logic of Late Capitalism.* Durham: Duke UP, 1991.

Janaszek-Ivaničková, Halina. "Postmodern Literature and the Cultural Identity of Central and Eastern Europe." *Postcolonial Literatures: Theory and Practice / Les Littératures Post-Coloniales. Théories et Réalisations.* Ed. Steven Tötösy de Zepetnek and Sneja Gunew. Spec. issue of *Canadian Review of Comparative Literature / Revue Canadienne de Littérature Comparée* 22.3-4 (1995): 805-11.

Jewish Museum Berlin (2008): <http://www.jmberlin.de>.

Jewish Museum in Prague (2004-2008): <http://www.jewishmuseum.cz>.

Johnstone, Chris. "Czech Television Put On the Spot Over Anti-Roma Election Clips." *Radio Praha* (21 May 2009): <http://www.radio.cz/en/article/116495>.

Jordan, Jennifer A. *Structure of Memory: Understanding Urban Change in Berlin and Beyond.* Stanford: Stanford UP, 2006.

Judt, Tony. *Postwar: A History of Europe Since 1945*. London: Penguin, 2006.

Kaminer, Wladimir. *Schönhauser Allee*. München: Goldmann, 2001.

"Kapuściana reklama stolicy wywołała burzę." *Dziennik.pl* (14 November 2008): <http://www.dziennik.pl/unused/wydarzeniapolsatu/article71871.ece>.

Kaschuba, Wolfgang. "Urbane Identität: Einheit der Widersprüche?" *Urbanität und Identität zeitgenössischer europäischer Städte*. Ed. Vittorio Magnago Lampugnani. Ludwigsburg: Wüstenrot Stiftung, 2005. 8-28.

Kilb, Andreas, and Heinrich Wefing. "Ein republikanisches Versprechen." *Faz.net* (26 April 2007): <http://www.faz.net/sRubEBED639C476B407798B1CE 808F1F6632/Doc~ED7D8B6928E2048C99F1A9708BF7CBDCE~ATpl~Ecom mon~Scontent.html>.

Kiler. Dir. Juliusz Machulski. Warszawa: Canal+ Polska, 1997.

King, Anthony D. "Actually Existing Postcolonialisms: Colonial Urbanism and Architecture after the Postcolonial Turn." *Southeast Asian Cities and Global Processes*. Ed. Ryan Bishop, John Phillips, and Wei-Wei Yeo. London: Routledge, 2003. 167-83.

Klausmeier, Axel and Leo Schmidt. *Mauerreste—Mauerspuren. Der umfassende Führer zur Berliner Mauer*. Berlin: Westkreuz, 2005.

Klein, Naomi. *The Shock Doctrine: The Rise of Disaster Capitalism*. London: Penguin Books, 2007.

Knallhart. Dir. Detlev Buck. Berlin: Boje Buck Produktion, 2007.

Knöfel, Ulrike, Joachim Kronsbein, and Michael Sontheimer. "Vorwärts in die Vergangenheit." *Spiegel* 49 (2008): 178-81.

Knowles, Jonathan. "The Role of Brands in Business." *Brands: Visions and Values*. Ed. John Goodchild and Clive Callow. Chichester: John Wiley & Sons, 2001. 21-90.

Kohout, Michal, Vladimír Šlapeta, and Stephan Templ, eds. *Prague: 20th Century Architecture*. Vienna: Springer, 1999.

Kolja. Dir. Jan Svěrák. Prague: Biograf Jan Svěrák, 1996.

Konwicki, Tadeusz. *Mała apokalipsa*. Warszawa: Niezależna Oficyna Wydawnicza Nowa, 1993.

Koolhaas, Rem. "The Generic City: Guide, 1994." *S, M, L, XL*. Rem Koolhaas and Bruce Mau. New York: The Monacelli P, 1995. 1238-69.

Kowalska, Agnieszka. "Burza o pole kapusty." *Gazeta.pl Warszawa* (16 November 2007): <http://miasta.gazeta.pl/warszawa/1,34861,4673547.html>.

Kowalska, Agnieszka and Izabela Szymańska. "Jedno logo za drugim." *Gazeta.pl Warszawa* 10 May 2008: <http://miasta.gazeta.pl/warszawa/1,34862,5198698. html>.

Kozak, Michał. "Kino Skarpa trafiło pod kilof." *rp.pl* (*Rzeczpospolita*) (18 February 2008): <http://www.rp.pl/artykul/94361.html>.

Kracauer, Sigfried. *Theorie des Films. Die Errettung der äusseren Wirklichkeit*. 1960. Trans. Friedrich Walter and Ruth Zellschan. Frankfurt am Main: Suhrkamp, 2009.

Krosnar, Katka. "A Tribute to Barren Shops." *Newsweek International* (11 February 2002): <http://www.newsweek.com/id/63751>.

Krzemiński, Ireneusz. "Fatalne skutki niezamkniętych spraw." *Dziennik.pl* (12 August 2007): <http://www.dziennik.pl/opinie/article49570/Krzeminski_Fatalne_skutki_niezamknietych_spraw.html>.

Kubiczek, André. *Die Guten und die Bösen*. Reinbeck: Rowohlt, 2004.

Kulish, Nicholas. "Trumping the Unbearable Darkness of History." *NYTimes.com* (20 March 2008): <http://travel.nytimes.com/2008/03/30/travel/30Footsteps.html?pagewanted=print>.

Kumar, M. Satish. "The Evolution of Spatial Ordering in Colonial Madras." *Postcolonial Geographies*. Ed. Alison Blunt and Cheryl McEwan. London: continuum, 2002. 85-98.

Kundera, Milan. "The Tragedy of Central Europe." Trans. Edmund White. *The New York Review of Books* 31.7 (26 April 1984): 33-38.

Lackó, Miklós. "Budapest During the Interwar Years." *Budapest: A History from Its Beginnings to 1998*. Trans. Judit Zinner, Cecil D. Eby, and Nóra Arató. Ed. András Gerő and János Poór. New York: Columbia UP, 1997. 139-90.

Ladd, Brian. *The Ghost of Berlin: Confronting German History in the Urban Landscape*. Chicago: U of Chicago P, 1997.

Lange-Müller, Katja. *Die Enten, die Frauen und die Wahrheit. Erzählungen und Miniaturen*. Köln: Kiepenheuer & Witsch, 2003.

Lemańska, Magda. "Syrenki dwie." *Rzeczpospolita Warszawa* (21 Sept. 2004): a7.

Lefebvre, Henri. *The Urban Revolution*. Trans. Robert Bononno. Minneapolis: U of Minnesota P, 2003.

Levin, Nora. *The Jews in the Soviet Union since 1917*. New York: New York UP, 1988.

Lola Rennt. Dir. Tom Tykwer. Berlin: X-Filme Creative Pool, 1998.

Long, Colin. "What is to Be Done with the Heritage of Communists? The Uses of Heritage in Post-Communist and Transitional-Communist Societies." *On Both Sides of the Wall: Preserving Monuments and Sites of the Cold War Era*. Ed. Leo Schmidt and Henriette von Preuschen. Berlin: Westkreuz-Verlag, 2005. 105-07.

Lungescu, Oana. "Chirac Blasts EU Candidates." *BBC News* (18 February 2003): <http://news.bbc.co.uk/2/hi/europe/2774139.stm>.

Lynch, Kevin. *The Image of the City* (1960). Cambridge: MIT P, 1993.

Magris, Claudio. "Praga cancellata." *Corriere della Sera.it* (8 November 2007): <http://www.corriere.it/spettacoli/07_novembre_08/praga_magris_miti.shtml>.

Marsovszky, Magdalena. "Cultural Essentialism in Post-1989 Hungary." *The New Central and East European Culture*. Ed. Steven Tötösy de Zepetnek, Carmen Andras, and Magdalena Marsovszky. Aachen: Shaker, 2006. 268-76.

Masłowska, Dorota. *Między nami dobrze jest*. Warszawa: Lampa i Iskra Boża, 2008.

Masłowska, Dorota. *Paw królowej*. Warszawa: Lampa i Iskra Boża, 2005.

McClennen, Sophia A., and Earl E. Fitz, eds. *Comparative Cultural Studies and Latin America*. West Lafayette: Purdue UP, 2003.

Memento Park Budapest (2008): <http://www.szoborpark.hu/index.php?Lang=en>.

Metropolis. Dir. Fritz Lang. Berlin: Universum Film (UFA), 1927.

Miłosz, Czesław. "Central European Attitudes." *Cross Currents* 5 (1986): 101-08.

"Minister Sikorski: Chcę zburzyć Pałac Kultury." *Dziennik.pl* (9 May 2008): <http://www.dziennik.pl/polityka/article170213/Minister_Sikorski_Chce_zburzyc_Palac_Kultury.html>.

Mitchell, William J. *Placing Words: Symbols, Space, and the City*. Cambridge: MIT P, 2005.

Modrzejewski, Filip and Monika Sznajderman, eds. *Nostalgia. Eseje o tęsknocie za komunizmem*. Wołowiec: Czarne, 2002.

Moszkva tér. Dir. Ferenc Török. Budapest: Budapest Film Kft., 2001.

Müller-Funk, Wolfgang. "Kakanien revisited. Über das Verhältnis von Herrschaft und Kultur." *Kakanien revisited. Das Eigene und das Fremde in der österreichisch-ungarischen Monarchie*. Ed. Wolfgang Müller-Funk, Peter Plener, and Clemens Ruthner. Tübingen: Francke 2002. 14-32.

Müller-Funk, Wolfgang, Peter Plener, and Clemens Ruthner, eds. *Kakanien revisited. Das Eigene und das Fremde (in) der österreichisch-ungatischen Monarchie*. Tübingen: Francke, 2002.

Municipality of Budapest. *Budapest Portál* (2008): <http://english.budapest.hu>.

Murawski, Jarosław. "Ucieczka na wieże." *Polityka* (29 September 2007): 94-96.

Museum of Communism (2008): <http://www.muzeumkomunismu.cz/>.

Museum of the History of Polish Jews (2009): <http://www.jewishmuseum.org.pl/index.php?lang=en>.

Musil, Jiří. "City Development in Central and Eastern Europe Before 1990: Historical Context and Socialist Legacies." *Transformation of Cities in Central and Eastern Europe: Towards Globalization*. Ed. F.E. Ian Hamilton, Kaliopa Dimitrovska Andrews, and Nataša Pichler-Milanović. New York: United Nations UP, 2005. 22-43.

Musil, Jiří. "Prague Returns to Europe." *Transformation of Cities in Central and Eastern Europe: Towards Globalization*. Ed. F.E. Ian Hamilton, Kaliopa Dimitrovska Andrews, and Nataša Pichler-Milanović. New York: United Nations UP, 2005. 281-317.

Nascimento, Amos. "On the Global Inter-location of a Postcolonial City." *City* 10.2 (2006): 149-66.

Nawratek, Krzysztof. *Miasto jako idea polityczna*. Kraków: Korporacja ha!art, 2008.

Nawratek, Krzysztof. "Wajda—kandydat na Wielkiego Urbanistę." *Krytyka Polityczna* (11 May 2008): <http://www.krytykapolityczna.pl/Naszym-zdaniem/Nawratek-Wajda-Kandydat-na-Wielkiego-Urbaniste/menu-id-34.html>.

Olszewski, Krzysztof. "Syrenka nam się rozmazała." *eMetro.pl* (21 September 2004): <http://www.emetro.pl/emetro/1,50145,2295711.html>.

Oppman, Artur. "Syrena." *Legendy warszawskie*. 1925. Warszawa: Krajowa Agencja Wydawnicza, 1982.

Ostkreuz. Dir. Michael Klier. Berlin: Michael Klier Film, 1991.

Ouroussoff, Nicolai. "Let the 'Starchitects' Work All the Angles." *NYTimes. com* (16 December 2007): <http://www.nytimes.com/2007/12/16/weekinreview/16ouroussoff.html?scp=1&sq=starchitect&st=cse>.

Palace of Arts Budapest (2005): <http://www.mupa.hu/epiteszetileiras.jsp>.

Palonen, Emilia. "Creating Communities: The Postcommunist City Text of Budapest." *Tr@nsit online* (2006): <http://www.iwm.at/index.php?option=com_content&task=view&id=416&Itemid=516>.

Parei, Inka. *Die Schattenboxerin*. Frankfurt am Main: Schöffling & Co., 1999.

Patke, Rajeev S. "Benjamin's *Arcades Project* and the Postcolonial City." *Southeast Asian Cities and Global Processes*. Ed. Ryan Bishop, John Phillips, and Wei-Wei Yeo. London: Routledge, 2003. 287-302. First published in *Diacritics* 30.4 (2000): 3-14.

Peltzer, Ulrich. *Teil der Lösung*. Zürich: Ammann, 2007.

Piątek, Tomasz. *Heroina*. Wołowiec: Czarne, 2002.

Pilch, Jerzy. *Miasto utrapienia*. Warszawa: Świat książki, 2004.

Pinkas, Aleksandra and Michał Kozak. "Miasto traci ikony architektury." *Życie Warszawy* (7 August 2008): <http://www.zw.com.pl/artykul/2,276548_Miasto_traci_ikony_architektury.html>.

Plac Zbawiciela. Dir. Jerzy Krauze and Joanna Kos-Krauze. Warszawa: Canal+ Polska, 2006.

Podzimková, Dina. "Názvy ulic: jak Palach porazil Rudou armádu." *Týden.cz* (8 August 2008): <http://www.tyden.cz/rubriky/domaci/historie/nazvy-ulic-jak-palach-porazil-rudou-armadu_18664.html>.

Poláková, Sylva. "Freedom as a Side-Product." *Visegrad Group* (2007): <http://www.visegradgroup.eu/main.php?folderID=1111&articleID=13034&ctag=artic lelist&iid=1>.

Pollesch, René. *Tod eines Praktikanten*. Berlin: Volksbühne im Prater, 2007.

Polyák, Levente. "Alternative Use of Public Space in Budapest." *Exindex* (2006): <http://www.exindex.hu/index.php?l=en&page=3&id=358>.

Polyák, Levente. "Coherent Fragmentation: Finding and Remembering in Central Europe's Confused Cities." *Visegrad Group* (2007): <http://www.visegradgroup. eu/main.php?folderID=1111&articleID=13030&ctag=articlelist&iid=1>.

Polyák, Levente. "Heritage as Argument, Heritage as Authority: Notions and Positions in Contemporary Budapest Urban Planning Discourse." *Levente Polyák's Page* (2008): <http://polyaklevente.wordpress.com/>.

"Pomnik Dmowskiego pomalowany na różowo." *Wyborcza.pl* (11 November 2006): <http://serwisy.gazeta.pl/kraj/1,34397,3729927.html>.

Popescu, Simona. "All that Nostalgia." *Nostalgia: Eseje o tęsknocie za komunizmem*. Ed. Filip Modrzejewski and Monika Sznajderman. Wołowiec: Czarne, 2002. 93-111.

Prague City Hall. *Portál hlavního města Prahy* (2006-2008): <https://www.praha. eu/jnp/en/home/index.html>.

Prague Information Service. *Prague Information Service*. 2008. <http://www.pis.cz/a>.

Presse und Informationsamt des Landes Berlin. *Berlin-Sygnet* (CD-ROM). 2002. 1-31.

Prigge, Walter. "Mythos Architektur: Zur Sprache des Städtischen." *Mythos Metropole.* Ed. Gotthard Fuchs, Bernhard Moltmann, and Walter Prigge. Frankfurt: Suhrkamp, 1995. 73-86.

Przypadek. Dir. Krzysztof Kieślowski. Warszawa: P.P. Film Polski, 1987.

Psy. Dir. Władysław Pasikowski.Warszawa: Agencja Produkcji Filmowej, 1992.

Psy 2: Ostatnia krew. Dir. Władysław Pasikowski. Warszawa: Agencja Produkcji Filmowej, 1994.

Radisch, Iris. "Zwei getrennte Literaturgebiete: Deutsche Literatur der neunziger Jahre in Ost und West." *DDR-Literatur der neunziger Jahre.* Ed. Heinz Ludwig Arnold. *Text+Kritik* Sonderband 9 (2000): 13-26.

Re: Warsaw 2016 Reborn by culture (2007): <http://pl.youtube.com/watch?v=0j-qIp28Fmg>.

Regener, Sven. *Herr Lehmann.* Frankfurt am Main: Eichborn, 2001.

Reimann, Kerstin E. *Schreiben nach der Wende—Wende im Schreiben? Literarische Reflexionen nach 1989/90.* Würzburg: Königshausen & Neumann, 2008.

Rév, István. *Retroactive Justice: Prehistory of Communism.* Stanford: Stanford UP 2005.

Rezerwat. Dir. Łukasz Palkowski. Warszawa: Paisa Films, 2007.

Richie, Alexandra. *Faust's Metropolis: A History of Berlin.* London: Harper Collins Publishers, 1998.

Richter, Christine. "Gut und gar nicht gut." *Berliner Zeitung* (12 March 2008): <http://www.berlinonline.de/berliner-zeitung/archiv/.bin/dump.fcgi/2008/0312/berlin/0050/index.html>.

Ritzer, Georg. *Enchanting a Disenchanted World.* Thousand Oaks: Pine Forge P, 2005.

Röggla, Kathrin. *Irres Wetter.* Salzburg: Residenz, 2000.

Royal Heraldry Society of Canada. *Royal Heraldry Society of Canada.* <http://www.heraldry.ca/>.

Rybczynski, Witold. "The Bilbao Effect." *TheAtlantic.com* (September 2002): <http://www.theatlantic.com/doc/200209/rybczynski>.

Said, Edward W. *Culture and Imperialism.* New York: Vintage, 1993.

Said, Edward. *Orientalism.* New York: Vintage, 1978.

Sassen, Saskia. "Locating Cities on Global Circuits." *Global Networks, Linked Cities.* Ed. Saskia Sassen. London: Routledge: 2002. 1-36.

Sassen, Saskia. "The New Centrality: The Impact of Telematics and Globalization." Sassen, Saskia. *The Global City: New York, London, Tokyo.* Princeton: Princeton UP, 1991.

Saunders, William S., ed. *Reflections on Architectural Practices in the Nineties.* New York: Princeton Architectural P, 1996. 206-18.

Schmidl, Erwin A., and László Ritter, eds. *The Hungarian Revolution 1956.* Oxford: Osprey Publishing, 2006.

Schmidt, Leo, and Henriette von Preuschen, eds. *On Both Sides of the Wall: Preserving Monuments and Sites of the Cold War Era.* Berlin: Westkreuz, 2005.

Schmidt, Siegfried J. *Foundations for the Empirical Study of Literature: The Components of a Basic Theory.* Trans. Robert de Beaugrande. Hamburg: Buske, 1982.

Schmidt, Siegfried J. "Literary Studies from Hermeneutics to Media Culture Studies." *CLCWeb: Comparative Literature and Culture* 12.1 (2010): <http://docs.lib.purdue.edu/clcweb/vol12/iss1/1>.

Schmidt, Siegfried J. "Empirical Study of Literature: Why and Why Not?" *The Systemic and Empirical Approach to Literature and Culture as Theory and Application.* Ed. Steven Tötösy de Zepetnek and Irene Sywenky. Edmonton: Research Institute for Comparative Literature, U of Alberta and Siegen: Institute for Empirical Literature and Media Research, Siegen U, 1997. 137-53.

Schmidt-Häuer, Christian. "Unter der Fahne der Faschisten." *Die Zeit* 20 (2009): 3.

Schomaker, Gilbert. "Der Volksaufstand vom 17. Juni unter Glas." *Berliner Zeitung* (17 June 2000): <http://www.berlinonline.de/berliner-zeitung/archiv/.bin/dump.fcgi/2000/0617/none/0070/index.html>.

Senatsverwaltung für Stadtentwicklung. *Alexanderplatz Berlin: History—Planning—Projects.* Berlin: Senatsverwaltung für Stadtentwicklung, 2001.

Senatsverwaltung für Stadtentwicklung Berlin. "Änderungsverfahren-Bebauungsplan I-200-1 Akademie der Künste." *Senatsverwaltung für Stadtentwicklung Berlin* (1996): <http://www.stadtentwicklung.berlin.de/planen/staedtebau-projekte/pariser_platz/de/b_plan/verfahren_i200_1.shtml>.

Senatsverwaltung für Stadtentwicklung Berlin. "Rückbau Palast der Republik" (2008): <http://www.stadtentwicklung.berlin.de/bauen/palast_rueckbau/index.shtml>.

"Siegelordnung der Deutschen Demokratischen Republik. Vom 28. Mai 1953." (2009): <http://www.documentarchiv.de/ddr.html>.

Sierakowski, Sławomir, and Slavoj Žižek. "Slavoj Žižek w Warszawie." (2007): <http://www.youtube.com/watch?v=pFW1uLgz0d4>.

Sigel, Paul. "Dealing with GDR-Era Monuments." *Goethe Institut—Contemporary Monuments Concepts in Germany* (2008): <http://www.goethe.de/kue/arc/dos/dos/zdk/en204232.htm>.

Simmel, Georg. "Die Großstädte und das Geistesleben." 1903. Frankfurt: Suhrkamp, 2006.

Shiel, Mark, and Tony Fitzmaurice, eds. *Cinema and the City: Film and Urban Societies in a Global Context.* Oxford: Blackwell, 2001.

Shiel, Mark. "Cinema and the City in History and Theory." *Cinema and the City: Film and Urban Societies in a Global Context.* Ed. Mark Shiel and Tony Fitzmaurice. Oxford: Blackwell, 2001. 1-18.

Short, John Rennie and Yeong-Hyun Kim. *Globalization and the City.* New York: Longman, 1999.

Shteyngart, Gary. *The Russian Debutante's Handbook.* London: Bloomsbury, 2002.

Skórczewski, Dariusz. "Postkolonialna Polska—projekt (nie)możliwy." *Teksty Drugie* 1-2 (2000): 100-12.

Soja, Edward. "Los Angeles 1965-1992: Six Geographies of Urban Restructuring." Los Angeles: Center for Social Theory and Comparative History, 1994: <http:// escholarship.org/uc/item/30s8h806>.

Sommer vorm Balkon. Dir. Andreas Dresen. Berlin: Peter Rommel Productions, 2005.

Sonnenallee. Dir. Leander Haußmann. Berlin: Boje Buck Produktion, 1999.

Sparschuh, Jens. *Der Zimmerspringbrunnen*. Köln: Kiepenheuer & Witsch, 1995.

Śpiewak, Paweł. *Pamięć po komunizmie*. Gdańsk: słowo/obraz terytoria, 2005.

Spivak, Gayatri Chakravorty. "Are You Postcolonial? To the Teachers of Slavic and Eastern European Literatures." *PMLA: Publications of the Modern Language Association of America* 121.3 (2006): 828-29.

Stanilov, Kiril. "Political Reform, Economic Development, and Regional Growth in Post-Socialist Europe." *The Post-Socialist City: Urban Form and Space Transformations in Central and Eastern Europe After Socialism*. Ed. Kiril Stanilov. Dordrecht: Springer, 2007. 21-34.

Stanilov, Kiril. "Taking Stock of Post-Socialist Urban Development: A Recapitulation." *The Post-Socialist City: Urban Form and Space Transformations in Central and Eastern Europe After Socialism*. Ed. Kiril Stanilov. Dordrecht: Springer, 2007. 3-17.

Stanilov, Kiril, ed. *The Post-Socialist City: Urban Form and Space Transformations in Central and Eastern Europe After Socialism*. Dordrecht: Springer, 2007.

Stanisławski, Piotr. "Miasto w mieście." *Przekrój* (24 January 2008): 54-55.

Stasiuk, Andrzej. *Dojczland*. Wołowiec: Czarne, 2007.

Stiftung Denkmal für die ermordeten Juden Europas (2008): <http://www.stiftung-denkmal.de/>.

Stiftung Gedenkstätte Berlin-Hohenschönhausen (2008): <http://www.stiftung-hsh.de/>.

Strauss, Stefan. "Lenins Fall." *Berliner Zeitung* (13 November 2001): <http://www.berlinonline.de/berliner-zeitung/archiv/.bin/dump.fcgi/2001/1113/berlin/0199/index.html>.

Sýkora, Luděk. "Gentrification in Post-Communist Cities." *Gentrification in a Global Context: The New Urban Colonialism*. Ed. Rowland Atkinson and Gary Bridge. London: Routledge, 2005. 90-105.

Sýkora, Luděk. "Office Development and Post-Communist City Formation: The Case of Prague." *The Post-Socialist City: Urban Form and Space Transformations in Central and Eastern Europe After Socialism*. Ed. Kiril Stanilov. Dordrecht: Springer, 2007. 117-45.

Szczygieł, Mariusz. *20 lat nowej Polski w reportażach według Mariusza Szczygła*. Wołowiec: Czarne, 2009.

Szczygieł, Mariusz. *Gottland*. Wołowiec: Czarne, 2006.

Szczygieł, Mariusz. "Wkurzacz czeski." *Gazeta Wyborcza* (12 August 2008): <http://wyborcza.pl/1,75480,5579849,Wkurzacz_czeski.html>.

Tangen, Jr., Ole. *Brokedown Palast* (2006): <http://video.google.com/videoplay?docid=-4282263054701767415&hl=en>.

Terror Háza (2008): <http://www.terrorhaza.hu/>.

Thomsen, Jan. "Sei Welt, sei offen, sei Berlin." *Berliner Zeitung* (12 March 2008): <http://www.berlinonline.de/berliner-zeitung/archiv/.bin/dump.fcgi/2008/0312/berlin/0029/index.html>.

Three Colors: White. Dir. Krzysztof Kieślowski. Paris: MK2 Production, 1994.

Till, Karen E. *The New Berlin: Memory, Politics, Place*. Minneapolis: U of Minnesota P, 2005.

Till, Karen E. "Re-Imagining National Identity: 'Chapters of Life' at the German Historical Museum in Berlin." *Textures of Place: Rethinking Humanist Geographies*. Ed. Paul Adams, Steven Hoelscher, and Karen Till. Minneapolis: U of Minnesota P, 2001. 273-99.

Timm, Uwe. *Johannisnacht*. Köln: Kiepenheuer & Witsch, 1996.

Tosics, Iván. "City Development in Central and Eastern Europe Since 1990: The Impacts of Internal Forces." *Transformation of Cities in Central and Eastern Europe: Towards Globalization*. Ed. F.E. Ian Hamilton, Kaliopa Dimitrovska Andrews, and Nataša Pichler-Milanović. New York: United Nations UP, 2005. 44-78.

Tosics, Ivan. "Post-Socialist Budapest: The Invasion of Market Forces and the Response of Public Leadership." *Transformation of Cities in Central and Eastern Europe: Towards Globalization*. Ed. F.E. Ian Hamilton, Kaliopa Dimitrovska Andrews, and Nataša Pichler-Milanović. New York: United Nations UP, 2005. 248-80.

Tötösy de Zepetnek, Steven. "Bibliography of Work in Contextual (Systemic and Empirical) Approaches in Comparative Cultural Studies." *CLCWeb: Comparative Literature and Culture* (*Library*) (1992-): <http://docs.lib.purdue.edu/clcweb/vol3/iss3/7>.

Tötösy de Zepetnek, Steven. "Comparative Cultural Studies and the Study of Central European Culture." *Comparative Central European Culture*. Ed. Steven Tötösy de Zepetnek. West Lafayette: Purdue UP, 2002. 1-32.

Tötösy de Zepetnek, Steven. *Comparative Literature: Theory, Method, Application*. Amsterdam: Rodopi, 1998.

Tötösy de Zepetnek, Steven. "Configurations of Postcoloniality and National Identity: Inbetween Peripherality and Narratives of Change." *The Comparatist: Journal of the Southern Comparative Literature Association* 23 (1999): 89-110.

Tötösy de Zepetnek, Steven. "Constructivism and Comparative Cultural Studies." *CLCWeb: Comparative Literature and Culture* (*Library*) (2002): <http://docs.lib.purdue.edu/clcweblibrary/ccsconstructivism/>.

Tötösy de Zepetnek, Steven. "From Comparative Literature Today toward Comparative Cultural Studies." *Comparative Literature and Comparative Cultural Studies*. Ed. Steven Tötösy de Zepetnek. West Lafayette: Purdue UP, 2003. 235-67.

Tötösy de Zepetnek, Steven. "Systemic Approaches to Literature: An Introduction with Selected Bibliographies." *Canadian Review of Comparative Literature / Revue Canadienne de Littérature Comparée* 19.1-2 (1992): 21-93.

Tötösy de Zepetnek, Steven, ed. *Comparative Cultural Studies and Michael Ondaatje's Writing.* West Lafayette: Purdue UP, 2005.

Turnock, David. "Regional Development with Particular Reference to Cohesion in Cross-Border Regions." *Foreign Direct Investment and Regional Development in East Central Europe and the former Soviet Union.* Ed. David Turnock. Burlington: Ashgate, 2005. 141-83.

"Twożywo autorem logo Warszawa 2016—Europejska Stolica Kultury." *Krytyka Polityczna* (10 May 2008): <http://www.krytykapolityczna.pl/Aktualnosci/Twozywo-autorem-logo-Warszawa-2016-Europejska-Stolica-Kultury/menu-id-48.html>.

Tykwer, Tom. "Anything Runs." (2004): <http://www.tomtykwer.de/03_filmographie/34_lola_rennt/index.shtml>.

Umbenennungen Berliner Straßen, Plätze, Bahnhöfe (1995-): <http://userpage.chemie.fu-berlin.de/diverse/doc/umbenennungen.html>.

Urzykowski, Tomasz. "Muzeum Komunizmu powstanie w Pałacu Kultury." *Gazeta.pl Warszawa* (18 June 2008): <http://miasta.gazeta.pl/warszawa/1,95190,5327203,Muzeum_Komunizmu_powstanie_w_Palacu_Kultury.html>.

Urzykowski, Tomasz. "Szpetne, banalne, nielubiane." *Wyborcza.pl* (21 November 2008): <http://wyborcza.pl/1,75478,5970981,Szpetne__banalne__nielubiane.html>.

Urzykowski, Tomasz and Jerzy S. Majewski. "Najgorsze i najlepsze pomniki z ostatnich lat." *Gazeta.pl Warszawa* (14 June 2005): <http://miasta.gazeta.pl/warszawa/1,34862,2766562.html>.

Varga, Krzysztof. *45 pomysłów na powieść.* Wołowiec: Czarne, 1998.

Varga, Krzysztof. *Bildungsroman.* Wołowiec: Czarne, 2000.

Varga, Lászlo. "The Devastation of Budapest in War and Its Role in the Revolution, 1945-1956." *Budapest: A History from Its Beginnings to 1998.* Trans. Judit Zinner, Cecil D. Eby, and Nóra Arató. Ed. András Gerő and János Poór. New York: Columbia UP, 1997. 191-232.

Varga, Krzysztof. *Gulasz z turula.* Wołowiec: Czarne, 2007.

Varga, Krzysztof. *Nagrobek z lastryko.* Wołowiec: Czarne, 2007.

Velinger, Jan. "Sixteen Years after Velvet Revolution Few Communist Relics Remain." *Radio Prague* (16 November 2005): <http://www.radio.cz/en/article/72799>.

Verheyen, Dirk. "Straßennamenpolitik und städtische Identität in Berlin." *Kultur—Identität—Europa: Über die Schwierigkeiten und Möglichkeiten einer Konstruktion.* Ed. Reinhold Viehoff and Rien T. Segers. Frankfurt: Suhrkamp, 1999. 333-69.

Viehoff, Reinhold. "Literature and Cultural Identity." *The Systemic and Empirical Approach to Literature and Culture as Theory and Application.* Ed. Steven Tötösy de Zepetnek and Irene Sywenky. Edmonton: Research Institute for Comparative Literature, University of Alberta and Siegen: Institute for Empirical Literature and Media Research, Siegen University, 1997. 181-88.

Wajda, Andrzej. "Świątynia Józefa Stalina czy zabytek sowieckiej architektury z lat 50?" *Gazeta.pl Warszawa* (6 May 2008): <http://wiadomosci.gazeta.pl/Wiadomosci/1,80269,5194903.html>.

Wall Street. Dir. Oliver Stone. Hollywood: Amercent Films, 1987.

Warsaw City Hall. *The Official Website of the City of Warsaw* (2008): <http://e-warsaw.pl>.

Warsaw Rising Museum (2005-): <http://www.1944.pl/>.

Warsaw Tourist Information. *Warsaw—Official Web Portal* (2008): <http://www.warsawtour.pl>.

Warszawa. Dir. Dariusz Gajewski. Warszawa: Agencja Produkcji Filmowej, 2003.

Was tun, wenn's brennt. Dir. Gregor Schnitzler. München: Claussen & Wöbke Filmproduktion, 2001.

Węcławowicz, Grzegorz. "The Warsaw Metropolitan Area on the Eve of Poland's Integration into the European Union." *Transformation of Cities in Central and Eastern Europe: Towards Globalization*. Ed. F.E. Ian Hamilton, Kaliopa Dimitrovska Andrews, and Nataša Pichler-Milanović. New York: United Nations UP, 2005. 223-47.

Wheeler, Alina. *Designing Brand Identity: A Complete Guide to Creating, Building, and Maintaining Strong Brands*. Hoboken: John Wiley & Sons, 2003.

Williams, Allan M. and Vladimír Baláž. *Tourism in Transition: Economic Change in Central Europe*. London: I.B. Tauris, 2000.

Winters, Laura. "A Rebel With Red Hair Rumples Stuffed Shirts." *The New York Times* (13 June 1999): 17.

Witte, Bernd, ed. *Topographien der Erinnerung: Zu Walter Benjamins Passagen*. Würzburg: Königshausen & Neumann, 2008.

Wowereit, Klaus. "Rede des Regierenden Bürgermeisters von Berlin, Klaus Wowereit, zum Start der Markenkampagne *be* Berlin." Berlin Partner GmbH. be *Berlin - Die Hauptstadtkampagne* (2008): <http://www.sei.berlin.de>.

Zając, Marek. "Quo vadis? Do Europy!" *Tygodnik Powszechny* (23 March 2003): <http://www.tygodnik.com.pl/numer/tp/zajac.html>.

Zander, Peter. "Das Drehen auf einer Baustelle—Berlin als Filmkulisse." *Text der Stadt—Reden von Berlin: Literatur und Metropole seit 1989*. Ed. Erhard Schütz and Jörg Döring. Berlin: Weidler, 1999. 172-85.

Zawatka-Gerlach, Ulrich. "Wir alle sind Berlin." *Tagesspiegel.de* (12 March 2008): <http://www.tagesspiegel.de/berlin/Imagekampagne;art270,2493015>.

Zimmerspringbrunnen. Dir. Peter Timm. Berlin: Senator Film Production, 2001.

Žižek, Slavoj. "Post-Wall." *London Review of Books* 31.22 (19 Nov. 2009): 10.

Zukin, Sharon. *The Cultures of Cities*. Oxford: Blackwell, 1995.

Zukin, Sharon. *Loft Living: Culture and Capital in Urban Change*. New York: Rutgers UP, 1989.

Index

www.ingramcontent.com/pod-product-compliance
Lightning Source LLC
Chambersburg PA
CBHW071855270326
41929CB00013B/2244